Tolerance, Democracy, and Sufis in Senegal

Religion, Culture, and Public Life

Religion, Culture, and Public Life

Series Editors: Alfred Stepan and Mark C. Taylor

The resurgence of religion calls for careful analysis and constructive criticism of new forms of intolerance, as well as new approaches to tolerance, respect, mutual understanding, and accommodation. In order to promote serious scholarship and informed debate, the Institute for Religion, Culture, and Public Life and Columbia University Press are sponsoring a book series devoted to the investigation of the role of religion in society and culture today. This series includes works by scholars in religious studies, political science, history, cultural anthropology, economics, social psychology, and other allied fields whose work sustains multidisciplinary and comparative as well as transnational analyses of historical and contemporary issues. The series focuses on issues related to questions of difference, identity, and practice within local, national, and international contexts. Special attention is paid to the ways in which religious traditions encourage conflict, violence, and intolerance and also support human rights, ecumenical values, and mutual understanding. By mediating alternative methodologies and different religious, social, and cultural traditions, books published in this series will open channels of communication that facilitate critical analysis.

After Pluralism: Reimagining Religious Engagement,
    edited by Courtney Bender and Pamela E. Klassen
Religion and International Relations Theory, edited by Jack Snyder
Religion in America: A Political History, Denis Lacorne
Democracy, Islam, and Secularism in Turkey,
    edited by Ahmet T. Kuru and Alfred Stepan
Refiguring the Spiritual: Beuys, Barney, Turrell, Goldsworthy,
    Mark C. Taylor

Tolerance, Democracy, and Sufis in Senegal

EDITED BY
MAMADOU DIOUF

Columbia University Press *New York*

Columbia University Press
Publishers Since 1893
New York   Chichester, West Sussex
cup.columbia.edu
Copyright © 2013 Columbia University Press
All rights reserved

Library of Congress Cataloging-in-Publication Data

Tolerance, democracy, and sufis in Senegal / edited by Mamadou Diouf.
   p. cm. — (Religion, culture, and public life)
   Includes bibliographical references and index.
   ISBN 978-0-231-16262-3 (cloth: alk. paper) — ISBN 978-0-231-16263-0
   (pbk.: alk. paper) — ISBN 978-0-231-53089-7 (e-book)
 1. Islam — Senegal. 2.   Sufism—Senegal. 3.   Senegal — Social conditions.
        4.   Senegal — Religion.   I.   Diouf, Mamadou.
                     BP64.S4T65   2013
                     297.409663 — dc23
                          2012035168

Columbia University Press books are printed on permanent and durable acid-free paper.
This book is printed on paper with recycled content.
Printed in the United States of America

References to Internet Web sites (URLs) were accurate at the time of writing. Neither the author nor Columbia University Press is responsible for URLs that may have expired or changed since the manuscript was prepared.

Contents

Acknowledgments vii
Abbreviations ix

1. Introduction: The Public Role of the "Good Islam": Sufi Islam and the Administration of Pluralism
   Mamadou Diouf 1

2. A Secular Age and the World of Islam
   Souleymane Bachir Diagne 36

3. Islam's New Visibility and the Secular Public in Senegal
   Beth A. Buggenhagen 51

4. Dakar's Sunnite Women: The Dialectic of Submission and Defiance in a Globalizing City
   Erin Augis 73

5. Sovereign Islam in a Secular State: Hidden Knowledge and Sufi Governance Among "Taalibe Baay"
   Joseph Hill 99

6. The Senegalese "Social Contract" Revisited: The Muridiyya
Muslim Order and State Politics in Postcolonial Senegal
Cheikh Anta Babou   125

7. Religious and Cultural Pluralism in Senegal: Accommodation
Through "Proportional Equidistance"?
Etienne Smith   147

8. Islam, the "*Originaires*," and the Making of Public Space
in a Colonial City: Saint-Louis of Senegal
Mamadou Diouf   180

9. Stateness, Democracy, and Respect: Senegal in
Comparative Perspective
Alfred Stepan   205

10. Negotiating Islam in the Era of Democracy: Senegal in
Comparative Regional Perspective
Leonardo A. Villalón   239

Glossary   267
Contributors   269
Index   273

Acknowledgments

This volume has its origin in a 2008 conference held at Columbia University to celebrate the reopening of the Institute of African Studies (IAS) at Columbia. A Sufi recital with the great Senegalese Sufi singer Musa Dieng Kala, and an art exhibition "Saint in the City," Senegalese Sufi urban art curated by Allen Roberts and Polly Nooters Roberts at the Arthur Schomburg Center for Research in Black Culture, accompanied the conference. The IAS reopening celebration benefited from the generous support and sponsorship of several institutions: the Institute for Religion, Culture, and Public Life; the Committee on Global Thought; the Institute of African Studies; the School of International and Public Administration; the Center for the Study of Democracy, Toleration, and Religion; and the Henry R. Luce Initiative on International Affairs and Religion. I would like to thank these institutions for their support.

I would like to thank the participants for writing and editing their texts for this book and the audience for their engagement and contribution to the discussion. Although Mansour Sy Djamil's contribution to the conference is not included herein, the presentation and the debate it provoked nevertheless shaped this volume.

I would like to gratefully acknowledge the contributions of Musa Dieng Kala, Allen Roberts, Polly Nooters Roberts, and Howard Dodson to the success of the conference. They added to the discussion a much needed aesthetic and cultural dimension. I would like to especially thank Sarah Walsworth, then at the Institute of African Studies, and Emily Brenner at the Institute for Religion, Culture, and Public Life for efficiently handling the complex administrative tasks associated with organizing an international conference, recital, and art exhibit.

It is a pleasure to express my indebtedness to many colleagues for their constructive criticism and very useful feedback on many versions of the introduction to the volume, in particular Jinny K. Prais and Trica D. Keaton. The reviewers for Columbia University Press offered thoughtful and useful commentaries on the introduction and the individual chapters, for which I am also extremely grateful.

At different stages of the production of this volume, three of my graduate and undergraduate students, Katie Hickerson, Mary McDonald, and Alioune Badara Dia, played a crucial role in helping me with the details—formatting, proofreading, and checking endnotes and bibliographies—of getting the volume ready for publication. I am indebted to them for their assistance.

Finally, I am most grateful for the support and enthusiasm of Anne Routon, my editor at Columbia University, who expedited production of the book and made it an enjoyable experience.

Abbreviations

AEEMS	Association des Élèves et Étudiants Musulmans du Sénégal
AEMUD	Associations des Étudiants Musulmans de l'Université de Dakar
AMEA	Association Musulmane des Étudiants Africains
CIRCOF	Comité Islamique pour la Réforme du Code de la Famille
DEM	Dahira des Étudiants Mourides
DMM	Dahira al-Mustarchidin al-Mustarchidat
FAIS	Fédération des Associations Islamiques du Sénégal
FAL	Front pour l'Alternance
HT	Hizb al Tarqiyya
JIR	Jama'at Ibadu Rahman
MFDC	Mouvement des Forces Démocratiques de Casamance
MMUD	Mouvement Mondial pour l'Unicité de Dieu
PDS	Parti Démocratique Sénégalais
PS	Parti Socialiste
PUR	Parti de l'Unité et du Rassemblement
PVD	Parti de la Vérité pour le Développement
UCM	Union Culturelle Musulmane

Tolerance, Democracy, and Sufis in Senegal

[1]

Introduction

The Public Role of "Good Islam": Sufi Islam and the Administration of Pluralism[1]

MAMADOU DIOUF

The prevailing predictions of the nineteenth century and the beginning of the twentieth century incorrectly announced that religions would suffer a continuous and irreversible decline due to democracy, tolerance, dialogue, and pluralism. Secularism, in particular, will be one of the key drivers of the process of economic and social development. On the contrary, as averred by Ashis Nandy, with a genuine irony:

> Many wrote obituaries of religions as early as the middle of the nineteenth century. Since then, it has been the triumph of one secular ideology after another, though steep decline or ignominious fall has usually followed the triumph. Religion has re-emerged at the end of what could only be called an age of ideologies, not in its pristine form but bearing the imprint, and, sometimes, even the garb of the age of secular ideologies. At the beginning of the twenty-first century, religion has turned into a phoenix that has risen from its own ashes as a sign of its new triumph.[2]

Sufism as an Antidote to Political Islam

The visual expressions, infrastructures, and sacred places of Sufism are currently called upon to oppose the rise of political Islam in this new environment, which is strongly characterized by the presence of religions in the public space, Islam in particular. This detour marks a paradox, very acutely anchored in the idea that the strengthening of the presence of a certain form of religiosity in the public sphere could ensure respect for pluralism, favor the development of an open society,[3] and establish democracy in the political and social landscape. In the case of Senegal, it is important to understand the political and religious dynamics as well as the meshing of and exchanges between the Western-educated elite and the various traditional leaders, the two groups that have strongly contributed to the Senegalese success story. The Senegalese case study is a historical construction in which a social contract has brought religious and political authorities together since colonial times. Why have brotherhood marabouts been able to offer formulas and forms of vernacularization of discourses and political practices to the state and to the political elites? Why is the return to Sufism an answer to the mobilization, inspired by political Islam (equated to fundamentalism, conservatism, traditionalism, and terrorism)? What lessons can we learn by strengthening or restoring Sufi organizations, practices, and spirituality, all of which are conceived as antidotes or responses to the rise of religious fundamentalism in a society in which Muslims form a majority?[4]

Dismantled during the process of building modern nation-states in Pakistan, Egypt, and Tunisia, Sufi associations are being reestablished as critical elements in strategies aimed at containing the advance of political Islam.[5] In chapter 9, Alfred Stepan illustrates the return to Sufi Islam in the case of Senegal because that "particular form of Islam [. . .] fosters 'rituals of respect' by emphasizing those parts of the Qur'an's multivocality that urge tolerance as a response to diversity." No one he interviewed during his fieldwork felt comfortable with the concept of an "apostate," and all felt comfortable with the famous Catholic Cardinal Thiandoum's Muslim roots. Additionally, he notes that in the city of Popenguine, he found Catholics and Sufi disciples who helped build one another's mosques and churches.

Zidane Meriboute, one of the most vocal advocates of the restoration of Sufism as a modernizing Islamic force[6] able to contain the expansion of political Islam, provides an analytical framework that powerfully contrasts the "liberal, rational, enlightened and tolerant" Sufi tradition with fundamentalist Islam. He makes a strong case that Sufism can be viewed as "an antidote" because it has a prose, a grammar, and modern practices that circumscribe and support a space of pluralism and tolerance. It represents

Introduction

the safest way to facilitate the admission of Muslim societies into today's world, considering its doctrinaire track record, "from the work of some of the most brilliant Muslim thinkers of the Middle Ages and from the Sufis. Such men included Ibn Rusch (Averros), Ibn Sina (Avicenna), sal Khawarizwi, Al-Hallaj, Ibn Al-Arabi, and Rumi. Centuries later, Jamal Ad-Din Al Afghani and Muhammad Abduh followed on from their work. Contemporary thinkers, such as Egypt's Abdullah Badawi and Mohammed Al-Jabri in Morocco, continue to play their part. It continues to be the only way Islam will be able to coexist with the West. Neither orthodox theologians nor Muslim politicians, however, have yet come to terms with these reformers and unconventional mystics whose activities tend to destabilize dogmatic Islam."[7] On the contrary, Meriboute continues, analyzing the current situation, "[I]n much of North Africa, Eurasia, and Africa proper, religious fundamentalism and Sufi coexist, either in uneasy cohabitation or outright conflict. In some countries, such as Algeria, Tunisia, and Turkey, for historical reasons, that have never been fully examined, there has been hostility to Sufi orders. The results were soon to be seen. The vacuum left by the withdrawal of the Sufis was swiftly filled by other expressions of Islam, often of the most hard-line Islamist variety."[8] Thus, the prevailing turn to *"Western-style nationalism, based on modernizing liberalism,"*[9] legitimized the destructive head-on attacks upon Sufi organizations and provided grounds to the expansion of "radical Islam."

In contrast to the dismantling of the Sufi brotherhoods, which benefited radical Islam, Meriboute discerns three events as key moments in the political trajectory of Sufi Islam: the reestablishment of Sufi associations in Egypt by Nasser, at the beginning of the 1950s;[10] the active participation of Algerian president Abdel Aziz Bouteflika in the revitalization of the Zawiyas social and charitable activities to serve as "bulwarks against fundamentalism . . . calling upon them to correct false ideas about Islam and to inform public opinion, particularly among young people;"[11] and, finally, the position of African nationalist regimes "that emerged from the process of decolonization [that] have refrained from allowing themselves to be persuaded by the traditionalist ulema to try to stamp out the brotherhoods, as was the case under President Bourguiba in Tunisia, and Boumédienne in Algeria. The unintended consequences of Boumédienne's policies were to complete the work begun by Sheikh Ben Badis who had persecuted bastions of liberal Sufism in Algeria, which could have been rampart against religious extremism."[12]

Regarding the Senegalese case study examined in this volume, an African country sandwiched between "Islam and the West"—referring to the title of Sheldon Gellar's book[13]—the challenge posed by the rise of "Islamist religious fundamentalism" is addressed by turning to a specific type of Islamic religious formation, Sufi Islam. The cooperation between the political power and the Sufi leadership is considered to be the foundation that ensured political stability in an African environment, stricken by military coups, civil wars, and ethnic conflicts. This singularity in Africa and the Senegalese exception has been qualified as a "quite remarkable success story,"[14] a "construction of a liberal democracy" by Robert Fatton,[15] a "quasi-democracy,"[16] or "an unfinished democracy."[17]

However, the combination of the hard blows to Sufism in the Middle East and Asia, combined with the assaults from the partisans of secularism and the rise of political Islam, seemed to announce the unquestionable decline of the Sufi tradition, according to the social science scholarship and the opinions of the observers of the political scene in sub-Saharan Africa. It is, for example, the argument of the British historian J. S. Trimingham who concludes his study of the influence of Islam in Africa insisting upon *"the weakening of the Sufi spirit,"* attacked by both political Islam and secularism, whose irresistible progression and hegemony characterize modern times.[18] E. E. Rosander, who draws a clear distinction between "African Islam" and "Islam in Africa," espouses this conclusion.[19] She suggests that African Islam reappropriated local forms and resources, thus retaining an African quality. Open to local cultures, it accommodates other spiritualities. Islam in Africa, which launched an attack against the increasingly retreating African Islam, according to Rosander, has set two goals for itself: the purification of Islam and the removal of any Western or local impurities.[20] Even if they do not believe political Islam will adversely affect the Senegalese political arena and society, C. Coulon and D. Cruise O'Brien observe that despite President Abdou Diouf's denial of the existence of an Islamic threat in Senegal, "to stay just a few days in Dakar is to realize that the tranquil and moderate Islam which has long prevailed in this country is now in question. One finds in Senegal the atmosphere of Islamic agitation that marked the early years of colonial rule, a period when the economic, social, and political upheavals introduced by the European presence produced large scale religious movements and gave birth, for example, to the Muridiyya of Amadu Bamba."[21]

Further examining the long-term changes undergone by the relationships between the state and the brotherhoods, from the improvement of their relationship during the colonial period with the establishment of a form of indirect administration of the rural population by the clerics to the postcolonial era, and their increasing role in political parties' access to voters and recruitment of militants, Coulon and Cruise O'Brien conclude by observing the closure of the harmonious sequence, during which "everything seemed to be for the best in the Islamic and patrimonial world." They stressed that "for the last ten years or so, and since the accession of Abdou Diouf as head of state, Islam seems to be a more and more autonomous force. The Islamic awakening is apparent in all social strata and manifests itself in a variety of ways. The increase in number of Islamic associations of all kinds is one sign of this renewal, whether they are traditional da'iras grouping the disciples of a single marabout or modernist groups with social and political goals influenced by reformist ideas."[22] Less than ten years after the publication of Coulon and Cruise O'Brien's article, L. Villalón argues that despite the threat, "*the system has proven durable,*"[23] even though he also notes a new wave of Muslim religious demonstrations within the Senegalese public sphere, as well as the rise in destabilizing risks, while recognizing that Islamic groups tend to exclusively reach the urban segment of the population.

Islam and National Culture: Revisiting the Social Contract

The long Senegalese history, which started with the establishment of the French colonial administration, is precisely the subject of this volume. It began as a conference hosted by the Institute of African Studies; the Institute for Religion, Culture, and Public Life; the Center for Democracy, Toleration, and Religion; and the Committee on Global Thought on the theme of Tolerance, Democracy, and Sufis in Senegal at Columbia University in 2008. The volume examines the different turns, twists, and facets of the complex trajectory of the Senegalese state and society; these contours are continuously reconstituted by the circumstances, social segments, and fragments through their confrontations, and cooperation within and between the various brotherhoods, as well as between the aforementioned state.

Introduction

The different chapters aim to identify and analyze the effects of Sufism on the Senegalese society, the public sphere, upon democratic procedures, and on the respect of pluralism, including religious pluralism. The numerous social, cultural, and religious arrangements highlighted by the authors attest to the existence of what is identified by many scholars as the "Senegalese exceptionalism." Building on his previous work on the Murid brotherhood, Donal Cruise O'Brien treats this exceptionalism using the simple, but nonetheless very revealing, concept of the "success story,"[24] achieved by a social contract binding the *taalibe*, the marabouts, the colonial administration (before independence), and the postcolonial political elite. Such a "success story," according to Coulon and Cruise O'Brien,

> was attributed to the emergence of an authentic national culture, to relatively viable linkages between the communities (local, religious, or ethnic) and the state. The success was manifest in the capacity of the governmental party as an effective political machine. The quality of the political leadership made the Senegalese state a uniquely effective apparatus, and an instrument of stability although still unable to initiate an effective development policy. The state in Senegal at least was not a political artifact, working in a void, without effective links with society at large.[25]

Cruise O'Brien's theoretical and methodological approaches as well as his main conclusions are now subjected to an intense questioning and revision. The new scholarship on the Murid in particular suggests specific revisions, as shown, for example, by Cheikh Babou in chapter 6. He investigates the "underlying assumption [that] the social contract theory relates to the willingness of the state, colonial and postcolonial, to share power or at least to recognize an autonomous domain of authority to the leadership of the Muslim orders of Senegal."

This volume juxtaposes different disciplines and various methods and theories to shed light on the different forms of vernacularization of democracy, tolerance, and pluralism, to participate in an effort to trace in detail the contours of the debate. The end result is a *longue durée* perspective, focusing on the changes and adjustments made to the social contract between the *taalibe* and marabouts, as well as between the marabouts and the state. Its ambition is to reexamine the Senegalese experience, a particular political enterprise, by revisiting its history, possibilities, mutations, and limitations and whose very unique Senegalese character is the reason for celebration by the Senegalese themselves and the researchers working on Senegal.

Introduction

The space within which the authors of the various contributions evolve is constituted by their critical reassessment of the theories and methods upon which is predicated the

> remarkable political stability, even a degree of democracy, based on a peculiar socio-political system in which Islamic institutions have been central but have coexisted with a nominally secular state and have made no significant challenge for the control of the state, at least not until recently [. . .]. A well entrenched system of trilateral relations between the state, the religious elite, and a well-organized religious society have provided for a measure of reciprocity in Senegalese state-society relations, providing the country with its singular political system.[26]

The elaborate available interpretations reconstruct the different instruments and ideological and material mechanisms, based on how the religious and political powers continue to define one another in time and in space. However, even if the authors of this volume did not consciously try to reach a methodological and theoretical agreement, none of them lose sight of the historical context, the transformations of the cultural and institutional frames, and the identification discourses adopted by the actors. Their analyses converge to draw multiple facets of the Senegalese political and religious economies, and their reciprocal interactions.

The historical and political picture that I would like to present in this introduction aims at providing the context and the space within which the different analyses offered in the chapters might be read. It traces the building of the Islamo-Wolof model,[27] the different shapes it took, the (re)adjustments and contestations it faced, and the contribution of Muslim institutions in the consolidation and the legitimization of the colonial state initially, and later that of its successor, the Senegalese postcolonial state.

West African Sufi Tradition: A Genealogy

The presence of the Sufi religious tradition in Western Africa is an ancient one. Since at least the beginning of the eighteenth century, it has prevailed in Islamic regional expressions in various forms, ranging from esoteric and ascetic to mystic expressions carried out by a very select elite. It would later become a mass religion—a brotherhood—during the twentieth century, following a militant jihad phase led by warrior marabouts such as Al Hajj

Umar Tall at the beginning of the nineteenth century, and Mamadou Lamin Drame, at the end.

The active intervention of Muslim leaders gave birth to a solid Muslim educational regional network and to the rise of a moral economy, sustained kinship affinities, and shared knowledge during this period. This provided the Muslim Senegambian communities with a solid social and political organization, successfully appropriated by the warrior marabouts, as a basis for the creation of theocratic states, or as the moral and ideological motive to disengage themselves from the traditional political system and thus bolster the defense of their autonomy. The successive leaders of Sufi Islam in the West African region initiated the redrawing of the political and linguistic boundaries of communities, while refashioning ethnic and religious amalgamations, which continually reinvented affiliations, identifications discourses, practices, and representations. In fact, the rooting of Sufism in the spiritual landscape began to translate into very elaborate transactions inexorably intertwined with social structures, matrimonial rules (including the preeminence of matrilineage and the power of women in some regions),[28] and with the rites and rituals of local religions. These arrangements pinpoint the still-prevailing Sufi brotherhoods' versatility, and their abilities to make use of solid clientelist networks, which in turn guarantee them some measure of autonomy, therefore allowing them to compromise on both political and social levels.

Colonial expansion terminated the warrior marabouts' activities. Most of the Islamic states crumbled before the military colonizers' eyes. In West Africa, even though France had already proclaimed itself "a Muslim power"[29] following the storming of Algiers in 1830, it remained hostile to the marabouts, because they were suspected of accumulating wealth and disciples for "jihad." The failure of the indirect government option that was built on the subordinated inclusion of traditional chiefs, and the important contribution of the Sufi orders in the success of the groundnut production, quickly provided the material foundation for the social contract binding the colonial (and subsequently postcolonial) state to the marabout leadership and their rural disciples.[30]

France's Islamic policy took shape with the conquest of Morocco in 1912. It drew a rigid categorization between the fundamentalist Muslims (the reformists) and the tolerant Muslims. It argued that "this conscious effort to control Islamic societies, select Muslim leaders and allies, and put a secular and tolerant face on imperialism was essential to whatever success colonial rule enjoyed. When the ancient regimes fell, the French could point to their acceptance of the institutions of Muslim civil society, particularly Islamic law and Sufi orders."[31] The many transactions that occurred during the colonial period when the visions, practices, and political and intellectual conceptualizations were informed and influenced by the radical distinction between a tolerant and flexible *Black Islam* and a fundamentalist *Moorish Islam* helped build the Islamo-Wolof model.[32] The first brand of Islam ("good" Islam) provides accommodation to colonial rule, while the second remains hostile to the West. The Islamo-Wolof model binds the state and the brotherhoods in a complex web of social, cultural, economical, and political relationships. It covers the whole social field and, moreover, guarantees the hegemony of a modernity that is Wolof inspired and driven, both at the ideological level and at the social level in the public sphere. The French colonial state used the Sufi brotherhoods to ensure that duties such as tax collection were performed. It also guaranteed the submission of the faithful to the religious and administrative orders and their continuous involvement in the colonial business economy.

The social contract, which was firmly anchored in the formal institutions of the colonial administrative and political apparatuses and in the institutions of brotherhood Islam, has a very deep sociological resonance. This resulted in the establishment of a colonial social order mainly administered at the local level by the marabouts, in association with, and certainly subordination to, the colonial administration, and resulted also in the exercise of power at the local level. They thus became essential intermediaries in the daily exercise of colonial power, particularly in the relationships between the colonial state and the peasantry. Thanks to their presence within the colonial administrative apparatus, and their influence in the shaping of colonial politicies, the marabouts translated the patterns and language of command and submission in Wolof.

The significance of this institutional coproduction lies in the fact that, unlike in situations that occurred during the construction of the modern state, one does not observe a differentiation within and a total control of the public sphere by the state structures and institutions, which strive to radically dissociate the religious loyalties from the political apparatus.[33] Religious power does not clash with the political structures and the state apparatus anymore, with the goal of building an Islamic society, as advocated by political Islam.[34] On the contrary, Sufi marabouts manage to fit their ceremonies, rituals, pilgrimages, sacred places, and commemorations in the colony's republican calendar, library, and geography. As shown by Alfred Stepan in chapter 9, "the historical pattern in Senegal of French and Sufi mutual accommodation in the rural areas, and the urban dialetic between French colonial 'concessions' and Senegalese 'citizen's voting conquests,' helped socially construct a workable consensus concerning once conflicting divisions within Senegalese society." Instead, the marabouts and their major clients obtained the recognition of their Islamic institutions by the colonial state, their inclusion in the colonial space and administrative architecture, and they benefit from a material assistance that would be partially redistributed to the disciples. They became the vital intermediaries between the colonial state and the rural masses.

Theorizing the Islamo-Wolof Model

The Islamo-Wolof model takes definite shape, appropriating Wolof idioms and discursive composition within a French colonial syntax. The death of the two main brotherhood founders, Al Hajj Malick Sy in 1922 and Amadu Bamba Mbacke in 1927, gave an opportunity for the colonial administration to reinforce the mechanisms and multiply the infrastructures that firmly bound the brotherhoods and the colonial state. In fact, in both cases, the colonial administration strongly influenced the succession of the founders by promoting the sons to the detriment of the brothers. In this manner, it ensured the unity of the brotherhoods, their bureaucratization, and their strong centralization.

The chapters of this volume explore in great detail the social contract linking the state and the brotherhoods, beyond considering the economic and political dimensions that have been the focus of the social scientists and political observers of the Senegalese political scene. They reexamine its constituent elements to identify and interpret the logistics of control and cooperation, as expressed through the demands of the colonial administration; these elements are: the respect of the autonomy of discursive space of each of the partners—a space within which they act jointly or separately in the execution of administrative tasks; the guidelines regulating their interactions; and the public display of their signs, images, language, and identity. The marabouts' recourse to the religious cosmology of Islam has been crucial in the enterprise. The coproduction of the Islamo-Wolof model, while guaranteeing the success of the colonial project, simultaneously consolidates the solid social grounding and the powerful efficiency of the brotherhoods.

The institutional systems of the social contract were forged as early as the first decade of the establishment of the colonial administration.

Introduction

The colonial state leaned on the Sufi brotherhoods in order to guarantee the accomplishment of certain tasks, such as tax collection, submission of disciples to the administrative and religious commands, and also their involvement with the colonial economic machine. In order to follow its metamorphosis over time, and to account for its strategies and constant repositioning of its political and religious actors, it is crucial, after describing the Islamo-Wolof model, to carefully define the true nature of its mode of institutionalization. In this system, Sufi brotherhoods simultaneously functioned as religious and administrative institutions.

This dual administrative and religious institutionalization establishes the contours of a colonial governance, which on one hand relies upon an indirect government of the communities, executed by the delegated brotherhoods (who are in charge of the management and the policing of the borders inside their specific territory and the common space they share) and on the other hand relies upon the colonial administration, which ensures the cohesion and stability of the system. It is precisely this capacity for maintaining law and order and executing the tasks assigned by the colonial administration, in an efficient and productive manner, which guaranteed the stability and cohesion of the colonial governance established by the Islamo-Wolof model. The coercive authority exercised upon the *taalibe*, on one hand, and on the other hand, the trust and the support of the colonial system, rested upon the responsibilities assigned to the Sufi marabouts. Its principal function was the meticulous monitoring of the relationships, transactions, and social protocols within its religious community and between the different brotherhoods—operations that J. D. Frearon and D. D. Laitin define as *"institutionalized in-group policing."*[35] In the absence of this authoritarian exercise of power, the system weakens. Its success validates the existence of parallel structures designed to govern the segments of a fragmented, but homogeneous, colonial society. The paradox of the situation is that the colonial state succeeded in including in its administrative realm all social fragments, thus guaranteeing a powerful sense of toleration, indulgence, and diversity within and among multiple religious groups and brotherhoods. In effect, the conjunction of different facets of pluralism, administered both in the colonial administrative domain and in the brotherhood territories, and also in the space that solidly binds them, maintains the difference and diversity and establishes the shared rules of cooperation, coexistence, and toleration.

Introduction

These procedures, in turn, provide the particular language and rules for managing a pluralistic culture. According to Ingrid Creppell, an administration that is the foundation of tolerance, based upon the authorization to freely deploy a variety of religious practices in the political realm, articulates the religious discourse according to the political climate.[36] The interesting point of Creppell's analysis, in our case, resides in the identification of the constituent elements of toleration, the recognition of the diversity of religious engagements, and the assignment of a specific space to each religious group to feature its rituals, liturgies, adoration of saints, and commemorations in order to guarantee its individuality, coexistence, and cooperation. In startling opposition to the European case examined by Creppell, rather than law, which is the main instrument in the establishment of the politics of religious coexistence that strongly enforced tolerance in the political process at the beginning of modern Europe, the Senegalese social contract of pluralism examined in this volume relied heavily on extralegal, Sufi Islamic, Wolof cultural, and French political and administrative resources.

The religious institutionalization considers each brotherhood separately. It offers specific religious references, signs, and rituals of identification, and a strictly confined territory, which contains daily social practices for disciples and the spiritual indicators of the brotherhood. The establishment and acknowledgment of expressions specific to each brotherhood unit—their differences—assigns to each of them the mission of rigorously controlling the disciples, the task of assuring the strict respect of order and discipline, and, above all, the task of imposing the incontestable word of the Khalife Générale. The administrative institutionalization provided a mechanism, at the disposal of the marabout and the state, that solidly anchored the disciples to the administrative apparatus. Each brotherhood's marabout grants himself the role of incontrovertible mediator between parties, with the consent of the disciples and the state. He mediates between the disciples and the state, and translates the language of each to the other. To make the state legitimate in the eyes of the disciples, the marabout enhances his spiritual authority by establishing a tutelage and a right to supervise the disciples' lives on earth. Because of this, the Senegalese-Sufi marabout's identity is defined dually through both the recognition of the state and the disciples; this duality is indispensable to his authority, prestige, and material success, all of which are signs and public expressions of his *baraka*. However, the particular religious identities of

Introduction

each of the brotherhood units simultaneously participate in the configuration of a territory of inter-brotherhood engagement in cooperation and mutual respect among all. The implementation of the inter-brotherhood resources was particularly apparent in the political scene, much before the colonial subjects acquired the right to vote, with the adoption of the 1946 Lamine Gueye law. The Murid marabouts, for example, were influential in the election of Blaise Diagne, the first black Senegalese elected to the French National Assembly in 1914; they did this through financial support and by asking their *taalibe*, who were French citizens, to vote for him. In the eyes of the colonial administration, the common space it shared with the brotherhoods constituted the productive core of the marabout common front. Seydou Nourou Tall, the grandson of Al Hajj Ourmar Tall, was their spokesman and principal mediator, initially between the colonial administration and the brotherhood system, and later between the postcolonial administration and the brotherhood system.[37]

The dual political and religious institutionalization contributed jointly to the creation of a political order that operated within the social and legal registers that have acquired a strong legitimacy. It initiated a pluralism that fed the Islamo-Wolof model and its own modernity. Accounting for the expressions of the pluralistic administration of the Senegalese social contract relative to its second component, which bound the *taalibe* to the marabout, is far more difficult. This second component relied upon a paradox, caused on one hand by the total obedience of the *taalibe* to his master and spiritual guide, as captured by the image portraying his behavior toward the latter as a "corpse in the hands of the embalmer," and, on the other hand, caused by the various options at the disposal of the *taalibe*, including the possibility of switching spiritual guides, precisely because of the conditional nature of the marabout's authority.[38] Such a paradox highlights the litmus test of pluralism, which provides two indicators. The *taalibe* is not a passive actor but rather a very active agent in the brotherhood sphere. He has a capacity for negotiation and resourcefulness in the face of the marabout who must show a strong willingness to compromise. Cruise O'Brien rightfully insists upon this tension, in observing, "Nonetheless, close attention to Sufi practice can show how misleading the outward display of an abject subservience can be. Not only may the apparently absolute spiritual master be on occasion chosen by the disciples, but it is generally the case that the master must satisfy at least some of the disciple's desires if he is to maintain control over his sacred clientele. The saintly master may even reach a tacit doctrinal understanding with his disciples, sacrificing the demands of Islamic purity to the requirements of acceptable tutelage. The appearance of total mastery and absolute subjection can thus conceal what is in effect a conditional authority, something close to a Sufi social contract."[39]

The various contributions to this volume emphasize this central aspect, neglected by most studies, which instead focuses upon the ideological content of the *Sufi* social contract and its political consequences, in particular, the *ndiggël*.[40] They emphasize the complexity of the relationship, its instability, and the numerous options at the disposal of the *taalibe*. In particular, they insist upon the vacant spaces that opened up with the decline of "restricted literacy"[41] that began over two decades ago, the intensification of the competition with fundamentalist and political Islam, the intensification of power and prestige conflicts within and between familial branches of the brotherhood, and the growing of the *taalibe* social demands in a time of economic crisis.

While continually adapting to the aforementioned circumstances, the arrangements of the social contract survived the transfer of power from the Senegalese colonial state to the Senegalese postcolonial state. The profound mutations undergone by the material foundation of the Senegalese social, economic, and political groups, henceforth dominated by the urban economy, the migratory movements, and the financial and social resources they generated at the expense of groundnut production, led to the alteration and revision of the constituent elements of the contract and the introduction of new economic, aesthetic (literary and textile), and ethical models. The main issue of the metamorphosis of the Islamo-Wolof model in the transition toward the Senegal national state is the maintenance and adaptation of the administrative pluralism, and of religious and administrative tolerance and flexibility, which consecrates the reciprocal exchanges between the religious discourse and the political demands and vice versa. The transition to the national state was not easy because of political, economic, and cultural projects carried out by different segments of the political class, who entered into a fierce competition for power and influence, which was attentively monitored by the *Sufi* marabouts, who actively took sides.

When Senegal became independent in 1960, the nature of the state to be built, the organization of society, and the administrative infrastructures, as well as of the representative institutions—ranging from the district administrative units to the highest ranks of government—were the main concern of the ruling class. The Senegalese political class was forced to face such issues as the place and the role of the Muslim religion and of Sufi brotherhoods in the new political, economic, social, and cultural structures of the new state, and of the ruling party, the Senegalese Progressive Union (UPS), before independence. In 1974, the UPS, the only officially recognized party from 1966 to 1974, became the Socialist Party (PS), following the transition to democracy and the beginning of multipartism. Initially limited to three parties by President Léopold Sédar Senghor, an unlimited multiparty democratic system was restored by his successor Abdou Diouf, after President Senghor's resignation in December 1980.

Toward a Wolof and Islamic Modernity

Several episodes are indicative of the evolution that was spurred by independence. The shape, both material and discursive, of the relationships between the political classes (both in power and in the opposition) and within and between the different segments of the Sufi religious communities, took form through attempts to propose a common language and references that would remain very flexible. This oral and written library, which sought Wolof and Islamic resources to define the marabout-*taalibe* relationship as well as French values regarding the responsibilities and rights of the new citizen, set the stage for a dialogue that sought new ways—both symbolic and literal—of behaving, speaking, dressing, perfuming, and exchanging in public or private spaces, creating a Senegalese modernity that hinged upon the Wolof grammar of civility. This modernity took on a national mission to take control of or silence the spirits of the non-Wolof and non-Muslim ethnic peripheries[42] through a permanent dialogue between the administrative, political, and religious entrepreneurs on one hand, and the various Senegalese communities on the other hand. Such a dialogue gave form to material, discursive, and leisure economies, whose Wolof references constituted the public emblems of the state and representations of the nation.

The first episode was started by the referendum organized by General Charles de Gaulle upon his return to power in 1958. He proposed the immediate independence or autonomy of the French "black" African colonies within the framework of the French Union. As the political class tergiversated, and was unable to reach consensus, neither at the federal level of French West Africa nor at the level of the individual territories, the Sufi marabouts—who were very sensitive to the central place they occupied in the colonial system, as well as to the multiple material privileges they received, including the indirect government of their disciples and the administration of the regions of groundnut production, the quintessential product of the colonial economy—sided with the Gaullist proposal. They created their own organization to campaign in favor of independence within the French Union and the adoption of the new constitution, proposed by General de Gaulle, placing their disciples' electoral force in opposition to that of the militants of the Senegalese political parties. This initial confrontation between political and religious leaders benefited the marabouts. The political classes were forced to align their positions with the marabouts. They called to vote "yes" to de Gaulle's proposal of the constitution of the French Union.

The second episode happened when Senegal became a sovereign state. The constitution of the new state was the subject of discord. Led by Seydou Nourou Tall, the Sufi marabouts attempted yet again to coerce the political class into adopting their positions by proposing a Muslim-inspired constitution. The confrontation this time favored the politicians, who were divided by the nation-building project. Regarding the inclusion of the marabouts in the administrative, political, and structural design of the new state, one may say that the deep disagreements within and between the religious and political leaderships were publicly expressed. The politicians espoused the following positions. Lamine Gueye was in favor of a rather rigid separation between the state and the "mosque"—as a veteran of the French Socialist Party, a freemason, and, above all, as the champion of the French citizens of the Four Communes, who were granted the right to vote and be represented. My contribution to this volume examines the main motivations for the civility of the *originaires*, which was a major influence upon Lamine Gueye's interventions in the local and imperial institutions. Mamadou Dia, president of the council for a new state, and coleader with Senghor of the Union Progressiste Sénégalaise (UPS, Senegalese Progressive Union), advocated the total exclusion of the marabouts from the political sphere to allow the party direct access to the masses; he was in favor of the modernization of Islam, which needed to rid itself of the scourge of traditional beliefs and of Sufi mysticism, to drastically reduce the control of the disciples by the marabouts. He established "a state institution, the Conseil Supérieur Islamique, having responsibility for the coordination of the country's Islamic religious life. Among the responsibilities assigned to this council was the drafting of a new family law in accordance with the

Introduction

provisions of the *sharî'a*, the development of a coherent system of Islamic religious education, and the organisation of the pilgrimage to Mecca."[43] Dia wanted to construct a secular state inspired by Islamic law and morals.[44] Dia, according to V. Y. Mudimbe, was a politician and a "theologian . . . exploring the Islamic heritage in its transmission through generations, balancing the tension between modernism and conservatism in terms of interpretative exegeses (1975), and invoking a socio-anthropology of Islam that would respect and could fulfill both the Prophet's word and the wellness of African cultures (1979, 1980)."[45] By contrast, at the time of his resignation from Gueye's Socialist Party and the creation of his own political party, Bloc des Masses Sénégalaises (BDS, Senegalese Masses Coalition), in 1948, Senghor constructed his political program, drawing heavily from the language and the symbols of the Islamo-Wolof model. In chapter 2, this volume, Souleymane Bachir Diagne uncovers the philosophical foundations of the Senghor/Dia spiritualist socialism project, tracing its genealogy and cultural and ideological resources to the philosophical and intellectual discourse of Muslim elites and intellectuals as well as to the "practical response" whereby "democratic and secular states are being built in the Muslim world."

The logics of accommodation, of fusion, and/or branching out of, which set the tone of the new political approach, helped Senghor gain control of the ruling party and of the presidency. The disagreements between the three dominant actors of the Senegalese political scene fall into the judicial and cultural foundations of the new citizenship and the rights responsibilities associated with them, along with the contours of the representative assemblies and the electoral processes upon the basis of which they are formed.

The victory of Léopold Sédar Senghor over Lamine Gueye and Mamadou Dia established the central position of the UPS as the dominant party, and the consolidation of the Islamo-Wolof model as the defining armature of the Senegalese political system. Senghor carried out his political operations by incorporating the ethnic (in particular, *Lebu* and *Joola*) and marabout elites in the political apparatus, as auxiliary and subaltern partners at all levels: ideological, political, economical, and administrative. The dissidence of Ibrahima Ñas (Niasse) of the Kaolack *Tijanyya*, of Cheikh Tidiane Sy (the son of the first caliph of the Tivaouane zawyia, Babacar Sy) and of Cheikh Mbacke Gainde Fatma (the son of the first Khalife Générale of the Murids, Moustapha Mbacke) combined with the total retreat from the political scene of the oldest son of Babacar Sy, Moustapha Sy Djamil, established in Dakar, did not have any negative effect upon the successful stabilization of the political system put in place by Senghor.

Senghor's project, based upon the manipulation of the triple political culture of legitimization power, the republican state, the Sufi brotherhoods, and of the regional traditions, favored personal relationships at the expense of political institutions. Senghor built his political networks on "the small motherlands,"[46] the vernacular logistics, and the instrumentation of the symbols of power. According to Janet Vaillant, Senghor acted in a "pretentious" manner, but he was the sort of prince who would rise to the local expectations and practices.[47] The strongest indicator of this political strategy was the adoption of the Islamo-Wolof model color "green" that signaled a solid grounding in the rural area, as opposed to the adoption of the urban "red" of the *originaires* of the Four Communes. This new strategy rested upon the displacement of the political center of gravity from the Atlantic façade to the Wolof brotherhood country (Waalo, Baol and Kajoor, Njambuur) and the regions of groundnut production (Saalum), as well as upon the firm relocation of the Islamo-Wolof model at the center of the public sphere, in particular, after the elimination of Mamadou Dia from the presidency of the government council; he had attempted to weaken the Sufi marabouts' grip on their *taalibe*, using modern techniques of education[48] in order to decrease the level of the "restricted literacy," which maintained the power of the marabouts over the *taalibe*. Senghor celebrated the vernacularization of the state by systematically manipulating ethnicity, religion, and autochthony, and the cultural codes with which they were associated. Playing upon the pluralism administered through disparate elites, he managed to build a coalition of local interests, to simultaneously reinforce his power and the stability of the state. In chapter 7, Etienne Smith examines the Senegalese state's policies from above (how it tries to accommodate both cultural and religious pluralism), as well as the soft and informal social practices of the interaction from below (kinship ties and joking kinship pacts) that craft tolerance. He argues that religious leaders rank alongside state and patrias "heroes" to conclude that the religious sphere is not the most distinctive feature of Senegal's exceptionalism. He promotes three frameworks to explore building community processes, either the community of "citizens" (citizenship as loyalty to the state), "believers" (faith as loyalty to God and its representatives), and "ethnics"' (local patriotism as loyalty to the *terroir*).

Smith's analysis of the "Senegalese exception" echoes Leo Villalón's contribution, chapter 10, which is written through a West African comparative perspective of Senegal, Mali, and Niger. He makes two observations. First, the claim that the relative tolerance of Sufism produces a greater affinity for a democratic political system than other forms of Islam is simply a variant of a "compatibility" argument. Villalón finds this approach unsatisfying, given that Sufism is "multivocal." Second, by examining Mali and Niger, he argues that Senegal's political experience is less exceptional than often stated, and that the country was not always democratic. Like elsewhere on the continent, Senegal moved quickly after independence to a single party system, and even the presidencies of Senghor and Abdou Diouf were not democratic. It was only in the 1990s that Senegal transitioned to a more "democratic" state, much like Mali and Niger.

The third episode begins with the appearance of the first fissures, due to the crisis of the groundnut economy, which was provoked by the fall of the price of the peanut at the end of the 1960s, the death of the Murids' Khalife Générale, Falilou Mbacke, the rise to power of his brother, Abdou Lahat Mbacke in 1968, and the beginning of the drought cycle in the first half of the 1970s. The new Murid caliph proposed innovative solutions in response to the new situation. Confronting the state, he sought a renegotiation of the administration of the pluralism of the social contract by the state, and ideological autonomy for the brotherhood, by constructing a library and a printing shop in Touba in order to keep the loyalty of his disciples who became migrants, who are now circulating the songs and prayers written by the founder. By taking the terms of the social contract in hand, both internally and externally, he questioned the inter-brotherhood cooperation and pushed the brotherhoods to compete for control of the state, of economic sites of accumulation and redistribution, authoritative positions, and prestige, the most solid pillars of the pluralistic administration of diversity. This drifting was reinforced by the attempts of the Senegalese technocracy, which progressively took the reins of the political and economic power after the nomination of Abdou Diouf as prime minister in 1970 to control the state and the ruling party.

The founding of Abdoulaye Wade's Senegalese Democratic Party in 1974, and the advent of the regime change, which provoked the downfall of the Socialist Party in 2000, after forty years in absolute power, amplified the breakup of the cohesion, the crumbling of the mutual respect, and of the collaboration between the Sufi brotherhoods. The genuflection of the newly elected president during his first visit after his election to Murid Khalife Générale, and the constant references to Touba, were signs of a new episode in the relationships between the political power and the Sufi brotherhoods. They opened the way to a political polarization, strongly inspired by the brotherhood identities, thus questioning what Mansour Sy Djamil, one of the heirs of the Senegalese *Tijanyya*, considered to be "an assault against Senegalese exceptionality, i.e., the coexistence in a perfect communion of all the brotherhood confessions and the religious beliefs of a country,"[49] questioning the "harmony"[50] and "the reciprocal respect between different confessions,"[51] as well as the neutrality of the state and its leader.[52]

Smith also questions this new turn of events, showing that it is Wade's reconsideration of the equidistant position of the state with regard to the brotherhoods, and the preeminence that he gives to the Murid, that are criticized, rather than his apparent religiosity. While recognizing the existence of theoretical justifications and ritualized features for the policy of equal respect, he argues that it has not been properly institutionalized. To illustrate such a fact, he mentions the conflicts in the south since the 1980s and the Comité Islamique pour la Réforme du Code de la Famille (CIRCOF) demand for a revision of a family code. These readjustments were foreseeable as noted by Joseph Hill in chapter 5 in his very rich ethnographic contribution focusing on the Tijanyya Ñasen (Niassen), identifying "a kind of pragmatic pluralism" not grounded in a supposedly neutral "liberal" approach to tolerance but in the negotiated and even symbiotic coexistence of multiple, mutually irreducible claims to truth and authority and understandings of community. In one example, Hill explains the Taalibe Baay community's engagement and disengagement from the state as presented during the community's religious celebrations.

The crisis of the groundnut economy had disastrous social and economical consequences in the *ndiggël* in the Wolof regions. It provoked a radical reconfiguration of Muridism's political economy. In chapter 3, Beth Buggenhagen traces, for example, the evolution of the Murid brotherhood, from its largely agricultural beginnings through the fall of the groundnut in 1968, the drought cycle and the environmental crisis of the 1970s, the structural adjustments of the 1990s, and migrations to urban centers and abroad. Even the trade liberalization of 1997, designed to curb the unofficial markets the Murid benefited from, reinforced the articulation between the formal and informal economies and the intertwining of personal and commercial networks. The reshaping of the Murid public codes, indicators or tracers of, as well as representations of the visual economy, and the knowledge associated with them, constituted the community references for the increasing number of Murid migrants settling in Senegalese, African, and Western cities. This migration introduced a new basis for economic accumulation, notably through the informal sector, driven by the rural migrants' dynamics and creativity, with the spread of lawful and unlawful networks and circuits, creating a new way to live in, exploit, and occupy the African city. It also favored the configuration of new associative systems, giving birth to new types of leadership, which attempted to open new horizons, outside of the genealogical transmission of power. New associations and new leadership began writing new chapters in the history and mission of the *Sufi* brotherhood founders, shifting the emphasis from the *baraka* to the *library*, defining anew the control of knowledge developed by the founders, the mystic power of the sacred sites and the commemorations, and finally, recasting the function of the caliph. These new spiritual sites, as well as the knowledge and ethics associated with them, became the critical weapons, directed in particular against the third generation of the Sufi clerical families.

The growth of the brotherhood networks, the diversification of their references and affiliations, combined with their continuous fragmentation—each fragment building progressively a solid material and ideological foundation in order to claim their autonomy from the brotherhood central power—was to some extent served by the passing away of the first generation (the sons) of the descendants of the brotherhood founders, and the coming to power of the second generation (the grandsons); this process unfolded at a time when the different branches, each of which had a member who assumed the role of caliph, began showing a desire for autonomy. The caliph position seems to have been used to launch a process of primitive accumulation of disciples, of financial and land resources, and to put into place networks inside the state and economic apparatuses to assure autonomy and the capacity to intervene in the post-caliph tenure. The abundance of new sites of agency in which actors could transgress the constraints posed by genealogy, to act independently from the caliph, introduced conflicting voices in the religious realm. What was then witnessed was the diffusion of loyalty to the brotherhood, which was either limited to the founder (and his library) or to the position of the caliph, the sacred sites or the miracles, and commemorations. All of these manifestations led to the closure of the solidarity ethos and the weakening of the logistics of unquestionable obeisance to the word of the Khalife Générale, who lost his indisputable authority.

The proliferation of the interpretations of collective identities and brotherhood cultures opened the way to literary, visual, acoustic, and dress code representations that were set in a common context but have different expressions. They led the way to new combinations and to a creativity that employed all resources at its disposal, constantly reinventing the different faces of the founders and their heirs. The competition among the grandsons and the scarcity of the redistributed resources led for the first time to possibilities for contesting, or refusing to implement the *ndiggël*, even within the marabout families. The main actors in this new power struggle were the youth, women, and city dwellers; they were the segments of the population that demanded to be treated differently than the rural disciples, who formed the majority of disciples before the crisis of the 1970s. These new developments raised more questions regarding the constitution of the political and moral realms in times of profound crisis. Buggenhaggen's chapter deals with this theme by reconstructing the trajectory of the Murid migrant women. Thus, what composed the strength and stability of this model—its centralization, the unity of its leadership, infallibility, and incontestable assurance—along with its capacity for negotiation with the state, then disintegrated within the brotherhood system.

The fragmentation of the public space has been continuously accentuated by the liberalization of the political regime since 1974 and the creation of an incredible number of political parties. The diversification of the political scene reinvigorated competition within the different segments of the Sufi brotherhoods, which bitterly negotiated their support, or attempted to directly establish themselves in the political sphere by creating their own parties or by presenting candidates at elections. Some marabouts became worldly marabouts (*marabouts mondains*).

The Future of the Social Contract: New Actors and New Roles—Women and Youth

The chapters in this volume define both the political and religious fields in a rather broad manner in order to include the interactions between politics and religion, each differently expressed, through different dress codes and

Introduction

discursive expressions, and discourses that are their own, and also through the imagining of the national community and the conceptualization of citizenship. This represents a cooperation that assured the success of the Senegalese social contract. The continuous remodeling of the Senegalese social contract has had various consequences upon democracy and tolerance. The first rearrangements started the succession and leadership disputes, which fragmented the *Tijannyya*, following the death of Seriñ Babacar Sy (1957), the consolidation of the autonomy of the *Tijanyya* of Kaolack, and the death of Seriñ Falilou Mbacke (1968). They were followed by the social, political, and economic adjustments consecutive to the political modernization, initiated by Senghor's National Domain (1964), and the Family Code (1974) laws. They mark the first intervention of the state in the fields of civil law. In chapter 9, Alfred Stepan shows that the Family Code—as well as the reform of the local and territorial administration (1974)—has become the core of the antigovernment rhetoric, represented by dissident religious groups, opposing the state and the *Sufi* brotherhood. The unstable trajectories that characterized the Senegalese political economy after the succession of Senghor by Abdou Diouf, and the regime change of 2000, with the election of Abdoulaye Wade, successively led to the consolidation of a political system that was open and plural. This signaled various changes in the Senegalese business sector, following the adoption of new economic policies, the metamorphosis of the Muslim Brotherhood, and the diversification of the economic and political actors and leaderships, the transformation of the languages of allegiance, subjugation, command, and contestation, along with the theories and practices of neo-patrimonialism and clientelism. The realities and fictions of the neoliberalism opened the way to very creative initiatives, supporting an urban economy, which sought new and old religious idioms, allowing new relationships with the state and the entrepreneurial economy. New procedures and relationships of power established themselves and profoundly transformed the political landscape and one of its underpinnings, the social contract.

Erin Augis's chapter 4 follows the emergence of the Sunnite movement in Senegal, during a time of rapid privatization, globalization, and economic liberalization, comprised of global flows of goods along with media, capital, and charitable flows from the West, China, and the Middle East. According to Augis, it is within Dakar's shifting socioeconomic context that orthodox Muslim Senegalese women's agency can be problematized. While arguing that the emphasis on the political and material sides of female adherents' accomplishments does not give proper place to their religiosity, she highlights the way Senegalese Sunnite women view Islam from Arab countries as being closer to a pure form of religion, idealizing imported ideas as a means of cultivating piety. She also suggests that while Sunnite women are unlikely to shun modernity, they will attempt to embrace it on their own terms, even if this means creating new subjectivities with commodities ushered in by some of the very capitalist forces they defy.

Two instances merit particular attention in this context: the interventions of women, highlighted in Buggenhaggen's chapter; and the interventions of the youth, who used strategies of revision, renewal, or of definitive closure of the Islamo-Wolof model.[53] They deployed new logistics of autonomy and formed lobbies and pressure groups to amass increasingly colossal gains, and present increasingly diverse forms of association and intervention.

Overview of the Volume

For many years, the study of relationships between the political power and Sufi marabouts' power and influence focused primarily upon a theoretical and empirical perspective, which unveiled the infrastructures and the mechanisms that articulated the two spheres. This volume juxtaposes diverse methodological and theoretical approaches in order to trace the contours of the debate about the role and place of religion within the public sphere.

The contributions in this volume aim to follow the trajectory of the transformations of the Senegalese social contract over a long period of time, on one hand emphasizing the processes of readjustments and revisions, and, on the other hand, emphasizing the crises that shook Senegal since the departure of Senghor, the difficulty of construction of Diouf's power, and the regime change in 2000 with the election of Abdoulaye Wade as the head of the Senegalese state, and his reelection in 2007 after the victory of his party, the Parti Démocratique Sénégalais (PDS, Senegalese Democratic Party) in the legislative elections of 2001 and 2007. The authors utilize a vast array of empirical resources in order to present their arguments and to examine very theoretical issues.

In chapter 2, Souleymane Bachir Diagne observes that the secularization narrative emerged as a criticism of Islam by some nineteenth-century thinkers such as Ernest Renan who regarded Islam, which he calls "Islamism," as incompatible with the idea of a well-elaborated science that explains well the "universe" and lays the foundations of a political organization of the state that allows the individual to freely choose its destiny and enjoy the right to "disbelief" and to "freedom of conscience." According to Diagne, Muslims' reaction to such a call that considers the secular state as an imperative "political philosophy" for fostering order and progress in society has been twofold: (1) the philosophical and intellectual discourse that recognizes the demise of the religious state, namely the irrevocable death of the Islamic caliphate to the detriment of new modern and positivist political forms that constitute the basis of the secular state inherited from the West, and (2) practical response whereby "democratic and secular states are being built in the Muslim world." Senegal's exceptionalism, the country's *"laicite bien comprise"* (well-understood secularism) exemplified the latter. Senegal is a particular case of a "Sufi-secular mutual respect"/ Islamic-Christian secular political system in which religious leaders— Muslim and Christian as well—join the state for cooperation in many political and socioeconomic activities, participate in public policy debates, and act as "firefighters of the political arena." However, as Diagne notes, such a vision of a working collaboration between the state and religions is more and more threatened by the tenuous and thin line that exists between the marabouts' religious obligations to educate their disciples and followers and their equally important role and moral obligation to intervene.

Beth A. Buggenhagen discusses the role of Islam in the public sphere in Senegal, focusing specifically on religion-based media, including radio programs, videocassettes, DVD productions, textiles, clothing, texts, and photography. In so doing, she explores "gendered and corporeal" practices that have exhibited remarkable traction among Muslims over the last decade. She begins with the following two questions: How is value produced through aural and visual components of religious videocassettes, dress codes, and images, and how are ideas about proper religious comportment, wealth, and status constituted by and shared among the *taalibe*? Drawing from a meticulous survey of the media landscape, the central role of the Internet, digital recording and broadcasting, as well as desktop publishing, Buggenhagen describes how secular and Muslim groups have been addressing the presence and increased role of religion in the public debate and the growing presence of Muslim candidates vying for public office in general elections. Further, as she illustrates, the representations by Murid male and female disciples of Sufi circuits act as mechanisms for offering access both to the future of eternal prosperity as well as economic and financial gains in the present. Analyzing the past decades, Buggenhagen provides a vivid demonstration of how the imaginative uses of Murid migrants' new wealth enable Murid to reconstitute and display in the urban landscape their distinctive signs and emblems of economic success. In so doing, they appear to be reshaping the social ethos and moral standing of the Muridiyya in terms of new technologies, ranging from photocopiers, radio programs, and videocassettes to DVDs, YouTube, and social networking sites. Buggenhagen's examination of the critical role of migrant women offers a distinctive picture of the itinerant lifestyles of Murids in transition and represents a significant shift from the dominant focus on male migrant to the role of technologies in creating a space for women, wherein they gain recognition as both visible and viable religious actors.

Using interviews with young, educated Sunnite women in Dakar, in chapter 4 Erin Augis analyzes the ways in which they negotiate between capitalist forces globalizing Western commodities on one hand, and the development of the rhetoric and "signs and symbols of transnational Islam," on the other. She highlights how these young women's reference to critiques of secularism by the male leadership serves to carve out an Islamist femininity that transforms them spiritually. Moreover, Augis demonstrates how the veil operates among these women as both a symbol of their orthodoxy and faith-generating, even as it is also a liability in the workforce. As her informants reveal, the more they cover, the more they demonstrate a disciplined feminine modesty for themselves and before men, in keeping with divine expectations. Often these women meet discrimination in the workforce for their outward displays of religiosity (i.e., certain kinds of veils), modesty in male/female relations (such as refusal to shake a man's hand), and recourse to Islamic morality in dress and forms of greetings (such as handshaking), which support their religious ethics and sense of self in a rapidly changing capital city. Although her chapter focuses on women with high school or college diplomas, Augis's Senegalese Sunnite informants come from varied ethnic, socioeconomic, and educational backgrounds. Through their actions, they represent the ideological legacy of a protest movement that originated in the 1930s against the perceived wasteful spending of the Sufis' disciples and leaderships.

Joseph Hill's chapter 5 questions the one-directional view of the relation between "Islam" and "the secular state," often presented as a conflict between two mutually irreconcilable grounds of sovereign legitimacy rather than a vast expanse of possibilities. Senegalese Muslims, for example, question this dichotomy, argues Hill, by exercising religious sovereignty while participating in secular state politics. Whereas liberal secularism depoliticizes and privatizes religion, Hill attempts to repoliticize Islam by showing it to be inseparable from questions of subject formation, moral order, and governance. "Taalibe Baay," or disciples of Shaykh Ibrahim Ñas (Niasse), employ the Sufi opposition between "apparent" (āhir) and "hidden" (bā) truths to accommodate multiple sovereignties, networks of governance, and interests within their community. Hill's chapter focuses on specific case studies in which Sufi language and practice serve to negotiate competing notions of sovereignty and claims to truth and authority that reflect a kind of "pragmatic pluralism," one that negotiates multiple, mutually irreducible claims without translating them into a supposedly neutral ground, as in the case of liberalism. Hill takes seriously both Muslims' claims about the nature of truth and authority and Islam's inseparability from forming subjectivities and moral order. Rather than undermine liberal aspirations to coexistence, tolerance, pluralism, and democracy, these examples suggest that such aspirations (which are not uniquely liberal) may find realization in unexpected, nonliberal ways. These alternative configurations are not "survivals" on the road to a liberal world, but are alternative answers to the problem of coexistence.

In chapter 6, Cheikh Anta Babou critically engages the so-called Senegalese "social contract." That is, Muslim clerics provide the government with legitimacy to ensure the loyalty of its citizens who, in return, receive recognition and material support from the state. Babou complicates this simplistic explanation by examining the extent of the cleric's self-determined role in Senegalese society and the degree to which disciples and laypeople's expectations are met by their religious leaders, as political brokers. Babou uses the Muridyya as a case study to examine how religious political power is rooted in the cohesion and discipline of the organization that is, in turn, dependent on the preservation of the sheikh's religious authority and the disciples' spiritual and material interests. Babou contends that the French did not welcome the establishment of an autonomous Muslim leadership, as the emphasis of colonial rule focused almost exclusively on subjugation, order, and obedience. He argues that the negotiation of space was a central component of the Muridiyya policy of cultural compromise—although by French culture they achieved symbolic and cultural autonomy from the colonial realm through creating the *daar al Murid*, where they physically occupied the land and culturally reshaped its landscape through the use of Islamic sacred architecture and rituals.

Mamadou Diouf's chapter 8 presents a portrait of the larger social group, the Muslim traders of Saint-Louis in the nineteenth and early twentieth centuries. As a community with a highly developed sense of civic culture, the *doomu ndaar*, as Diouf contends, drew as much from the wellsprings of Islam as from the political, economic, and social rights that they enjoyed, owing to their legal status as *originaires*. The economic and philanthropic activities of the *doomu ndaar*, along with knowledge of how they ran their households, allow us to question the ways in which they combined, recombined, and ultimately created their own culture out of the various social, economic and political milieus around them. Their highly developed and urbane civic culture borrowed as much from the traditions of the Senegambia—in particular its Wolof and Halpulaar dimensions from the "religious library" of the Muslim world (North Africa, Egypt, and the Middle East)—as from the administrative, political, and institutional sources and resources of the French colony of Senegal. As Diouf documents, despite collaboration with the colonial administration, the *doomu ndaar* carved out an autonomous civic space for themselves. As Diouf further shows, the inhabitants of Saint-Louis shaped for themselves a collective representation in sharp distinction to that presented to the colonial authorities. As Diouf argues, in challenging the authoritarianism of the administration, the *doomu ndaar* subverted colonial formulas that sought to foster cultural assimilation by institutionalizing the *mission civilisatrice*. Consequently, observes Diouf, scriptural and literary Islamic modernity evolved to contain and resist the hegemonic pretentions of this colonial "mission" through introducing a civility born of multiple heritages with an Arabic and Muslim textuality at its core. This civic culture contrasted dramatically with that of the Sufi Wolof region of central Senegal.

Etienne Smith's chapter 7 is both a theoretical diagnostic of the literature explicating Senegal's peaceful ethnic, cultural, and religious pluralism and a constructive analysis of the Senegalese "social contract." By particularly focusing on the "republican model" and the "Islamo-Wolof model" approaches to the "contract," Smith points to its defining attribute: tolerance. He identifies in the "Senegalese model" three interlocking spheres: the republican sphere of the modern state (colonial and postcolonial), the religious sphere (including the Christian minority), and the cultural sphere of the patrias (Senegalese *terroirs* and precolonial polities). Smith argues forcibly that the study of religion in Senegal can be usefully compared to the study of ethnicity because there is a patterned relationship between the state and the spheres of ethnicity and of religion. Smith argues that while religion plays an important role in Senegal, it is not the only factor determining Senegal's peaceful ethnocultural and religious pluralism. Smith also suggests that kinship is the major conceptual framework irrigating Senegalese political culture, one that cuts across cleavages based on religion, language, or ethnicity. The chapter discusses how social uses of kinship are used to transcend other cleavages. While results varied between geographic locations and religious groups, Smith shows how kinship groups transcend religious affiliations in different religious groups. Consequently, ethnicity and kinship may have more to do with religion in terms of being among the many convenient tools available in daily life to create social connections.

In chapter 9, Alfred Stepan surveys four salient epistemological and methodological findings in the available comparative literatures on secularism, human rights, citizenship, and democratization. He incorporates Senegal's experience into modern democratization theory to challenge the assumption that complete separation of church and state, as reflected in the American or the French model (however tenuous), is the most conducive arrangement for building democracy and the protection of human rights. He then argues that where specific human rights violations are defended as intrinsic to the country's religion, the most efficacious actions are those coordinated by the state as well as religious campaigns against such practices. Through his theory of "rituals of respect"—recurrent, reciprocated, public performances that foster a "common knowledge among relevant actors" Stepan argues that such "rituals" function to ensure a group's recognition of mutual dignity. As Stepan shows, the consistent displays of mutual respect between religions and the state have facilitated a policy of cooperation in cases of human rights abuses, such as the Campaign Against Female Genital Mutilation and anti-AIDS policies. Stepan credits the diminishing presence this practice as well as the low levels of AIDS in the country to coordinated measures undertaken by the religious leadership and the state. Further, he contends that there is not much interest in Wahhabi or Iranian styles of Islam, since this formation would go against their spirit of religious tolerance and their belief that fundamentalists grow best under repressive politics. While neither the state nor Sufis seek to contain political Islam by repression, observes Stepan, because most Senegalese view these schools as culturally alien competitors, they are in low demand.

While scholars and observers point to the supposed "incompatibility" between Islam and democracy, Leonardo A. Villalón, in chapter 10, focuses on Senegal's role in relation to the future of democracy in the Muslim world, as articulated in debates emanating from academic and policy-oriented circles. Although Senegal is often cited as both a devoutly Muslim and democratic country, some scholars consider that Islam in Senegal is an "African Islam," and is more hospitable to democracy than other variants of Islam. Villalón's work seeks to place Senegal's supposed "exceptionalism" in a comparative regional perspective by examining the democratic developments of two of its Sahelian neighbors, Mali and Niger. Mali and Niger both followed the model of postindependence authoritarianism, with single party regimes that gave way to military ones, and were toppled in the 1990s by popular mobilization. As Villalón demonstrates, these newly liberalized spaces allowed for the organization and mobilization of new, empowered social groups whose efforts to exert control over the political agenda shaped the outcomes of social reform. Villalón maintains further that specifically in Senegal, with its clericalized marabout system, the democratic liberalization of the public sphere has brought significant transformations in the religious domain that could be identified as "democratization of religion." In Niger and Mali, one witnesses the emergence of an explosion of religious associations of varying kinds, including those from Salafist or Wahhabi inspiration. Villalón's chapter shows how, on fundamental levels, the interaction of religion with politics in Senegal parallels the situation of its neighbors in this era of democratization. Villalón concludes that democracy will move the Senegalese state closer to local cultures and lived realities, though a democracy still rooted more in religious values than many secularists would like, particularly in terms of gender and sexuality.

Notes

1. This introduction was translated by Nathalie Porter (Vanderbilt University) and revised by the author. My friend and colleague Trica Keaton, also from Vanderbilt University, assisted in revising it formally and substantively.

Introduction

I would like to thank both of them. The notion of "administration of pluralism" is borrowed from Karen Barkey's work, in particular, *Empire of Difference: The Ottomans in Comparative Perspective*; and "In the Lands of the Ottomans: Religion and Politics," in *Religion and the Political Imagination*, eds. Ira Katznelson and Gareth Stedman Jones.

2. Nandy, *The Return of the Sacred*, p.1.
3. Diagne, *Islam et société ouverte*.
4. Meriboute, *Islam's Fateful Path*, trans. John King.
5. Ibid., p. 13.
6. In his "work of synthesis" *Muslim Communities of Grace: The Sufi Brotherhoods in Islamic Religious Life*, p. 4, Jamil M. Abun-Nasr also reconstructs the history of the Sufi tradition to examine the attacks the Sufi are subject to by Muslim reformers and "Modernizing Muslim rulers," from Ataturk (Turkey) to Mamadou Dia (Senegal) and Boumédienne (Algeria) (pp. 243–251) in the early nationalist period. Since the 1970s, the political leadership in countries such as Algeria and Pakistan began supporting Sufi brotherhoods in order to offset the influence and political operations of Muslim reformers and the threat of Islamist movements (pp. 251–255).
7. Zidane Meriboute, *Islam's Fateful Path*, p. 13. It is worth noting that, in the Senegalese case, the politician who won the power struggle following independence was Léopold Sédar Senghor, a Catholic. He defeated two Muslim politicians, Lamine Gueye and Mamadou Dia, by espousing, regarding the brotherhoods, the position advocated by Meriboute. I will come back to this issue later in the introduction.
8. Ibid., p. 177.
9. Ibid.
10. Ibid., pp. 179–180.
11. Ibid., p. 187.
12. Ibid., p. 193.
13. Gellar, *Senegal*.
14. Coulon and Cruise O'Brien, "Senegal," p. 187. On the political stability of the Senegal state and the role of the Muslim brotherhoods, see also L. Creevy, "Muslim Brotherhoods," in addition to the books and articles mentioned earlier.
15. Fatton, *The Making of a Liberal Democracy: Senegal's Passive Revolution, 1975–1985*.
16. Coulon, "Senegal: The Development and Fragility of a Semi-Democracy."
17. Diop and Diouf, *Le Sénégal sous Abdou Diouf*.
18. Trimingham, *The Influence of Islam Upon Africa*, p. 142.
19. Rosander, "Introduction: The Islamization of 'Tradition' and 'Modernity.'" Using her very solid ethnography of the expansion of Shi'a Islam and the

constitution of a Shi'a community in Senegal, Mara Leichtman questions Eva Rosander's rigid cartography of Islam in Africa. See her chapter "The Authentication of a Discursive Islam: Shi'a Alternatives to Sufi Orders," in eds. Diouf and Leichtman, *New Perspectives on Islam in Senegal: Conversion, Migration, Wealth, and Femininity*, p. 114.

20. Rosander, "Introduction."
21. Coulon and Cruise O'Brien, "Senegal," p. 156.
22. Ibid., pp. 156–157.
23. Villalón, "Generational Changes," p. 130.
24. Coulon and Cruise O'Brien, "Senegal," p. 145.
25. Ibid.
26. Villalón, "Generational Changes," p. 130.
27. The Islamo-Wolof model is composed of the political, social, and cultural arrangements (infrastructures and ideologies) that have been supporting both the operations of the colonial and the postcolonial states and providing the sources and resources for the legitimacy of their power.
28. See, for example, the work of Guèye, *Touba: La capitale des Mourides*. He shows in a very convincing way the role of matrilineal family branches in the struggle for power and influence among the Murids.
29. Julien, *Histoire de l'Algérie contemporaine*; Ageron, *Les Algériens musulmans et la France*.
30. See Cruise O'Brien, *The Mourides of Senegal*; Copans, *Les marabouts de l'arachide*; Coulon, *Le marabout et le Prince*.
31. Robinson, *Paths of Accommodation*, p. 77.
32. See Diop and Diouf, *Le Sénégal*; Diouf, *Une histoire du Sénégal*.
33. Asad, "From the History of Colonial Anthropology to the Anthropology of Western Hegemony."
34. Roy, *The Failure of Political Islam*.
35. Frearon and Laitin, "Explaining Interethnic Co-operation."
36. Creppell, *Toleration and Identity*.
37. Garcia, "Al-Hajj Seydou Nourou Tall: 'Grand Marabout' Tijani," and Clark and Colvin, *Historical Dictionary of Senegal*.
38. Cruise O'Brien, *Symbolic Confrontations*, p. 181.
39. Ibid.
40. The *ndiggël* is the political instruction given to the *taalibe* by his marabout during elections. The Sufi marabout indicated very clearly to the disciples which candidate to vote for in exchange for spiritual and material gains. In exchange for delivering the votes, the former have been constantly rewarded by the state and the ruling class. On the *ndiggël*, see Diop and Diouf, *Le Sénégal*.

41. Goody, "Restricted Literacy in Northern Ghana," pp. 198–265.
42. Diouf, *Une histoire du Sénégal*.
43. Abun-Nasr, *Muslim Communities of Grace*, pp. 245–246.
44. Dia, *Islam société Africaines et culture industrielle; Essais sur l'Islam: Socio-anthropologie de l'Islam; Islam et civilisations Négro-Africaines*.
45. Mudimbe, *Tales of Faith: Religion as a Political Performance in Central Africa*, p. 91.
46. Smith, "Des arts de faire sociétés."
47. Vaillant, *Vie de Léopold Sédar Senghor*.
48. Mudimbe, *Tales of Faith*. Mudimbe traces how "against the classical style and its combatively intolerant policy, the faithful graduates from Al-Azhar Ben Badis in Tunisia and Qarawiyyin in Fes [emerged] a clairvoyance coming out of the Qur'an proposed a call to modernity: how can we reorganize Islamic schools in today's context? How and why Islam should be an African challenge and a response to modern cultures, and thus really present in the city, and not be perceived only as a far-away religious reference, accepted or tolerated for civility reasons and reserved to a marginal group of practitioners," p. 91.
49. Déclaration de Serigne Mansour Sy Djamil sur les derniers événements nationaux: "*Wade na dem, dafa doy*," *L'Obs* sur *Seneweb.com*, *Actualités*, January 5, 2010, p. 1.
50. Ibid.
51. Ibid., p. 3.
52. Ibid., p. 4.
53. On this issue, see Marie Broissier's excellent dissertation, *Quand la mobilisation produit de l'institution*.

Bibliography

Abun-Nasr, Jamil M. *Muslim Communities of Grace: The Sufi Brotherhoods in Islamic Religious Life*. New York: Columbia University Press, 2007.

Ageron, Charles Robert. *Les Algériens musulmans et la France, 1871–1919*. 2 vols. Paris: PUF, 1968.

Asad, Talal. "From the History of Colonial Anthropology to the Anthropology of Western Hegemony." In *Colonial Situations*, ed. George Stocking, 314–324. Madison: University of Wisconsin Press, 1991.

Broissier, Marie. *Quand la mobilisation produit de l'institution: Pratiques de la famille et organisations religieuses au Sénégal*. PhD dissertation. Ecole doctorale de science politique. Université de Paris 1, 2010.

Clark, Andrew F. and Lucie Colvin. *Historical Dictionary of Senegal*. Metuchen, N.J.: Scarecrow, 1994.

Copans, Jean. *Les marabouts de l'arachide*. Paris: Le Sycomore, 1980.

Coulon, Christian. *Le marabout et le prince*. Paris: Editions Pedone, 1981.

———. "Senegal: The Development and Fragility of a Semi-Democracy." In *Democracy in Developing Countries*, eds. Larry Diamond, Joan Linz, and Seymour M. Lipset, Vol. 4, 141–187. Boulder, Colo: Lynne Rienner, 1988.

Coulon, Christian and Donal B. Cruise O'Brien. "Senegal." In *Contemporary West African States*, eds. John Dunn and Richard Rathbone, 145–164, Cambridge: Cambridge University Press, 1989.

Creevey, Lucy. "Muslim Brotherhoods and Politics in Senegal in 1985," *Journal of Modern African Studies* 23 (1985): 715–721.

Creppell, Ingrid. *Toleration and Identity, Foundations in Early Modern Thought*. London: Routledge, 2003.

Cruise O'Brien, Donal B. *The Mourides of Senegal: The Economic and Political Organization of an Islamic Brotherhood*. Oxford: Clarendon Press, 1971.

———. "Senegal." In *West African States: Failure and Promise*, ed. John Dunn, 173–188. Cambridge, Mass.: Cambridge University Press, 1979.

———. *Symbolic Confrontations. Muslims Imagining the State in Africa*. New York: Palgrave-Macmillan, 2003.

Dia, Mamadou. *Islam société Africaines et culture industrielle*. Dakar, Senegal: Nouvelles Editions Africaines, 1975.

———. *Essais sur l'Islam. Socio-anthropologie de l'Islam*. Dakar, Senegal: Nouvelles Editions Africaines, 1979.

———. *Islam et civilisations Négro-Africaines*. Dakar, Senegal: Nouvelles Editions Africaines, 1980.

Diagne, Souleymane Bachir. *Islam et société ouverte. La fidélité et le mouvement dans la philosophie de Muhammed Iqbal*. Paris: Maisonneuve et Larose, 2001.

Diop, Momar Coumba and Mamadou Diouf, *Le Sénégal sous Abdou Diouf*. Paris: Karthala, 1990.

Diouf, Mamadou. *Une histoire du Sénégal: Le modèle Islamo-Wolof et ses périphéries*. Paris: Maisonneuve et Larose, 2001.

Frearon, James D. and David D. Laitin, "Explaining Interethnic Co-operation," *American Political Science Review* 90 (1996): 715–735.

Garcia, Sylvianne. "Al-Hajj Seydou Nourou Tall 'Grand Marabout' Tijani: L'histoire d'une carrière, c. 1880–1980." In *Le temps des marabouts: Itinéraires et stratégies Islamiques en Afrique Occidentale Française, v. 1880–1960*, eds. D. Robinson and J. L. Triaud, 247–275. Paris: Karthala, 1997.

Gellar, Sheldon. *Senegal: An African Nation Between Islam and the West*. Boulder, Colo.: Lynne Rienner, 1995.

Introduction

Goody, Jack. "Restricted Literacy in Northern Ghana." In *Literacy in Traditional Societies*, ed. J. Goody, 198–265. Cambridge, Mass.: Cambridge University Press, 1968.

Julien, Charles-André. *Histoire de l'Algérie contemporaine. 1, La conquête et les débuts de la colonisation, 1827–1871*. Paris: PUF, 1964.

Leichtman, Mara. "The Authentication of a Discursive Islam. Shi'a Alternatives to Sufi Orders." In *New Perspectives on Islam in Senegal. Conversion, Migration, Wealth, and Femininity*, eds. Mamadou Diouf and Mara A. Leichtman, 111–138. New York: Palgrave-Macmillan, 2009.

Meriboute, Zidane. *Islam's Fateful Path. The Critical Choices Facing Modern Muslims*. Trans., John King. New York: I. B. Taurus, 2009.

Mudimbe, V. Y. *Tales of Faith. Religion as a Political Performance in Central Africa*. London: Althone Press, 1997.

Nandy, Ashis. *The Return of the Sacred. The Language of Religion and the Fear of Democracy in a Post-Secular World*. The Mahesh Chandra Regmi Lecture 2007. Kathmandu: Social Science Baha, Himal Books, 2007.

Robinson, David. *Paths of Accommodation: Muslim Societies and French Colonial Authorities in Senegal and Mauritania, 1880–1920*. Athens: Ohio University Press, 2000.

Rosander, Eva Evevs. "Introduction: The Islamization of 'Tradition' and 'Modernity.'" In *African Islam and Islam in Africa. Encounters Between Sufis and Islamists*, eds. D. Westerlund and E. E. Rosander, 1–27. Athens: Ohio University Press, 1997.

Roy, Olivier. *The Failure of Political Islam*. London: Tauris, 1994.

Smith, Etienne. *Des arts de faire sociétés: Parentés à plaisanteries et constructions identitaires en Afrique de l'Ouest (Sénégal)*. PhD dissertation, Institut d'Etudes Politiques, 2010.

Trimingham, J. Spencer. *The Influence of Islam Upon Africa*. 2nd ed. London: Longman, 1980.

Vaillant, Janet. *Vie de Léopold Sédar Senghor: Noir, Français et Africain*. Trans., Roger Meunier. Paris: Karthala, 2006.

Villalón, Leonardo, "Generational Changes, Political Stagnation, and the Evolving Dynamics of Religion and Politics in Senegal," *Africa Today* 46 (3/4) (Summer/Autumn 1999): 129–137.

[2]

A Secular Age and the World of Islam

SOULEYMANE BACHIR DIAGNE

Islam's responses to the secularization narrative are of two different kinds: intellectual responses and practical ones.

What is to be understood as an intellectual response by the philosophical and political discourse that was produced by the self-examination of Muslim societies conducted by their intellectual elites following the encounter with European modernity and secularism in the nineteenth century?

A practical response is the process by which democratic and secular (in their own way) states are being built in the Muslim world. I will consider here the case of Senegal as it exemplifies the project of constructing a version of secularism, characterized as a "well understood and properly practiced *laïcité*"[1] by its second president, Abdou Diouf, who succeeded L. S. Senghor in 1980 and remained in office until 2000.

The Senegalese case has been taken by Alfred Stepan to be one of the examples that should lead "empirical democratic theorists [to] abandon the idea of a singular secularism and advance research concerning 'the multiple secularisms of modern democracies.'"[2] The secularization narrative referred to can be summarized, in the words of Charles Taylor, as the story of "a change . . . needs to be a nonbreaking ellipsis which takes us from a society in which it was virtually impossible not to believe in God, to one in which faith, even for the staunchest believer, is one human possibility among others."[3]

That raises the question of the intellectual and practical responses to that story coming from societies, where, at least statistically, it is virtually impossible "to take religion off the agenda," to quote Rawls's watchword that Stepan questions from the point of view of an empirical democratic theorist.[4] What understanding of secularism and what types of secular projects do those societies produce?

Intellectual Responses

Calling for a New Cosmology

Charles Taylor writes that there is something new in the turn to unbelief witnessed in the middle or late nineteenth century in Europe that makes this era more than just a continuation of the eighteenth century. The "intellectual formulations" of Comte, Mill, Renan, and Feuerbach, he explains, mark that turn in a "deeper . . . qualitatively different" way than what can be found in Bentham, Helvétius, or Holbach.[5]

Consider, for example, a "formulation" by Ernest Renan that Taylor quotes at least twice in the book *A Secular Age* and for which he provides the following English translation: "A day will come when humanity will no longer believe, but it will know: a day when it will know the metaphysical and moral world, just as it already knows the physical one."[6,7] The day evoked in this quotation is precisely that of the colonial spread of Western modernity in the world, in the Muslim world in particular.

Renan delivered a famous lecture in 1884 called *L'Islamisme et la science*, in which he developed the thesis that Islam, which he called "Islamism," was in essence incompatible with the spirit of science. The societies in Islam's grip could not have produced the same story that unfolded in Europe and culminated in a modernity in which the future belonged to science. Renan started with what was for him a fact: "l'infériorité naturelle des Etats gouvernés par l'Islam"—the natural inferiority of the States under the rule of Islam—a consequence, according to him, of "the inevitably narrow mind of a true believer, of this sort of iron circle which wraps up their heads, making them absolutely closed to science and incapable of learning or opening up to any new idea."[8]

He also dismissed the notion that some golden age existed during which Islam had produced prominent scientists and thinkers. As a consistent positivist, he considered it a fallacy to think that Islam could have produced them.

As scientists and thinkers, they necessarily thought within an un-Islamic or at least a-Islamic framework.[9] The first Abbasid caliphs who opened up the Muslim world to Greek and Indian science and philosophy, he affirmed, were "à peine musulmans"—barely Muslims. He also called Avicenna and Averroes "those great infidels who have represented for five centuries the tradition of the human spirit."[10]

It is worth noting the circumstances of the lecture: the visit in Paris of Jamal ad-Din Al-Afghani, a Muslim intellectual and political activist, who, for most of his life, traveled tirelessly in the "East" and in the "West" to promote the independence and the modernization—modernization as the only means for independence—of Muslim lands. The response by Afghani to Renan was not what his followers expected. In fact, Afghani basically acquiesced to what Renan said, asking him only not to single out Islam when in fact all religions stood in the way of the promise of science.

In that agreement, one could read a form of response to the question posed to Muslim elites by the secularization narrative. Two years before that conference, in a lecture he gave in Albert Hall Calcutta, Afghani had himself chided the "ulema of India," the traditional elite, for having lost the sense of science when they established a distinction between "European science" and "Islamic science." He invited them to stop living in an Aristotelian world, to leave the "cosmos" and embrace the "universe."[11]

One could see this call for a new cosmology—which will be echoed later in Muhammad Iqbal's philosophy of a continuously emerging universe open to the action of human beings—as promoting a secular outlook on the world: The world does not have to correspond to the geocentric picture that seems to translate the cosmology of the Qur'an. How about the philosophical and political implications of such a call?

Calling for a New Political Philosophy

The response to that question had to address the precise question of the caliphate and what it represented. Here we need to examine a work, the importance of which, for the discussion of secularism in Islam, cannot be emphasized enough: Egyptian thinker Ali Abderraziq's (1888–1966) *L'Islam et les fondements du pouvoir* (*Islam and the Foundations of Power*).

A Secular Age and the World of Islam

After the proclamation founding in October 1923 of the Republic of Turkey, the Ottoman caliphate, which, until then, nominally remained the symbol of the unity and continuity of a Muslim world (*Umma*), was abolished. That was the official end of the history of an Islamic community created by the prophetic message, even though, in fact, the notion of a central government effectively in charge of such a community had been a fiction for a long time.

So ultimately the abolition of the caliphate did not change the reality of things much. The event nevertheless was a shock. The notion had been integral to the idea of an Islamic community that transcended national borders. The caliph was the "protector of *shari'a*." The Qur'anic notion of *khalifatullah* applied to man—lieutenant of God—with political weight when applied to the caliph.

We can think here of the Indian *Khilafat* movement created with the goal of safeguarding the institution of the caliphate after World War I and the Allied victory. The fear was that the Allies would abolish the caliphate. The irony is that a few years later the abolition would come, not from Great Britain, but from the nationalist movement of Mustafa Kemal Ataturk.

The abolition of the caliphate created the obligation to rethink the political question of government. In fact, the Turkish National Assembly, justifying the end of the caliphate and inviting Muslim peoples to freely define the forms of government that suited their particular situations, commissioned a manifesto. There were responses from many ulema claiming that an Islamic model of political organization existed on the basis of an "implicit constitution," both the model and the constitution going back to the Prophet himself, and they therefore demanded that the Muslims eternally strive to conform to them.

Abderraziq opposed those ulema. He took seriously the challenge of rethinking the political question, or rather, of thinking of it for the first time, as it was not obfuscated by the issue of the caliphate anymore. Until the point when "who should be the caliph?" was no longer the unique question of political philosophy, the reflection on the nature and types of governments had remained underdeveloped.

In his book, published in 1925—the year after the caliphate was abolished—Abderraziq observed that philosophical thought in the Islamic world, even at the time when it was flourishing, seriously neglected such topics. The reason was political. According to the author, caliphates, powerful leaders, or dictators—thrones do not like to entertain questions about the foundations of power because they could reveal that power ultimately rests on force and draws no real legitimacy from what rulers pretend to be a continuation of the Prophet's accomplishments. It is, in fact, the very notion of continuation that needs to be questioned because, after all, Abderraziq asks, in a deliberately provocative way, "Was the Prophet a king?"

Abderraziq demonstrates, *more geometrico*, as his Moroccan commentator Abdou Filali-Ansary describes his argument,[12] that there has never been such a thing as an ideal government establishing a norm to be followed by Muslim populations in their efforts to create political institutions. The historical facts are that the Prophet of Islam did not set out to constitute a political state. Of course, he lead the radically new type of community that his message had created. But he was not preoccupied with instituting the principles of a system of government with all the basic rules for its functioning.

So if we do not know anything about the procedures by which the system was supposed to perpetuate itself, it is not because of a lack of historical information—it is because things had been left open for human reason and judgment.

What Abderraziq reads when revisiting the early history of Islam is not the will to institute a model of indissoluble unity between state and religion, but the intention to start a society in which nothing prevents the people from imagining and building the systems of government adapted to the conditions that the movement of life continuously creates. It is certainly the pressure of modernity that has triggered such a retrospective reading of the events of early Islam. But that does not mean that there is anything "inauthentic" in an approach that demonstrates that nothing in the *fundamentals* of the religion is opposed to the modern demand of a separation between the state and the mosque and to the development of an autonomous science of the political.

Ali A. Allawi, who served as a minister in postwar Iraqi governments, writes: "The institution of the caliphate symbolizes the former world power of Islam. The yearning for its reinstatement has been a constant theme for radical islamists. . . . [T]he idea of the caliphate continues to exert a powerful pull on Muslims and its restitution has been skillfully employed by Islamists of all hues as a shorthand for the emergence of a Muslim super-state able to bestride the world stage."[13]

Allawi also writes that "the reality is such that the caliphate, at least in its historical form, is unlikely to be resuscitated. The current division of the Muslim World into nation-states, republics and monarchies, democracies and autocracies, is far too advanced to assume that they could ever be regrouped within a single empire or super-state inspired by religion."[14]

This is to say that ultimately the response to the narrative of secularization will consist of practical responses at the level of the nation-states—namely, the members of the Organization of the Islamic Conference.

The challenge is to create democracies based on secularism that will take different forms provided that core principles are present: (1) moral equality of persons and (2) freedom of conscience and religion.[15] This raises a fundamental question: Is such a freedom of conscience part of the intellectual response to the secularization narrative?

Affirming the Need for Freedom of Conscience

Law professor Abdullah Ahmed An Na'im articulates that need well when he writes in the concluding chapter of his latest book:

> As a Muslim, I need a secular state in order to live in accordance with *shari'a* out of my own genuine conviction and free choice, personally and in community with other Muslims, which is the only valid and legitimate way of being a Muslim. Belief in Islam, or any other religion, logically requires the possibility of disbelief, because belief has no value if it is coerced. If I am unable to disbelieve, I will not be able to believe. Maintaining institutional separation between Islam and the state, while regulating the permanent connection of Islam and politics is a necessary condition for achieving the positive role of shari'a now and in the future.[16]

This claim that one needs a secular state committed to pluralism and tolerance because one is a Muslim and because, as a consequence, one's faith becomes meaningful only in such a state is, in fact, based upon the principle expressed in the Qur'an (al-Baqarah 2:256).[17]

What An Na'im is ultimately drawn to conclude necessarily follows from the notion that compulsion is incompatible with religion. So "yes, no, and it does not matter" would be the right answer to the question he raised earlier in the book about whether his position and theses were influenced by "Western" liberalism and modernity. Such an influence is *also* certainly the case, but that does not make his reading of the Qur'anic principle upon which his claims and advocacy are founded any less "authentic."

A Practical Response: Senegal's Construction of a "Well-Understood *Laïcité*"

With the example of Senegal as a practical response to the challenge presented by secularization to Muslim societies, I will examine a case outside of what is generally considered in orientalist scholarship to be the world of Islam. Quite often when one thinks of Islam one thinks of the Arab or Persian or South Asian worlds, relegating, for example, the sub-Saharan part of the African continent to the margins. As a consequence, when the question of the compatibility of Islam with secularism, considered a cornerstone of democracy, is raised, examples of countries such as Senegal, a West African Sahelian country that, against all the odds of extreme poverty, still manages to have a fairly democratic and free political system, seldom comes to the mind of most political scientists or empirical democratic theorists.

But many reasons make Senegal an interesting case to consider. First, although the Muslim faith was present very early, massive Islamization is relatively recent. Second, its heritage of French colonialism and French *laïcité* (a very specific brand of secularism) make the country a special case. Third, is the role played by Léopold Sédar Senghor, who led the country to independence and played a crucial role in establishing its institutions and defining the state's *laïcité*. Although he belonged to the Catholic minority in an overwhelmingly Muslim country, Senghor tried to realize in practice what has been called the *Muslim intellectual response* to the challenge of secularization by placing his project of building a modern state under the auspices of modernist Muslim philosophers such as Al Afghani, Muhammad Abduh, and Muhammad Iqbal, and, on the Christian side, Father Pierre Teilhard de Chardin.

Senghor wanted to define a form of modernity and secularism that would be inspired by the spirit of a "reconstruction of Islam's religious thought"—to borrow Iqbal's title—as a response to the "secular age," in many respects comparable to what Habib Bourguiba wanted for Tunisia. But, of course, unlike Bourguiba, Senghor as a Catholic would face a more difficult task of calling the Muslim majority of Senegal to the kind of Islamic *ijtihad* that he had in mind.

A Secular Age and the World of Islam

Islamization of Senegal and the Challenge to French Laïcité

The Islamic presence in the valley of the River Senegal was already a reality when, at the beginning of the eleventh century, in the kingdom of Tekrûr, then situated in the northern part of modern-day Senegal known as *Fuuta Tooro*, Wârjâbî became the first king to convert to Islam. He adopted Islamic law for Tekrûr, and it was a Muslim territory by the time he died in 1040. The Muslim faith then steadily spread toward the southern regions, where learning centers were founded and flourished and through which Islamic knowledge and practices were disseminated.

A phase of accelerated Islamization occurred at the end of the eighteenth century and throughout the nineteenth century. In northern Senegal, a new regime known as *almaamiyya* took power in 1776. The leadership was headed by an *almamy*—a local title in the Fulani language coming from the Arabic *imam*—who was elected from among the members of a new class of religious families known as *Torodo*.

Fuuta Tooro is also the homeland of Shaykh Umar al Fûtî, who led a religious war for the expansion of Islam in the regions east of the River Senegal. Umar also fought against French armies and died in a war in 1864 in Bandiagara, a region in present-day Mali.

The massive Islamization of West Africa occurred during French colonization. The colonial administration constructed roads and railways and thus helped Muslim traders to travel widely, preaching Islam to local populations. At the same time, the people who had witnessed the collapse of the traditional kingdoms they lived in and the disruption of the social order they were used to in their homelands were willing to stand behind the new religious leadership offered by spiritual guides known as shaykhs or marabouts. As their influence grew rapidly, these leaders became the target of the colonial administration's suspicion and ire. Marabouts headed the *Sufi* (mystical) orders, which provided education to new converts to Islam, as they integrated the social structure of a fraternity organized around a *shaykh* (master) and a religious center where recurrent gatherings would take place. This history explains why Islam in West Africa is mostly mystical in which the role of Sufi orders is paramount.

This importance of the Sufi orders is found particularly in Senegal. Thus, *Qadiriyya* (or the path of Abd al Qadir Jîlânî, who died in the eleventh century in Bagdad) and *Tijjaniyya* (the path of Abul Abbass Ahmad at-Tijjânî, who died in 1815 in Fez, Morocco) are important Sufi orders in the country.

Their local leaders, called shaykhs, *seriñ*, or *ceerno*, have many followers in Senegal. Two other important orders, known as Muridiyya and Laayeen, can be considered specific contributions of Senegal to the continuous proliferation of mystical orders in the Islamic world in general because they were locally created. The Murid path—the second most important by number of followers after the Tijaniyya—was founded by the Senegalese Shaykh Amadu Bamba (1853–1927) in the late-nineteenth century. Seydinâ Limâmu Laay (1843–1909), who led a movement eponomously named Laayeen. Initially begun as a *mahdism*—the belief that the *mahdi* or the messiah has come—it rapidly became just another Sufi path.

After Senegal officially became a territory of France following the Berlin Conference (1884), the French colonial administration found itself having to find a path of accommodation with Islam, in particular with the Sufi orders.

It is an irony of history that France, where, in 1905, *laïcité* was articulated as a conception of secularism founded on a history of anticlericalism and on a haughty opposition to any manifestation of religion in the public sphere, had to think of itself in its colonies, and in Senegal in particular, as a "Muslim power" and had to find a "path of accommodation" with Islam and the Sufi orders. It thus had to preside over the creation of Qur'anic schools,[18] organize the *hajj* (pilgrimage to Mecca), create Muslim tribunals, appoint Islamic judges (*qadis*), and guarantee the particular personal status of the Muslim populations in spite of the decision, made in 1840, to apply the civil and penal codes to the colony (then the city of Saint-Louis), and despite the decree made in 1903 that instituted uniformity in justice applied to *metropolitains, originaires,* and *assimilés*. The right for the populations to keep their customs, "if not contrary to humanity and civilization," was recognized within a de facto regime of legal pluralism. In a word, the difference between direct and indirect rule associated, respectively, with French and British imperialisms, real in theory, became somewhat irrelevant in practice as "the administrator, as the 'man on the spot,' often had to be pragmatic if he wanted French authority to take root."[19] Pragmatism, for the French colonial administration, meant associating the Sufi marabouts to its policies.[20]

The Spiritual Socialism for a Modern Secular State of Léopold Sédar Senghor and Mamadou Dia

Léopold Sédar Senghor, the first president of newly independent Senegal, and Mamadou Dia, its président du conseil—equivalent to the prime minister in the French system of government before the Fifth Republic—inherited that situation of accommodation between the state apparatus and the Sufi orders. They believed deeply in secularism while thinking at the same time that religious fervor could and should play a role in bringing a cultural energy to the task of achieving modernization and development. As Senghor stated:

> The aim of Islamism and of Christianity is to fulfill the will of God. In order to fulfill this will, which is to gain heaven, we must achieve brotherhood among men, through justice for all men here on earth. Indeed, what is such justice if not equality of opportunity given from the beginning to all men regardless of race or condition; and, along with work, the equitable distribution of national revenue among citizens, of world revenue among nations and finally, the equitable distribution of knowledge among all men and all nations?[21]

Senghor was expressing a profound conviction concerning the role that the two Abrahamic religions (he realized that traditional African belief systems were inevitably going to fade out), at least as organized religions, fully reconciled with their own commitment to realize social justice and development, could play in building the new nation. That conviction is echoed in the following lines written by Mamadou Dia:

> Islam must remind the Muslim world, at this juncture when it is taking its Promethean leap, that *if it is required to act, it is so that one may fulfill oneself, that one may achieve even richer being.* For industrial development to be a boon and not the ruin of mankind, it is crucial that it retain a human dimension, that it not give rise to a new kind of slavery under the pretense of promoting productivity or efficacy, that it not create progress that is in reality perversion, desire of well-being and not of better-being, that it not produce a world where ethics is sacrificed to power and spirit to matter, a world of inanimate objects. Islam cannot accept just any model of economic development without denying itself. It will give its blessing only to a development program that tends toward an order of social justice and human solidarity and is founded upon a code of ethics.[22]

Senghor's and Dia's philosophy of dynamic religions contributing to the task of educating the nation out of poverty and ignorance and into modernity is reflected in the definition of Senegal's secularism articulated by

Senghor in 1963—after the separation of the two men, who had until then presided together over Senegal's destiny—when he made it clear that it had nothing to do with French *laïcité*. On the contrary, Senghor explained, although the sphere of politics and that of religion must be separated, religions are invited by the state, in equal respect for all of them, to be present in the public square in order to contribute to the edification of the nation.

The successor of Senghor as president of Senegal, Abdou Diouf, often referred to the conception of secularism he inherited from the founding fathers (Senghor and Dia) as "laïcité bien comprise" (well-understood secularism), such as in the following statement:

> *Laïcité* in itself is a manifestation of respect of others. It acts in this way if it is *laïcité* well understood and properly practiced. Such *laïcité* cannot be anti-religious, but neither, if it is a true *laïcité*, can it become a state religion. I would say further that such a *laïc* state cannot ignore religious institutions. . . . Respect of religion does not only mean tolerance, it does not mean only to allow or to ignore, but to respect the beliefs and practices of the other. *Laïcité* is the consequence of this respect for the other, and the condition of our harmony.[23]

Conclusion: Whither Senegal's Exceptionalism?

Speaking of the system he labeled "Sufi-secular mutual respect," Stepan presents the Senegalese case as evidence that, contrary to Rawls, sometimes it would be a mistake to "take religion off the agenda."[24] He and A. Kuru give as an example the fact that "the constant mutual display of respect between religions and the Senegalese state has facilitated policy cooperation on issues such as anti-AIDS and anti-female genital mutilation policies. It has created an atmosphere where religious leaders have felt free to make arguments from within Islam against practices and policies that violate human rights."[25]

The authors could have added that there was religious-secular dialogue on the Senegalese family code too, although the continuous controversy about the code, since its adoption in 1972—the marabouts have rejected it—is also a sign that Islamic-Christian-secular state cooperation to achieve the Senegalese modernity envisioned by Senghor cannot be taken for granted but must be pursued as a perpetual goal.

Scholars who have studied the functioning of Senegal's "well-understood secularism" often maintain that it manifests a "Senegalese exceptionalism," explaining the high degree of democracy and stability in the African context achieved by the country. The view that a certain "Senegalese social contract"[26] in which the Sufi orders' role of social moderator, their function as peacemakers in the public arena, is deemed necessary certainly corresponds to the reality. A well-known Shaykh of the Tijani order, Abdou Aziz Sy, Jr., thus described the intervention of religious leaders or marabouts in the public sphere:

> We are the firefighters of the political arena. . . . In the present situation in Senegal our role remains and those who protest that religious leaders should not speak out on the political situation do not understand the meaning of our action. We do not speak of politics. The marabout who interferes in politics is someone seeking privileges or positions of responsibility from those in power. The marabout must not interfere with politics in this way; his mission is to assume his responsibilities in matters of religion. But if the political game begins to create negative consequences for the people then our role is to intervene in order to preserve peace.[27]

This statement does correspond to the ideal that the founders had in mind, but what about its application? How can the line be drawn between "interference in politics" and "assuming the religious responsibility" to intervene? The system imagined by Senghor and Dia in continuity with the colonial policy of accommodation supposes from the religious and the state actors the discipline that would preserve the not-always-visible line of separation that still exists in the Senegalese brand of secularism between religion and politics. That not everybody has that discipline is something real today, especially when the dire situation of poverty is favorable to all sorts of populisms.

Particularly worrisome to many is the fact that a few marabouts are now tempted to create political parties while the current president, unlike his predecessors, does not shy away from putting on display his connection to the Murid order, eliciting protests from secularists and adherents of other Muslim brotherhoods that there is a bias in favor of one particular segment of the country's religious community.

In his *Les laïcités dans le monde* (*Secularities in the World*) Jean Baubérot recalls the significant fact that after Abdoulaye Wade, Senegal's third president, rose to power, he intentionally leaked a draft constitution in which the explicit use of the word *laïcité* was omitted; two days later, in the face of hostile reactions, the reference was reintroduced in the draft.[28]

Obviously the principle needs to be reassessed, as Senegal's "well-understood secularism" remains an ongoing task and demands precisely to be continuously *understood* by all actors in the public sphere.

Notes

1. These words of Abdou Diouf are quoted in *Constitution of Senegal*, ed. Doudôu Ndoye, 68–69.
2. Stepan, chapter 9, this volume.
3. Taylor, *A Secular Age*, p. 3.
4. Stepan, *Arguing Comparative Politics*, p. 227.
5. Taylor, *A Secular Age*, p. 322.
6. Ibid., pp. 434, 574.
7. "Il viendra un jour où l'humanité ne croira plus, mais où elle saura; un jour où elle saura le monde métaphysique et moral, comme elle sait déjà le monde physique." Ibid., pp. 434, 574.
8. Renan, *Oeuvres complètes*, 1:946. My translation.
9. Taylor writes: "Stigmatizing the religious societies as hostile to modern values as many Europeans tend to do today with the United States; and even more with Islam" (*A Secular Age*, p. 770).
10. Renan, *Oeuvres complètes*, 1:961.
11. I am alluding here to the title of the book on modern science by Alexandre Koyré, *From the Closed World to the Infinite Universe*. Baltimore and London: Johns Hopkins University Press, 1957.
12. Filali-Ansary, *L'Islam est-il hostile à la laïcité?*
13. Allawi, *The Crisis of Islamic Civilization*, p. 163.
14. Ibid, p. 165.
15. I am referring here to the principles established in the report cowritten by Charles Taylor and Jocelyn Maclure for the government of Quebec in which it is stated that "any secular system achieves some form of balance between the following 4 principles: two purposes: (1) Moral equality of persons, (2) Freedom of conscience and religion. Two essential institutional structures: (3) Separation of Church and State, (4) State neutrality in respect of religions and deep-seated secular convictions." They advocate an "open secularism" that develops the essential outcomes of the first and second principles by defining institutional structures (3 and 4)

A Secular Age and the World of Islam

in light of this objective. Maclure, *Secularism and Freedom of Conscience*, pp. 19–20.

16. An Na'im, *Islam and the Secular State*, p. 268.
17. The Holy Qur'an (al-Baqarah 2:256).
18. Between 1880 and 1890 the number of Muslim schools in Saint-Louis doubled while there was a dramatic increase in the market for Arabic books printed in Beirut or Smyrna (Klein, *Islam and Imperialism in Senegal*).
19. Ibid. Klein adds that "adapting to African realities" could be seen as "a bizarre footnote to 'mission civilisatrice.'" Hence the frustration of the purists of such a "mission" as that of Le Chatelier who, at the end of the nineteenth century, wrote (his *L'Islam dans l'Afrique Occidentale*, published in 1899, is quoted by Klein): "Every day it becomes harder and harder to tear down the barrier that rises between us. They are conscious of their role as a part of the Muslim world, in opposition to Christian society. Without reaching the point of applying reformist formulas to us [*nous appliquer les formules réformistes*], many look forward to a political revolution that will eventually give their party hegemony in the country."
20. One illustration of the collaboration between the French colonial administration and the Muslim leaders is the letter to Governor William Ponty from the three *qadis* (judges) of the tribunals of Dakar, Rufisque, and Saint-Louis during World War I, after Turkey, then the site of the Islamic caliphate, allied itself with Germany. The purpose of the letter was to assure the French authorities that Turkey's alliance with Germany was condemned by the Islamic leadership in Senegal; the signatories also acknowledged that "the French Republic had bestowed its peace and all sorts of good deeds to this Muslim country of [theirs], building mosques and Islamic schools . . . appointing *qadis* and supporting them in their task of ensuring justice." The letter, dated February 1, 1915, is reproduced in Djibril Samb's *Comprendre la laïcité* (pp. 237–238). In his book Samb also reproduces letters of accommodation to French rule and French "peace" from El Hadj Malick Sy, Shaykh Amadu Bamba, and El Hadj Abdoulaye Niass.
21. Senghor, *Liberté I*.
22. Dia, *Islam, sociétés Africaines, et culture industrielle*, p. 164. My emphasis.
23. Quoted in Ndoye, *Constitution du Sénégal*, pp. 48–49. The English translation is by Stepan, who quotes this passage in his *Rituals of Respect*.
24. Stepan, *Rituals of Respect*, pp. 227–229.
25. Stepan and Kuru, "*Laïcité* as an Ideal Type and a Continuum." In *Democracy, Islam, and Secularism in Turkey*, eds. A. Kuru and Al Stepan, 95–121.
26. Cruise O'Brien, "Le contrat social Sénégalais à l'épreuve." *Politique Africaine* 45, 1998.

27. *Echos de la Banque Mondiale, Magazine du Bureau régional de Dakar (Sénégal, Cap-Vert, Gambie, Guinée-Bissau, Niger)*, 9 (November 2007): 14–17.
28. Baubérot, *Les laïcités dans le monde*, p. 93.

Bibliography

Allawi, A. A. *The Crisis of Islamic Civilization*. New Haven and London: Yale University Press, 2009.

An Na'im, A. *Islam and the Secular State: Negotiating the Future of Shari'a*. Cambridge, Mass.: Harvard University Press, 2008.

Baubérot, J. *Les laïcités dans le monde*, 2nd éd. Paris: PUF, 2009.

Cruise O'Brien, D. B. "Le contrat social Sénégalais à l'épreuve." In *Politique Africaine*, no. 45, 1992.

Dia, M. *Islam, sociétés Africaines et culture industrielle*. Dakar: NEA, 1975.

Filali-Ansary, A. *L'Islam est-il hostile à la laïcité?* Casablanca, Morocco: Ed. Le Fennec, 2000.

Klein, M. *Islam and Imperialism in Senegal: Sine Saloum, 1847–1914*. Stanford, Calif.: Stanford University Press, 1968.

Ndoye, D. (ed.). *Constitution du Sénégal*. Dakar, Senegal: EDJA, 2001.

Renan, E. *Oeuvres complètes*, T I. Paris: Calmann-Lévy, 1947.

Samb, D. *Comprendre la laïcité*. Dakar, Senegal: NEAS, 2005.

Senghor, L. S. *Liberté I : Négritude et humanisme*. Paris: Seuil, 1964.

Stepan, A. *Arguing Comparative Politics*. Oxford and New York: Oxford University Press, 2001.

Taylor, C. *A Secular Age*. Cambridge and London: Harvard University Press, 2007.

[3]

Islam's New Visibility and the Secular Public in Senegal

BETH A. BUGGENHAGEN

Cosmopolitan Dakar and Islam's New Publicity

Every evening a Dakar radio station, Radio Dunyaa, hosts a show in which Senegalese can call in and ask questions pertaining to Islam. Radio Dunyaa also broadcasts announcements concerning the events, projects, and conferences of the Sufi congregations in Senegal. Popular Muslim scholars or young shaykhs usually host the show, but every so often, a prominent shaykh will make an appearance in an attempt to rally disciples in support of a major event. During his appearance, the shaykh will ask his disciples: "*Do you want me to plug this in? Do you want me to plug this circuit into God?*" I first heard these words spoken in a videocassette I watched more than a decade ago in Chicago, Illinois—a Senegalese television production covering the annual pilgrimage of disciples of the Murid Sufi order to their sacred city of Touba, in the desert interior of the country. The circuit of which the elder shaykh spoke was the ambit of spiritual power by which blessings (*baraka*) radiate outwards from God to those who have submitted to God through homage to Sufi shaykhs. He might as well have been talking, though, of the circuits of cash that Murid disciples remit as offerings (*addiya*) to their shaykhs from their earnings as merchants and workers of the diaspora in Europe, the United States, the Middle East, and China.

Islam's New Visibility and the Secular Public in Senegal

This video displayed the many proceeds of the money sent to Touba—bowls overflowing with food for pilgrims and dignitaries, the many forms of public and private transport that brought close to three million disciples there, and the development of a vast infrastructure to channel electricity into and sewage out of the city that disciples had come to witness. The cassette itself is circulated annually to disciples around the world who are unable to journey in person to the center, for them, of the globalized networks in which they seek fortunes no longer available in Senegal's barren ecology and economy. The videocassette is at once the motivation and the outcome of disciples' hard work abroad and desire to devote their earnings to this Muslim way. The medium of the videocassette and the practice of viewing and being viewed are central to the production of values for Murid disciples.[1]

Murid adepts also circulate other Muslim paraphernalia in addition to videocassettes, such as audiocassette sermons, DVDs, portraits, textiles and clothing, and texts. Through these diverse media forms, Muslims abroad are plugged into life at home, in Senegal, where Islam has gained new visibility in the last decade. In particular, Muslim men and women strive to create a pious, prosperous, and morally correct persona through video recordings and photographs that are viewed among kin and community in Senegal. In this chapter, I analyze the gendered and corporeal practices underpinning Islam's new visibility and focus on the production and circulation of videocassettes and portraiture. I consider how value is produced through aural and visual components of religious videocassettes and the ways in which dress and images of dressing well communicate ideas about proper religious comportment, wealth, and status.

In addition to the emergence and proliferation of new media, in the Senegalese capital of Dakar, the signs of Islam are everywhere. Piety is for sale not just in the form of religious paraphernalia such as prayer beads, mats, and head coverings, but also in the form of mass-produced home fashions such as calendars, clocks, bumper stickers, key rings, and decals for store windows and vending stalls. In homes and shops, one often sees the portraiture of important religious figures adorning the walls. In navigating the city, one is struck by the prominence of Muslim themes in urban expressive forms such as public murals and graffiti that have transformed secular spaces and places of work (Roberts et al. 2003), and in popular and religious music heard in shops and on public transportation.[2] Even the modernist rational layout of the city—its grids, boulevards, and round points—carries the names of Muslim figures and iconography of the Sufi congregations. The signs of Islam index urban and domestic spaces as Muslim spaces and their occupants and those who pass through them as potential beneficiaries of grace (*baraka*). These religious objects are not mere commodities—they are endowed with a particular efficacy; they are protective, generative of prosperity, and enable the bearer to escape misfortune.[3]

Muslim thought and practice has, in part, gained heightened visibility through the liberalization of broadcast media such as television and radio, but also through new media technologies such as the Internet, digital recording and broadcasting, facsimile machines, and desktop publishing. These new developments have been deeply contested in Senegal by both secular and Muslim publics. The terms of public debate in Dakar have come to turn on such matters as the increasing visibility of religious affiliations of candidates for public office,[4] sartorial practices and new Muslim media, including the use of radio, television, and Internet. Moreover, the liberalization and independence of the media has been hotly debated in Senegal. During the presidency of Abdoulaye Wade, independent media has been at odds with the government leading to questions about the freedom of the press in this secular republic.[5] And the proliferation of small media in particular, such as radio broadcasting, has permitted new religious figures who may not have the criteria for leadership, such as genealogical claims and scholarship, to land a larger audience.[6] Religious figures themselves have also come to question the interpenetration of the religious and public, especially with regard to popular cultural practices such as the invocation of Muslim themes in music, films, and novels. For example, the Mbalax star Youssou Ndour's 2004 album *Egypt* was widely criticized in Senegal for combining popular music with religious expression.

Many scholars have considered the penetration of Islam into economic and political life in postcolonial Senegal. It is now conventionally accepted that the intertwining of secular and religious forces has led to the establishment of one of the best-functioning democracies in West Africa. Other scholars have focused on the emergence of Muslim cities and towns in colonial and postcolonial Senegal.[7] Yet how do we understand Islam's new visibility with respect to the cultural politics of the capital city, at once secular and modern, but now saturated with new Muslim media and consumption practices oriented toward the creation of the proper, pious, and prosperous body? Clearly the emergence of new media has provided a platform for religious voices destabilizing the association of modernity and modern technologies with the decline of religion.[8] Technological innovations, global infrastructures, inexpensive media technologies, and state liberalization have facilitated the emergence of a Muslim public sphere, or as Charles Hirschkind[9] argues, a Muslim *counterpublic*. Hirschkind uses this term to index the multiplicity of voices and positions occupying these newly mediated spaces that counter both the singular authority of the state and of a religious hierarchy. As much as new media have provided a platform for Muslim leaders and challenged religious authority by providing spaces for new voices, they have also put the mundane activities of followers on display. Disciples watch videos and television programming and view portraits not only to learn from renowned scholars and leaders and to benefit from their *baraka*, but also to see themselves and others participating in these events. Of great interest are the sartorial displays of women, how their piety is enacted through dressing for religious occasions on which they will be photographed and videotaped.

Do the appeal of Muslim fashions and media challenge the secular republic and attendant notions of the significance of a secular public sphere? Certainly in this age of the global war on terror Islam seems to be more visible everywhere. But does this mean that where Islam is more visible democracy is less certain? In places such as France and Turkey, religious signs and symbols have been banned outright in municipal spaces. Is this an "excess of secularism," and is the contemporary concern with secularism a "fetish of modernity"?[10] Many certainly argue that secularism is under attack in Senegal, as well as personal liberties and women's rights, in part due to the long history of the intertwining of religious and state interests. Though I do not seek to undermine such claims, it is worth noting that in some ways the notion of a Muslim public sphere is not new. Although new modes of communication have fostered new Muslim publics, Muslim thought and practice has historically had public visibility in many parts of the globe in part through efforts at mass education.[11] As I said before, as the state relinquishes its control over the media, new religious actors have emerged in these newly opened spaces. Yet, visual and aural practices have long been incorporated into Sufi life in Senegal. Religious leaders have long been acquainted with the microphone, the telephone, the radio, the photocopier, and the camera. For example, the supreme leader of the Murid way, the Khalife Générale, has long given an address over the radio at the start of the rainy season to signal the beginning of the planting season for the faithful and on the occasion of the *Mággal* pilgrimage to Touba.[12]

Islam's New Visibility and the Secular Public in Senegal

The radio addresses of the Khalife Générale are seen as commentary on relations with the state and carry broad appeal.

How do we understand the increasing visibility and publicity of Islam as it unfolds in contexts of political uncertainty and fiscal turbulence? For adepts of the Murid Sufi way, in particular, visuality has been at the heart of Murid devotion and has taken on new meaning as adepts search for moral renewal in the context of global volatility. Importantly, photography, videography, tailoring, and the trade in merchant goods, such as household objects, are tied to the growth of a religious economy in the past thirty years. In the context of prolonged economic uncertainty, devotees of the Muslim Sufi order, Tariqa Murid, create long-term value through carefully crafted financial strategies including the construction of global trade networks, religious offerings, and the circulation of valued objects. The desire to create long-term value is related to the new prominence of Muslim commodities. Here I focus in particular on the gendered politics underpinning these new visualities. I consider the visual culture of religious videos and television programming and portrait photography. These visual forms and practices mark urban spaces typically thought of as modern and secular with a new Muslim cosmopolitanism.[13] I focus on the production, circulation, and reception of these visual objects to understand how processes of social production unfold in contexts of transnational migration marked by political uncertainty and fiscal turbulence.

Global Circuits of Senegalese Muslims

To be "plugged in" to Sufi circuits was to be part of a recognized way of achieving divine union, and to be "connected" was to receive the esoteric litanies (*wird*) that would bring one closer to God. For the millions of Murid men and women, to be "plugged in" offers not just the promise of eternal prosperity, but also access to the forms of trade and production through which that prosperity is crafted in the present. The high circulation of signs of wealth and well-being including cloth, homes, and cars as well as mosques, clinics, and schools is remarkable in the context of a declining postcolonial state following two decades of structural adjustment programs, devaluation of the currency, failed privatization schemes of state-managed transportation and communications industries, the decline in peanut production in the 1970s on which Senegal's export-based economy depended, and the closing of the few local manufacturing plants, most notably textiles.[14] Yet despite the influx of remittances from Murid traders, Dakar was also in flux. Murid traders who had been based overseas returned home to participate in the emergent affluence of the capital city spurred by investments of Chinese, Indian, and Gulf states in national infrastructure and natural resource extraction that focused upon phosphates, gold, and iron ore. Grandiose homes, hotels, and casinos were under construction, walling off and privatizing previously public beachfronts.

Many in the urban community turned to the signs of Islam to index a new prosperity for some and moral renewal for others. Many devotees had suffered the stigmatism of race abroad and for them Islam at home held a sort of nationalist appeal for men and women alike. Murid men at home sought moral renewal at a time when the conventional forms of male value were untenable, such as control over land, labor, and brides.

The Murid way emerged at the turn of the twentieth century as an agricultural movement. But by the 1960s, Murid peasant families were among the hardest hit by the declining price for peanuts in the world market due, in part, to the European community's end to preferential prices for Senegalese peanut and oil producers in 1968,[15] and were further devastated when, in the 1970s, due to a prolonged period of monocropping, poor environmental management, severe drought, and a series of locust plagues, the country experienced a destructive famine. To escape rural devastation and mounting debt many disciples migrated to the urban centers from the central agricultural regions of the country. In Dakar, they populated the city with self-built dwellings[16] and became employed in the burgeoning unregulated sectors of the urban economy.[17] At first, Murid agricultural migrants were mere scavengers in the urban areas of Thies and Dakar, recycling cleaned-up bits of string, bottles, and cans for sale in the market at the religious injunction (*ndiggël*) of Seriñ Abdou Lahat Mbacke, the third oldest son of Bamba who inherited the spiritual leadership of the Murid way. Over time, Murids transformed the strategy of trading in the dry season to make ends meet in lean agricultural cycles into full-time urban settlement.

Although it might have seemed that urban disciples had moved beyond the rural grasp of their religious guides and that they were in the process of becoming further entrenched in the world market through their trade, "they made a conscious effort to incorporate their unique temporality and rationality into world time by using their own vocabulary, grammar and worldview to understand the world and operate within it."[18] In the urban areas, disciples congregated into religious associations called *da'ira* through which they collected offerings that garnered them an audience with a shaykh and fostered social networks that facilitated their entry into the urban economy. Over time, as religious associations grew they began to invest in the rural region of Touba at the behest of shaykhs who came to recognize the importance of these new urban associations. For these disciples, Islam became the framework that encased their interactions in the new urban milieu. For example, the patronage of a senior member of the da'ira could enable one to engage in financial transactions within the sphere of that which was morally sanctioned in Islam, thus avoiding *riba* (interest or increase), which was associated with formal sector economic transactions. The Qur'an also advises adepts not to sacrifice religious practice for commercial gain in trade, that wealth should be used in the service of God, and that capital obtained through wrongdoing to others is to be avoided.[19] Moreover, adepts should not participate in gambling or speculation.[20] In the capitalist economy, such activities are difficult to avoid; participation in Murid circuits of exchange contributed to the strategies that good Muslims could employ in seeking a living within their moral aspirations and the financial constraints of their time.

Murid migrants to the city often became involved in the so-called informal sector transport and internal distribution networks since formal sector business was largely dominated by private French capital and state enterprise while Lebanese businesspersons controlled transport and real estate.[21] For those who did engage in the formal sector, they found that they could "work optimally when they had recourse to both kinds of systems, and therefore have a real interest in the maintenance of what the 'modern sector' may consider to be a 'traditional' form of moral authority and financial power."[22]

While many Murid families who had been engaged in farming in the peanut basin had picked up for the city, or at least sent a son to labor there on their behalf, others sojourned abroad. A labor shortage in postwar France drew many former colonial subjects abroad to work on docks, in maritime shipping, and in factories.[23] As former colonies gained independence, a multilateral agreement between France and Senegal allowed Senegalese to move without restriction.[24] While Murid disciples immigrated to France in this period in search of university degrees and wage labor, many more became involved in an international trade in African art perhaps inspired in part by the opportunities offered by the 1966 Paris *Exposition de l'Art Nègre*.²⁵ By the 1980s, Murid communities had grown in New York, Belgium, and Italy.²⁶ As immigration policies grew stricter in France, the U.S. Amnesty Law passed in 1986 facilitated a greater circular migration of these traders and disciples as their status was regularized, so the numbers of Murid in the United States grew steadily.²⁷ The 1990 Immigration Act, which introduced the Diversity Immigrant Visa Program that provided permanent resident visas to citizens of countries with low immigration rates to the United States, also contributed to the rising number of Senegalese there.²⁸

The overseas migration of Murids took place in the context of a declining Senegalese economy in the postcolonial period. An economic recession took hold in Senegal, due in part to the decline of agriculture and manufacturing, but also to the fact that the state was unable to derive revenue from the thriving import trade in contraband.²⁹ Beginning in 1985, the state implemented a series of reforms mandated by the International Monetary Fund in exchange for loans from the World Bank. These structural adjustment programs privatized state assets, removed trade barriers and constraints on financial flows, introduced fiscal discipline, reduced state involvement in the economy, ended agricultural subsidies, and led to the devaluation of the Senegalese currency, the C.F.A., in 1994.³⁰ The local impact of these reforms included an inflationary spiral—especially in the prices of tools, electricity, and fuel, as well as in imported rice and wheat, which were staples of the urban diet of rice, fish, and baguettes—that led to public protests and greater social and economic instability for Senegalese families.³¹ These new forms of impoverishment were matched by new forms of wealth as the gap between the rich and the poor increased over the decades as an unintended consequence of economic liberalization.³² Those who worked at the interstices of the formal and informal economies, such as Murid traders abroad and at home, did better in this changing political and economic environment. In time, government bureaucrats came to depend upon Murid trade.

Although trade liberalization in 1997 was designed to squeeze out parallel markets (where Murid activities, amongst others, thrived), liberalization in Senegal had the opposite effect of reinforcing the extralegal and unofficial economy.³³ Part of the explanation for this lies in the way in which the Murids successfully shifted between the formal and informal economies and in the intertwining of personal and commercial networks; Murid economic networks drew on da'ira membership, allegiance to shaykhs, lineages, villages of origin, caste membership, membership in neighborhood ritual associations, and the like.

I argue that in part Islam's success in the public sphere is related to the success of the Murid way in international trade. Although the forms of work in which Murids engaged became less visible as they began trading and moved abroad, the products of their labor in what they could build or buy became central to their moral standing at home. In Dakar, Murid merchants have come to control major markets, including the largest cloth market, *Marché H.L.M.* (*Habitations Loyers Modéré*)[34] as well as *Marché Sandaga*, the largest urban market in Senegal, which also serves as a gateway to hundreds of smaller markets throughout the city and its periphery.[35]

Pious Productions: Religious Media and Portrait Photography

Murid faithful have long turned to technology to express their mission, from using photocopiers and photo studios to produce and distribute religious texts and images to using audiocassette sermons and radio addresses. More recently, devotees have turned to videocassettes, DVDs, and the Internet where religious associations host Web sites, post videos on YouTube and Google Video, and participate in social networking sites. For Murid disciples and clergy, these new spaces are new territories to be conquered.[36]

In the decade after independence, the state had a monopoly over broadcast and print media. Television was introduced in the 1960s following independence to a largely urban population, consisting for the most part of francophone programming.[37] Unlike other West African countries that liberalized their media in the 1990s, such as Mali,[38] Senegal began to liberalize its print media as early as 1974. Today, though the government still has a monopoly on nationwide television stations through Radiodiffusion Television Senegalaise (RTS), state television recognizes the appeal of religious programming and often broadcasts Muslim conferences, pilgrimages, and speeches, as well as Muslim-themed entertainment such as question-and-answer programs aimed at providing guidance for a straight life. New private television stations are emerging, including RTS2 and Walf TV, but they are only available in the capital, Dakar. Attempts have been made to launch a Murid television station in Touba, but the state has not yet granted a broadcast license.[39] New commercial and community radio stations emerged in the 1990s; among them were the myriad of stations addressing Muslim themes and audiences. Muslim groups broadcast programs through both private and official media channels. There are radio stations that are officially Muslim such as Radio Al Hamdoulilah, Radio Touba Hizbut Tarqiyyah, and those that carry Muslim names such as Radio Dunyaa, Lamp Fall FM Dakar, and Touba.

Parents and grandparents can often be found listening to audio- and videocassettes of sermons and radio and television broadcasts. Through these aural and visual practices, disciples benefit from the *baraka* of the shaykh, receive religious merit from God, and receive guidance for a morally upright and meaningful life. At times, families and groups of neighbors or friends listen intently to such broadcasts, especially on their first airing. At other times, these audio- and videocassettes become a backdrop for conversations and gatherings much like a portrait of a shaykh that hangs on the wall gracing the space with its presence and endowing the bearer with a righteous persona. The religious videos are often part of a wider collection of frequently viewed media, including videos of life cycle ceremonies, video photo albums, and music videos.

Mággal *Videos*

Although media use—including radio, Internet, cell phones, and visual media—is common in religious circuits across West Africa, especially in light of the liberalization of formerly state-run media in many places,[40] it has become particularly crucial in Senegal as an increasing number of potential disciples reside abroad. The videocassette that I described at the beginning of this chapter indexes the economic power of the Murid way by making visible the offerings of the disciples of this religious order. Shaykhs' redistribution of these offerings is displayed in the videocassettes and DVDs that are produced annually to commemorate the yearly *Mággal* (pilgrimage) of Murid disciples to their sacred city of Touba in the desert interior of the country.

In addition to circulating cassettes, Murids broadcast their annual pilgrimage to the sacred city of Touba over the national television station, RTS, and unofficial copies of these productions are available in the market. Though this is a recording of a pilgrimage to a rural center, it is often watched and experienced in urban areas, in Dakar and in cities abroad where Murid faithful reside. In the 1990s, the RTS productions often opened with

Islam's New Visibility and the Secular Public in Senegal

scenes of thousands of aspirants crowding into Touba's main streets, which radiate out from the Grand Mosque at the center of the town. Most of the productions included images of the rural roads jammed with buses, *car rapide* minivans, and taxis meant for urban transport. As far as the eye could see, there would be *Ndiaga Ndiaye* minibuses intended for urban-rural commutes, the air-conditioned buses of the late Cheikh Mortalla Mbacke, as well as double-axle dump trucks with their trailers spilling over with disciples. RTS productions frequently captured iconic nationalist images of the baobab tree juxtaposed with a train headed for Touba, its boxcars overflowing with Murid disciples from the rural agricultural communes surrounding Touba. Voice-overs often explained that these disciples came from all over Senegal—indeed from all over the world—and that they were returning to Touba to thank their *wali* (holy person), Amadu Bamba, the founding figure of the Murid way. RTS cameras then took viewers into the mosque to witness the work of Sëriñ Saliou Mbacke, the late Khalife Générale (successor or caliph) of the Murid way. The most symbolic of his numerous public works projects in Touba was the gold leaf that he added to the mausoleum of Amadu Bamba along with a crystal chandelier. The camera also showed images of disciples tossing coins, banknotes, and kola nuts over the brass railing that separated them from Bamba's tomb as they prayed for good health, employment, fertility, and the like. Between these various scenes, the productions featured accomplished *rabb* (religious griots) whose wailing of Murid litanies established a historical genealogy for this media event, and among shots of political and military dignitaries from African and Middle Eastern countries and France, the viewer was instructed about the benefits that would accrue to those who follow the way of the Murid shaykhs.

After showing scenes of the mosque, the videos often included an interview with the custodian of the Murid archive and library at Touba. The custodian would take the viewer on a tour of the library, and the video focused on the stacks full of the numerous volumes of writings by key Muslim figures in Arabic as well as French. The custodian then discussed the corpus of writing produced by Bamba himself. The custodian showed the viewer a number of display cases containing the personal items that belonged to Bamba, including his bed and his suitcase, and then describes the *jikko ju baax* (pious comportment) of a good Murid and of a good Muslim. Finally, the custodian discussed the subject of offerings supplicated to the shaykh to signify submission to a path in the hope of achieving salvation, noting that the aspirant should make offerings to the shaykh because the person who holds money in his or her hand has nothing of *njariñ* (value). But once given to the shaykh, the money would acquire these qualities and, in return, the disciple will benefit from the shaykh's *baraka*.

This visit to the library is then followed by images of the offerings of prominent prayer circles that are devoted to the shaykhs. In Senegal, there are many da'ira associations that are composed of professionals, bureaucrats, and students; however, it is the contributions of the overseas disciples who sell their wares on the streets of major Western cities that are the focus of this video. These translocal organizations send yearly offerings to the Murid clergy from places such as Milan, Paris, New York, Chicago, and Washington, D.C. Not only do they send cash, but they also send crates of bleach, ammonia, and toilet paper. The camera records hospitals, sewage systems, port-o-potties, and rural electrification projects made possible by the *liggéey* (work) of disciples abroad. The broadcast continues to shift back and forth between scenes of the prayerful masses filling the streets to images of the myriad of ways in which they have contributed to developing the sacred city to views of long lines of dignitaries greeting the shaykhs. Condensed in the forms of wealth that circulate on the day of pilgrimage—food, money, and transport—is the work of the disciples and the magnitude of the shaykh's blessings, all of which are made possible by the grace of God. These offerings that circulate in the broadcasts, videocassettes, and DVDs are recognized as being not only signs of the *baraka* of the Murid shaykhs, but also as containing elements that produce the social system, that is, the Murid way itself. The *Mággal* is not only a display of all that the disciples have sacrificed for the development of the way, it is also a representation of all that the shaykhs have returned to their faithful incrementally and an index of the *baraka* that is Bamba's legacy.

Media productions such as the *Mággal* video are central to the Murid economy in which offerings are made and redistributed to the faithful. The video production plays a central role in the creation of value by Murid disciples. The video makes visible, and thus meaningful, the workers' investment in Touba. Importantly, the majority of this work takes place outside of Touba, in the unregulated spaces of the urban Dakar economy and abroad in major Western cities. The video is part of the repertoire of social labor that goes into rendering offerings meaningful. These meanings were produced in part through talk about the significance of the offering in the video, thus setting it aside from the mundane temporal world of work. Additionally, Murid men and women engaged in performances of devotion

Islam's New Visibility and the Secular Public in Senegal

often through talk about offerings to shaykhs, as part of a repertoire of possible economic practices that secured their vision of an Islamic modernity. They did so because an offering of money is an object and, like any other object, it is susceptible to different readings. The money form in particular can be characterized by its indeterminacy and openness.[41] Thus the representational quality of money is often fixed through talk; "objects require the reflexive capacity of language if they are to serve as fully efficacious media of social relations . . . the capacity of objects to serve semiotically as representations and economically as representatives of persons is unstable and requires constant effort to sustain."[42] When cash is given to a shaykh through the institution of addiya offerings, it is no longer an alienable commodity, a standard of value, or a symbol of the state; instead, it signifies both submission in this world and the next to the path to divine union and also the recognition of the shaykh as a worthy guide.

How do visual media, such as videocassettes and photography, figure in the construction of Muslim modernities[43] and give evidence of a critical Islamic practice?[44] In this section, I focus on the person and intimate use of portrait photography and of visuality itself as a practice. Dakar is considered by many across West Africa to be a fashion center, and Dakarois are described as cosmopolitan and urbane.[45] Dakar's orientation as a fashion city is reflected in the photographic practices of its inhabitants. Portrait photography is central to the project of making one's work abroad visible at home. It is also central to the politics of reputation. For women migrants in particular, work and travel are often seen as dangerous, potentially compromising their moral virtue and the honor of a family. Thus women often turn to media to project a pious image at home. Women abroad can be seen at home in the videocassettes of Muslim conferences held in New York and elsewhere, and in portraits from life cycle ceremonies and Muslim feast days that they send home.

Above all, these are images of Muslim women and can be read like the portraits of important religious figures as efficacious. They index the pious persona of their subjects, whose dress and accessories made visible the strength of their social networks, understood as products of their religious devotion. As in the portrait of the founding figure of the Murid way, Amadu Bamba, there is also a particularly Sufi way of seeing these images that understands these objects as generative of something else.[46] Women's portraits, which are often taken at religious and life cycle ceremonies, are documentary, commemorative, a form of reportage, persuasive, and everlasting.[47] They concretize vast social networks of circulation as well as becoming objects themselves that circulate. Senegalese portraiture is the ultimate expression of Annette Weiner's[48] notion of the paradox of keeping-while-giving. These portraits work the contradictory forces of conservation and change, of visibility and concealment, and the pleasures and pressures of give and take.

As displays of beauty (*rafet*), portraits are also displays of wealth (*alal*). Portraits allude to stores of wealth objects, such as cloth, and the desire to bestow these wealth objects on others. Such beauty speaks to the cult of elegance that characterized colonial urban Senegal and claims to high rank (*rafet judo*). These images are not only of well-dressed women but of women's worth as well, and piety plays an important role in the staging of these photographs. The qualities of wealth, grace, and rank can be read from the surface of the images. The images concretize a vast circulation of prestations of cloth and religious offerings, among other things, underpinning translocal circuits of wage labor and capital organized under the aegis of Tariqa Murid. These images can be found gracing the parlors of homes in and out of Senegal, hanging alongside portraits of religious figures and iconography of religious devotion such as Muslim calendars, wall clocks, and framed scripture.

Weiner cautions against thinking of the history *of* things, but rather, the history *in* things.[49] As early as the 1840s, French adventurers, missionaries, and ethnographers were "instrumental in affirming visual codes and stereotypes through which the West interpreted Africa and its peoples."[50] The images of François-Edmond Fortier, one of the largest producers of European postcards in Africa between 1899 and 1920, exemplify this tendency. While colonial officers employed photography to document the activities of Muslim shaykhs, these photographs became devotional images whose presence "gets things done . . . they are endowed with *Baraka* . . . Murid visuality is above all directed toward *practice*."[51]

At the turn of the century in Saint-Louis, personal photo albums became popular for urban residents through the work of the photographer Meissa Gueye. By mid-century, the photographer Mama Casset had opened a photography studio in the Medina neighborhood of Dakar, where he applied skills learned from his service in the French air force. As West African photographers turned cameras on their own societies, the novelist Aminata Sow Fall remarked: "The arrival of photography must have been seen as a gift from the gods, to conspire against the grotesque and often insulting caricatures produced by the colonists. We could finally all enjoy looking at ourselves in a snapshot of happiness; immortalized on a card . . . a photograph should only reflect the beautiful, admirable, dazzling side of our existence. That is why we were photographed for major ceremonies."[52]

Casset's portraits can be characterized by tight framing, structured composition, a preference for slants and diagonals, the skillful arrangement of cloth and clothing as well as attention to bodily expression. Both the Malian photographer Seydou Keïta and the Senegalese photographer Mama Casset employed the angled bust portrait as "in this pose the sitter's face was captured in a three-quarter view, with the body appearing to lean toward the edge of the picture frame"[53] or according to Mercer to "lean out of the frame."[54] These mid-century portraits became the inspiration for the *peintures sous verre*, or reverse glass painting, which captured the poses popular in studio photography. Glass paintings were also used to enhance studio portraits, framing them with religious iconography. The photographs and the paintings often draw on Muslim thought such as the tension between *zahir*, the visible, and *batin*, the invisible.[55]

In relation to Stephen Sprague's work on Yoruba images, Christopher Pinney remarks upon subjects' "concern with the surface of the image and its production after its photographic moment is manifest"[56] and how in Indian photography subjects seek to "come out better." Rather than being "a window on reality," contemporary portraits are "a surface, a ground, on which presences that look out toward the viewer can be built."[57] The shallow picture space brings attention to what Pinney and Oguibe[58] describe as the surface, or the substance respectively, or what emerges after the moment that the photograph is taken. Similarly, contemporary Gambian photography, Liam Buckley[59] argues, is also concerned with, "the mysteries of exterior appearance,"[60] and "multiplying surfaces."[61] This is in contrast to the way in which mid-century West African portrait photographers sought to capture the inner persona, or *jikko*, of the client. Today, *jikko* has come to be seen as too volatile and too dangerous to handle.

Photographers seek to "multiply surfaces" to produce multiple views, and thus meanings, by cutting the photographs into montages.[62] What is the relation then between how images look and why they work?[63] Clearly, the meaning of these images is not fixed. The relationship between "discursive formations and image worlds" is ever shifting, allowing for what Pinney calls the "transformational potentialities"[64] and "volatility"[65] of photographic practices.

These portraits imparted visual evidence of hard work and masculine grace; they also intimated the desire to impart the tactile manifestations of grace on others. As wealth objects and representations of wealth, portraits have a "density" to use another of Weiner's terms.[66] Senegalese portrait photographers captured the complex Wolof notion of beauty as self-mastery and grace.[67] Yet, as Deborah Poole argues, portraiture has as much to do with "shared meanings and community" as with "inequality and power."[68] One must be careful about viewing these portraits as images of wealth. The forms of women's wealth, their woven underwraps, were never made visible.[69] Photographs, indeed all aspects of Sufi life, are thought to "posses a secret side," or *batin*, "the insightfulness of *not* seeing, then, is often believing."[70] The three-quarter bust portrait obscured the strip-woven underskirts that served as the basis of women's wealth and served as exchange objects. Thus there is a politics of suggestion and concealment at play in the image. It is this relationship between "display and secrecy [that is] essential to Mouride Visuality."[71] Visual objects, such as portraiture and cloth, are ideal media through which to discuss the production of social futures and fortunes in contemporary Senegal given their role, as Weiner notes, as a "visual substitute for history, ancestors and the immortality of human life."[72]

Conclusion

Islam's new visibility is in part related to the success of the Murid way in international trade. Although the forms of work in which Murid women and men engaged became less visible as they began trading and moving abroad, the products of their labor in what they could build or buy became central to their moral standing at home. Murid disciples create long-term value in contexts of global volatility through the production and circulation of valued objects such as religious paraphernalia. Muslim media practices, the viewing of audiocassettes and portraiture, are central to the creation of the proper, pious, and prosperous body in times of moral and fiscal uncertainty. The heightened visibility of Islam was also facilitated by access to new media technologies and state liberalization of broadcast media. Muslim media practices in urban Dakar challenge the association of modernity with the decline of religion. In global Senegal, as I have argued, the signs of Islam are to be found everywhere. Yet it is important

Islam's New Visibility and the Secular Public in Senegal

to acknowledge that those signs index a multiplicity of voices competing to fill public spaces and garner an audience, and that they are as often discordant as they are harmonious.

Notes

1. For further discussion of Murid videocassettes, see Beth Buggenhagen, "Islam and the Media of Devotion in and out of Senegal." *Visual Anthropology Review* 26 (2) (2010): 81–95.
2. McLaughlin, Fiona. "Islam and Popular Music in Senegal."
3. Roberts, A. "Displaying Secrets"; Starrett, "The Political Economy."
4. Mbow, "Senegal."
5. Ibid., p. 163.
6. Schulz, "Morality, Community, Publicness."
7. Babou, *Fighting the Greater Jihad*; Ross, "Tuba."
8. See Meyer and Moors, *Religion, Media*, p. 4, for further discussion of Habermas's view of the public sphere and religion.
9. Hirschkind, "Cassette Ethics."
10. Gole, "Islam in Public."
11. Eickelman and Anderson, *New Media*.
12. Gueye, "New Information."
13. Diouf, "The Senegalese Murid Trade Diaspora."
14. For a further discussion of the textile industry, see Catherine Boone, *Merchant Capital and the Roots of State Power in Senegal, 1930–1985*.
15. Babou, *Fighting the Greater Jihad*; Babou, "Urbanizing Mystical Islam"; Gueye, "New Information."
16. Creevey, "Muslim Brotherhoods"; Diouf, "The Senegalese Murid Trade; Gueye, "New Information."
17. Cruise O'Brien, "Charisma Comes to Town," pp. 135–156; Diop, "Fonctions et activités des dahiras"; Gueye, "New Information"; Roberts, "The Ironies of System D."
18. Diouf, "The Senegalese Murid Trade Diaspora," p. 695.
19. Hunwick, "Islamic Financial Institutions," pp. 72–96.
20. Ibid., p. 82.
21. Thioub, Diop, and Boone, "Economic Liberalization," pp. 63–89.
22. Stiansen and Guyer, "Introduction," pp. 1–14.
23. Bowen, "Does French Islam Have Borders?"
24. Diop and Michalak, "'Refuge' and 'Prison,'" p. xix.
25. Cruise O'Brien, "Charisma Comes to Town," pp. 135–156.

26. Diouf, "The Senegalese Murid Trade Diaspora."
27. Babou, "Brotherhood Solidarity."
28. Beck, *Brokering Democracy in Africa.*
29. Thioub et al., "Economic Liberalization."
30. Diouf, S., "The West African Paradox," pp. 268–298; Hesse, "The Peugeot and the Baobab"; Perry, "Rural Ideologies."
31. Creevey, Vengroff, and Gaye, "Devaluation of the CFA."
32. Ibid., p. 671.
33. Hibou, "The 'Social Capital,'" pp. 69–113.
34. Mustafa, "Practicing Beauty."
35. Diouf, "The Senegalese Murid Trade Diaspora."
36. Gueye, "New Information."
37. Fair, "Francophonie and the National Airwaves," pp. 189–210.
38. Schulz, "Morality, Community, Publicness"; Soares, "Notes."
39. Gueye, "New Information."
40. Ibid.; Schulz, "Morality, Community, Publicness"; Soares, "Notes."
41. Maurer, "The Anthropology of Money."
42. Keane, "Money is No Object."
43. Larkin, "Degraded Images."
44. Bowen, *Muslims Through Discourse*; Soares, "Notes."
45. Heath, "Fashion, Anti-Fashion"; Mustafa, "Portraits of Modernity"; Roberts and Roberts, "L'aura d'Amadou Bamba"; Scheld, "The City in a Shoe: Redefining Urban Africa"; and Scheld, "Youth Cosmopolitanism."
46. Roberts, A., "Displaying Secrets."
47. Mustafa, "Practicing Beauty," p. 172.
48. Weiner, *Inalienable Possessions.*
49. Steiner, "Rights of Passage."
50. Lamunière et al., *You Look Beautiful Like That.*
51. Roberts, A., "The Ironies of System D"; Roberts, A., "Displaying Secrets"; Roberts, A. et al., *A Saint in the City.*
52. Fall, "Vague Memory of a Confiscated Photo," pp. 64–65.
53. Lamunière et al., *You Look Beautiful Like That.*
54. Mercer, quoted in Bell and Solomon, *In/sight: African Photographers.*
55. Roberts et al., *A Saint in the City*, p. 95.
56. Pinney and Peterson. *Photography's Other Histories.*
57. Ibid., p. 219.
58. Bell and Solomon, *In/sight: African Photographers*, p. 246.
59. Buckley. "Self and Accessory."
60. Ibid., p. 71.
61. Ibid., p. 83.

62. Ibid., p. 1.
63. Roberts et al., *A Saint in the City*, p. 22.
64. Pinney and Peterson, *Photography's Other Histories*, p. 3.
65. Ibid., p. 6.
66. Weiner, "Art and Material Culture."
67. Mustafa, "Practicing Beauty."
68. Poole, *Vision, Race, and Modernity*.
69. Roberts et al., *A Saint in the City*, p. 48.
70. Ibid., p. 47.
71. Ibid., p. 80.
72. Weiner, "Inalienable Wealth."

Bibliography

Babou, Cheikh Anta. "Brotherhood Solidarity, Education, and Migration: The Role of the Dahiras Among the Murid Muslim Community of New York." *African Affairs*, 101 (2002): 151–170.

———. *Fighting the Greater Jihad: Amadu Bamba and the Founding of the Muridiyya of Senegal, 1853–1913*. Athens: Ohio University Press, 2007.

———. "Urbanizing Mystical Islam: Making Murid Space in the Cities of Senegal." *International Journal of African Historical Studies* 40 (2) (2007): 197–223.

Beck, Linda. *Brokering Democracy in Africa: The Rise of a Clientelist Democracy in Senegal*. New York: Palgrave, 2008.

Bell, Clare and Solomon R. Guggenheim Museum. *In/sight: African Photographers, 1940 to the Present*. New York: Guggenheim Museum, 1996.

Bowen, John. *Muslims Through Discourse*. Princeton, N.J.: Princeton University Press, 1993.

———. "Does French Islam Have Borders? Dilemmas of Domestication in a Global Religious Field." *American Anthropologist* 106 (1) (2004): 43–55.

Buckley, Liam Mark. "Self and Accessory in Gambian Studio Photography." *Visual Anthropology Review* 16 (2) (2000): 71–91.

Creevey, Lucy. "Muslim Brotherhoods and Politics in Senegal, in 1985." *Journal of Modern African Studies* 23 (4) (1985): 715–721.

Creevey, Lucy, Richard Vengroff, and Ibrahima Gaye. "Devaluation of the CFA Franc in Senegal: The Reaction of Small Business." *Journal of Modern African Studies* 33 (4) (1995): 669–683.

Cruise O'Brien, Donal B. "Charisma Comes to Town: Mouride Urbanization, 1945–86." In *Charisma and Brotherhood in African Islam*, eds. C. Coulon and D. B. Cruise O'Brien, 135–156. Oxford: Clarendon Press, 1988.

Diop, Momar Couba. "Fonctions et activités des dahira Mourides urbains (Sénégal)." *Cahiers d'Etudes Africaines* 20 (1-3) (1981): 79–91.

Diop, Mustapha and Laurence Michalak. " 'Refuge' and 'Prison': Islam, Ethnicity, and the Adaptation of Space in Workers' Housing in France." In *Making Muslim Space in North America and Europe*, ed. B. D. Metcalf, 19. Berkeley: University of California Press, 1996.

Diouf, Mamadou. "The Senegalese Murid Trade Diaspora and the Making of a Vernacular Cosmopolitanism." *Public Culture* 12 (3) (2000): 679–702.

Diouf, Sylviane. "The West African Paradox." In *Muslims' Place in the American Public Square*, eds. Z. Bukhari, S. Nyang, M. Ahmad, and J. Esposito, 268–298. Lanham, Md.: AltaMira Press, 2004.

Eickelman, Dale F. and Jon W. Anderson. *New Media in the Muslim World: The Emerging Public Sphere*. Bloomington: Indiana University Press, 2003.

Fair, Jo Ellen. "Francophonie and the National Airwaves: A History of Television in Senegal." In *Planet TV: A Global Television Reader*, ed. L. Parks, 189–210. New York: New York University Press, 2003.

Gole, Nilufer. "Islam in Public: New Visibilities and New Imaginaires." *Public Culture* 14 (1) (2002): 173–190.

Gueye, Cheikh. "New Information and Communications Technology Use by Muslim Mourides in Senegal." *Review of African Political Economy* 98 (2003): 609–625.

Heath, Deborah. "Fashion, Anti-Fashion and Heteroglossia in Urban Senegal." *American Ethnologist* 19 (1) (1992): 19–33.

Hesse, Brian J. "The Peugeot and the Baobab: Islam, Structural Adjustment and Liberalism in Senegal." *Journal of Contemporary African Studies* 22 (1) (2004): 4–12.

Hibou, Béatrice. "The 'Social Capital' of the State as an Agent of Deception." In *The Criminalization of the State in Africa*, eds. J.-F. Bayart, S. Ellis, and B. Hibou, 69–113. Bloomington: Indiana University Press, 1999.

Hirschkind, Charles. "Cassette Ethics: Public Piety and Popular Media in Egypt." In *Religion, Media and the Public Sphere*, eds. B. Meyer and A. Moors, 29–51. Bloomington: Indiana University Press, 2006.

Hunwick, J. O. "Islamic Financial Institutions: Theoretical Structures and Aspects of Their Application in Sub-Saharan Africa." In *Credit, Currencies and Culture: African Financial Institutions in Historical Perspective*, eds. E. Stiansen and J. I. Guyer, 72–96. Stockholm: Nordiska Afrikainstitutet, 1999.

Keane, Webb. "Money is No Object: Materiality, Desire and Modernity in an Indonesian Society." In *The Empire of Things: Regimes of Value and Material Culture*, ed. F. R. Meyers, 65–90. Santa Fe, N.M.: School of American Research Press, 2001.

Lamunière, Michelle, et al. *You Look Beautiful Like That: The Portrait Photographs of Seydou Keïta and Malick Sidibé*. Cambridge, Mass., New Haven, Conn, 2001.

Larkin, Brian. "Degraded Images, Distorted Sounds: Nigerian Video and the Infrastructure of Piracy." *Public Culture* 16 (2) (2004): 289–314.

Maurer, Bill. "The Anthropology of Money." *Annual Review of Anthropology* 35 (2006): 15–36.

Mbow, Penda. "Senegal: The Return of Personalism." *Journal of Democracy* 19 (1) (2008): 156–169.

McLaughlin, Fiona. "Islam and Popular Music in Senegal: The Emergence of a 'New Tradition.' " *Africa* 67 (4) (1997): 560–581.

Meyer, Birgit and Annelies Moors. *Religion, Media, and the Public Sphere*. Bloomington: Indiana University Press, 2006.

Mustafa, Huda Nura. *Practicing Beauty: Crisis, Value and the Challenge of Self-Mastery in Dakar, 1970–1994*. PhD dissertation, Harvard University, 1998.

———. "Portraits of Modernity: Fashioning Selves in Dakarois Popular Photography." In *Images and Empires: Visuality in Colonial and Postcolonial Africa*, eds. Paul Stuart Landau and Deborah D. Kaspin. Berkeley: University of California Press, 2002.

Perry, Donna. "Rural Ideologies and Urban Imaginings: Wolof Immigrants in New York City." *Africa Today* 44 (2) (1997): 229–260.

Pinney, Christopher and Nicolas Peterson. *Photography's Other Histories*. Durham, N.C.: Duke University Press, 2003.

Poole, Deborah. *Vision, Race, and Modernity: A Visual Economy of the Andean Image World*. Princeton, N.J.: Princeton University Press, 1997.

Roberts, Allen F. "The Ironies of System D." In *Recycled, Re-Seen: Folk Art from the Global Scrap Heap*, eds. C. Cerny and S. Seriff. New York: Harry Abrams for the Museum of International Folk Art Santa Fe, 1996.

———. "Displaying Secrets. Visual Piety in Senegal." In *Visuality Before and Beyond the Renaissance: Seeing as Other Saw*, ed. R. S. Nelson. Cambridge, UK: Cambridge University Press, 2000.

Roberts, Allen F. and Mary N. Roberts, "L'aura d'Amadou Bamba: Photographie et fabulation dans le Senegal urbain." *Anthropologie et Sociétés* 22 (1) (1998): 15–40.

Roberts, Allen F., et al. *A Saint in the City: Sufi Arts of Urban Senegal*. Los Angeles: UCLA Fowler Museum of Cultural History, 2003.

Ross, Eric. "Tuba: A Spiritual Metropolis in the Modern World." *Canadian Journal of African Studies* 29 (2) (1995): 222–259.

Scheld, Suzanne. "The City in a Shoe: Redefining Urban Africa Through Sebago Footwear Consumption." *City and Society* 15 (1) (2003): 109–130.

———. "Youth Cosmopolitanism: Clothing, the City and Globalization in Dakar, Senegal." *City and Society* 19 (2) (2007): 232–253.

Schulz, Dorothea E. "Morality, Community, Publicness: Shifting Terms of Public Debate in Mali." In *Religion, Media and the Public Sphere*, eds. B. Meyer and A. Moors. Bloomington: Indiana University Press, 2006.

———. "Competing Sartorial Assertions of Femininity and Muslim Identity in Mali." *Fashion Theory* 11 (2/3) (2007): 253–280.

Soares, Benjamin F. "Notes on the Anthropological Study of Islam and Muslim Societies in Africa." *Culture and Religion*, 1 (2) (2000): 277–285.

Starrett, Gregory. "The Political Economy of Religious Commodities in Cairo." *American Anthropologist* 97 (1) (1995): 51–68.

Steiner, Christopher. "Rights of Passage. On the Liminal Identity of Art in the Border Zone." In *Empire of Things. Regimes of Value and Material Culture*, ed. F. Meyers. Santa Fe: School of American Research, 2001.

Stiansen, Endre and Jane Guyer. "Introduction." In *Credit, Currencies and Culture: African Financial Institutions in Historical Perspective*, eds. E. Stiansen and J. Guyer, 1–14. Stockholm: Nordiska Afrikainstitutet, 1999.

Thioub, Ibrahima, Momar Coumba Diop, and Catherine Boone. "Economic Liberalization in Senegal: Shifting Politics of Indigenous Business Interests." *African Studies Review* 41 (2) (1998): 63–89.

Weiner, Annette B. "Inalienable Wealth." *American Ethnologist* 12 (2) (1985): 210–227.

———. *Inalienable Possessions: The Paradox of Keeping-While-Giving*. Berkeley: University of California Press, 1992.

———. "Art and Material Culture: A Conversation with Annette Weiner." In *The Empire of Things: Regimes of Value and Material Culture*, ed. F. Myers. Santa Fe: School of American Research, 2001.

[4]

Dakar's Sunnite Women

The Dialectic of Submission and Defiance in a Globalizing City

ERIN AUGIS

The capitalist forces that propel the globalization of Western commodities and those that disseminate the implements and symbols of transnational Islam are cut from the same cloth, and sub-Saharan African youths who become orthodox Muslim activists often negotiate vigorously between the two to find themselves. This is particularly the case for educated, young women in Dakar, Senegal's Sunnite movement, who use their male leadership's critiques of secularism to carve out an Islamist femininity that not only transforms them spiritually but buffers their entry into Dakar's rapidly liberalizing labor force. As such, female Sunnites' constructions of self as pious Muslim women are not passive accommodations of Islamist men's dominance, nor are they rationalist manipulations of local power hierarchies. Instead, participating in a global, capitalist Sunni reform movement enables young Senegalese women to undertake processes of subjectivation where they define themselves in simultaneously religious and political terms, while negotiating an urban context of dramatic cultural and economic change.

This chapter will first describe the demography and philosophies of Senegal's Sunnites, and then address how new neoliberal and transnational forces in the country set the stage for a dialectic of political and moral activism not yet addressed in academic studies of orthodox women.

Finally, Sunnite women's means of surpassing their male leadership's inversions of secular arguments on family law, by exercising their own forms of protest when they enter Dakar's formal labor market, will be shown to exhibit this moral and political dualism.¹

Who are Dakar's Sunnites?

Female Sunnites living in Senegal's capital city are a heterogeneous group of young women ranging from about fourteen to thirty-five years of age, who come from highly varied class, educational, and ethnic backgrounds. They most often claim Pulaar, Sereer, Wolof, or Halpulaar roots, and they are residents of some of the city's poorest suburbs, in addition to mixed-class popular neighborhoods and wealthy residential *quartiers*. Sunnite university students' origins also represent a wide class variation, as some hail from the country's impoverished rural areas, others from middle class families of merchants or state *fonctionnaires*, and still others from Dakar's nouveau riche. Although the women featured in this chapter hold high school or college diplomas, it is important to note that Sunnite women from very diverse educational backgrounds, including those whose only formal schooling has been at a local Qur'anic school, or *daara*, endeavor to define themselves as pious women in an orthodox movement that extends beyond Senegal's borders. It is perhaps the experience of being urban—with its inherent dislocations but also multitudinous possibilities for new forms of affiliation—that inspires young women to seek out the spiritual, social, and political affirmations of being Sunnite.

The origins of Senegal's Sunni orthodox reform movement are in fact urban, and they date from the 1930s, when small groups organized to promote Qur'anic literacy in Arabic and condemn religious innovations introduced by Sufi brotherhood practices. The Brigade de la Fraternité Musulmane, an organization founded by Abd al-Qadir Fall and Abd al-Qadir Diagne, for instance, undertook these efforts. They endeavored to fight "*gaspillages familiaux*," or the wasteful spending of Sufi brotherhood adherents' (*taalibe*) tithes by the wealthy families of brotherhood leaders, or marabouts.² By the 1940s and 1950s, a number of young Qur'anic scholars sympathetic to diminishing Sufi leaders' political sway left Senegal to attend theological schools in Algeria and Saudi Arabia, where they studied the works of thinkers such as Rashid Rida, who espoused the Salafist philosophy that Islam was flawless and whole during the lifetime of the Prophet Muhammed and the first three generations of Muslims who followed him (*sahaba, tabi'in, tabi'at-tabi'in*). This view maintains that an accumulation of centuries of undesirable cultural and political innovations have tarnished an original, pure Islam. Senegalese theologians who studied abroad, such as Shaykh Mohammed Touré, Alioune Diouf, and Al Haj Mahmoud Ba, began to see the *taalibé*-marabout relationship as an exploitative tie that prevents Muslims from cultivating a one-to-one relationship with God through the Qur'an. They returned to Senegal to found the Union Culturelle Musulmane, Jama'at Ibad ar-Rahman (Organization of the Servants of God), and Harakat al-Falah (Movement for Success), respectively, where they advocated Qur'anic literacy in Arabic and challenged Sufi brotherhoods' clientelist ties to the state. These scholars each became disabused of the tactics of the secular colonial and postcolonial administrations that, fearing the influence of orthodox reformist thought, attempted to control their studies or subsequent activism.[3]

Although Senegal's reformist movement was born of challenges to local religious and political hierarchies, since the 1950s, Sunnite organizations have operated in constant negotiation with the country's secular government. Alioune Diouf in fact founded the Jama'at Ibad ar-Rahman because he split with the Union Culturelle Musulmane when it was co-opted by the administration of President Léopold Sédar Senghor during the 1970s. Today, Jama'at Ibad ar-Rahman, Harakat al-Falah, and their descendant, multifarious student, neighborhood, and umbrella Sunnite groups represent a broad diversity in demographic characteristics, doctrinal requirements, and public positions on the Senegalese state and Sufi influence. Halpulaar merchants who receive support from Saudi Arabia, Kuwait, and Egypt, yet who take a largely apolitical stance, for example, mostly organize Harakat al-Falah. On the other hand, the Jama'at Ibad ar-Rahman encourages secular political participation, drawing inspiration from Algerian ulema associated with Albelhamid Bin Badis in the 1930s.[4] Sunnite groups take various approaches to Islamic education as well; female students at al-Falah Collège in Dakar's popular neighborhood of Colobane are required to veil during classes and rigorously study jurisprudence (*fiqh*) in Arabic, whereas members of Sunnite groups at Dakar's Université Cheikh Anta Diop (UCAD) are encouraged to veil only when they are ready. University Sunnites typically discuss the Qur'an by shifting their speech between French and Wolof, only peppering their discourse with Arabic religious phrases.

Despite their organizational diversity, Senegalese Sunnites commonly advocate the essential elements of universal orthodox Sunni philosophy and practice: perfecting one's personal relationship to God through Qur'anic and Hadith literacy, the proper execution of ritual practices such as prayer and ablutions (*ibadat*), modesty in dress as well as relations with the opposite sex (*haya*), bringing others to Islam through proselytizing (*dawa*), and teaching about the uniqueness of God (*tawhid*) as well as the sinfulness of innovations in religious practice (*bida*). Adherents today refer to themselves as "Sunnites" to indicate that they work to correctly practice the Sunnah, or traditions of the Prophet Muhammed. Despite many blurred philosophical and political boundaries between orthodox and Sufi groups in Senegalese as well as West African history, this self-reference serves as a semantic distinction for Sunnite activists, implying that their religious practices are more pure than those of brotherhood adherents and the vast majority of Senegalese, who are nonetheless also Sunni Muslims.[5]

Dakar's young Sunnites distinguish themselves as proper Sunnis not just through religious practice, or semantics for that matter, but through consuming an ever-expanding collection of transnational ideological exchanges, such as visits from reformist thinkers such as Tariq Ramadan and Islamic Web sites produced in the West as well as in Muslim countries. They also purchase commodities manufactured by companies in the Gulf, North Africa, and the Middle East, which include imported veils, videos, books, posters, and cassettes. This movement in goods, ideas, and people serves as a primer to interested Senegalese youth for how to *enact* orthodoxy and *feel* piety, but also animates their imaginations of life in Muslim countries abroad and their beliefs in the possibility for global solidarity among orthodox Sunnis.

Many of the distinctions enacted by Sunnite youth exist, however, in tension with increasingly conciliatory discourses of their older Sunnite leadership. Though movement leaders still challenge secular governance and *bida*, or innovations, in local Islamic practice, they publicly voice this defiance in nuanced discourses of reconciliation with Sufi leaders and in cooperation with President Abdoulaye Wade's strong state. Instead of directly confronting the brotherhoods or attempting to organize a revolution reminiscent of Iran in 1979, Sunnite officials often focus their doctrinal speech on the virtues of proper ritual practice and their political discourse not on scrutinizing the whole Senegalese government but on challenging secular policies that address women's roles as sexual beings and as mothers.

These discourses are negotiations on the part of Sunnite leadership, however, and not simply evidence of a benign reformist impulse. As Alidou[6] observes in Niger, orthodox Sunnis are reformists not necessarily because they adhere to the philosophy that conversion to proper Islamic comportment must come only from an individual's change of heart but because they are constrained in their political options for any more revolutionary action. Many Senegalese Sunnites, including *imams* and Qur'anic teachers, speak idealistically within orthodox circles about the Iranian revolution, Saudi theocracy, and the complete installation of *sharî'a* in Senegal. Thus, "reform" for a number of Senegal's Sunnite leaders may be a public ideology of necessity, imposed by the powerful political and social sway of Sufi brotherhoods, and also by widespread popular attachment to a secular pluralism that allows Senegal's diverse peoples to adhere to a range of Islamic, Christian, and traditional forms of worship.[7]

However, the dual processes of neoliberal economic change and globalization in Senegal vibrantly transform the Sunnite leadership's muted critiques of Sufism and inconsistent attacks on the secular state through discourse on female sexuality for youth. These two forces bring new meaning to the spiritual and contestatory nature of being Sunnite, particularly for young women. While Sunnites of all backgrounds encounter and address their effects, educated female adherents shape specific religious and political subjectivities as they navigate the pitfalls of formal employment in Dakar's new environment. The following discussion of the cultural and economic changes that have dramatically altered the city's landscape will contextualize how these young women recast their leadership's discourses on secularism in order to reconcile their personal identities with Senegalese modernity, creating a moral and political hybrid of feminine Islamic activism.

Neoliberal Ethics, Transnational Commerce, and Islamist Women's Agency

Capitalist change in addition to the expansive, rapid globalization of urban markets and communications networks has radically altered not only Senegal's economy and class structure but the ways Senegalese people understand themselves in relation to the contemporary world. It is well documented that Senegal's faltering agricultural sector in the 1970s and

1980s, concomitant with sharp increases in oil prices, began a downward economic spiral for the country, where the state's borrowing from international banks and subsequent defaults led to its acceptance of structural adjustment agreements with the International Monetary Fund, World Bank, and Paris Club. These agreements forced the removal of subsidies that maintained the affordability of food, gas, utilities, and transport; the elimination of 20,000 public sector jobs; the installation of fees for schooling and formerly free health services; and the sale of large portions of nationalized telecommunications, water, and electricity firms to private companies overseas. This near thirty-year process has only been compounded by the 1994 devaluation of the CFA, resulting in drops in rural productivity by up to 200 percent, the diminution of the average Senegalese purchasing power by at least one-third, and a massive exodus of villagers to cities and towns already strapped for municipal services.[8] Although Senegal is now held up as a moderate success by the World Bank and the International Monetary Fund for proving the efficacy of structural adjustment, its economy has grown only in secondary and tertiary sectors, which employ a minimum of Senegal's work force and are monopolized by wealthy entrepreneurs.[9] Nongovernmental organizations and Senegalese banks touting the miracles of microcredit and small business claim to stand ready to enrich those left behind by structural adjustment, but these new plans tend to further parcel out poor countries' already piecemeal division of labor and frequently bolster just a few *petits commerçants* while continuing to subjugate those who become their underpaid employees.[10]

Accompanying Senegal's privatizing trend and its consequent increases in poverty is globalization, where liberalized markets, growing numbers of families entirely dependent on the remittances of their *ressortissants*, and disenfranchised youth seeking new dreams and identities open up to the transnational process. Outpacing every other sub-Saharan country besides Ghana and Botswana, Senegal ranks fifty-first out of *Foreign Policy's* seventy-two most-globalized countries for 2007, with 69.4 percent of its gross domestic product (GDP) made up by trade, forty minutes of international phone traffic per capita, and total remittances as 6.24 percent of GDP, placing the country thirteenth in the world for money sent home by relatives from overseas.[11]

Dakar's markets and street life offer colorful evidence of these global currents, where clothing, DVDs, electronic equipment, and books imported from around the world are displayed for purchase, and signs for Western Union and MoneyGram hang on every rentable public space.

Television channels broadcast music videos and films from the West, as well as cell phone companies' new offers for Senegalese to send free text messages to their friends in Europe to pay for their phone minutes. Young consumers of varied class backgrounds purchase imitations of clothing brands such as DKNY and BabyPhat, listen to Beyoncé and Alicia, and as Buggenhagen[12] points out, watch Latin American soap operas about women who defy their communities' norms to marry the men of their dreams. Nearly every Senegalese youth can recite the English phrase "time is money" when conversing with American visitors, and those with university diplomas vie for jobs as telemarketers in French-owned call centers, as connection specialists in French cell phone companies, and as cashiers in European-style convenience marts.

Yet Senegal's economic liberalization, in both goods and jobs, is not just comprised of global flows from the West. Perhaps the most recent trend is China's infiltration: Les Allées du Centenaire, Dakar's large boulevards leading to its bustling Sandaga market, are now lined with the tiny garage shops of Chinese merchants who sell plastic shoes, kitchenware, and clothes. Equally present and for many more years, however, have been items for sale from Muslim countries in North Africa, the Gulf, the Middle East, and even Southeast Asia. These include veils of all colors and styles from the Iranian tchador to pastel scarves typical of those worn by Turkish women with pantsuits, posters of Mecca, clocks with Islamic calligraphy, videos on proper comportment for Muslim women, cassettes and CDs of international imams' sermons, books by Tariq Ramadan, pamphlets listing innovations to be avoided as well as rituals to perfect, and Internet Web sites that offer chat sessions with *usthaths* all over the world. Young people's imaginations of Muslim countries beyond West Africa are further enlivened by television programs ranging from infomercials on shopping complexes in Dubai, Egyptian and Saudi soap operas, and Gulf-produced series on the life of the Prophet.

Images and ideological messages travel not just through markets and media but along educational vectors as well. Private Islamic schools, and now public Franco-Arab schools, employ teachers who hold orthodox Sunni values, and who sometimes come from Morocco and Egypt. In the reverse, countries such as Morocco, Saudi Arabia, and Sudan offer scholarships to young Senegalese who are outstanding in Arabic. Government officials and wealthy private citizens in Saudi Arabia, Kuwait, Egypt, Turkey, and Libya donate money to the Senegalese government for public works such as health clinics and banks, but also to private Islamic academies such as Al-Falah College.

Other investments from the Arab world play a role in Senegal's transnational growth as well. In 1999, the Foire Afro-Arabe (Afro-Arab Fair) was held in a large, newly built complex close to Dakar's airport, where twenty-two African and Arab countries sold their wares. Sunnite women who shopped there returned with bags of Islamic clothing and home décor, which they used themselves or marketed to their peers. In March 2008, the Organization of the Islamic Conference (Organisation de la Conférence Islamique, or OCI), communed in Dakar. This collective of fifty-seven Muslim countries declared that it would work to promote economic advancement and security amongst member states, coordinate efforts to safeguard Islamic Holy Lands, and support the Palestinian nationalist struggle. Massive refurbishments of Senegal's Méridien President Hotel were paid for by the Saudi Bin Laden Group to house leaders from the member countries in comfort, and Kuwait donated $33 million (the first phase of $100 million promised), for the improvement of, as stated by its government, "mobility, security, accessibility, and the environment of Dakar." The president of the OCI, Ekmeleddin Ihsanoglu, also promised significant charitable contributions to Senegal's Digital Solidarity Fund, established by President Wade to increase access to information technology for peoples of the developing world.[13]

In this context of two-directional globalization from the West as well as the East, comprising media, capital, and charitable flows, Dakar's youth currently broker selves. The valorization of private accumulation, in concert with increased inequality, has created a new landscape for the politics of inclusion and exclusion—for who succeeds, who fails, who lives their dreams, and who languishes, and hence, for the constitution of personhood.[14] Amplifying the transformations in this altered socioeconomic terrain is an influx of global commodities and networks that offer, as Weiss[15] states, the promise of "compelling forms of identification and affiliation," expedited by new media images, modalities of worship, discourses on the rights of citizenship, and constellations of cultural goods from which to cobble together new identities. These implements inspire young Africans as they pursue what Buggenhagen[16] calls a "desire for self in the face of community"—a sense of oneself as an individual who confronts and accommodates the local and international changes that redefine her relationships, community, and future possibilities.

It is within Dakar's shifting socioeconomic context that the academic question of orthodox Muslim women and their agency can be problematized. For two decades, Muslim women's self-determination has been the center of a debate in the academy on whether it is a value-rational, political phenomenon, or whether it should instead be understood as a moral, ethical project. In efforts to move past early academic arguments that characterized orthodox Muslim women's choices as passive acceptance of male dominance or false consciousness,[17] a spate of work emerged, particularly in the 1990s, that interpreted their decisions as ways to gain leverage with men or acquire social and material power in broader society. Orthodox women's veiling, for instance, was explained as an effort to command male respect while maintaining religiously prescribed femininity in the public spheres of the street, the market, the school, and the workplace.[18] *Hijab* was also described as a tool of feminine resistance to Western domination in both colonial and postcolonial eras.[19] Other works shed light on the economic motives of women in Islamist groups that supported populist causes, such as Turkey's Refah party and Bahrain's Jamiyat al-Islah, or on the interests of women in groups that ushered in a new capitalist class, such as Sudan's National Islamic Front.[20]

Analyses of West African Muslim women have also addressed their gains in material and social capital. Many works credit Sufi Islam with opening cultural spaces for women to carve out leadership roles, public identities, and access to business opportunities. Female adherents of Sufi brotherhoods bestow honors upon one another, and provide mutual financial support in rotating credit clubs, groups that pool resources to celebrate religious pilgrimages and baptisms, and commercial exchanges at religious festivals.[21] In very rare cases, women even become marabouts, and they employ patrilineage, Qur'anic knowledge, and physiologically male traits to amass their religious followings.[22]

Access to these forms of power is not only reserved for Sufi women; female Sunni reformists in the region have also been shown to achieve political influence. Alidou[23] argues that Nigerien reformist women reclaim Islamic knowledge from men by learning Qur'anic views on women's domestic roles and sexuality for themselves. Le Blanc[24] highlights the ways Ivorian reformist women confront generational and class relations, whereas Masquelier[25] suggests that Izala youth contest their elders' corrupt materialism, particularly the problem of bride wealth. Miran[26] shows that through reformist organizations in Benin and Ghana, women respond to democratization and public discourses on human rights, while in Ivory Coast, they engage in discussions about gender equality.

The foregoing analyses point up important forms of Muslim women's agency, yet a danger exists in emphasizing just the political and material sides of female adherents' accomplishments. Women's religiosity can be easily relegated to mere decoration for materialist motives, and where value-rational action is associated with self-determination, spiritual inspiration can become tied to false consciousness. No matter what their material attainment through religious activity, orthodox women are often perceived in Western academic circles to perpetually subjugate themselves by succumbing to patriarchy. Perhaps Nancy Hirschmann's comment[27] best typifies this point of view: "To say that women veil as a way to reconcile work with traditional values . . . may recognize women's agency but circumvents a larger question: Is it a mark of women's agency to uphold values or codes that oppress women?"

A rebuttal to this rhetorical question is represented by an important contention from the other side in this debate: To assess Muslim women's interests in the secular humanist terms of personal freedom is to apply a rubric that has little historical basis in the development of social thought in the Islamic world. Mahmood[28] proposes this critique in her study of Sunni reformist women in Cairo, where she argues that female adherents do not build religious subjectivities that are politically identitarian, nor do they confront male dominance. Instead of becoming reformist for nationalist reasons, to rebuke Western power, to sympathize with a global Islamic identity, or to defy patriarchy, Cairo's "mosque women" endeavor foremost to cultivate a pious lifestyle based on self-control, regulation of their emotions, modesty and shyness, and reflection on God. If they must defy secular institutions or their husbands' reproaches, then these are political effects incidental to their spiritual and ethical efforts, faced by any group that advocates a moral program that conflicts with broader society's hegemonic institutions.

Mahmood[29] reminds us that desires, and the forms of subjectivity and agency they breed, are human constructs tied to specific sociohistorical contexts. For this reason, she argues, it is unreasonable to evaluate Egyptian reformist women's efficacy with the Western criterion of personal liberation, given that these women understand the world in communitarian terms. Yet, if we can agree with Mahmood[30] that sociohistorical contexts help shape human desires, the identitarian affiliations and political sensibilities that lack for Cairène women may play crucial roles alongside pious sentiments for reformist females in other empirical contexts.

Roy[31] points out that universalist orthodox Islamic ideology, while not attached to any particular state, is political in that many of its young adherents worldwide see themselves in a struggle for the ascendance of a global *ummah* that would defy Western, capitalist hegemony as well as the social and economic constraints of their local communities. Perhaps paradoxically, activists in globalized cultural movements frequently use the commodities of transnational capital in their defense against these very forces. The international commodities of orthodox Islam marketed in Dakar—such as veils, pamphlets, Web sites, scholar exchange programs, and CDs of internationally known *ustaths*—not only become implements for Sunnite women to build outward identities as Muslims in solidarity with orthodox Sunnis in other parts of the world but also become tools for female adherents to build a sense of spirituality and righteousness. The appropriation of these goods, and the practices they teach, are not passive or alienated processes whereby consumers become classified into categories without social bonds, or where they use material things to compete for status with others.[32] Commodities, when imbued with cultural meaning, can represent oppositional ideologies and contribute to sentiments of piety, as religious adherents incorporate goods' symbolic values into their conceptions of self.[33]

Because young Sunnite women often view Islam from Arab countries as being close to an original, pure version of the religion, and because they idealize Arab and Middle Eastern societies as more strictly enforcing orthodox practice, they use items imported from these places as a means for cultivating piety.[34] Veils require one to concentrate on virtue, pamphlets teach the proper way to pray, and recordings of international speakers imply that Muslims everywhere can be bound together by faith and striving for ethical as well as ritual perfection. These transnational commodities, and the sense of international connection they inspire, become bound up in many Sunnite women's notions of their own religiosity. Female adherents' subjectivities are thus twofold: Being orthodox is a private, individualist project in spiritual and moral cultivation, while it is simultaneously a political, identitarian assertion of self amidst the capitalist influxes of Western popular culture, transnational Islamic goods, and a liberalization of markets and the workforce that has resulted in increased social inequalities.

To create oneself as a modern individual with specific tastes and convictions, and in relief from capitalist, globalizing forces that threaten to fragment familiar affiliations, is to engage in a process of subjectivation that characterizes many people's involvement in collective action today, and which comprises the dual religious and political choices of women in Dakar's Sunnite movement.[35] Touraine[36] points out that in a world where humans depend not only on production but also on consumption and communication, people seek to salvage their singular existences as free actors entitled to universal rights and personal liberties. These sentiments are shaped in part by secular thought, which has defined the separation of the citizen from the community through the separation of the state from the church. In efforts at self-preservation, contemporary activists often create institutions and demands in order to defend their personal creativity and cultural rights against the effacing forces of governments and global markets. In Senegal, male Sunnite leaders actually make claims on the virtues of secularism to critique the secular state as they insist on the cultural freedom to adjudicate women's bodies according to their conception of Islam. Young female adherents, on the other hand, surpass this dispute as they create personal subjectivities through which they cultivate piety, stand in solidarity with a global Sunni movement they envision exists beyond Senegal, and negotiate the challenges of Dakar's changing labor force.

Defending the New Code: Sunnite Women's Discourses on the State, Sexuality, and the Nature of Faith

Data for the remainder of this chapter was collected consistently from 1998 to 2008 by the author in the form of archival research on Senegalese newspapers and Sunnite publications, as well as in participant observation, focus group, and life history narratives with female adherents, their male counterparts, and movement leaders of both genders. The vast majority of Sunnites interviewed belonged to the following organizations, which represent the diversity of adherents' ethnicities and socioeconomic backgrounds: the Association des Étudiants Musulmans de l'Université de Dakar, the Association des Élèves et Étudiants Musulmans du Sénégal, the Jama'at Ibadu Rahman, and Harakat al-Falah, as well as three neighborhood groups, referred to by the pseudonyms Mosquée à Rond Point, Association Rabi Sarr, and Association Thiaroye.[37] Before introducing female Sunnites' discourses, this section will address the male leadership's challenges to the secular state with respect to the governance of women. The chapter will conclude that while Sunnite men do test Senegalese democracy by calling forth a public debate on secularism, female adherents create a broader, more quotidian challenge to the liberalizing state that combines political and moral perspective.

During the 1980s, Sunnite male leaders began to contest the Senegalese government's legal authority over women's bodies and family roles. Viewing these domains as private and only legitimately regulated by the Qur'an and the Sunnah, orthodox heads questioned the viability of secular governance in this realm, and in general. In 1983, for instance, the Jama'at Ibad ar-Rahman published this statement likening President Abdou Diouf's prohibition of religious political parties to immoral stewardship: "We know that the system [Diouf] directs is not the 'best' nor is it acceptable from an Islamic point of view. Isn't it this regime that instituted the health card for prostitutes? Isn't it he who forbade Islam to form a political program?"[38]

Ten years later, the Jama'at still blamed the state for the mismanagement of women in matters of sex and the family, making the following claims: "[The national administration has]—maintained a law, which, under the cover of secularism, forbids Muslims to attempt the political alternative of their religion—closed Muslim courts tolerated by the ex-colonizer and banalized the function of *qadi* [Islamic judge]—legalized prostitution, despite the axioms of our creed and the values of our civilization—adopted a Family Code of Judeo-Christian essence."[39]

For Sunnites, the Family Code—a body of legislation passed in 1972 during the Senghor presidency and amended by the Diouf administration in 1981—is not a defense of women's rights, which they argue are adequately addressed in the Qur'an but represent an unacceptable separation of faith from law. The Code, presented as a compromise between local Islamic traditions and secular French statutes concerning women, raised the legal age of marriage to sixteen for girls and required all couples to register their marriages with the state, upon which the husband, presumably with his wife's consent, would sign how many wives he could take during the course of their marriage. Wife repudiation was outlawed, and a secular judge would arbitrate divorces, custody, and the separation of assets.[40]

The Sunnite leadership's public objections to the state's intrusions into religious and family life have stayed strong since the Code was instated. In April 1997, President Abdou Diouf announced to a group of foreign journalists at the United Nations Population Fund "the balanced family is a monogamous family. We must [as a society] come prudently to monogamy."[41]

In response, members of the Association de Quinze, an umbrella organization for fifteen prominent Sunnite associations in Dakar, wrote an open letter to the president arguing that polygamy provides for "the solidarity, the equilibrium, and the strength of our family system." They continued: "We will not be [the] object of enraged attacks . . . This recurrent crusade against our religion and its most sacred institutions is due to the fact that its traditional enemies hardly react."[42]

While Sunnite spokesmen responded with similar indignation to the Senegalese state's accord with international agencies to legally ban female circumcision in 2000,[43] by 2003 the leadership returned squarely to the domestic question of the Family Code. An organization of seventeen groups called the Collectif des Associations Islamiques au Sénégal helped form the Comité Islamique pour la Réforme du Code de la Famille, or CIRCOF. This body proposed that the executive and legislative branches of the Wade administration adopt a 276-article Code du Statut Personnel Islamique. Based on *sharî'a* and inspired by similar legislation in Morocco, Algeria, and the Gulf, the suggested laws would prohibit rights of inheritance to children born outside of marriage, decrease the amount of daughters' and wives' inheritances, require women to seek male family members' permission to marry, reinstate divorce by repudiation, and legalize female excision.[44] The Code, CIRCOF maintained, would not be a violation of religious freedom in Senegal because it would apply only to Muslims.

In response to CIRCOF's recommendation, President Abdoulaye Wade issued a public statement from his diplomatic mission in Japan asserting that the measure would never be considered, and that it was a threat to secularism.[45] Rejected and embarrassed by Wade's international rebuff, Sunnite leaders took recourse to arguments *for* secular pluralism in order to assert their rights to propose the law. Contending that the Code did not threaten secularism because non-Muslim Senegalese would not have to adhere to it, leaders such as Imam Mbaye Niang of the Mosquée Inachevée de l'Aéroport argued that in a free society, Muslims should have the right to request governance by religious law.[46] And in a three-page essay for the July 2003 issue of the Islamic newspaper *Al Yawmou*, Maitre Babacar Niang, the president of CIRCOF, asked Senegalese to consider the secular pluralism of numerous countries in the European Union as well as the United States, enjoining that exceptions are made in those places for religious heterogeneity and that Senegal should not have to imitate the anomaly of French secularism, which delimits diversity in the name of republican solidarity.[47]

Sunnite leaders' calls for the Wade administration and the Senegalese people to reflect upon the liberties offered by a secular state—that in this case, paradoxically, would allow for the passing of an anti-secular Code—touched off a debate in the media where Muslim and Christian laypersons, religious leaders, professors, and politicians hotly disputed the meanings of Senegalese secularism, its departures from the French model, and the limits of democracy. Sunnite females, who widely supported the proposed Code, also participated in this conversation, and like their leadership, appealed to the universal and cultural rights a secular government should afford each citizen. Take, for example, the words of Mme Aichatou Fall Diagne, an elementary school teacher who lives in Guediawaye: "Peace in the 'cité' should be constructed in diversity and in respect for diversity . . . Why, free and sovereign, do we fail in our desire to live together, when, during our moment of subjugation and domination, we lived together in a comfort of conscience, belief, and mutual respect for our reasons for being? Who would want to secularize Senegalese Islam only to take the parts of it that suit them? . . . Is it so difficult for a woman to reconcile her sincere faith as a Muslim, and by consequence, her status with a respectable modernity?"[48]

Here, Mme Diagne relies on the pluralist possibilities of secularism to allow orthodox Muslims the right to live as they see fit, but she simultaneously criticizes secularizing Islam as destructive to religion itself and to the abilities of Muslim women to practice their religion properly. Mme Diagne's concerns second those voiced by Ndèye Faty Sarr, a recent graduate of the Université Cheikh Anta Diop with a bachelor's degree in sociology.

Ndèye Faty asserts in her defense of the proposed Code that "Islam assures to the woman a grace that the modern world has taken from her." Women, like all Muslims, she continues, are required to individually comprehend God's word. The place of the woman in Islam is a high, protected place, where she should dress modestly as a protection "against the crooks which infect and fester the streets." Progressing to a justification of unequal inheritance rules included in the new Code, Ms. Sarr reasons that given women's protected status, "nothing is more normal than to give the largest part of the [inheritance] to the man and a lesser part to the sister, who is cared for by her husband . . . one will object that women participate more and more in the domestic economy (which is true). However, one must recognize that this phenomenon only really appears in the cities with the emergence of this new generation of women coming from the occidental school."⁴⁹

Arguing similarly to Mme Diagne that Islam provides a spiritual grace to women who must confront the erosions of modern life, Ndèye Faty associates values antithetical to the new Code—such as women's equal participation with men in household finances—as Western and external to Islam. This identitarian defense of Islam vis-à-vis the West also resounds with Mme Diagne, who asks, "Is there a 'supranationality' of faith? Should we, under the pretext of signed and ratified international conventions, permit everything here? When is our national assembly going to lean toward legal propositions like 'civil unions' allowing marriage for homosexuals, or authorizing the adoption of children by lesbians?"⁵⁰

It is clear that Mme Diagne, in her support for the proposed Code, also endeavors to defend Islam against deterioration by Western influences, which, she worries, have already made inroads to Senegalese Islamic culture. Ndèye Faty similarly endeavors to galvanize Islam against external attack, as well as internal assault by Senegalese Muslims who "have been charmed by the evils that Satan has rendered beautiful to their eyes." She instructs fellow Muslims who disapprove of the Code to "stop criticizing your religion because if you are the first to do it, what do you think the others will do? Well, they won't be the least bit bothered to criticize you [as Muslims] and they'll do it better than you do yourselves."⁵¹

Mme Diagne's and Ndèye Faty's efforts to defend the proposed Code by reminding Muslim women that they must reconcile their faith with contemporary times and help protect Islam from corrupting external forces highlight the moral and political dualism of Sunnite discourses. Their words also point up the fact that female adherents actually have to find and effect answers in their daily lives to the hypothetical posed by Sunnite men in their dispute with the state on femininity. As Sunnite women endeavor to cultivate piety as a means to build a modern, orthodox life, which includes negotiating Dakar's burgeoning neoliberal economy, they engage in the dual task of private spiritual development and defiance of new capitalist forces that threaten to erode their Islamic ethics. In the next section, educated Sunnite women who hail from the middle class narrate their experiences in Dakar's formal labor market, centering on the moral and political dialectics of veiling, shaking hands with men, and telling the truth at work.

Women, Work, and the Moral-Political Dialectic of Sunnite Ethics

Sunnite women do not simply view veiling as a symbol of their orthodoxy but use the veil as a tool to build faith. The more one covers, the more one disciplines herself in the domains of feminine modesty, reserve before men, and reflection on God. In 2000, when Coumba,[52] who had recently graduated from Université Cheikh Anta Diop, stopped wearing colorful headscarves and began to wear a black *tchador*, she explained: "I had been veiling for a long time with just a short veil and long sleeves with loose pants or a dress, but I did not feel my faith growing. Everyone was shocked when I began to wear this veil à l'Iranienne (Iranian style), but I finally feel good now; I feel good in my own skin, so to speak." Coumba's commitment to veiling is echoed by Majigeen, an MBA student whose story highlights the sacrifices Sunnite women make when navigating Dakar's transnational job market, because of their decisions to never unveil: "When looking for work, [veiling complicates things]. [My private marketing school] makes us do internships each year, and so one day they put me in contact with a multinational that had offices almost everywhere in the world. I had an interview with [the boss]. It was a recruiting interview, and he was really interested in my CV, and then when he saw my veil, he was a little surprised! 'Well,' he said, 'you're dynamic, you have a good CV, a good education, but it would surprise me if you could work in France.' He had an export branch there. 'That just won't work out in France with you wearing the veil.' . . . Then he asked me if one day he hired me, would I ever take my veil off. I said that was out of the question. I would keep my veil for the rest of my life . . . They understood, but they did not give me the job . . . I was a little disappointed but I expected it. A girl wearing miniskirts will get a lot further than me. So if that girl makes fifty percent of an effort, I'll have to make one hundred percent, and I'm ready to do that."

As a sign of personal strength, tenacity, and faith, Majigeen veils to maintain her orthodox convictions, and she values overcoming the discrimination against her dress and beliefs in Dakar's globalizing workforce. However, she also points out that "Westernized" young Senegalese women represent a tough form of competition in her search for work in multinational companies. Her veil is a liability in a market that demands secular conformity, but Majigeen intends to steel herself against these pressures, guard her identity as a pious Muslim, and not fold before the demands of a transnational labor market she is determined to enter.

Majigeen also tells of times when she was refused jobs and even interviews because she would not shake hands with her prospective boss. Sunnite women argue that it is a sin to shake hands with someone of the opposite sex, and they cite Hadiths that promise severe punishment for this forbidden physical contact with men. For female adherents, abstaining from handshaking is a duty to protect their virtue, and thus their piety. Additionally, they feel responsible for protecting men in the *ummah* from experiencing any form of unwarranted sexual attraction through the touch of a woman's hand. Young Sunnite women also criticize shaking hands as a colonial remnant, and they challenge those who practice this custom as lacking the Islamic knowledge held by orthodox Muslims in places beyond Senegal. Here is the perspective of Aminta, an undergraduate student at the Université Cheikh Anta Diop: "It is against Islam for men and women to shake hands . . . The French came over here and started shaking hands with everyone. So the only difficulty I have is that my father tries to insist that I shake hands with my uncle . . . you know, our parents were colonized men."

Rabi Sarr, a well-known *arabisant* and Qur'anic teacher, stood up for her convictions about handshaking against pressures for her to yield to workplace hierarchy and the bruised ego of her male boss, who did not share her religious perspective on the matter. She explained: "It was at Senelec [electric company] where my boss at the time created trouble for me. One day, he ran into me at the infirmary, where I was with my daughter, who was sick. He wanted to shake my hand, and I refused, with great politeness, as is recommended in Islam. His response was "I will fire you" . . . He called my local level boss in Rufisque to tell him to process my removal . . . When I got home, I told my husband, saying that I would seek justice. He categorically refused, saying that God, the Real Judge, was on our side. So I obeyed. I stayed home for five years without losing faith, without regrets. Then one day, a high-ranking official at Senelec and a close friend of my husband, stopped by to say that my old boss was demoted. I came back to Senelec as a temporary employee . . . [and] I worked there [until] I chose to leave. When I did, thank God, I was able to open a school where I teach the Holy Qur'an."[53]

Rabi relates that she maintained her faith and her honor by refusing her boss, and also by obeying her husband's wishes and believing that God would ultimately rectify her loss of work. Ultimately, she rejoined Senelec, left this secular position when she chose to, and followed her passion by opening an Islamic school. Sunnite women's recourse to Islamic morality in dress and handshaking defends their religious ethics and, consequently, their sense of self in a capital city rife with economic and globalizing changes that alter the terrain of relationships, social behavior, and personal identities. Standing by one's Sunnite convictions is thus not simply a matter of ritual purity in dress or greetings but a question of conscience.

In the following extract, a UCAD graduate named Aisha describes some of her own experiences that personify the tension between many Sunnite women's desires to work and the moral dilemmas inherent in Dakar's new labor market:

> I worked in a call center that had contracts with French marketing companies. We called people in France to ask them what products they would buy . . . we even worked with Orange. We had to pretend we were French; a French phone number appeared on the recipients' phones. It was a company built on lies. I had to say my name was Chantal Duval, and we had scripts to follow if our accent gave us away, like "I live with my grandmother who is from Haiti." If French people figured out we were doing jobs their own unemployed youth could do they would be frustrated . . . but I would come home and think, "I'm making my living by lying," which is forbidden in Islam. . . . The youth who worked there acted so westernized. The girls smoked and wore revealing clothes. It was a loss of values, so I quit.

On the basis of Islamic morality, Aisha took a stand in opposition to global and neoliberal forces that now permeate Dakar. Rather than have her identity completely effaced by a marketing firm that required her to lie about her true self and keep company with youth who did not share her values about dress and behavior, Aisha chose to wait for a job where she could work without compromising her beliefs.

Sunnite women such as Aisha support the Islamic ideals of feminine modesty and submission in the communitarian vision addressed by Mahmood (2005). However, they also take political stands against cultural changes that they view as contrary to Islam, supporting their senses of solidarity with other Muslims worldwide. They assert, furthermore, an individualism specific to being inhabitants of a twenty-first-century, globalizing city rife with the contradictions of neoliberalism, the cultural tools to mold new subjectivities, and discourses on secularism and the universal right of self-expression. In a group conversation among some female graduates of Al Falah high school, Niarra—whose favorite quote is Dolly Parton's "dream what you want to be, then be it"—asked her colleagues to give her an Islamic answer to this question: "If God said, 'each person is responsible for his own actions,'" but He also said, "'You shall follow the destiny I have traced for you,' what exactly is my role?"

Niarra's query is emblematic of contemporary, young Sunnite women's efforts to shape themselves as individuals and pious Muslims in Dakar's volatile social context. The buttressing of self practiced by Majigeen, Rabi, and Aisha as they navigate Dakar's labor market is a dialectic of private piety and defiance that extends the Sunnite male leadership's paradoxical discourse on secularism to a negotiation of the transnational, capitalist forces reshaping Dakar today. While not an organized test of Senegal's democracy, these women's responses represent some of the quotidian, consistent ways female Sunnites confront changes introduced by the Senegalese state's neoliberal era.

Sunnite women's moral and political sensibilities invite us to look beyond value-rational explanations of their choices as well as past analyses that understand subjectivation as only a project in personal ethics. Dakar's female Sunnites do endeavor to continually improve their spirituality through proper ritual practice, modesty, and religious reflection, but they also engage Sunnite ideologies, in addition to the transnational ideals and goods of global Sunni orthodoxy, to shape bounded selves in an urban climate of immense economic and social transformation. And while Sunnite women are unlikely to ever shun modernity, they will attempt to embrace it on their own terms, even if this means creating new subjectivities with commodities ushered in by some of the very capitalist forces they defy.

Notes

1. Research for this chapter was funded with the generous support of Fulbright IIE, the National Science Foundation, Social Science Research Council, Princeton University's Transregional Institute for the Study of North Africa and the Middle East, and the Ramapo College's Separately Budgeted Research program.
2. Loimeier, "The Secular State."

3. Augis, *Dakar's Sunnite Women: The Politics of Person*; Brenner, *Controlling Knowledge*; "La vie et l'œuvre d'Al-Hajj Mahomoud Ba Diowol," D. Robinson and J. L. Triaud (eds.). *Le temps des marabouts: Itinéraires et stratégies islamiques en Afrique occidentale française*. Paris: Karthala, 1997; Loimeier, "Cheikh Touré."
4. Augis, *Dakar's Sunnite Women*; Piga, "Neo-Traditionalist Islamic Associations."
5. Soares, "Islam in Mali in the Neoliberal Era"; Kane, *Muslim Modernity in Post-Colonial Nigeria*; and Leonardo Villalón, "Generational Changes" have pointed out that differences between orthodox reformist and Sufi groups are frequently indistinct, and that groups' espousals of doctrine or approaches to hegemonic powers often depend on highly nuanced political, religious, and historical contexts. It is important to note, however, that many Sunnites discursively (while perhaps not always in practice) attempt to distinguish themselves from other Muslims and that there are important local and geopolitical causes behind their efforts to do so.
6. Alidou, *Engaging Modernity*.
7. Villalón, "Generational Changes."
8. Gellar, *Senegal*; O'Bannon, *Confronting the Development Dilemma*; Somerville, "Reaction and Resistance."
9. Programme des Nations Unies pour le Développement, *Découvrir le Sénégal* (Dakar: Sénégal, PNUD, 2001).
10. Davis, *Planet of Slums*.
11. *Foreign Policy* (November/December 2007). The globalization index 2007 (www.foreignpolicy.com).
12. Buggenhagen, "Domestic Objections."
13. *Le soleil multimedia*. February 4, 2008 (www.lesoleil.sn).
14. Comaroff and Comaroff, "Afromodernity"; Davis, *Planet of Slums*; Weiss, "Contentious Futures: Past and Present."
15. Weiss, "Contentious Futures," p. 8.
16. Buggenhagen, "Domestic Objections."
17. See, for instance, El Saadawi, "Fundamentalism"; Mernissi, *Beyond the Veil*; Mernissi, *The Veil and the Male Elite*.
18. Hessini, "Wearing the Hijab in Contemporary Morocco"; MacLeod, *Accommodating Protest*; Odeh, "Post-Colonial Feminism and the Veil."
19. Ahmed, *Women and Gender in Islam*.
20. Hale, *Gender Politics in the Sudan*; Seikaly, "Women and Religion in Bahrain."
21. Augis, *Dakar's Sunnite Women*; Coulon, *Femmes, Islam et Baraka*; Coulon, "Women, Islam, and *Baraka*"; Heath, "Fashion, Anti-Fashion, and Heteroglossia in Urban Senegal": Laborde, *La confrérie Layenne*; Villalón, *Islamic Society and State Power in Senegal*.

22. Coulon, *Femmes, Islam et Baraka*; Coulon and Reveyrand-Coulon, *L'Islam au féminin*; Gemmeke, "Women Reconfiguring Esoteric Economies."
23. Alidou, *Engaging Modernity*.
24. Le Blanc, "The Production of Islamic Identities"; Le Blanc, "Hadj et changements identitaires."
25. Masquelier, "The Scorpion's Sting."
26. Miran, "D'Abidjan à Porto Novo"; Miran, *Islam, histoire, et modernité en Cote d'Ivoire*.
27. Hirschmann, *The Subject of Liberty*.
28. Mahmood. *The Politics of Piety*.
29. Ibid.
30. Ibid.
31. Roy, *Globalized Islam*.
32. Baudrillard, *Selected Writings*; Bourdieu, *Distinction*.
33. Augis, *Dakar's Sunnite Women*; D'Alisera, "I Love Islam"; Janson, "Roaming About for God's Sake"; Schulz, "Promises of (Im)mediate Salvation."
34. Augis, "Jambaar or Jumbax-Out?"
35. Augis, *Dakar's Sunnite Women*; MacDonald, *Global Movements*.
36. Touraine, *Un nouveau paradigme*.
37. Given ongoing debates in the academy about the necessity of the ethnographer to address the effect of her presence on respondents' presentations of self and social problems, I am frequently asked to explain the impact of my identity as a white, non-Muslim American on Sunnite women's representations of themselves and their religious activism. While some Sunnites have declined to speak with me because of suspicions about my motives for research (which validly come from real experiences Africans have had with Westerners in their midst)—ranging from espionage for the CIA to concerns about my publishing mischaracterizations of Islam—those who agreed to participate in my study viewed my position as an outsider as an opportunity to explain their own feelings of difference from other Senegalese, to discuss their conceptions of "true" Islamic piety versus other forms of Islamic practice, and to describe their sense of solidarity with a global *ummah*, often with respect to a negative vision of the West and the United States. The amount of time I have spent in Sunnite milieus and with Sunnite respondents has allowed me to observe breaches in their presentations of self as pious Muslims. Yet many of my respondents, in the spirit of open conversation and humility, and the Islamic philosophy that "no Muslim is perfect," have not even tried to present themselves as monolithically pious or principled. They, and I, are more interested in the process by which adherents work to improve themselves according to hopes and ideals inspired by the movement.

38. Jama'at Ibad ar-Rahman, *Le Musulman* 7 (May–June) (1983).
39. Jama'at Ibad ar-Rahman, *Le Musulman* 43 (1993).
40. Sow, "Famille et loi au Sénégal."
41. Diop, "Querelle de ménage avec Abdou Diouf," *Walfadjri*, July 24, 1997.
42. Ibid.
43. Augis, *Dakar's Sunnite Women*.
44. Abdoullah, "Regards sur le projet de code de statut personnel Islamique," *Le Soleil*, May 26, 2003, pp. 18–19. Document du code du statut personnel (www.lequotidien.sn/dossiers/index.cfm?var_doss=13).
45. Kama, "Les difficultés à mettre en oeuvre la réforme," *Walfadjri*, April 10, 2003, p. 2.
46. Dieng, "Quitus au code du statut personnel, veto contre le sénat," *Walfadjri*, May 8, 2003, p. 4.
47. Maitre Babacar Niang, "La laïcité? Parlons-en," *Le Jour: Al Yawmou*, July 2003, pp. 8–10.
48. Mme Aïchatou Fall Diagne, "Qui a si peur du code musulman et pourquoi?" *Walfadjri*, May 7, 2003, p. 10.
49. Ndèye Faty Sarr, "Les musulmans sont les premiers ennemis de l'Islam," *Walfadjri*, May 6, 2003, p. 10.
50. Mme Aïchatou Fall Diagne, "Qui a si peur du code musulman et pourquoi?" *Walfadjri*, May 7, 2003, p. 10.
51. Ndèye Faty Sarr, "Les musulmans sont les premiers ennemis de l'Islam," *Walfadjri*, May 6, 2003, p. 10.
52. Pseudonyms have been used to protect the privacy of all respondents.
53. Rougui Sy Kane, "J'ai été licenciée pour avoir refusé de serrer la main à mon patron," *Sud Quotidien*, September 4, 1999.

Bibliography

Ahmed, Leila. *Women and Gender in Islam*. New Haven, Conn.: Yale University Press, 1992.

Alidou, Ousseina. *Engaging Modernity: Muslim Women and the Politics of Agency in Post-Colonial Niger*. Madison: University of Wisconsin Press, 2005.

Augis, Erin. *Dakar's Sunnite Women: The Politics of Person*. PhD thesis. Ann Arbor, Mich., 2002, University Microfilms.

_____. "Jambaar or Jumbax-Out? How Sunnite Women Negotiate Power and Belief in Orthodox Islamic Femininity." In *New Perspectives on Islam in Senegal*, eds. M. Diouf and M. Leichtman, 211–233. New York: Palgrave Macmillan, 2009.

Baudrillard, Jean. "Consumer Society." In *Selected Writings*, ed. Mark Poster, 32–59. Stanford, Calif.: Stanford University Press, 1988.

Bourdieu, Pierre. *Distinction*. Cambridge, Mass: Harvard University Press, 1984.

Brenner, Louis. *Controlling Knowledge: Religion, Power, and Schooling in a West African Muslim Society*. Bloomington: Indiana University Press, 2001.

Buggenhagen, Beth. "Domestic Objections: The Senegalese Murid Trade Diaspora and the Politics of Marriage Payments, Love, and State Privatization." In *Producing African Futures; Ritual and Reproduction in a Neoliberal Age*, ed. B. Weiss, 21–53. Boston: Brill, 2004.

Comaroff, Jean and John Comaroff. "Afromodernity and the New World Order." In *Producing African Futures; Ritual and Reproduction in a Neoliberal Age*, ed. B. Weiss, 329–346. Boston: Brill, 2004.

Coulon, Christian. *Femmes, Islam et Baraka*. Bordeaux: CEAN, 1985.

———. "Women, Islam, and *Baraka*." In *Charisma and Brotherhood in African Islam*, eds. Donal B. Cruise O'Brien and Christian Coulon, 113–133. Oxford: Clarendon, 1988.

Coulon, Christian and Odile Reveyrand-Coulon, *L'Islam au féminin: Sokhna Magat Diop cheikh de la confrérie Mouride, Sénégal*. [Talence, France: Centre d'études d'Afrique Noire (Institut d'études politiques de Bordeaux), 1990.]

D'Alisera, Joann. "I Love Islam: Popular Religious Commodities, Sites of Inscription, and Transnational Sierra Leonean Identity." *Journal of Material Culture* 6 (3) (2001): 365.

Davis, Mike. *Planet of Slums*. New York: Verso, 2006.

El Saadawi, Nawal. "Fundamentalism: A Universal Phenomenon." *WAF Newsletter* 1 (November) (1990): 12–13.

Gellar, Sheldon. *Senegal: An African Nation Between Islam and the West*. Boulder, Colo.: Westview Press, 1982.

Gemmeke, Amber. "Women Reconfiguring Esoteric Economies." *ISIM Review* 19 (2007): 36–37.

Hale, Sandra. *Gender Politics in the Sudan*. Boulder, Colo.: Westview Press, 1996.

Heath, Deborah. "Fashion, Anti-Fashion, and Heteroglossia in Urban Senegal." *American Ethnologist* 19 (1992): 19–33.

Hessini, Leila. "Wearing the Hijab in Contemporary Morocco." In *Reconstructing Gender in the Middle East*, eds. F. Goçek and S. Balaghi, 40–56. New York: Columbia University Press, 1991.

Hirschmann, Nancy. *The Subject of Liberty: Toward a Feminist Theory of Freedom*. Princeton, N.J.: Princeton University Press, 2003.

Janson, Marloes. "Roaming About for God's Sake: The Upsurge of the Tabligh Jama'at in the Gambia." *Journal of Religion in Africa* 35 (4) (2005): 450–481.

Kane, Ousmane. *Muslim Modernity in Post-Colonial Nigeria: A Study of the Society for the Removal of Innovation and the Reinstatement of Tradition*. Leiden, the Netherlands: Brill, 2003.

Laborde, Cécile. *La confrérie Layenne et les Lébous du Sénégal: Islam et culture traditionelle en Afrique*. Bourdieux: CEAN, 1995.

Le Blanc, Marie Nathalie. "The Production of Islamic Identities Through Knowledge Claims in Bouakè, Côte d'Ivoire." *African Affairs* 98 (1999): 485–508.

———. "Hadj et changements identitaires: Le jeunes musulumans d'Abidjan et deBouaké, en Côte d'Ivoire dans les années 1990." In *L'Islam politique au sud du Sahara: Identités, discours, et enjeux*, ed. Muriel Gomez-Perez, 131–158. Paris: Karthala, 2005.

Loimeier, Roman. "The Secular State and Islam in Senegal." In *Questioning the Secular State*, ed. D. Westerlund, 183–197. London: Hurst and Co., 1996.

———. "Cheikh Touré, un musulman Sénégalais dans le siècle du réformisme a l'Islamisme." In *Islam et Islamismes au sud du Sahara*, eds. O. Kane and J. L., 155–168. Paris: Karthala, 1998.

MacDonald, Kevin. *Global Movements: Action and Culture*. Malden, Mass.: Blackwell, 2006.

MacLeod, Arlene. *Accommodating Protest*. New York: Columbia University, 1991.

Mahmood, Saba. *The Politics of Piety: The Islamic Revival and the Feminist Subject*. Princeton, N.J.: Princeton University Press, 2005.

Masquelier, Adeline. "The Scorpion's Sting: Youth, Marriage, and the Struggle for Social Maturity in Niger." *Journal of the Royal Anthropological Institute* 11 (371) (2005): 59–83.

Mernissi, Fatima. *Beyond the Veil*. Bloomington: Indiana University Press, 1987.

———. *The Veil and the Male Elite*. Reading, Mass: Addison-Wesley, 1991.

Miran, Marie. "D'Abidjan à Porto Novo: Associations Islamiques et culture religieuse réformiste sur la Côte de Guinée." In *Entrepreises religieuses transnationales en Afrique de l'Ouest*, eds. L. Fourchard and A. Mary, R. Otayek, 43–72. Paris: Karthala, 2005.

———. *Islam, histoire, et modernité en Cote d'Ivoire*. Paris: Karthala, 2006.

O'Bannon, Brett. *Confronting the Development Dilemma: Decentralized Cooperation, Governance, and Local Responses to Neoliberal Reform in Rural Senegal*. PhD thesis. Ann Arbor, Mich.: University Microfilms, 2004.

Odeh, Lama Abu. "Post-Colonial Feminism and the Veil." *Feminist Review* 43 (1993): 26–37.

Piga, Adriana. "Neo-Traditionalist Islamic Associations and the Islamist Press in Contemporary Senegal." In *Islam in Africa*, eds. G. Stauth and T. Bierschenk, 43–55. Münster: London: Lit, 2003.

Roy, Olivier. *Globalized Islam: The Search for a New Ummah.* New York: Columbia University Press, 2004.

Schulz, Dorthea. "Promises of (Im)mediate Salvation: Islam, Broadcast Media, and the Remaking of Religious Experience in Mali." *American Ethnologist* 33 (2) (2006): 210–229.

Seikaly, May. "Women and Religion in Bahrain." In *Islam, Gender, and Social Change*, eds. J. Esposito and Y. Haddad, 169–189. New York: Oxford University Press, 1998.

Soares, Benjamin. "Islam in Mali in the Neoliberal Era." *African Affairs* 105 (418) (2006): 77–95.

Somerville, Karen. "Reaction and Resistance: Confronting Economic Crisis, Structural Adjustment, and Devaluation in Dakar, Senegal." In *Globalization and Survival in the Black Diaspora*, ed. C. Green, 15–42. Albany, N.Y.: SUNY Press, 1997.

Sow, Fatou. "Famille et loi au Sénégal: Permanences et changements." *WLUML* dossier spécial no. 1, 1996.

Touraine, Alain. *Un nouveau paradigme pour comprendre le monde d'aujourd'hui.* Paris: Fayard, 2005.

Villalón, Leonardo. *Islamic Society and State Power in Senegal: Disciples and Citizens in Fatick.* New York: Cambridge University Press, 1995.

———. "Generational Changes, Political Stagnation, and the Evolving Dynamics of Religion and Politics in Senegal." *Africa Today* 46 (3-4) (1999): 129–147.

Weiss, Brad. "Contentious Futures: Past and Present." In *Producing African Futures: Ritual and Reproduction in a Neoliberal Age*, ed. B. Weiss, 1–20. Boston: Brill, 2004.

[5]

Sovereign Islam in a Secular State

*Hidden Knowledge and Sufi Governance
Among "Taalibe Baay"*

JOSEPH HILL

Over the past decade, questions about whether Islam can coexist with secularism, democracy, modernity, other religions, and Western civilization have proliferated in Europe and the United States. Once marginal claims that Islam imminently threatens Western civilization have moved into mainstream news media, policy circles, and even some academic settings.[1] Arguments that Islam is fundamentally incompatible with secular governance rely on the claim that Islam demands submission not only to a belief system but also to an integrated political, legal, and cultural system.[2] A burgeoning right-wing literature even purports to unveil a vast conspiracy of Muslim immigrants to violently replace Western democracy with Islamic law (*sharî'a*).[3] As outlandish as such claims probably seem to nearly all Muslims, certain Islamist groups share with these alarmists at least a general prognosis that God's unchanging law cannot coexist with the man-made laws of a secular or democratic state. Salafis in post-Mubarak Egypt, where I currently live, reminded me of this belief when I saw them distributing pamphlets warning Muslims that to support the increasingly powerful tides of democracy and secularism was to sin against God.

Any serious examination of Islam's history, its traditions of scriptural interpretation, and its many uses in various contexts shows that Muslims do not execute a predetermined and unchanging script. Rather, they participate in a "discursive tradition"[4] through which they relate current projects to an authoritative past. As legal scholars have shown, Islamic jurisprudence (*fiqh*) has long accommodated multiple interpretations of *sharî'a*, including those that present *sharî'a* as compatible with modern notions of religious freedom, democracy, human rights, and gender equality.[5] Furthermore, in addition to the diverse conclusions reached through "*sharî'a* reasoning,"[6] *Sharî'a* has coexisted in various contexts with other systems of reasoning and regulation, including *siyâsa* (legal regulations instituted by a nonclerical political authority),[7] rationalistic *falsafa* (philosophy), and the modern adaptation of European codes of law and administration.[8] Among Muslims more generally, surveys suggest that the vast majority desire a democratic state not influenced by religious clerics.[9] This widespread desire for democracy in the Muslim world became apparent to those who watched largely prodemocratic protests bring down several dictators during the 2011 "Arab Spring."

Seen in this light, the pluralistic orientation of the Senegalese Sufis discussed in this chapter stands out not as an exception but as a clear illustration of the many practical approaches to pluralism encountered in the Muslim world. These Sufis look to *Sharî'a*—understood not as a predetermined politico-juridical order but as God's prescriptions derived from the Qur'an and the Prophet's example—to guide acts of worship (*'ibâdât*) and social behavior (*mu'âmalât*). Yet they do not consider all past prescriptions to be relevant to their circumstances, and in some situations they describe transcendent Islamic principles of reality (*ḥaqîqa*) as superseding distinctions made by *sharî'a*.[10] They disagree with Islamists not over *whether* to apply Islamic principles in governance but over *how* to do so and, more particularly, over whether *sharî'a* is the sole authoritative principle governing all circumstances.

Consequently, I believe it is more analytically helpful to think of such disagreements in terms of "pluralism" versus "monism" rather than in terms of "moderation" versus "extremism" more often heard today. By "pluralism," I mean not a liberal multiculturalism that politically neutralizes difference by transforming it into culture but a pragmatic pluralism equipped to accommodate and contest multiple claims and principles of truth and authority. My purpose in shifting emphasis away from moderation and nonpolitical Islam is neither to deny Sufi Muslims' moderation, which they present as a core value of Islam, nor to support the claim that so-called moderate Muslims are closet Islamists. To the contrary, to recognize

Sovereign Islam in a Secular State

a political dimension in religious practice is to challenge the monistic religious-secular dichotomy that informs the perception of a "clash" between an intrinsically theocratic Islam and intrinsically secular Western cultural values.[11] Especially since September 11, 2001, discourse on "moderate" Muslims has called on Muslims to renounce any political aspect of their religious practice[12] in order to become good secular subjects.[13] Western political actors seek alliances with moderate Muslims to combat extremism both at home and abroad, and some commentators present Sufi Muslims in West Africa as ideal moderate allies in combating Islamic militancy.[14]

Today, West African Sufis indeed often define themselves as moderates in contrast to puritanical Salafi reformists who present themselves as defenders of orthodoxy and *sharî'a*.[15] Although several nineteenth-century Sufi leaders led Islamic revolutions against a decaying aristocracy,[16] the quietist tradition of separation from state corruption has been far more prevalent among West African Muslim leaders.[17] This tendency only strengthened when they confronted the overwhelming force of European colonial power.[18] Senegal sometimes serves as a paradigmatic example of moderate, nonpolitical West African Sufism. Its immensely influential Sufi communities, clearly uninterested in Islamizing the state, contribute to relative peace and stability through providing many civil society functions.[19] Senegal's curiously hybrid mode of governance, which emerged over the course of the French colonial period, combines formally secular state institutions with informal Islamic governance in its interior.[20] This pragmatic entente resulted not from any theory of government but from trial and error as colonial administrators discovered they needed Muslim leaders to rule and Muslim leaders discovered the colonial state's potential uses.[21]

This chapter examines cases of religious governance among Taalibe Baay,[22] or followers of the Senegalese Sufi leader Shaykh Ibrahim Niass (1900–1975), better known as "Baay" ("Father"). These cases show Taalibe Baay approaching Islamic authority as the highest authority yet simultaneously participating in Senegal's formally secular nation-state. They recognize *sharî'a* as an obligatory, yet not the only, source of authority, and religious leaders who intervene in conflicts appeal more often to mystical discourses of transcendence than to formal legal provisions. Disciples appeal to Islamic authority and discourses when responding to actual or potential violence, especially in small towns and villages, challenging the state legal system's monopoly over such cases. Senegalese Sufi groups, as a long and rich literature has shown, deeply shape Senegalese state politics.[23]

Yet, as these cases show, their political significance consists not only in their influence on the state but in their exercise of forms of "informal sovereignty."[24] Such cases challenge the distinction between "political" and "nonpolitical" Islam.[25]

Although historically less visible in national politics than Murids and the Tijanî disciples of Al-Hadj Malîck Sy, Taalibe Baay engage increasingly in national politics and global institutions. A son of Baay (Mamoune, who died in October 2011) founded a secular political party, and many Taalibe Baay *muqaddams* (representatives of the Sufi order) have founded nongovernmental organizations and partner with international organizations in development projects.[26] While those Taalibe Baay delegated to act as liaisons with nonreligious entities learn the languages of neoliberal development and secularism, they do not merely become "secular subjects."[27] Rather, their visible engagement in neoliberal and secular regimes of governance serves less visible religious projects founded on Islamic notions of truth and authority.[28] Rather than attempt to minimize or reconcile such tensions, Taalibe Baay accommodate and contest competing claims through mystical discourses of apparent (*zâhir*) and hidden (*bâtîn*) truths.

The remainder of this chapter relates several narratives showing how Taalibe Baay living in a secular Senegalese State subject themselves to Islamic governance. These cases illustrate three aspects of the religious community's constitution under Islamic authority: (1) its performances of engagement and disengagement with state authority; (2) mystical language serving to negotiate competing truth claims; and (3) religious governance acting to resolve local conflicts.

When the State Goes Home: Performing Sovereignties

Perhaps the most dramatic performances of Taalibe Baay community and its engagement and disengagement with the state occur during nightlong celebrations of the Prophet Muhammad's birth, or *Mawlid* (*Gàmmu* in Wolof). The principal *Mawlid* takes place on the twelfth night of the Islamic month of *ar-Rabî' al-awwal*, when hundreds of thousands of disciples from around the world gather in Medina Baay, the Taalibe Baay religious center founded by Baay Niass on the outskirts of the regional city of Kaolack. The state provides equipment, a delegation including government ministers, and press coverage for this event and the annual events of other nationally recognized Islamic groups. Throughout the year, disciple associations around Senegal organize *Mawlids* of various sizes that replicate the same structure on a smaller scale, the smallest local *Mawlid* "metonymically figur[ing] the structure of the grandest."[29] Lower-level politicians similarly form delegations and may even conspicuously sponsor these local events. At these events, the *Mawlid* proper begins after midnight, its centerpiece a stylized narrative of the birth and life of the Prophet Muhammad interspersed with sung poems praising Muhammad, *dhikrs* (chanting God's name), and religious speeches. Anyone organizing a *Mawlid* seeks the authorization and, ideally, participation of Medina Baay's leaders. Baay's sons and grandsons spend much of their year attending *Mawlids* in Senegal and around the world.

During a public afternoon "conference" before the *Mawlid* proper, representatives of the state and other entities present themselves to show respect to religious leaders. Whereas the more sacred *Mawlid* itself is, among many things, an enactment of a spiritual chain of authority, the more worldly conference is a point of engagement between the religious community and its others: the state, the nation (through print and broadcast media), and in many cases other Sufi groups through their delegations. The hierarchy is ambiguous: Where politicians may see themselves as seeking religious leaders' political support, the religious community may see political leaders performing obeisance to religious leaders.

The following is an account of a regional *Mawlid* my neighbor Mamadou invited me to attend in 2004, hosted by his personal shaykh, Daam Diop, in the village of Kër Móodu east of Kaolack where Diop is the village shaykh.[30] This account, along with another following, illustrates three roles that Daam Diop plays: as his disciples' advocate with state institutions, as a representative and disciple of Medina Baay's central authority, and as the spiritual leader and de facto governor of a rural disciple community, many of whom see him as bearing unique spiritual capabilities.

By late afternoon, chartered buses from throughout Senegambia have brought thousands of people to the village, and a handful have gathered in the giant tent in Kër Móodu's central square, knowing that the afternoon conference will soon begin. My host, Mamadou, a 20-year-old student at the Islamic Institute in Kaolack who studies concurrently at several informal Islamic schools, is a close disciple of Daam Diop and aspires to himself become a religious leader.[31] After a late lunch, Mamadou and two fellow students hurry to the tent to open the afternoon's activities with

Wolof speeches quoting the Qur'an and Hadîth to teach about proper Muslim behavior.

An hour into the meeting, attendees have filled most of the seats (the men on the right side and the women on the left). A piercing siren interrupts, and a large, black sport-utility vehicle crawls toward the tent. Beside the truck walks a dreadlocked fifty-year-old man in colorful, patchwork clothing, carrying the megaphone emitting the siren sound.[32] Daam Diop emerges in a flowing robe and enters the tent escorted by the siren and a train of young men chanting, "*Lâ ilâha illâ-Llâh*" ("There is no God but Allâh").[33] He sits in a large, plush armchair front and center, surrounded by about ten still unoccupied armchairs. The young preacher tentatively resumes, but ten minutes later the siren heralds a white Jeep carrying several government officials—the mayor, the subprefect, the prefect, and a deputy to the national assembly—who sit beside Daam Diop. Their arrival definitively ends my friends' warm-up activities.

The master of ceremonies, president of the local *daayira* (religious association) attached to Diop, now welcomes each notable by name, including the producer and crew from the Senegalese radio and television (RTS). One cameraman pans across the audience as another focuses on the subprefect who elaborately greets the audience and lists members of the government delegation. He conveys apologies from President Abdoulaye Wade, who was unable to attend. After similar words from the mayor, a television producer from RTS greets and prays for the congregation. The deputy follows, saying he would never miss this important event and reminding attendees of his efforts to improve the road to the village. The department prefect then greets Daam Diop and others present, saying that government leaders (*kilifay aada*) are one with the religious community and religious leaders (*kilifay diine*), sharing the same religion and hopes, and he briefly prays for the congregation. He apologizes for the government's lateness in paying farmers for their peanuts, assuring them that all will soon be arranged.

After a posse of young chanters performs a brief *dhikr*, Daam Diop takes the microphone and thanks the government leaders for attending. He then addresses them sternly: They must work harder to help farmers and must listen to them to understand and address their concerns. As the Qur'an says, if you help God's servants, God helps you. Members of the audience snap their fingers and call out their approval. After praying at length over the audience, Diop cedes the floor to the chanters for a few minutes until the sun nears the horizon, when he arises and the siren accompanies him back to his truck. Government leaders follow, boarding their truck for home, and the television crew packs up their material. Visitors adjourn to their hosts' houses for a festive dinner and perhaps a nap before the all-night meeting. Meanwhile, thousands flock to Daam Diop's house seeking cures to *jinn* problems, advice, or his divine blessing (*barke*). His guards only let a couple of hundred people into his courtyard and a few dozen, mostly visitors with connections, into his hot and crowded receiving room.

After midnight, a far larger congregation gathers for the *Mawlid* proper, minus government leaders and camera crew. Welcoming speeches now center around dignitaries from Medina Baay. A famous Taalibe Baay chanter and his posse perform extended chants, alternating with a high-profile Medina Baay leader who emulates Baay Niass's stylized, chanted *Mawlid* narrative of the Prophet Muhammad's life. Some attendees' cries, tears, and electrified leaps suggest states (*haal*) of "divine knowledge" (*xam-xamu Yàlla*) acquired through Baay Niass's mystical education (*tarbiya*).[34] After the sun rises, dozens of chartered buses return attendees to various parts of Senegambia.

Government leaders had followed their televised performance as public servants and disciples with a second performance: their exit from the scene, leaving religious authorities as the night meeting's uncontested authorities. Whereas national media publicized the performance of Islam-state engagement, what followed was the gathering's primary purpose for disciples. Where a state-centered optic presents a "vertical topography of power"[35] with religious authority as a layer of indirect rule mediating state sovereignty, a view from inside this religious community presents religious authority as the ultimate authority governing daily life while presenting the state as one set of resources and constraints among others. Religious groups engage with the state yet do not necessarily perceive state authority as above religious authority. As I show in the following, in many cases appeals to state coercive power would lack both legitimacy and efficacy.

Simultaneous Succession: Hiddenness as Resistance and Disengagement

The mystical opposition between visible (*ẓâhir*) and hidden (*bâtîn*) truth claims is central to Taalibe Baay internal political negotiations and to their interactions with the state and other fields of political power.[36] Effectively, this binary opposition does not divide the world into two opposing realms but accommodates multiple and shifting claims to truth and authority. This pair is widespread in Sufi discourse; these Taalibe Baay discourses often exemplify an "aesthetics of ambiguity"[37] widespread in West Africa, where "cultures of secrecy" have arisen to conceal certain practices from the powerful.[38] In the case of the Taalibe Baay, Baay Niass's techniques of mystical education (*tarbiya*) have transposed Sufi discourses and reasoning into large numbers of disciples' everyday practice, providing a repertoire of ways of talking about, accommodating, and undermining competing truth claims. To advance a *bâtîn* claim often serves as an act of resistance, yet not necessarily as a "weapon of the weak,"[39] since hidden tactics of resistance can serve both the powerful and the weak.

My puzzlement over Baay Niass's succession compelled me to contemplate how mystical discourses negotiate competing claims to authority. In 2001, I arrived in Medina Baay to begin research, confused by conflicting accounts of who succeeded Baay Niass after his death in 1975. Most sources named Baay's eldest son, Al-Hadj Abdoulaye Niass,[40] while others named his right-hand man, Seriñ Aliou Cissé. Succession disagreements are common, yet what confused me was that no one seemed to acknowledge any disagreement at all. Considering the enormous political consequences of the title *Khalîfa* (Khalife Général), such ambiguity seemed like confusion over who was president of the republic. My confusion only grew as, like the texts I had encountered, religious leaders and disciples casually named one or the other as *Khalîfa* yet mentioned no disagreement.

Asked to account for the competing history, proponents of either side would initially shake their heads and say the other version was simply not true. When confronted with the other side's evidence, each would explain why their favored successor was Baay's hidden (*bâtîn*) successor while leaving open the possibility of the alternative claim as an apparent (*zâhir*) explanation. One of Cissé's sons quoted Baay Niass's letters, poems, and will, universally accepted as authentic, that name Cissé as Niass's successor. I mentioned the alternative explanation, that Seriñ Aliou Cissé had summoned Baay Niass's sons following Baay's death and relinquished any claim to successorship. He responded that "that didn't happen," yet without specifying which details may have occurred, and explained that Seriñ Aliou Cissé had no power to transfer Baay's spiritual mantle anyway.

Sovereign Islam in a Secular State

In a speech at a conference in Banjul honoring Seriñ Aliou Cissé, Cissé's son and successor as Medina Baay's Imam,[41] Shaykh Hassan Cissé (1945–2008), said:

> The white man [colonial authorities] wrote: whoever wants to fight Baay must eliminate Sëriñ Aliou Cissé first, and only then Baay, because he [Cissé] is the one who publicizes Baay's work to society. . . . That shows that those two beings were not two beings but are one being. . . . The Prophet and Seydinaa Baabakar [Abû Bakr, Muhammad's first *khalîfa*] have no relation—they were only together in God. Likewise, Sëriñ Aliou and his spiritual leader (*sëriñ*) have no relation—God alone brought them together. That relationship in God is stronger than a blood relationship.[42]

Nowhere in the speech does Cissé overtly mention his father's successorship. Instead, he invokes a series of mystical identities suggesting a spiritual transmission: first, the mystical union between Muhammad and his successor Abû Bakr, and then the mystical union of Baay and Seriñ Aliou Cissé. Listeners certainly recall Baay's mystical oneness with Muhammad and draw the connection.

Shaykh Hassan Cissé's own spiritual status as Baay Niass's oldest grandchild probably contributed significantly to his recognition as most prominent Tijanî leader worldwide even though he could not be nationally recognized as Baay Niass's *Khalîfa* due to Senegal's routinized patrilineal system. Similarly, Baay Niass himself, a junior son, disengaged from this system and made his name in Mauritania, Nigeria, and beyond[43] without claiming his father's successorship or appointing a son as his own successor. Like his grandfather, Cissé cultivated a global disciple base and relationships with international organizations. His photographic résumé shows him not meeting with national leaders but posing with United Nations Secretary General Kofi Annan, attending international development summits, and receiving the keys of the cities of Cleveland and Detroit.

The title *Khalîfa* has multiple referents partly because its meaning shifts in relation to different contexts, although speakers invariably maintain this ambiguity. As mentioned earlier, in the Senegalese nation-state context, the title *Khalîfa* or *Khalife Générale*[44] came to designate someone recognized by the state as representative of a corporate body of disciples, a national "Islamic brotherhood." Seeking stable interlocutors among Muslim leaders, the colonial administration helped routinize the pattern of succession by a leader's eldest son and then subsequent sons, ruling through a *Khalîfa* much as an indirect ruler under British colonialism. This political arrangement is entirely different from spiritual succession in a Sufi path (*tarîqa*). Cissé's partisans emphasize spiritual succession while remaining silent about the notion of *Khalîfa* as an indirect ruler in the national context.[45] Thus, Cissé's partisans portray him as the *Khalîfa* in the less visible (*bâtîn*) sense as opposed to the more visible (*ẓâhir*) *Khalîfa* formally recognized on the national scene.

Those whom I asked to explain Al-Hadj Abdoulaye Niass's succession as *Khalîfa* also invoked a *bâtîn* reality. Baay had indeed recognized Seriñ Aliou Cissé's great contribution by outwardly naming him as successor, knowing that the humble Cissé, attuned to Baay's deeper intention, would defer to Baay's family. They described Seriñ Aliou as a reclusive scholar constantly in Baay's shadow, uninterested in the public office of *Khalîfa*. As a village elder who lives near Kaolack told me, defending Al-Hadj Abdoulaye Niass's successorship, "when a Sufi says red, he means black"; behind Baay's literal pronouncements lay a hidden (*bâtîn*) intent. When I heard a close companion of Al-Hadj Abdoulaye Niass referring to him as Baay's *Khalîfa*, I asked him to explain. He described a relationship devoid of rivalry and concluded that both acted together as a single *Khalîfa* with a miraculous unity. In a diverse community that prizes harmony, Sufi discourses of *ẓâhir* (apparent) and *bâtîn* (hidden) truths offer a way to maintain one's position without openly challenging a competing position. Yet each side claims to represent the deeper *bâtîn* reality, revealing a hierarchy between simultaneous truth claims.

Islamic Authority in Local Governance

These succession narratives illustrate how many Taalibe Baay continually appeal to the flexible mystical logic of *ẓâhir* and *bâtîn* as a framework for handling conflicts that inevitably arise in a global movement that must accommodate multiple factions in rural communities and groups of disciples from diverse cultural backgrounds. After sketching the Taalibe Baay network of authority in the Saalum region of Senegal, I will narrate two cases in which religious authority and mystical principles served to resolve potentially violent conflicts, allowing each side to maintain its narrative.

Sovereign Islam in a Secular State

The distribution of Taalibe Baay governance is largely geographical and sometimes follows the state's administrative divisions (region, department, rural community). The governance network centers around *muqaddams*, or those appointed to transmit the Sufi litanies, and lay leaders such as village heads and *daayira* (religious association) presidents. *Muqaddams* in each area report to the *muqaddam* designated to represent Medina Baay there, often the person or the son of the person delegated by Baay Niass over that area. For example, his son Shaykh Tidiane Niass and his Mauritanian Arab representative Hâdî wuld Sayyid represented him in Hausaland, and other sons act as liaisons to other parts of West Africa.46 Shaykh Hassan Cissé later represented the movement in the United States; Baay's son Muḥammad al-Amîn ("Baaba Lamin") is the movement's *Khalîfa* in the Dakar region, as other sons oversee other Senegalese regions. Just as the term *Khalîfa* can imply both political and spiritual succession, many residents follow their village's appointed *muqaddam* in village matters but become spiritual pupils of another *muqaddam* outside the village. Within the village, any other *muqaddam* typically refrains from dispensing *tarbiya* to respect the appointed *muqaddam*. In contrast, cities such as Dakar and Kaolack can accommodate many active *muqaddams* so long as they are approved by the area's Medina Baay representative.47

Taalibe Baay religious governance is most pervasive in Western Saalum, a predominantly Taalibe Baay area south and east of Kaolack. In nearly all these villages, elders tell of a late-nineteenth-century Islamic leader—in some cases a Sufi *muqaddam*—founding the village and its Qur'anic school after leaving some other region with his disciples.48 The village head (*boroom dĕkk*), usually the oldest male member of the founding clerical lineage and often a Quaranic teacher or esoteric healing specialist, makes or approves routine decisions affecting the village. Each village is under the moral authority of a *muqaddam* appointed to represent Medina Baay. Generally not from the village's founding lineage, this leader intervenes in less routine matters such as serious disputes and petitioning government and nongovernmental institutions for improvements. The *muqaddam* may live in Medina Baay or elsewhere, especially if a son of Baay Niass or of one of his close followers, delegating everyday affairs to one or more local religious specialists. Otherwise, the *muqaddam* may live in the village and more actively oversee the village's affairs and report to another leader in Medina Baay. In either case, villagers collect monetary and in-kind offerings (*àddiya*) to present to the *muqaddam*, who in turn donates to needy residents, religious schools, and mosque construction. Some charismatic local *muqaddam*s become famous in their own right, and zealous disciples may ascribe to them a spiritual stature rivaling Baay's sons. To counter accusations of "wanting to be Baay," such leaders must carefully demonstrate submission to Medina Baay.

Local governance and conflict resolution in these villages is left almost entirely to village heads and *muqaddam*s who report to Medina Baay. Mayors and prefects in nearby administrative towns are seen not as authorities but as administrators of state funds for infrastructure development. Villagers speak of these funds not as abstract civic goods but as resources for improving and showing devotion to sacred sites. The community insisted that Baay Niass's birthplace of Tayba Ñaseen get priority in receiving electricity, water, and a well-maintained road, and years later, disciples lamented that Kóosi Mbittéyeen, where the Taalibe Baay movement first emerged, still had no electricity or running water. In every village I visited, residents attributed the presence or hope of electricity or running water to the efforts of their *muqaddam*.

Conflicts between disciples who are not close kin may require local mediation by the village head and religious leaders, and cases of potentially major rupture require the intervention of Medina Baay's central leadership, namely a senior son or grandson of Baay Niass. Although police may be summoned temporarily to maintain the peace until a religious authority arrives, to follow through with a legal proceeding would constitute a definitive repudiation of the shared religious community and would likely fail. Conflicts between Taalibe Baay and non-Taalibe Baay that could not be resolved through the combined leadership of both Sufi groups have occasionally resulted in village schism.[49] As with many informal conflict resolution processes,[50] religious authorities attempt to restore harmony without overtly assigning blame, although their pace or manner of intervention may subtly favor one party.

Case 1: A Village Divided

I spent much of the 2004 rainy season in a predominantly Taalibe Baay village south of Kaolack called Cekkeen.[51] Along with a number of other Njolofeen villages in the area, emigrants from the northern Jolof kingdom founded this village during the mid-to-late nineteenth century around the

III
Sovereign Islam in a Secular State

time of Màbba Jaxu Ba's jihad, which founded a short-lived Islamic state.[52] Njolofeen identify their villages as sites of Islamic knowledge and correct practice and typically ban drums and other profane entertainment in favor of religious chants. Baay Niass himself hailed from the most prominent Njolofeen clerical family, and many of his first disciples were Njolofeen.

My host, the village head, was a peanut farmer and an esoteric healer of some renown. He told me that in 1950 his father had been living in a nearby village when the *chef de canton*, a hereditary position occupied by Màbba Jaxu Ba's grandsons, alerted him that his ancestral village of Cekkeen lacked a village head. Since the previous head had died several years earlier, leaving no elders of the founding Seck family, an elder from another prominent lineage had been acting as "provisional" village head. Yet Cekkeen's headship rightfully belonged to members of the founding Seck lineage.[53] When my host's father agreed and moved back to Cekkeen, the other lineage refused to cede the headship to the newcomer. One member of this lineage was a *muqaddam* and close friend of Baay, perhaps contributing to their sense of leadership. Yet the *chef de canton* told the rival family, in my host's words: "If you want your own village, go to your ancestral village, NGueyeeen." A violent struggle nearly ensued, and the rival family even attempted to enlist Baay's support, but Baay refused to go against the established hereditary pattern of succession. However, as a compromise, Baay named an elder from the Gueye family as the principal imam. Both families thus maintained some claim to village primacy: the Seck family remained the village's uncontested heads while the Gueye family could claim to be the village's hidden spiritual leaders.

I arrived just as the large Friday mosque was to be inaugurated. Villagers prepared for the inaugural Friday prayer, which would draw numerous Medina Baay notables and people from neighboring villages without Friday mosques. The principal imam whom Baay had appointed from the Gueye family was losing his sight and hearing and could not speak clearly. Unsure that the old imam could lead the grander Friday prayer gracefully, the head proposed to the village elders that they appoint a new principal imam to lead Friday prayers while retaining the current imam for the ordinary prayers. After discussing several candidates, the head proposed a twenty-five-year-old son of the village, a member of neither rival family, who was finishing his studies with a famous *muqaddam*-teacher in the Gambia.

The Gueye family decried the appointment of such a young man above the current imam, likely perceiving the move as a grab for the spiritual role Baay had given their family. Despite their objections, village elders voted to appoint the young man, agreeing on his ample knowledge despite his youth. My host, marveling that this young man was everyone's elder in knowledge and wisdom, cited a Wolof proverb: "Being old and enduring many rains are not the same."[54] The village's *muqaddam* approved the decision, although his approval did not inspire universal confidence. He himself was a young man who had studied and worked in the Middle East for several years. Despite festering discontent, the new imam began to lead Friday prayers.

On the morning of the Feast of Sacrifice (*Tabaski, 'Îd al-'adhâ*), the villagers donned their finest clothes and gathered under the giant fig tree for the Feast Prayer. Arriving as the principal imam to lead the prayer and deliver the sermon, the new imam approached the congregation flanked by young men chanting *Allâhu 'akbar!* and *Lâ 'ilâha 'illâ-Llâh*. But members of the Gueye family had already gathered around the old imam and ordered the new imam to defer to their elder. Uneasy about taking the job in the first place, the new imam froze, but my host urged him on. When he moved before the congregation to begin the prayer, young men of the Gueye family bore machetes. Someone used the single working telephone in the village to call the police from the nearest administrative town. They arrested those who had threatened the young imam, and the prayer proceeded despite the Gueye faction boycotting.

Shortly thereafter, a senior son of Baay Niass arrived by car from Medina Baay, ordered the young men's release, and called the two parties together to work out their differences. The leader reminded both sides that all disciples are one in Baay and God. He proposed that the new imam lead Friday prayers but that the old imam continue to lead feast prayers. Both sides accepted, whether or not they thought this an ideal solution.

In both conflicts, the three contrasting authorities—Sufi authority, customary hereditary headship, and state representatives—owed their position to descendance from Islamic authorities. The state played a role in both conflicts: In the first, its representative insisted on customary succession, and in the second, police intervened to prevent injury. Yet in both cases it was Sufi authorities' intervention that not only proved binding but advanced a solution to accommodate clashing narratives of authority. It is almost unthinkable that any party might have prosecuted these cases in a legal court rather than accept religious leaders' mediation. These incidents show, first, the unique legitimacy of religious authority even in mundane matters and, second, how Sufi authorities invoke mystical discourses of hidden truths to divert competing narratives from open collision. Thus, each side can imagine its narrative as the deeper, *bâtîn* narrative and their opponents' as the more superficial, *zâhir* one.

Case 2: Cultural Difference and Divine Unity

The second case involves a potentially more decisive rift between a regionally important Taalibe Baay *muqaddam* and the Medina Baay community. There is an ongoing cultural tension between Njolofeen of Western Saalum and certain eastern Saalum-Saalum. I have often heard Njolofeen, who see themselves as more orthodox Muslims, characterize many eastern Saalum-Saalum as barely Muslim and fanatical about local religious leaders at the expense of Baay and Islam more generally.

Daam Diop (whom we encountered before at his village's *Mawlid*) is a thirty-eight-year-old *muqaddam* from Kër Móodu in eastern Saalum where, he once told me, most people only began practicing Islam seriously within his lifetime. He is famous beyond his years as a specialist of *jinn*, *dëmm* (soul-eaters, sometimes translated as "witches"), and other unseen problems. A *muqaddam* of the Imam of Medina Baay, Shaykh Hassan Cissé, Diop owes his formidable reputation perhaps at least as much to esoteric knowledge from his father and from his special relationship with *jinn* as to his relationship to Medina Baay.[55] Many Njolofeen residents of Medina Baay describe Diop's disciples, mostly from recently Islamized eastern Saalum-Saalum families, as fanatically devoted to Daam Diop and marginally loyal to Baay Niass and Islam.

Soon after arriving in Medina Baay, I began to hear conflicting opinions of him. Some residents questioned whether he had become too independent of Medina Baay to be considered a *taalibe* (disciple). Yet my neighbor Mamadou, himself an eastern Saalum-Saalum, was his disciple and insisted that Diop surpassed even Baay Niass's sons in knowledge and spiritual gifts. When I asked him about his studies, Diop told me that God had granted him the ability to learn books without studying them as others do. Many saw this as a hollow claim, as he has founded no Islamic school as most major *muqaddam*s have (he tells me he plans to organize a school soon, although he will surely not be its teacher).

One Friday afternoon, I heard that there had been a fight at the Medina Baay mosque. Young Njolofeen men from Medina Baay described the situation: Daam Diop was leaving the mosque surrounded by disciples chanting the *dhikr* loudly, and several walked ahead to clear a path for him. One man sat counting prayer formulas on his prayer beads and would not budge when Daam Diop's disciples ordered him to clear the way. According to these young men, when the man ignored them and remained seated, Daam Diop's disciples grabbed him and started beating him. It turned out that the man was one of the younger sons of Baay Niass. The young men telling me the story insisted that the attackers must have known who he was, hence heightening the outrage, although not all of Baay's dozens of children are well known.

The young men continued their story: later that day, as word spread through Medina about this "attack on Baay Niass's family," outraged Medina residents came and seriously damaged Daam Diop's house and sport-utility vehicle (which I remembered carried him to Kër Móodu's *Mawlid*). Medina Baay authorities made no haste to intervene, and some accounts depict certain sons of Baay Niass encouraging the destruction. Imam Hassan Cissé came that evening to express his horror that these disciples would so mistreat a son of Baay Niass. Daam Diop and his disciples returned to his village that night, soon sold the house in Medina Baay, and for eight months did not appear openly in Medina, including my friend Mamadou.

A week later, Mamadou returned surreptitiously to Medina Baay and recounted an entirely opposite story. I told him I had heard of problems, and he nodded—yes, big problems. When I prodded, he said that when the disciples of Daam Diop had politely asked the son of Baay Niass to make way, he had become angry and yelled at them, yet they had gone their way without violence. Hence his astonishment that night when the son of Baay Niass brought his friends to Daam Diop's house and violently attacked Diop and his younger brother. Diop's disciples stood to defend their leader, yet Diop ordered them to forbear and not to strike back. But, Mamadou lamented, as people in Medina Baay love controversies (*histoires*), rumors spread quickly, and many joined the son of Baay Niass in damaging Diop's cars, one of them beyond repair, and causing part of the roof of his house to collapse. The destruction so dismayed the imam that he visited Daam Diop and cried bitterly over Medina Baay residents' lack of hospitality.

Afterwards, one of my housemates, a Njolofeen high school student from Medina Baay, assured me that although he had not witnessed the event, he was certain that Mamadou's version was grossly twisted and that the son of Baay Niass, whom he knows well, had not lifted a finger against Daam Diop or his disciples. Why was Baay Niass's son treated at the hospital that evening for a wound above his eye? I said I hoped at least that Mamadou was not involved, and my housemate (also a friend of Mamadou) laughed and assured me that Mamadou was a fanatic and had surely struck the first blow. Likewise, most Medina Baay residents I spoke with were convinced that Daam Diop's followers bore the blame and had shown themselves to be "impolite" (*reew*) and to lack discipline (*yar*). Some blamed Diop while others said his disciples were merely hard to teach.

When I brought up the case with young people in Medina Baay, they doubted that Daam Diop's disciples would dare show themselves again. Yet this situation was untenable for both sides: Diop needed Medina Baay's blessing to represent the Taalibe Baay movement, and Medina Baay depended on him as an enormously influential link to a large rural constituency. To be restored to the community of disciples, Diop first had to perform his place as a disciple.

Daam Diop convened a large religious meeting in his village and invited the son of Baay Niass involved in the conflict to come and speak. Buses and cars packed with Medina Baay notables and the religious associations (*daayiras*) affiliated with them trekked from Medina Baay to Kër Móodu.⁵⁶ Before the public meeting, Daam Diop received and addressed the guests in his sitting room. He indexed his discipleship to the "family of Baay"—represented metonymically by Baay's son—by sitting on the floor while seating Baay's son in an armchair. His speech called for unity over division using the mystical opposition between the *zâhir* ("the world") and *bâtîn* ("God," "unity"):

> The fact that the family of Baay has come here today to give us a speech about God is a momentous act of unity for God. Because—you know how the world is today—if he were following the world he would never dream of coming here. But God is all he sees, God is all he experiences, and God is all he finds here too. All he finds here are his disciples and his loved ones who have nothing to offer him but peace. They place everything they have in his arms and tell him that he has come home to his family. We are listening to you—wherever you point us, that's where we go; whatever you say, that's how it is; whatever you want, that's how it will be.⁵⁷

Later, during the meeting in the public square, other speakers similarly invoked the mystical principle of *bâtîn* unity, as well as the mystical unity between Baay, his family, and the community of disciples. Daam Diop's younger brother declared: "one might say that a son of Baay did not come here today, but rather Baay himself came." Speakers commonly say that Baay is literally attending a meeting, as his family and even the community of disciples are mystically one with Baay. One might read this statement in more than one way. If these disciples still believed the narrative they told me, submitting to Baay's mystical embodiment would certainly be more bearable than submitting to the individual who had wronged them. In this case, as in the village conflicts described before, mystical language and Islamic authority address violent conflicts in ways that avert community rupture, restore moral community, and maintain multiple competing narratives.

Conclusion

The ethnographic examples presented in this chapter demonstrate a kind of pragmatic pluralism not grounded in a supposedly neutral "liberal" approach to tolerance but in the negotiated and even symbiotic coexistence of multiple, mutually irreducible claims to truth and authority and multiple understandings of political and moral community.[58] The cases presented here do not fully exhaust the political dimensions of Taalibe Baay participation in Islamic, state-centered, or global regimes—which are far more extensive than this discussion might suggest—much less of an overarching "Islam in Senegal." What I have attempted to show using these examples is how Muslims creatively draw on religious discourses to accommodate multiple imperatives, competing interests, and authoritative institutions and discourses. This pragmatic pluralism undermines prevalent monistic assumptions that Muslims must either subordinate religious belonging to the nation-state or engage in projects to Islamize the nation-state. It also problematizes liberal ambitions to provide a neutral ground of secularism, tolerance, and democracy. Rather than undermine these ideals themselves, these cases suggest that such aspirations (which are not uniquely liberal) may find realization in unexpected ways. Far from "survivals"[59] on the road to a liberal world, hybrid approaches to authority are among many answers to the problem of coexistence. Pluralism here is not the comfortable, colorful multiculturalism of liberalism but a pluralism that inevitably causes "vertigo"[60] by refusing to situate difference on a single authoritative common ground.

Notes

1. Carr, "You Are Now Entering Eurabia."
2. Lewis, "The Roots of Muslim Rage."
3. To name but a smattering: Bat Ye'or, *Eurabia: The Euro-Arab Axis*; Fallaci, *The Rage and the Pride*; Fallaci, *The Force of Reason*; Gaubatz and Sperry, *Muslim Mafia*; Wilders, "Warning to America"; see Wajahat Ali et al., "Fear, Inc." for a discussion of the financing behind this literature.
4. Asad, "The Idea of an Anthropology of Islam."
5. For example, An-Na'im, *Toward an Islamic Reformation*; An-Na'im, *Islam and the Secular State*; for discussions of feminism and Islamic jurisprudence, see Ali, *Sexual Ethics and Islam*.
6. Kelsay, *Arguing the Just War in Islam*.
7. Schacht, *An Introduction to Islamic Law*. Note that this term has come in contemporary Arabic to mean simply "politics."
8. Tibi, "John Kelsay and 'Sharia Reasoning.'"
9. For a synthesis of these studies, see Tessler, "Arab and Muslim Political Attitudes."
10. For examples of how this language serves to abrogate certain gender distinctions, see Hill, "'All Women Are Guides.'"
11. Huntington, *The Clash of Civilizations*; Lewis, "The Roots of Muslim Rage"; see Mamdani, *Good Muslim, Bad Muslim* for a critique of using essentializing "culture talk" to account for political problems.
12. Mamdani, *Good Muslim, Bad Muslim*; Mahmood, "Secularism, Hermeneutics, and Empire"; Bowen, *Can Islam Be French?*; Asad, *Formations of the Secular*.
13. It is important to note that those who call most loudly for a secular Islam are not secularists but those who claim to be protecting the West's Judeo-Christian heritage from Islamization. See the authors listed in note 3 above.
14. For example, see Hill, "Sufism in Northern Nigeria."
15. Kane, "Le réformisme musulman au Nigeria du Nord"; Kane, *Muslim Modernity in Postcolonial Nigeria*; Kane and Triaud, eds., *Islam et Islamismes au sud du Sahara*; Loimeier, *Islamic Reform and Political Change*; Loimeier, "Cheikh Touré"; Loimeier, "L'Islam ne se vend plus"; Masquelier, *Women and Islamic*

Revival; Augis, "'They Haven't Even Mastered the Qur'an:'"; Augus, "Dakar's Sunnite Women"; Augus, "Jambaar or Jumbax-Out?"

16. Klein, *Islam and Imperialism in Senegal*; Klein, "Social and Economic Factors in the Muslim Revolution in Senegambia"; Robinson, *The Holy War of Umar Tal*; Curtin, "Jihad in West Africa"; Hiskett, *The Sword of Truth*.
17. Sanneh, *The Jakhanke Muslim Clerics*; Sanneh, *The Crown and the Turban*.
18. Babou, *Fighting the Greater Jihad*.
19. For a synthesis of a long literature demonstrating this phenomenon, see Villalón, *Islam and State Power in Senegal*.
20. Behrman, *Muslim Brotherhoods and Politics in Senegal*; Cruise O'Brien, *The Mourides of Senegal*; Copans, *Les marabouts de l'arachide*; Coulon, *Le marabout et le prince*; Samson, *Les marabouts de l'Islam politique*; Villalón, *Islam and State Power in Senegal*.
21. Robinson, *Paths of Accommodation*; While this accommodation may appear to contradict France's secularism, French politicians today follow a similar paradoxical principle, patronizing "moderate" Muslim leaders and organizations to ensure a "French Islam" they perceive as more compatible with secular ideals. See Bowen, *Why the French Don't Like Headscarves: Islam, the State, and Public Space*.
22. Outsiders most often call them "Ñaseen" ("of the Ñas [Niass] family"; French spelling: "Niassène"), although many Taalibe Baay object to this term.
23. See the references listed in note 20.
24. Hansen and Stepputat, eds., *Sovereign Bodies*; Hansen and Stepputat, "Sovereignty Revisited."
25. Roy, *The Failure of Political Islam*; Roy, *Globalized Islam*; Roy, *Secularism Confronts Islam*.
26. See Hill, "The Cosmopolitan Sahara," for an example in nearby Mauritania.
27. Mahmood, "Secularism, Hermeneutics, and Empire."
28. Hill, "Mystical Specialists, Institutional Specialists, and the Construction of an Urban Sufi Movement in Senegal"; Hill, "The Cosmopolitan Sahara."
29. Douglas, "Deciphering a Meal."
30. I have changed the names of people and places.
31. Since this event, unsurprisingly, Mamadou has been appointed a *muqaddam* of Daam Diop and has begun to initiate his own disciples.
32. The zealous disciple in a uniform of dreadlocks, colorful patchwork, and a pendant bearing a Shaykh's photo seems influenced by "Baay Faal," Murids who emulate Shaykh Ibra Fall. In Eastern Saalum, I have encountered several quasi-Baay Faal Taalibe Baay. One called himself a "Baay Faal of Baay" and peppered his speech with Baay Faal-isms.

Sovereign Islam in a Secular State

33. This phrase, the first half of the *shahâdah* or testament of faith, is central to many Sufi rituals and is often chanted in a stately tempo to herald an important leader.
34. Hill, *Divine Knowledge and Islamic Authority*; Seesemann, *The Divine Flood*.
35. Ferguson and Gupta, "Spatializing States."
36. See Hill, chapter 1, this volume, for more details regarding these terms' connotations and uses.
37. Ferme, *The Underneath of Things*.
38. Lattas, *Cultures of Secrecy*; see also de Certeau, *The Practice of Everyday Life*.
39. Scott, *Weapons of the Weak*.
40. Al-Hadj Abdoulaye Niass bears Baay Niass's father's name. To distinguish them, Taalibe Baay often call the former "Pàppa Aas" and the latter "Maam Al-Hadj."
41. Shaykh Hassan Cissé (1945–2008) was not Seriñ Aliou Cissé's oldest son but was the oldest he had with Fatoumata Zahra Niass, Baay Niass's oldest child, and hence Baay Niass's oldest grandson. See Hill, "All Women Are Guides," on his spiritual succession through his mother's side.
42. Hassan Cissé gave this speech in Banjul, Gambia, in 2005. Cheikh Baye Thiam recorded and transcribed it in Wolof.
43. Paden, *Religion and Political Culture in Kano*; Seesemann, "The 'Shurafa' and the 'Blacksmith,'" "The History of the Tijâniya," and *The Divine Flood*; Hiskett, "The 'Community of Grace' and Its Opponents."
44. In early Islam, *Khalîfa* ("Successor") designated the *Amîr al-Mu'mînn* (Commander of the Faithful). In Senegal, it maintains the quasi-political connotation of head of a particular religious community.
45. As I have argued elsewhere, Taalibe Baay did not constitute one of these national "Islamic brotherhoods" until the 1980s. See Hill, "Mystical Specialists, Institutional Specialists."
46. Baay's son Makki is Medina Baay's liaison to parts of Niger, partly because his full sister, Oumoul Khayri, married the Zarma *muqaddam* Abubakar Kyota (d. 2004) who became the movement's representative in Niger.
47. The relatively flexible space of authority in cities has allowed a growing number of women and men not from clerical backgrounds to become religious leaders. See Hill, "All Women Are Guides."
48. See Hill, "Divine Knowledge and Islamic Authority," on the oral history of some of these villages.
49. For example, Caameen Waalo's Taalibe Baay residents founded Caameen Sanc after tensions with followers of Baay Ñas's older brother Muḥammad.
50. Clarke, *Fictions of Justice*.

51. Again, I have changed the names of people and places.
52. Klein, *Islam and Imperialism in Senegal*.
53. Cekkeen is a nominal form of the family name Seck, in the same pattern as Ñaseen (Niasseen) deriving from Ñas (Niass).
54. "*Doo mag ak yàgg tawte duñu benn.*"
55. Relationships with *jinn* are often cited as occult knowledge sources and signs of formidable powers.
56. Adi Aïdara Fall, a member of the Medina Baay Research Association, observed, recorded, and transcribed the events.
57. From Adi Aïdara Fall's Wolof transcription, my translation.
58. Chakrabarty, *Provincializing Europe*.
59. Tylor, *Primitive Culture*.
60. Needham, *Belief, Language and Experience*; Pels, "The Magic of Africa."

Bibliography

Ali, Kecia. *Sexual Ethics and Islam: Feminist Reflections on Qur'an, Hadith, and Jurisprudence*. Oxford: Oneworld, 2006.

Ali, Wajahat, Eli Clifton, Matthew Duss, Lee Fang, Scott Keyes, and Faiz Shakir. "Fear, Inc.: The Roots of the Islamophobia Network in America." Washington, D.C.: Center for American Progress, 2011 (www.americanprogress.org/issues/2011/08/islamophobia.html).

An-Na'im, Abdullahi Ahmed. *Islam and the Secular State: Negotiating the Future of Shari'a*. Cambridge, Mass.: Harvard University Press, 2008.

———. *Toward an Islamic Reformation: Civil Liberties, Human Rights, and International Law*. Contemporary issues in the Middle East. Syracuse, N.Y.: Syracuse University Press, 1990.

Asad, Talal. *Formations of the Secular: Christianity, Islam, Modernity*. Stanford, Calif.: Stanford University Press, 2003.

———. "The Idea of an Anthropology of Islam." In *The Social Philosophy of Ernest Gellner*, eds. John A. Hall and Ian Charles Jarvie, 381–403. Amsterdam and Atlanta: Rodopi, 1996.

Augis, Erin. "Dakar's Sunnite Women: The Politics of Person." In *L'Islam politique au sud du Sahara: Identités, discours et enjeux*, ed. Muriel Gomez-Perez, 309–326. Paris: Karthala, 2005.

———. "Jambaar or Jumbax-Out? How Sunnite Women Negotiate Power and Belief in Orthodox Islamic Femininity." In *New Perspectives on Islam in Senegal: Conversion, Migration, Wealth, Power, and Femininity*, eds. Mamadou Diouf and Mara A. Leichtman, 211–233. New York: Palgrave Macmillan, 2009.

———. "'They Haven't Even Mastered the Qur'an': Young Islamist Women's Negotiations of Social Change and Generational Hierarchies in Dakar." In *L'Afrique d'une génération à l'autre*. Paris: Karthala, forthcoming.
Babou, Cheikh Anta. *Fighting the Greater Jihad: Amadu Bamba and the Founding of the Muridiyya of Senegal, 1853–1913*. Athens: Ohio University Press, 2007.
Badran, Margot. *Feminism in Islam: Secular and Religious Convergences*. Oxford: Oneworld, 2009.
Bat Ye'or. *Eurabia: The Euro-Arab Axis*. Cranbury, N.J.: Associated University Presses, 2005.
Behrman, Lucy C. *Muslim Brotherhoods and Politics in Senegal*. Cambridge, Mass.: Harvard University Press, 1970.
Bowen, John Richard. *Can Islam Be French?: Pluralism and Pragmatism in a Secularist State*. Princeton, N.J.: Princeton University Press, 2009.
———. *Why the French Don't Like Headscarves: Islam, the State, and Public Space*. Princeton, N.J.: Princeton University Press, 2006.
Carr, Matt. "You Are Now Entering Eurabia." *Race & Class* 48 (1) (July, 2006): 1–22.
Certeau, Michel de. *The Practice of Everyday Life*. Berkeley: University of California Press, 1984.
Chakrabarty, Dipesh. *Provincializing Europe: Postcolonial Thought and Historical Difference*. Princeton, N.J.: Princeton University Press, 2000.
Clarke, Kamari Maxine. *Fictions of Justice: The International Criminal Court and the Challenge of Legal Pluralism in Sub-Sahara Africa*. 1st ed. Cambridge, UK: Cambridge University Press, 2009.
Copans, Jean. *Les marabouts de l'arachide: La confrérie mouride et les paysans du Sénégal*. Paris: Sycomore, 1980.
Coulon, Christian. *Le marabout et le prince: Islam et pouvoir au Sénégal*. Paris: Editions Pedone, 1981.
Cruise O'Brien, Donal B. *The Mourides of Senegal: The Political and Economic Organization of an Islamic Brotherhood*. Oxford: Clarendon, 1971.
Curtin, Philip D. "Jihad in West Africa: Early Phases and Inter-Relations in Mauritania and Senegal." *Journal of African History* 12 (1) (1971): 11–24.
Douglas, Mary. "Deciphering a Meal." *Daedalus* 101 (1) (Winter 1972): 61–81.
Fallaci, Oriana. *The Force of Reason*. New York: Rizzoli, 2004.
———. *The Rage and the Pride*. New York: Rizzoli, 2002.
Ferguson, James and Akhil Gupta. "Spatializing States: Toward an Ethnography of Neoliberal Governmentality." *American Ethnologist* 29 (4) (2002): 981–1002.
Ferme, Mariane C. *The Underneath of Things: Violence, History, and the Everyday in Sierra Leone*. Berkeley: University of California Press, 2001.
Gaubatz, P. David and Paul Sperry. *Muslim Mafia: Inside the Secret Underworld That's Conspiring to Islamize America*. Los Angeles: WND, 2009.

Hansen, Thomas Blom and Finn Stepputat, eds. *Sovereign Bodies: Citizens, Migrants, and States in the Postcolonial World.* Princeton, N.J.: Princeton University Press, 2005.

———. "Sovereignty Revisited." *Annual Review of Anthropology* 35 (October 2006): 295–315.

Hill, Jonathan N. C. "Sufism in Northern Nigeria: Force for Counter-Radicalization?" Strategic Studies Institute, May 2010 (www.strategicstudiesinstitute.army.mil/pubs/download.cfm?q=989).

Hill, Joseph. "'All Women Are Guides': Sufi Leadership and Womanhood Among Taalibe Baay in Senegal." *Journal of Religion in Africa* 40 (4) (2010): 375–412.

———. *Divine Knowledge and Islamic Authority: Religious Specialization Among Disciples of Baay Ñas.* PhD dissertation, Yale University, 2007.

———. "Mystical Specialists, Institutional Specialists, and the Construction of an Urban Sufi Movement in Senegal." Paper presented at the African Studies Association Annual Meeting, New York, October 21, 2007.

———. "The Cosmopolitan Sahara: Building a Global Islamic Village in Mauritania." *City & Society* 24 (2012): 62–83.

Hiskett, Mervyn. "The 'Community of Grace' and Its Opponents, 'the Rejecters': A Debate About Theology and Mysticism in Muslim West Africa with Special Reference to its Hausa Expression." *African Language Studies* 17 (1980): 99–140.

———. *The Sword of Truth: The Life and Time of the Shehu Usuman dan Fodio.* New York: Oxford University Press, 1973.

Huntington, Samuel. *The Clash of Civilizations and the Remaking of World Order.* New York: Touchstone, 1996.

Kane, Ousmane. "Le réformisme musulman au Nigeria du Nord." In *Islam et Islamismes au sud du Sahara*, eds. Ousmane Kane and Jean-Louis Triaud, 117–135. Paris: Karthala, 1998.

———. *Muslim Modernity in Postcolonial Nigeria: A Study of the Society for the Removal of Innovation and Restatement of Tradition.* Leiden: Brill, 2003.

Kane, Ousmane and Jean-Louis Triaud, eds. *Islam et Islamismes au sud du Sahara.* Paris: Karthala, 1998.

Kelsay, John. *Arguing the Just War in Islam.* Cambridge, Mass.: Harvard University Press, 2007.

Klein, Martin A. *Islam and Imperialism in Senegal: Sine-Saloum, 1847–1914.* Stanford, Calif.: Stanford University Press, 1968.

———. "Social and Economic Factors in the Muslim Revolution in Senegambia." *Journal of African History* 13 (1972): 419–441.

Lattas, Andrew. *Cultures of Secrecy: Reinventing Race in Bush Kaliai Cargo Cults.* Madison: University of Wisconsin Press, 1998.

Lewis, Bernard. "The Roots of Muslim Rage." *The Atlantic Online*, September 1990 (www.theatlantic.com/doc/print/199009/muslim-rage).

Loimeier, Roman. "Cheikh Touré: Un musulman Sénégalais dans le siècle, du réformisme à l'Islamisme." In *Islam et Islamismes au sud du Sahara*, eds. Ousmane Kane and Jean-Louis Triaud, 151–170. Paris: Karthala, 1998.

_____. *Islamic Reform and Political Change in Northern Nigeria*. Evanston, Ill.: Northwestern University Press, 1997.

_____. "L'Islam ne se vend plus: The Islamic Reform Movement and the State in Senegal." *Journal of Religion in Africa* 30 (2) (2000): 168–190.

Mahmood, Saba. "Secularism, Hermeneutics, and Empire: The Politics of Islamic Reformation." *Public Culture* 18 (2) (April 1, 2006): 323–347.

Mamdani, Mahmood. *Good Muslim, Bad Muslim*. New York: Pantheon, 2004.

Masquelier, Adeline. *Women and Islamic Revival in a West African Town*. Bloomington: Indiana University Press, 2009.

Needham, Rodney. *Belief, Language and Experience*. Oxford: Blackwell, 1972.

Paden, John N. *Religion and Political Culture in Kano*. Berkeley: University of California Press, 1973.

Pels, Peter. "The Magic of Africa: Reflections on a Western Commonplace." *African Studies Review* 41 (3) (December 1998): 193–209.

Robinson, David. *Paths of Accommodation: Muslim Societies and French Colonial Authorities in Senegal and Mauritania, 1880–1920*. Oxford: James Currey, 2000.

_____. *The Holy War of Umar Tal: The Western Sudan in the Mid-Nineteenth Century*. Oxford: Clarendon, 1985.

Roy, Olivier. *Globalized Islam: The Search for a New Ummah*. London: Hurst, 2004.

_____. *Secularism Confronts Islam*. New York: Columbia University Press, 2007.

_____. *The Failure of Political Islam*. Cambridge, Mass.: Harvard University Press, 1998.

Samson, Fabienne. *Les marabouts de l'Islam politique: Le Dahiratoul Moustarchidina wal Moustarchidaty, un mouvement néo-confrérique Sénégalais*. Paris: Karthala, 2005.

Sanneh, Lamin. *The Crown and the Turban: Muslims and West African Pluralism*. Boulder, Colo.: Westview, 1997.

_____. *The Jakhanke Muslim Clerics: A Religious and Historical Study of Islam in Senegambia*. Lanham, Md.: University Press of America, 1989.

Schacht, Joseph. *An Introduction to Islamic Law*. Oxford: Clarendon, 1979.

Scott, James C. *Weapons of the Weak: Everyday Forms of Peasant Resistance*. New Haven: Yale University Press, 1987.

Seesemann, Rüdiger. *The Divine Flood: Ibrāhīm Niasse and the Roots of a Twentieth-Century Sufi Revival*. Oxford: Oxford University Press, 2011.

———. "The History of the Tijâniya and the Issue of Tarbiya in Darfur." In *La Tijâniyya: Une confrérie musulmane à la conquête de l'Afrique*, eds. Jean-Louis Triaud and David Robinson, 393–437. Paris: Karthala, 2000.

———. "The 'Shurafa' and the 'Blacksmith': The Role of the Idaw Ali of Mauritania in the Career of the Senegalese Shaykh Ibrahim Niass (1900–1975)." In *The Transmission of Learning in Islamic Africa*, ed. Scott S. Reese, 72–98. Leiden, Netherlands: Brill, 2004.

Tessler, Mark. "Arab and Muslim Political Attitudes: Stereotypes and Evidence from Survey Research." *International Studies Perspectives* 4 (2) (May 1, 2003): 175–181.

Tibi, Bassam. "John Kelsay and '*Sharia* Reasoning' in Just War in Islam: An Appreciation and a Few Propositions." *Journal of Church and State* 53 (1) (January 1, 2011): 4–26.

Tylor, Edward Burnett. *Primitive Culture: Researches Into the Development of Mythology, Philosophy* (Two Vols.). Vol. 2. 3rd ed. London: John Murray, 1891.

Villalón, Leonardo A. *Islam and State Power in Senegal: Disciples and Citizens in Fatick*. Cambridge, UK: Cambridge University Press, 1995.

Wilders, Geert. "Warning to America." *YouTube*, September 19, 2009 (www.youtube.com/watch?v=NQOCcx5V9RI).

[6]

The Senegalese "Social Contract" Revisited

The Muridiyya Muslim Order and State Politics in Postcolonial Senegal

CHEIKH ANTA BABOU

The so-called Senegalese "social contract" has been the object of much scholarly interest. Most scholars credit the unusual stability of postcolonial Senegal in the politically chaotic West Africa to the role of Muslim orders (especially the Muridiyya). They argue that Muslim clerics provide the government with the legitimacy to ensure the loyalty of the citizens and in return receive recognition and material support from the state.[1] This system, it is argued, is rooted in the Muslim policy of the French colonial administration crafted by the famous Bureau of Muslim Affairs founded by Governor Roume in the first decade of the twentieth century. This policy, it is believed, recognized Sufi Muslim clerics as junior partners in the administration of the colony, especially regarding issues related to the rural population that formed the majority of their disciples.

The idea that the Muslim leadership enjoyed unfettered obedience and control over their disciples and that they had the power to make them endorse whatever deal they wished to strike with the state constitutes a cornerstone of the social contract theory. Proponents of the social contract approach, however, overlook two things that seem fundamental for the system to work even if one accepts their rather simplistic characterization of the relationships between disciples and masters in the Sufi orders. First, one needs to know to what extent the self-perception of the cleric's role in Senegalese society included a sense of sociopolitical responsibility and, second, to what extent the disciples and laypeople of Senegal entertained expectations from their religious leaders to play the role of political brokers and were ready to use them as intermediaries with the colonial administration, and later on with the rulers of independent Senegal.

Looking at the responses of the Muslim leadership to the British conquest of India, Barbara Metcalf has argued that Muslim ulemas (learned men) turned their attention away from issues of the organization of state and society and focused more closely on concerns with the moral qualities of individual Muslims.[2] In Senegal, the turning away from the politics of kings had started even earlier among some militant ulemas after devastating military defeats suffered at the hands of local rulers in the eighteenth and nineteenth centuries. Among quietist ulemas who specialized in teaching, the access and control of political power has never been a central preoccupation.[3] One of the reasons for the failure of militant Muslims to capture and establish enduring authority over the precolonial kingdoms of Senegal is that they were never able to convincingly establish in the eyes of the people their credentials (genealogical or ethical) as legitimate statesmen. People clearly distinguished between the ethics of government and the ethics of religion, although in practice the boundaries between these two ethics can be sometimes blurry. In effect, some clerics worked as advisers of kings and as judges and therefore shared responsibilities in the making and implementation of their policies. But by the end of the nineteenth century, which coincided with the French conquest of Senegal, there was a clear demarcation between the politics of kings and the politics of clerics, especially those Sufi clerics who would provide the leadership to the Muslim population during the colonial and postcolonial eras.[4]

Another important underlying assumption of the social contract theory relates to the willingness of the state, colonial and postcolonial, to share power or at least to recognize an autonomous domain of authority with respect to the leadership of the Muslim orders of Senegal. Jean Louis Triaud has convincingly argued that it was never the intention of the French colonial administration to govern through the Muslim clerics of its colonies, and they did not welcome the establishment of an autonomous Muslim leadership.[5] Triaud's argument is particularly germane here, especially if one agrees with Thomas B. Hansen and Finn Stepputat that the emphasis of colonial rule was rarely on forging consent and the creation of a nation-people, and almost exclusively on subjugation, order, and obedience through performance of paramount sovereign power and suppression of competing authorities.[6] One can argue that the goals of disciplining and subjugating all forms of authorities outside the state's purview was not an exclusive preserve of the colonial state—postcolonial rulers also aspired to achieve hegemonic status.

In this chapter, I present a more contrasted picture of the relationships between disciples and shaykhs in the Muridiyya and their impact on the order's relations with the postcolonial Senegalese state. I share scholars' view that the Muridiyya is one of the most powerful political players in Senegal and that it has historically played a major role in helping foster consent for government policies. However, I contend that the relationships between the Muridiyya and the Senegalese state are less stable and more complex than the social contract theory would let to believe. I further argue that what scholars describe as a social contract is rather a sort of modus vivendi (that is, a way of living and getting along) that gradually emerged as the culmination of a long process of tensions, compromises, and mutual adjustment between the Murids and the colonial and postcolonial Senegalese state.[7] And, it is because of the informal nature and fluidity of this modus vivendi that the relationships between the Muridiyya and the postcolonial government of Senegal are highly subject to the idiosyncrasy of leadership, the changing relations between disciples and shaykhs, and the vagaries of changes within the Murid order and the state.

Exploring the Roots of the Social Contract

Xavier Coppolani, a French administrator from Corsica posted in Algeria in the second half of the nineteenth century, could be credited for being the main influence behind what some scholars have come to call the Senegalese social contract. In contrast with Paul Marty, often seen as the originator of French Muslim policy in Senegal and West Africa, Coppolani was a field administrator who experienced firsthand the difficulties of establishing peace and achieving consent for colonial policies in a recently conquered colony populated by a large and hostile population of Muslims.[8]

The central preoccupation of Coppolani was security and maintenance of order, and he believed that this could be best achieved through negotiations and compromises rather than coercion. Coppolani was convinced that the Sufi orders, with their elaborate and ubiquitous networks of disciples and their rigid hierarchies dominated by powerful shaykhs, could be a great asset to the colonial administration. To turn these former and potential enemies into friends, or a least to secure their political neutrality, Coppolani proposed a policy based on two premises: first, the preservation of their interests; and second, the respect for their mores and religion.[9] Thanks to the support of Governor General Ernest Roume, he was able to experiment with this policy in West Africa where colonization was still in process and where the majority of the population, such as in Algeria, were Muslim and followers of Sufi orders. Although Coppolani did not live to witness the triumph of the policy he devised—he was murdered in Mauritania by a rebellious Moorish faction in 1905—his views continued to govern colonial policy. Governor General William Ponty (1908–1915), the successor of Roume, continued in the footsteps of his predecessor. In a memo dated April 22, 1909, he wrote, "It seems possible today to formulate this [Muslim] policy into a body of principles derived from the greater understanding that we have of the psychology of our subjects, from our constant concern not to offend them in their customs, in their beliefs, and even in their superstitions."[10]

It was the gradual abandonment of the controversial policy of assimilation and the adoption of the policy of cultural compromises inspired by Coppolani, implemented by Roume and continued by Ponty, that made possible the establishment of a modus vivendi with the Muslims of French West Africa. It should be mentioned, however, that this new policy of cultural accommodation was encouraged only when the Muslim communities involved wielded considerable power and authority and they were no longer thought of as an insurmountable political threat.

In the case of the Muridiyya, negotiation for space and the politics of space making was a central component of the policy of cultural compromise.[11] From 1889 to 1912, the Murids entertained tense relations with the colonial administration. Amadu Bamba Mbacke, the founder of the Murid order, was exiled twice and then confined to house arrest in Senegal, but out of his native land of Bawol. Murid villages were evacuated and the Murid leadership harassed by African chiefs and colonial administrators. But in 1912, the French realized the futility of coercion and decided to move Bamba back to Diourbel, in the heartland of the Muridiyya. The change of tactics was an effort to diminish the popularity of Bamba that they thought was fueled by his image as a freedom fighter and a martyr, and an attempt to create avenues for what the lieutenant governor of Senegal called a "policy of rapprochement."[12]

The ability of the Murids to build what could be called *daar al Murid* or house of the Murids in French dominated Bawol was central in achieving rapprochement. From 1913, the Murids endeavored to turn eastern Bawol into an enclave for Islam within the land of unbelief that Senegal had become after the consolidation of French rule. In pursuit of their agenda to carve out space for the Muridiyya in Bawol, they deployed a three-step strategy: first, physical occupation of the land by Murid disciples; second, the cultural reshaping of the landscape through the use of Islamic sacred architecture, geometry, and religious rituals; and third, the containment of French cultural influence. *Daar al Murid* did not contest French political and administrative domination; rather, it represented a project to achieve symbolic and cultural—and when possible, geographical—autonomy from the colonial realm. By stripping *daar al Islam* of its political content and infusing it with cultural meanings, the Murids created the condition for its preservation under French colonial rule and later on in postcolonial Senegal.

Reassured by the success of cultural compromise, the French went further by giving official recognition to Murid spatial autonomy. A deed issued in 1928 recognized the 400 hectares of land on which the tomb of Amadu Bamba was located and on which the Great Mosque of Touba was being built as private propriety of the Murid community. Gradually, the whole village of Touba was recognized as the holy city of the Murids, and as such was given, if informally, a special status.[13] The government of independent Senegal took this recognition even further by granting the village of Touba a status of quasi-extraterritoriality. Today Touba is Senegal's second largest city, with a population estimated at 600,000–1,000,000 inhabitants. However, despite its size and exponential development, Touba is still run by the leadership of the Murid community, and although the population pays taxes, the presence of the Senegalese state remains discreet and in some areas such as public morality, local customs take precedence over Senegalese law. For instance, since 1980, Touba remains Senegal's only city where drinking alcoholic beverages and smoking are forbidden. The preservation and reinforcement of the spatial autonomy of Touba is a central concern of the Muridiyya that plays a key role in the relationships with the state.

The Golden Age of the Social Contract

The years 1960–1968 marked the golden age of the social contract. This era coincided with the caliphate of Seriñ Falilou Mbacke, second caliph of the Muridiyya, and the rule of Senghor, first president of independent Senegal. Murids still remember the caliph's bold pronunciations in favor of the new president: *Senghor seng ca kaw; neelen ko jakk, buleen ko patu, buleen ko piis*, asking every Senegalese to remain steadfast and unwavering in their support of Senghor. Several factors related to tensions within the Muridiyya and the Senegalese state, the personalities of the two leaders, and the economic and political environment in Senegal explain why the social contract functioned so well during this period.

Falilou Mbacke accessed the caliphate in 1945 amid much contestation and tension.[14] His nephew, Cheikh Mbacke Gainde Fatma, elder son of his predecessor at the caliphate, refused to recognize him as paramount leader of the Muridiyya.[15] It took the mediation of powerful Murid notables, along with the help of the colonial administration, to bring peace back among the leadership of the Murid order.

When Senghor started his political career in 1948, he singled out Falilou as one of his major allies. He campaigned around the slogan "the quintal of peanuts at 5,000 F.CFA" (about $20 then). This political message was particularly appealing to the Murids, who were among the major peanut producers in Senegal, and especially the leadership that drew much its wealth from gifts given by peanut-producing disciples. Senghor also pledged to help the caliph complete the building of the Great Mosque of Touba, which had been in the making for two decades. The mosque was inaugurated in the presence of Senghor in 1963, and the president skillfully used the opportunity to stress the convergence between his political philosophy and Murid ideology. In the speech he delivered to the enthusiastic Murid crowd, he magnified the accomplishment of Amadu Bamba as a precursor of Negritude and depicted the Murid doctrine of hard work and sharing as epitomizing African socialism, the official economic policy of the state of Senegal.[16]

Senghor and Seriñ Falilou needed each other in a period of relative economic abundance when support for unpopular government policies did not require the investment of much political capital. Senghor was a Catholic competing with Muslim politicians in a country with a population more than 80 percent Muslim. Within two years after Senegal accessed independence, he had to face two major political crises: the dissolution of the Mali Federation that united the current-day states of Mali and Senegal; and a so-called coup allegedly perpetrated by Mamadou Dia, head of the government. He also had to earn the support or neutrality of the Sufi orders to implement his policy, which tried to strike a balance between the aspiration of Senegalese Muslims to have a constitution and state inspired by Islamic law and morality and his willingness to build a secular state.[17]

Falilou did oppose some state policies he deemed detrimental to the Murids and peasants of Senegal, such as the cooperative system, but overall he was a staunch backer of Senghor and his government. In May 1968, when the government of Senegal was on the brink of collapsing after a wave of leftist youth movements and strikes, Caliph Falilou was the most vocal supporter of the state. He called for calm and sent hundreds of Murid disciples into Dakar to help protect the government.[18]

Just as Senghor needed the caliph to consolidate his power and implement his policies, the caliph also needed the state for the consolidation of his power over the Muridiyya. He needed government recognition and material support to complete his projects in Touba: namely, bringing water and electricity to the village, finishing the building of the mosque, and securing jobs and governmental support for the growing number of Murid traders and businessmen living in Senegal's cities.[19] Falilou could take the risk of entertaining close relationships with the state only because he benefited from a certain aura that provided him with much symbolic and cultural capital, which also shielded him against accusations of collaboration with the state.

The Social Contract in Crisis

The social contract suffered a major crisis under Falilou's successor, Caliph Abdou Lahat Mbacke, who took the reins of the Muridiyya in 1968. Unlike Abdou Lahat's predecessor who was a staunch and vocal supporter of the Senegalese president, Senghor, mounting tensions with the government of Senegal marked the first years of Abdou Lahat's caliphate.[20] Two speeches by the caliph evidenced the shift in the relations with the state. In 1973, in his address to the Murids at the occasion of the *Mággal* (largest Murid religious event celebrated annually to commemorate Amadu Bamba's departure for exile in 1895), he observed, "We, the Murids, we live in an enclosure, our lives governed by the teachings of Shaykh Amadu Bamba, by work and prayer. Beyond the boundaries of this enclosure, we only see Satan and his works."[21] In a public meeting at the presidential palace in 1980, he conveyed the pain and sufferings of the Senegalese peasants, expressed his unwillingness to support government policies, denounced the embezzlement of governmental subsidies destined to farmers, rejected the government's long-term plan to address the problems of the rural economy of Senegal, and called for immediate action.[22]

Scholars differ in their interpretation of this shift in the attitude of the leader of the Muridiyya toward the state. Some see it as an effort to move the Murid order away from the dependency that had long characterized its relations with the state without causing a brutal separation.[23] One scholar characterized these tensions as "symbolic confrontations,"[24] but I believe that beyond what is viewed as a "showmanship" of the Murid leadership, important transformations under way within the Muridiyya and the state explain the dramatic change in the relationships between the Muridiyya and the state of Senegal under Abdou Lahat. These changes are best explained by looking at characteristics internal to the Murid order in the late 1960s and early 1970s.

Seriñ Abdou Lahat was a caliph with a different personality leading the Muridiyya in a period of rapid political and economic transformations. His standing in the Murid order was much different than that of Caliph Falilou. Falilu knew and interacted with his father, Amadu Bamba. His mother belonged to the Buso clan, a renowned clerical family that has been allied to the Mbacke for over a century. Amadu Bamba's mother was a Buso. Falilou performed the pilgrimage to Mecca and was celebrated as an accomplished poet who mastered the Arabic language. He had the reputation of a saint and miracle worker. Falilou also lead the Muridiyya in a time that is still remembered as that of *xeewal* or grace, marked by abundant harvests and prosperity.[25] Falilou was also able to unite the Muridiyya behind the project of finishing the building of the mosque of Touba, which was the most important project that Amadu Bamba had tasked his sons and disciples to accomplish on his behalf. Falilou therefore had enough spiritual and symbolic capital that could mitigate popular resentment for his support for unpopular government policies, as, for example, was the case during the strikes and riots of 1968.

Abdou Lahat, was, in turn, virtually unknown when he became caliph in 1968.[26] His mother was from the Jaxate clan of Mewndu that has a long tradition of Islamic learning, but he did not have the reputation of a great scholar and writer. He spent most of his lifetime in the village of Kabb in Kajoor. While the Senegalese government has maintained courteous relationships with most of the sons and potential successors of Amadu Bamba, it seems that Abdou Lahat did not benefit from government attention and generosity. He struggled to earn a decent living, like the common Murid disciples, and most of his friends were ordinary people in the village of Ndande and in Mbacke and Touba.

Moreover, in the early years of his caliphate, Abdou Lahat had to confront the opposition of two of his nephews, Cheikh Mbacke Gainde Fatma, son of the first caliph of the Muridiyya, and Moustapha Falilou, elder son of his predecessor, Falilou.[27] Cheikh Mbacke resisted the caliph's attempt at increasing centralization and control of the order, and Moustapha contested the new caliph's project to build a house on the esplanade of the Great Mosque of Touba. The caliphate of Abdou Lahat also coincided with the beginning of a cycle of droughts that devastated the rural economy of Senegal and the Sahelian belt of West Africa.

The lack of original symbolic and spiritual capital, contestation within the Murid order, and deteriorating ecological and economic conditions put Abdou Lahat in a situation of vulnerability where his caliphate could not afford to back unpopular government policies. In addition, unlike Falilou and some of his other half brothers, Abdou Lahat knew what it meant to struggle to make ends meet. He understood better the difficulties that ordinary Senegalese were going through. Facing the contestation of the two most powerful families in the Muridiyya, without much power of his own, he needed first to rally the disciples' support to build a power base and then assert his authority within the order.

Abdou Lahat achieved this by championing the struggle of the disgruntled Senegalese peasants hit hard by years of drought and the policy of structural adjustment imposed on Senegal by the International Monetary Fund and the World Bank. The caliph deplored government neglect of the farmers and pleaded for help on their behalf; he urged people to abandon cash crop cultivation for food crops and to give up superfluous luxuries such as coffee. He also presented himself as a modernizer and a defender of the Muridiyya. He mobilized the Murid community and raised large sums of money to build a library and a guesthouse, refurbish the mosque, and start an Islamic university.[28] Under his leadership, the village of Touba experienced an exponential growth, becoming Senegal's second largest city.

These investments earned him the affectionate nickname "The Builder." Abdou Lahat also stood up to the government when he felt that the Murids were under attack.[29] The tensions between Abdou Lahat and Senghor may have been a contributing factor to the latter's decision to retire in 1980.

The relationships between the Muridiyya and the government improved considerably under the presidency of Abdou Diouf, Senghor's successor.[30] Caliph Abdou Lahat gradually became a supporter of the president, who backed his projects in Touba by providing funding to dig deep-water wells, build roads, and extend the electrical and telephone networks. The autonomy of Touba was also reinforced. The caliph's decision in 1980 to ban the selling and use of tobacco and alcohol in Touba was supported by the government, which agreed to open a precinct for the gendarmes at the entrance of the village and dispatched officers to the main roads leading to Touba to enforce the interdiction.

Different factors explain the changing relations between Caliph Abdou Lahat and the government, and the gradual rapprochement with President Diouf. First, Diouf was in a position to have a fresh start in his relations with the caliph, although he had held the position of prime minister for a number of years. As a newly minted president without much popular support both within and outside his party, the Socialist Party, Diouf was certainly in a weaker political position than Senghor and therefore more willing to find areas of compromise to win the badly needed support of the caliph. Second, by the time Diouf became president in 1981, Caliph Abdou Lahat had accumulated much symbolic and spiritual capital that he could risk by investing some of it in support of the new president. He had established himself as an able and energetic leader who was willing to abandon the convoluted language and ambiguous political attitude of religious leaders in Senegal to bluntly criticize the government and forcefully advocate the Murid community's interests. Third, because of his style of leadership, the caliph had consolidated his authority within the Murid organization. He had successfully controlled the dissenting factions and concentrated much of the order's power in his hands.

However, the alliance between the caliph and the government did not translate into massive backing of the latter by the disciples as evidenced by the tally of Murid votes for the elections of 1983 and 1988. The mending of fences between the state and the Murid supreme leader did not yield much political gain, and Diouf did not benefit from the free ride he had perhaps expected, although the caliph's support may have helped him get away with rigged elections. Instead, many Murids, such as Senegalese elsewhere, remained critical of government policies and the caliph's political choices. Some of them, including those living in the city of Touba and its vicinity, expressed their discontent by sending angry anonymous letters to the caliph and by defying his recommendation at the ballot booth where many chose abstention or voted for the opposition PDS in 1988.[31]

Under Abdou Lahat's successor, Caliph Saliou Mbacke, who accessed the caliphate in 1990, the relationships between the state and the Muridiyya experienced a new chill. The relations between Shaykh Saliou, his younger brother, Shaykh Mortalla, and the Diouf government were not as close or cordial as the relations the president entertained with Caliph Abdou Lahat. Shaykh Mortalla, albeit discreetly, was very critical of government policies.[32] Caliph Saliou opted out of open involvement in politics, although the government of Diouf tried hard to earn his support.[33] He refused to ally himself with the ruling party and applied an open-door policy of receiving politicians of all stripes. Some among his entourage took advantage of this policy to openly work for opposition parties and even to run for elected offices. The caliph also remained neutral during elections, implicitly suggesting disciples vote their conscience. He declared his willingness to count exclusively on his labor and that of the Murid community to carry out the modernization projects he had for the city of Touba. He invested millions of dollars renovating and expanding the mosque of Touba, building new mosques and markets in the city, as well as new roads and development sites. He did not reject state investment in the town, but did not ask for it. Between 1990, when Shaykh Saliou accessed the caliphate, and 2000, the end of Diouf's presidency, the relationships between the leadership of the Muridiyya and the government of Senegal grew increasingly strained. And it seems that Diouf's refusal to renew and expand the deed on Touba that the colonial administration had granted the Murid order in 1928 ended up turning the option for political neutrality into implicit hostility toward the government.[34] By the time of the elections in 2000, which resulted in the victory of the opposition, many Murids were convinced that the leadership of the Murid order was in favor of the opposition.

The attitude of Caliph Shaykh Saliou vis-à-vis the state may be explained by lessons learned from the setbacks that his predecessor had experienced because of his close association with the ruling Socialist Party (PS) and President Diouf. It is also possible that he was aware of the new political environment created by the adoption of a new constitution and electoral code in 1991. This code instituted the secrecy of the ballots, mandatory identification of the voters, and a new system for collecting the votes, which made it more difficult to intimidate voters or rig the elections. In this context, where the results of an election could not be predicted and where the ruling party was no longer guaranteed automatic victory, it was wiser to adopt neutrality.[35]

But the caliph's attitude may also be explained by his personality. Shaykh Saliou was a Sufi quietist and educator. He was not primarily interested in the politics of government whether its outcome was negative or positive. He preferred prayers for change to recriminations and open criticism of government policies. He understood his stewardship of the Muridiyya in a narrow sense, by urging disciples to worship, work, and fulfill the order's projects, but counting first on their labor. He was more comfortable in his villages in the countryside surrounded by young disciples than in the limelight of the cameras and microphones of the press. In addition, Caliph Saliou accessed the caliphate at a relatively advanced age; he was in his mid-seventies and he understood that he did not have much time left to leave his mark on the history and collective memory of the Muridiyya. He did not want to divide his energy by giving too much attention to national issues.

However, the election in 2000 of President Abdoulaye Wade, leader of the political opposition and a self-styled Murid and disciple of Shaykh Saliou, considerably transformed public perception of the relationships between the Muridiyya and the state. As soon as he was inaugurated as president of Senegal, Wade traveled to Touba to thank the caliph, whose prayers he credited for his election victory. He broke with the protocol used by his predecessors, sitting on the floor, his head gear removed, kissing the Shaykh's hands as is customary among ordinary Murid disciples.[36] He developed a habit of visiting the caliph whenever he had an important political decision to make. He pledged government support to finance projects in Touba and included some prominent Murids in his government. While he was unsuccessful in convincing the caliph to openly enter the political arena by issuing recommendations of support on his behalf, he was able to secure the public support of the caliph's closest collaborators and aides. In doing so, he was able to use rumors and semiofficial channels to create the impression that he benefited from the caliph's support and that all of his major policy decisions were made in consultation with (and with the approval of) Murid's paramount leader.

The Senegalese "Social Contract" Revisited

Although in measurable terms the impact of Wade's policies on the Muridiyya did not differ substantially from those of his predecessors, through his behavior, declarations, and the astute manipulation of symbols, he quite successfully portrayed himself in the eyes of most Murids and Senegalese as a Murid president—that is, a president who was first and foremost at the service of Shaykh Amadu Bamba, and not only a president who happened to be a Murid. Wade's Murid supporters perceived any criticism of his policies as evidence of hostility toward the Muridiyya and Amadu Bamba. He successfully turned large segments of the Murid community, especially those living in the rural areas and the diaspora, into a solid bloc of support, and in this he was unwittingly helped by the newspapers and civil society of Senegal. In effect, Wade's opponents concentrated most of their criticism on his servile submission to the Murid caliph and in the process failed to apply rigorous scrutiny to his policy choices. Other Sufi orders, such as the Tijaniyya and the Qaridiriyya, also blasted the president although they greatly benefited from his presidency by playing the card of a marginalized group that needed attention. In all, the president's political maneuverings and the attacks on Wade's Murid identity created an emotional response among ordinary Murid disciples that blurred the boundaries between the politics of the government and the politics of the order, in the process, making the social contract less relevant.

Redefining the Social Contract

During the six decades covered in this research, the Muridiyya underwent important changes. Its social basis increasingly shifted from a peanut growing rural peasantry to an urban merchant constituency. Murids are found in all Senegalese cities and in the large cities of West and Central Africa. There is also a burgeoning Murid diaspora in the major metropolises of Europe and North America. Touba, the holy city of the Murid order, has a population of more than 500,000.[37] These transformations are having a gradual, but increasingly powerful, impact on the relations between shaykhs and disciples. The changing shaykh-disciple relations are in turn profoundly affecting the ways that the order's leadership does business with the state.

The urbanization of the Muridiyya and the transformation of the order's economy has resulted in the creation of new Murid religious institutions and sub-identities, a new role for the Murid in Senegalese civil society, a new understanding of the principle of *ndiggël* (religious ordinance), new ways of interacting with the shaykh, and a reevaluation of the power of the state and its rapports with the Murid leadership.

In the urban setting, Murid disciples created the *dahira*, or prayer circle, which originally functioned as an educational institution and an instrument for social and economic integration.[38] But with the internationalization of the Muridiyya, new *dahiras* appeared that were modeled on the international nongovernmental organizations, as shown by the example of *Hizbut Tarqiyyah* and *Matlabul Fawzayni*, and the Foundation Cheikhul Khadim, which are run by a board of secretaries accountable to the membership.

These new breeds of *dahiras* try to mobilize disciples around projects common to the order as a whole, across national boundaries, regardless of lineage allegiance. The Western-educated disciples, or sophisticated transnational migrants who manage them, deal directly with the caliph without intermediaries. International *dahiras* tap into the growing Murid diaspora and are able to raise large sums of money. *Matlabul Fawzayni* has funded a new modern hospital in Touba for the cost of more than $10 million. *Hizbut Tarqiyyah* runs a large school and community center in Touba and has chapters across the Murid heartland and abroad. *Hizbut* has emerged as a powerful player in the organization of the annual *Mággal* of Touba, the largest Murid religious gathering, which attracts more than one million pilgrims to the tomb of Amadu Bamba. *Maam Jaara Buso*, an all-female international institution, is an active partner in the organization of the annual pilgrimage at the tomb of their patron saint, who is also Amadu Bamba's mother. Members of this *dahira* are instrumental in the life of Murid communities abroad.[39]

All of these *dahiras* invest in education and have contributed to a substantial increase in literacy in Arabic among Murid disciples. A growing number of disciples now have direct access to the writings of Amadu Bamba and develop their own understanding and interpretations of his teachings.[40] They distinguish between legitimate and illegitimate *ndiggël*, the domain of the spiritual and that of the temporal. They seek their shaykhs' guidance in religious matters, but object to their involvement in political and state affairs. A growing number among these disciples claim direct affiliation with the caliph and do not recognize the authority of junior lineages. This is the case with *Hizbut Tarqiyyah*, which created a crisis within the Murid order when its leader denounced the preeminence of the Mbacke family and pleaded for the recognition of education and faithfulness to Amadu Bamba's teachings as the sole valid criteria for the choice of leadership.[41]

Murids are also active members of civil society. They play a major role in merchant trade unions. They spearheaded the founding of the most powerful union of traders in Senegal, National Union of Traders and Industrialists of Senegal (UNACOIS), which led the struggle for economic reforms in the tertiary sector of Senegalese economy and for the end of the government monopoly over the production and importation of some consumer goods such as rice, flour, sugar, oil, and garments.

Most of the time the grievances of Murid merchants are corporatist. But they have put the hierarchy of the order in an uncomfortable position where siding with the government also would mean opposing the interests of a powerful segment of their constituency upon which their financial well-being and that of the Murid order as a whole are, to a large extent, dependent.

The growing dependency of the Muridiyya on the financial contributions of the Murid diaspora in Africa, Europe, and the United States has had an even greater influence on the relations between the Muridiyya and the state. There are no available figures or estimates of the amount of money that Murid residing overseas contribute to the economy of Senegal and to the Murid order. But my educated guess is that it is millions of dollars a year.[42] This is more substantial than what the government of Senegal could afford to pay the order in a period of shrinking state resources, especially in the context of political pluralism where the state faces the aggressive scrutiny of the press and a largely secular-minded civil society that has grown hostile to government largesse to Muslim clerics.

The increasing financial autonomy of the Muridiyya has resulted in a reevaluation of its relations with the state and to more assertiveness on the part of the disciples. Murid disciples, particularly those living in the cities of Senegal and abroad, now want their voices to be heard and their views taken into account in the management of the order, especially with regard to the relations with the state. This aspiration has not yet resulted in an organized or concerted effort to change the way business is done in the order, but it constitutes a powerful, if not informal, undercurrent that increasingly affects the decision-making process in the Muridiyya. Disciples, particularly those living abroad, have easier access to their shaykhs through telephones and other electronic devices, and the physical distance makes it much easier for them to express feelings and concerns that direct contact may have otherwise made difficult to communicate. This physical distance also removes the protocol, ceremonies, and other trappings that add to the shaykh's charisma and make him somewhat closer to his disciples.

Exposure to political processes in host countries has also greatly enhanced the political consciousness of Murid immigrants. They have become a coveted constituency disputed by the government of Senegal and its opposition, especially since Abdoulaye Wade's rise to the presidency. The immigrants' open and muted criticism of the government puts pressure on shaykhs to keep a low political profile. Shaykhs who associate themselves too closely with the government are finding it more and more difficult to attract disciples. With the diversity of party affiliation among disciples, many important shaykhs have found it unwise to ostensibly take sides in the political contests in Senegal while peripheral and young shaykhs show greater political involvement to make up for the concentration of power and resources in the hands of their elders.

The then-new caliph of the Muridiyya, who was inaugurated in December 2007, seems to have drawn lessons from changes I have described herein. In his first major address to the Murid and Senegalese community at the occasion of the official ceremony of the *Màggal* of Touba that took place on February 28, 2008, the caliph urged the Murid shaykhs to respect and pay attention to the disciples whom he said are the real force behind the Muridiyya. And for the first time in the history of the Muridiyya, he invited the Catholic Church to the official ceremony of the *Màggal*.[43] He also abstained from making political statements, focusing instead on religious recommendations and calling for the unity of Senegalese of all creeds.

Conclusion

The Muridiyya has been and continue to be a powerful political force in Senegal. But shaykhs and disciples alike are aware that this power is rooted in the cohesion and discipline of the organization, which, in turn, depends on the preservation of the shaykh's religious authority and the disciples' spiritual and material interests. Although the contract of *njebbel* theoretically gives the shaykhs unlimited authority over the disciples, these shaykhs are also sensitive to the disciples' needs and feelings, and they know that there are boundaries not to be crossed. The idea of blind submission of disciples and unfettered power for the shaykh, which is at the core of the social contract approach, needs to be mitigated. The relation between shaykhs and disciples is not fixed and frozen in time. It is subject to continuous negotiations and transformations shaped by the changing economic and political environments in Senegal. And it is these transformations that in turn determine the nature of the relationships between the state and the order's leadership. But although the relationship between the state and the Murid leadership remains unstable and subject to many unpredictable factors, the preservation of the spatial autonomy of Touba continues to be a major bargaining chip at the disposal of the government that could be used to win the support or to secure political neutrality of the Muridiyya.

Notes

1. For more on the social contract theory, see Cruise O'Brien, *The Mourides of Senegal*; *Saints and Politicians*; Cruise O'Brien, "Le contrat social Sénégalais à l'épreuve"; Cruise O'Brien, *Symbolic Confrontations*; Cruise O'Brien, Diop, and Diouf, *La construction de l'etat au Sénégal*. The approach developed by Cruise O'Brien has had a major influence on scholarly exploration of the relationships between religious authorities and state power in Senegal, especially on the literature in the English language. See Coulon, *Le marabout et le prince*, for an attempt to apply the social contract theory to the wider Senegalese Muslim leadership. For a different perspective, see Vilallòn, *Islamic Society*. More recently, Robinson has introduced the concept of "accommodation" to mitigate the role of dependent subaltern that the social contract approach ascribed to the Muslim leadership in their dealings with the colonial and postcolonial state of Senegal and to provide a more balanced portrayal of these relationships. See *Paths of Accommodation*.
2. Quoted in Zaman, *The Ulama in Contemporary Islam*.
3. Cerno Bokar Taal, studied by Brenner, offers a good example of this type of Muslim leadership. See *West African Sufi*.
4. Coulon, *Les musulmans*.
5. Triaud, "Islam in Africa."
6. See Hansen and Stepputat, *Sovereign Bodies*.
7. In *Fighting the Greater Jihad*, I discuss the complexities of the relationships between the Muridiyya and the French colonial administration.
8. Marty, through his prolific writings and his ties with the major Muslim families of West Africa, has certainly exerted great influence on French colonial Muslim policy. But in reality, by the time he joined West Africa in 1912, the

shift from a Muslim policy based on repression to a policy based on cooperation had already taken place. For more on Coppolani and the policies he advocated, see Depont and Coppolani, *Les confréries religieuses musulmanes*.
9. See Frébourg, "Coppolani revisité," p. 623.
10. Quoted in Johnson, "William Ponty."
11. See Babou, "Contesting Space."
12. See Letter of Lieutenant Governor Cor to the director of public service and administration October 21, 1912, in Archives Nationales du Sénégal, dossier Ahmadou Bamba, 1912.
13. See Guèye, *Touba*, for a broader discussion of the deed of Touba and the place of the holy city of the Muridiyya in the politics of relationships between the Murid order and the state of Senegal.
14. Schmitz, "Un politologue chez les marabouts."
15. Cheikh Mbacke Gainde Fatma withheld the deed and documents concerning the building of the Great Mosque of Touba, which at the time was the most important project of the Muridiyya, and refused to surrender the papers to the new caliph. He was supported by some of his uncles, albeit discreetly. Seriñ Basiru, third in line for the caliphate, for example, kept his distance with his older half brother, Falilou, and managed to stay away from Touba.
16. See a complete transcription of the speech in Senghor, *Liberté 1*. Negritude is a major literary and philosophical movement founded in the 1930s by Senghor and black students in Paris from the French West Indies. It stressed the common identity of the black people and affirmed the contribution of blacks to universal civilization and humanism.
17. See Sy, *La confrérie Sénégalaise des mourides*.
18. Adriana Piga, *Dakar et les ordres soufis*.
19. Leaders of Murid religious organizations (*dahiras*) in Dakar are unanimous in stressing the role that Caliph Falilou played in solving conflicts with the local government in the cities of Senegal and protecting the interests of Murid traders. I refer here to my interviews with Ngagne Caam, one of the oldest Murid traders in Sandaga Market in Dakar on February 18, 1999, and Elhaj Bamba Diaw, leader of a powerful coalition of Murid *dahiras* in the region of Dakar, April 8 and May 13, 2000.
20. For Piga, the caliphate of Abdou Lahat marked the end of the social contract. See *Dakar*, p. 197.
21. See *Politique Africaine*, December 4, 1981, "Paroles mourides: Bamba, père et fils," p. 104.
22. See a transcription of the conversation between President Senghor and Caliph Abdou Lahat in *Politique Africaine*, Ibid., p. 109.
23. Ibid., 104.

24. Cruise O'Brien, *Symbolic Confrontations*.
25. The Falilou caliphate is much recalled in poetry and popular songs as a sort of Golden Age.
26. It is striking to note that his name does not appear on the list of Murid dignitaries compiled by the French colonial administrator and writer Abel Bourlon, in 1962. See Bourlon, *Mourides and Mouridisme*.
27. See Schmitz, "Un politologue."
28. For more on Caliph Abdou Lahat's projects in Touba and their significance, see Guèye, *Touba*. Though the guesthouse and the refurbishing of the mosque were completed, the university still remains a project that is resurfacing from time to time.
29. In 1984, he, for example, threatened to never speak through the national radio if they did not stop attacking Murid beliefs and religious practices. This threat was a response to what the caliph saw as anti-Murid propaganda promoted by some Islamists and disciples of other Sufi orders such as Shaykh Gassama, who said in one of his radio talk shows that "Those who kiss their sheikhs' hands and bow to them [these are well-known Murid practices] will resurrect with a donkey head." Bachir Kunta, one popular television commentator and member of the *Qadiriyya* hierarchy, commenting on the celebration of a disputed end of Ramadan said: "All the Muslims in Senegal have ended their fast today" whereas he was aware that there were discrepancies about the sighting of the moon and that the Murids were fasting that day.
30. To my knowledge, scholarly works have not been published on the relationships between President Abdou Diouf and the Muslim leadership of Senegal. Diop and Diouf's *Le Sénégal sous Abdou Diouf* provides a good assessment of Diouf's administration, halfway into his presidency.
31. See Beck, "'Patrimonial Democrats"; also Cruise O'Brien, *Symbolic Confrontations*, particularly the section entitled "the Mouride Brotherhood and the Social Contract, 1983–2001," pp. 202–210.
32. In a meeting with the president, he stressed that the Senegalese were suffering and that the government needed to do more to help them. Diouf, who was irritated by the shaykh's observations, terminated the audience prematurely. Personal conversation with A. S. B., who was Shaykh Mortalla's interpreter during the audience, Dakar, June 2000. During the elections of 2000, it is rumored that the shaykh told emissaries sent by the president who was seeking his support that he had already extended his prayers to his challenger.
33. A domain of 45,000 ha of forest in the region of Mbeuge was given to the caliph, who opened 15 *daaras* (or schools) and farms there despite the vociferous protest of environmentalists, international NGOs, and members of civil society in Senegal.

34. Personal conversation with Y. B., a well-known political and community activist in Mbacké, February 2000.
35. I thank my colleague Leonardo Villalón for calling my attention to the impact that the electoral reform enacted after the disputed elections of 1988 may have had on the attitude of the Murid caliph. New York, March 7, 2008.
36. This behavior created an outcry among the Senegalese civil society, especially among intellectuals who wrote fiery op-ed editorials and newspaper articles denouncing Wade for making the republic kneel and bow to a simple citizen.
37. The latest Senegalese census conducted in 2002 found that 31.7 percent of the population of Senegal residing in the country was Murid. With an estimated Senegalese population of 11 million in 2008, the Murid population in and out of Senegal has surpassed 4 million. A recent survey by Senegalese and American geographers found that there were 150,000 households in Touba. This information was given to me by Cheikh Guèye, a geographer and author of an important book on the city of Touba, who was a member of this team of geographers.
38. For more on the *dahira* and the transformations brought about by the urbanization of the Muridiyya, see Diop "La confrérie Mouride"; Cruise O'Brien and Coulon, *Charisma*; Babou, "Brotherhood Solidarity"; Babou, "Urbanizing Mystical Islam."
39. For more on the *Maam Jaara Buso* organization, see Evers-Rosanders, "Mam Diarra Bousso."
40. My attention was called to this by two Murid shaykhs: Elhaj Jaxate and Abdourahim Dem, whom I interviewed in Touba and Diourbel in June and July 2000.
41. See the dossier devoted to this crisis by the Senegalese independent newspaper *Sud-quotidien*, July 17, 1997.
42. The Senegalese Office for Economic Forecast and Statistics indicated that remittances sent by Senegalese in the diaspora had reached 410.5 billion CFA franc in the year 2006 ($1 was worth over 500CFA in 2006). See news dispatch by the government-owned Senegalese news agency, APS, of August 22, 2006, posted on Seneweb.com. I visited the Web site on August 23, 2006. Considering that more than 60 percent of this diaspora is constituted by Murids, and that these Murids also send a considerable amount of money to Touba, it is likely that a large portion of these remittances ended up in the coffers of Murid shaykhs or was invested in Murid projects in Touba and elsewhere in Senegal.
43. See the account of the official ceremony that ended the *Mággal* in the online version of *L'Observateur* (www.seneweb.com), February 28, 2008.

Bibliography

Babou, Cheikh Anta. "Brotherhood Solidarity, Education and Migration: The Role of the *Dahiras* Among the Murid Muslim Community of New York." *African Affairs* 403 (2002): 151–170.

———. "Contesting Space, Shaping Places: Making Room for the Muridiyya in Colonial Senegal." *Journal of African History* 46 (2005): 405–426.

———. *Fighting the Greater Jihad: Amadu Bamba and the Founding of the Muridiyya of Senegal, 1853–1913*. Athens: Ohio University Press, 2007.

———. "Urbanizing Mystical Islam: Making Murid Space in the Cities of Senegal," *The International Journal of African Historical Studies* 40 (2) (2007): 197–223.

Beck, Linda. "Patrimonial Democrats," in *A Culturally Plural Society: Democratization and Political Accommodation in Patronage Politics of Senegal*. PhD dissertation, University of Wisconsin Madison, 1996.

Bourlon, Abel. *Mourides and Mouridisme*. Paris: Peyronet, 1962.

Brenner, Louis. *West African Sufi: The Religious Heritage and Spiritual Search of Cerno Bokar Taal*. Berkeley: University of California, 1984.

Coulon, Christian. *Le marabout et le prince. Islam et pouvoir au Sénégal*. Paris: Pedone, 1981.

———. *Les musulmans et le pouvoir en Afrique Noire*. Paris: Karthala, 1988.

Cruise O'Brien, Donal B. "Le contrat social Sénégalais à l'épreuve." *Politique Africaine* 45 (1992): 9–20.

———. *The Mourides of Senegal: The Political and Economic Organization of an Islamic Brotherhood*. Oxford: Clarendon Press, 1971.

———. *Saints and Politicians*. Cambridge, UK: Cambridge University Press, 1975.

———. *Symbolic Confrontations: Muslims Imagining the State in Africa*. London: Hurst, 2003.

Cruise O'Brien, Donal B. and Christian Coulon (eds.), *Charisma and Brotherhood in African Islam*. London: Oxford University Press, 1988.

Cruise O'Brien, Donal B., M. C. Diop, and M. Diouf. *La construction de l'etat au Sénégal*. Paris: Karthala, 2002.

Depont, O., and X. Coppolani. *Les confréries religieuses musulmanes*. Alger: Jourdan, 1897.

Diop, M. C. *La confrérie Mouride: Organisation politique et mode d'implantation urbaine*. Thèse de troisième cycle unité d'études et recherches de psychologie et des sciences sociales, Université de Lyon 2, 1980.

Diop, M. C. and Mamadou Diouf. *Le Sénégal sous Abdou Diouf*. Paris: Karthala, 1990.

Evers-Rosanders, Eva. "Mam Diarra Bousso la bonne mère de Porokhane, Sénégal. *Africa* (Rome) Anno LVIII-3/4 (2003): 296–317.

Frébourg, Cécile "Coppolani revisité." *Cahiers d'Etudes Africaines*, 80 (1993): 615–626.

Guèye, Cheikh. *Touba, la capitale des Mourides*. Paris: Karthala, 2002.

Hansen, Thomas B., and Finn Stepputat (eds.). *Sovereign Bodies: Citizens, Migrants, and States in the Postcolonial World*. Princeton, N.J.: Princeton University Press, 2005.

Johnson, Wesley. "William Ponty and Republican Paternalism in French West Africa, 1908–1915." In *African Proconsuls*, eds. L. H. Gann and Peter Duignan. New York: Free Press, 1978, 127–157.

Piga, Adriana. *Dakar et les ordres soufis*. Paris: Harmattan, 2002.

Robinson, David. *Paths of Accommodation: Muslim Societies and French Colonial Authorities in Senegal and Mauritania, 1880–1920*. Athens: Ohio University Press, 2000.

Schmitz, J. "Un politologue chez les marabouts." *Cahiers d'Etudes Africaines* 91 (23) (1983): 329–351.

Senghor, Léopold Sédar. *Liberté 1: Négritude et humanisme*. Paris: Seuil, 1964.

Sy, Cheikh T. *La confrérie Sénégalaise des Mourides*. Paris: Présence Africaine, 1969.

Triaud, Jean Louis. "Islam in Africa Under French Colonial Rule." In *The History of Islam in Africa*, eds. N. Levtzion and R. Pouwels. Athens: Ohio University Press, 2000.

Vilallòn, Leonardo. *Islamic Society and State Power in Senegal: Disciples and Citizens in Fatick*. Cambridge, Mass.: Cambridge University Press, 1995.

Zaman, Muhammad Qasim. *The Ulama in Contemporary Islam: Custodians of Change*. Princeton, N.J.: Princeton University Press, 2002.

[7]

Religious and Cultural Pluralism in Senegal

Accommodation Through "Proportional Equidistance"?

ETIENNE SMITH[1]

Senegal's peaceful cultural and religious pluralism has been hailed by many analysts and is a common matter of pride in contemporary Senegal. Two types of explanation have been put forward: (1) the "external" argument, summoning factors from outside the realm of ethnicity or religion that constrain their supposedly intrinsic divisive elements, the "republican model," i.e., a strong republican state that created an encompassing political community downplaying the political salience of cultural and religious belongings; (2) the "majority" argument, emphasizing the homogenization processes of the Islamo-Wolof model, i.e., the unifying trend of the predominant Muslim religion and its organization in powerful Sufi orders that cut across ethnocultural cleavages, combined with the dynamic of Wolofization creating a new society that dissolves "peripheral" ethnicities.[2] Both explanations have converged into a single one: the accommodation between the republican state and the Sufi orders providing the missing link between state and society, allowing for a distinctively Senegalese "social contract."[3] The republican model and the Islamo-Wolof model, in their original combination, are indeed the key to Senegalese distinct political culture.

However, focusing exclusively on these two building blocks of the Senegalese polity and their combinative effects might at the same time obscure some other processes that are no less important in accounting for Senegal's relatively peaceful religious and cultural pluralism. In comparison with religion, the relative silence about ethnicity in the literature on Senegal, unless it becomes politically salient as in Casamance, contrasts with its omnipresence in daily life in the benign form of presentations of the self, patronymics, and joking interaction between individuals in public.[4]

In this chapter, I propose to think comparatively of the state accommodation of both religious and cultural pluralism. The Senegalese model is thus a broader picture, made of three interacting spheres: the republican sphere of the modern state (colonial and postcolonial), the religious sphere (including the Christian minority), and the cultural sphere of the patrias (Senegalese *terroirs* and precolonial polities). I argue that there is a common pattern of relations between the state and the two other spheres, which can be described as an informal and pragmatic policy of "proportional equidistance," not fully theorized yet quite remarkably efficient.[5] "Proportional equidistance" is the principle that tries to combine equal respect by principle and de facto acknowledgment of the different weights of the different communities.[6]

But this political accommodation process from above is only half of the story. I contend that the crafting of tolerance must also be thoroughly examined. The dynamics from below are too often left aside in the analysis because they do not "appear" in institutionalized forms that usually catch the observer's attention. Without falling into the pitfalls of reification on the one side, or mere anecdote on the other side, it is necessary, as anthopologists have argued, to study these "soft" or "informal" social practices of interaction that are critical to social connection in Senegal, e.g., kinship ties and joking kinship pacts.

In this exploration of some forms of religious and ethnocultural tolerance in Senegal, from above and from below, I shall first briefly emphasize the need to put religion in perspective, reminding us that it is not the only game in town and that the key element is the structure of crosscutting cleavages in the fabric of Senegal's sociocultural and religious landscape. Second, I will argue for the study of microprocesses of tolerance from below if one is to fully explain how pluralist worldviews are sustained. Finally, I assess the similarities in the pattern of accommodation of cultural and religious diversity by the Senegalese postcolonial state.[7] In the process, I wish to show that if we are to account for Senegal's tolerant political culture, we should not focus only on (Sufi) Islam or only on inclusive ethnicities or only on the *"sens de l'État,"*[8] but on the peculiar combination of the three.

Is Religion Everything? Bringing the State and the Patrias Back In

The Sufi orders have rightly been subjected to intensive scholarly inquiry and depicted as the building blocks of Senegalese society and politics.[9] The social dynamics of Islam and the Wolofized dominant cultural model to which it has become associated have indeed been essential in the shaping of Senegalese postcolonial political culture and imagery.[10] Islam is undoubtedly a potent source of mobilization as shown, for instance, by massive attendance to religious festivals, to the point that being Senegalese seems to have become synonymous with being a *taalibe*.[11] But religion is only one of the socialization frameworks. Besides the community of "believers" (faith as loyalty to God and its representatives), there is also the community of "citizens" (citizenship as loyalty to the state), and the community of "kin" and "ethnics" (kinship as loyalty to kin and local patriotism as loyalty to the *terroir*). All three spheres of socialization and practices are critical in the imagination of the Senegalese community and the crafting of its political culture. A brief look at emic perceptions collected in a survey carried out in Dakar in 2006 shows that we need to bring the state and the cultural patrias back in the political imagination.[12]

First, when we consider narratives about history and national identity, "heroes" of Senegal come from different spheres, as shown in table 7.1.[13,14] We notice that the "saints" figure prominently in the top list of heroes of Senegalese history. But much space is left to the heroes of secular modernity as well as the heroes of the cultural patrias.[15] Senegal's national self-image as it is portrayed by respondents of this survey through its heroes is threefold: the modern state, the religious faith, and the cultural patrias.

Second, the question on the reasons for Senegal's declared peaceful intercommunity relations[16] reveals that the "external" argument (the state) is strikingly absent and that the "majority" argument (Islamo-Wolof) does not figure prominently, as table 7.2 shows.[17]

As we can see, a common religion (and even common religiosity) comes fourth in explaining good relations between communities. Likewise, a common language (Wolof) comes fifth. It seems, therefore, that the dominant "Islamo-Wolof" model is not spontaneously used in emic discourse of the sample as the first explanation for good relations between communities. What we have instead are references to cultural values and practices (*teranga*, *kalante*, kinship) that are not group specific, that refer to a sociability ethos shared by many *terroirs*, cutting across linguistic or religious divides.

Table 7.1 Heroes of Senegalese history

Heroes of the cultural patrias	Heroes of Islam	Heroes of the modern state	Rank	%
Lat Dior Diop			1	52.4
	Cheikh Amadu Bamba		2	31.7
Aline Sitoe Diatta			3	23.4
Alboury Ndiaye	El Hadj Omar Tall		4 (tie)	21.3
		Léopold Sédar Senghor	6	19.5
		Cheikh Anta Diop	7	14.2
	El Hadj Malick Sy		8	13.3
Koumba Ndoffene Diouf			9	8.9
	Maba Diakhou Ba		10	8.6
		Lamine Gueye	11	4.7
	El Hadj Ibrahima Niasse		12	4.4
	Seydinâ Limâmu Laay		13	3.0

Note: "Heroes" listed in this table were prompted by the following open question: "For you personally, who are the heroes of Senegalese history?" Multiple answers were permitted.

Table 7.2 Causes for perceived good relations between communities in Senegal

Cause	%
Teranga (hospitality)	31.6
Kalante (joking kinship)	25.0
Kinship and marriage	14.5
Religion (Muslim majority, Sufi orders, religiosity of both Catholics and Muslims)	11.2
Language (Wolof as an unifying language)	3.2
Other ("understanding," "peace," "respect," "role of Senghor . . .")	14.5
Total	100

Note: Causes listed in this table were prompted by an open question for which only a single response was permitted.

Religious and Cultural Pluralism in Senegal

Table 7.3 Domains that set Senegal apart from other African countries

Domain	%
deggo (understanding)/*maaslante* (sociability)/*xamante* (knowing each other)/*kalante* (joking kinship)/*jappalante* (mutual help)/*savoir-vivre* (manners)	57.0
teranga (hospitality)/openness/tolerance	44.6
political stability/democracy/human rights/freedom of expression	19.3
religious stability/religious peace/religiosity/brotherhood/faith	19.0
jamm (peace, unspecified)	17.6
intellectuel/éduqué/civilisé/développé*	13.7
"ethnic peace"/absence of discriminations between groups	10.3
craftmanship/culture/arts	10.3
economy/commerce	5.2
gastronomy	1.7

Note: Domains listed in this table were prompted by an open question. Multiple answers were permitted.
* These words were, significantly, always in French.

This seems to point to a broader cultural matrix, which is the declared locus for positive social interaction, in which religion and lingua franca seem to play only a secondary role.

Third, when asked in which domains Senegal was different from other African countries, respondents argued that Senegal's so-called exceptionalism is not unidimensional, as table 7.3 reveals.[18]

Again, in emic discourse, it seems that the religious sphere or the political culture is not the most distinctive feature of Senegal's exceptionalism. Sociocultural practices and values come first.

This insight into emic discourse, through a sample from the Dakar region, should of course not be generalized. Yet it does show that religion, and especially Sufi orders, do not encapsulate the whole of Senegalese national identity, politics, and daily life.[19] Senegal's imagined nation, or imagi-nation, is a combination of a still omnipresent secular modern state, a lively religious society, as well as resilient cultural patrias and values.

The key feature, however, is the considerable overlap of the three spheres. First, as shown in the literature, the relation between the state and the Sufi orders has been one of mutual accommodation and intervention. Second, the state has tremendously affected the patrias with its modernization and territorialization projects while its daily workings got entangled in local historicities and "arts de faire." Finally, Islam has deeply influenced cultural patrias while being at the same time reformulated in the vernacular of these *terroirs*. Islam, since precolonial times, has been a potent tool in delocalizing imaginations of community and ethnohistorical landscapes. As a result, it has often been argued that the unifying trend and delocalized feature of vastly preponderant Islam explains the homogenization of Senegalese society as well as its stability. However, if some cultural boundaries were rendered less salient by the spread of Islam, differential Islamization also produced new boundaries altogether, new cultural markers available for differentiation. It brought about a reallocation of identities according to a new religious axis or "religious ethnography."[20] Still, nowadays, as surveys on stereotypes show, one of the key criteria used in emic discourse to distinguish ethnicities is that of Muslim religious practice, groups being differentially ranked along an axis of "Muslimness": long-standing Muslimness (Tukulor, Soninke, Wolof, Mandinka) and more recent Muslimness (Serer, Joola).[21] Thus, Islam, rather than simply being synonymous with homogenization and unification, is one of the very tools used to mark differences between ethnicities, according to the different Islamic credentials of groups.

Differential historical sequences of Islamization produced a diverse Muslim community but also resulted in some groups being only partially Islamized. The Serer and Joola patrias (whose historical process of forging of collective identities cannot be understood without taking into account Islamization and resistances to it) are such examples. If, historically, Islamization and its dialogics has helped delineate cultural boundaries, nowadays, religion and ethnicity are not reinforcing cleavages, but crosscutting cleavages. This is critical, since as we shall see, the Serer and Joola patrias are setting the example of positive interreligious relations. Moreover, the dividing lines of the Sufi orders themselves (Tijan, Murid, Qadir, Layen), create new crosscutting cleavages, as these diverse (and often competing) affiliations often cut across kinship or ethnicity (especially among Wolof, Serer, or Wolofized Mandinka with conversions to Muridism).[22]

Ultimately then, it is clear that under the umbrella of the dominant "Islamo-Wolof" model lies a more variegated picture: religious and cultural fragmentation. The combination of the two types of diversities certainly

Religious and Cultural Pluralism in Senegal

helps prevent the emergence of binary and exclusive reinforcing cleavages that would lead to open conflict.[23] But is the structure of crosscutting cleavages combined with a dominant Islamo-Wolof model a sufficient explanation of Senegal's seemingly peaceful religious and cultural pluralism?

Tolerance and Inclusion from Below: Social Uses of Kinship

I believe that one has to bring the ideology of kinship into the picture.[24] It is undeniable that many social relationships are conceptualized through the idiom of kinship and assessed according to the intensity of this kinship: it is the lens used most often to assess relations between religions and cultural groups. Kinship is still the major conceptual framework irrigating Senegalese political culture that cuts across cleavages based on religion, language, or ethnicity. It remains a powerful ideological tool in triggering or silencing conflicts.

For instance, in interviews, among Serer and Joola respondents, kinship bonds were systematically put forward to explain and justify feelings toward the religious other, who precisely was not so much of an "other," but a kin. In the Serer area of Senegal, as well as in the southern region of Casamance, where the Catholic communities are more important and where Islamization is more recent, many families have either Catholic or Muslim members that feel more bound by this kinship and the power of locality than divided by differences of faith.[25] Beyond the specificities of Joola or Serer *terroirs*, the Dakar survey shows that circles of sociability, if not kin, are religiously diverse. Sixty-eight percent of Catholic respondents have Muslim kin, and 100 percent have Muslim friends, which is no real surprise, Catholics being a minority (around 5 percent). But 16 percent of Muslims sampled have Catholic kin, and 72 percent Catholic friends.

Despite the absence of reliable data on this issue, interfaith marriages do occur in Senegal, and personal choices of faith inside the family—though often fiercely opposed by the family—do sometimes happen. One of the survey's questions, as it appears in table 7.4, gives us a glimpse about opinions of those sampled on the issue of marriage.

The contrasting results of religion and ethnicity seem to show that religion is still felt by respondents as a possible frontier on an important issue such as marriage, while ethnicity is not. However, as a whole, but for this significant qualification on the issue of marriage, neither ethnicity nor

Table 7.4 Criteria in marriage decision

	Yes (%)	No (%)
Ethnicity	29.4	70.6
Religion	74.5	25.5

Note: The question was "Would you marry/would you let your son or daughter marry . . . someone who is . . ." followed by a list. Results have been compiled with three categories: ethnicity, religion, and caste. Line one shows that for 29.4 percent of respondents, ethnicity of the future spouse is important in making a decision about marriage, and for 70.6 percent it is not. Line two shows that for 74.5 percent of respondents, religion of the future spouse is important in making a decision about marriage, and for 25.5 percent it is not. Results about "caste" are not indicated because the nonresponse rate was very high.

religion seems to constitute a salient cleavage in Senegalese society. A recent study on tolerance in Senegal points to this direction: in the question on "tolerance of others as neighbors," "peoples from other ethnic groups or races" ranks first (87.1 percent) and "people from another religious group" ranks third (78.3 percent). It means, that together with "foreign workers and immigrants" (second with 84.2 percent), the cultural other and the religious other are the most readily accepted by the Senegalese respondents,[26] although the "ethnic" other, the foreigner, and the religious other are usually the very categories around which intractable cleavages or conflicts are created around the world.[27]

In this respect, as an extension of kinship ideology, joking kinships are an essential part of the inclusive uses of ethnicity and patronymics. These joking alliances are practiced among all major cultural groups in Senegal and between many of them.[28] Whether based on patronymics or ethnocultural labels and stereotypes, they contribute to the structure of crosscutting cleavages. The classical functionalist and jural model in anthropology tried to theorize joking relationships as playing a functional role in maintaining social harmony by defusing conflicts between joking allies. Beyond the apparent hostility involved in mockery and the strong exchange of stereotypes, joking relationships were described as a means of creating friendship links and adjusting in a friendly fashion to cultural differences. Enacted disrespect would ultimately foster respect.[29]

However, fieldwork and empirical data show that joking kinships, as *practices* and not abstract theorization, are ambiguous and do not automatically have the pacifying functions attributed to them by the literature.[30] Nonetheless, joking pacts are reciprocal and routinized gestures of mutual recognition, familiar patterns of interaction available to individuals whenever the need is felt to cut across cultural or social boundaries and set interactions in a potentially inclusive framework. It is a fact that most people in Senegal enjoy practicing joking pacts and look for them also when they can help to solve a problem or provide advantages, to the point of sometimes inventing a joking kinship link with an individual not obviously connected through the well-known alliance networks.[31]

Surveys have also shown that joking kinship ties seem to have some effect on positive representations between the communities involved. Correlation between the existence of a joking kinship between two groups and a declared good relationship between them has been documented.[32] Joking kinship relations are often spontaneously invoked by respondents both as justifying their appreciations of the partner group and as being the explanation of the quality of the relation. As we have seen (table 7.2), for respondents, joking kinships also come second in explaining good relations between communities in Senegal. Although by no means accounting for all relations between communities and all statements about otherness, it does seem that joking kinships involve a peculiar channelling of stereotypes through a ritualization of comic display of difference that does foster tolerance in some contexts. It has been argued, for instance, that good relations between civil servants and populations in some regions were to be ascribed to joking kinships.[33]

It is exaggerated to assert, as many do, that joking pacts *create* peace between communities in Senegal, that it is a *cause* of good intergroup or interindividual relations. It seems rather that, historically, those joking alliances emerged as a *consequence* of the establishment of peace, that is, after a war between some segments of the communities involved, as well as from gradual transformations of asymmetrical power relations stemming from class domination, slave-master relations, conquests, or marriage alliances.[34] But nowadays, from a consequence or symptom of pacified relations, they may well have turned through performance and daily reiteration into an adjuvant of good relations. Joking alliances, as both practices and cultural/ideological repertoire, simultaneously confirm symbolic borders between groups and offer means to cross them. They provide codified peaceful patterns of interaction for whoever wants to tap into them. Joking pacts have turned into an extendible idiom that applies to groups and individuals who were not usually included, as a pattern of relation to otherness.[35] As a result, kinship and joking interethnic alliances, as well as religion, are the most convenient tools available in daily life to create social connections.

The case can therefore be made that horizons of tolerance and patterns of cooperation can be found within the thickness of local cultures and moralities. Tolerance may not only need be cast in the abstract liberal vocabulary of human rights and require uprootedness from local traditions. It can also emerge from within particular practices such as joking kinships that acknowledge the presence of the other and create a symbolically contested, but ultimately common, space.[36] It has been argued that Sufi Islam provides the means of such a pluralist and cosmopolitan worldview;[37] I think that the joking interstices of Senegambian (and more widely, Sahelian) ethnicities are also part of the picture, as vernacular cosmopolitanisms.[38]

All this being said, the social fabric of tolerance from below is not enough. The role of the state is obviously critical in maintaining societal tolerance or in crushing it. We now need to assess the role of leadership and state policies.

Tolerance and Inclusion from Above: The Postcolonial State Impossible Equidistance?

Leadership Practices

It is well known that religious leadership in Senegal, whether Catholic or Muslim, is ethnically diverse. Sufi leaders in Senegambia have a longstanding habit of marriage alliances and networks of *taalibe* that cut across cultural or linguistic markers. The Muslim/Christian frontier sometimes also cuts across families of religious leaders. Former Cardinal Thiandoum came from a Muslim family—it is even said that his uncle was an imam, and that the muezzin of the mosque in the famous Catholic pilgrimage village of Popenguine is one of his nephews.[39] Relations between the leaders of these communities take the form of respect owed to kin and friend. Mutual invitations, routine visits, and exchange of gifts are ordinary activities for Sufi and Catholic leaders. This display of respect between religious leaders is important as it is always public and routinized so as to make it the "normal" way.

Similarly, political leadership in Senegal is ethnically and religiously diverse. Political elites have often set the example of religiously diverse families: President Senghor was a Catholic, but he had Muslim sisters. President Diouf, a Muslim, married a Catholic, and their children prolonged this familial ecumenism. President Wade, a Muslim, married a Catholic too. As for ethnicity, the presidents of Senegal have been careful to stress their connections to all the major patrias of Senegal: Senghor "the Serer" traced his paternal ascent to the Mandinka nobility (and even the Portuguese) while his mother was Haalpulaar;[40] he connected himself to the Joola and the Haalpulaar through joking kinship, and insisted that he spoke Wolof more than Serer, while the Lebu were nothing else than "Serer with wet feet." Abdou Diouf presented himself as a Wolof with a Serer name and Haalpulaar maternal kin, connected through his Serer emblem with the Joola and Mandinka.[41] Finally, the Wolof Abdoulaye Wade likes to mention his mother of Mandinka origin from Casamance. While all this is part of political strategies—in which Senghor was a master—to appear as representative as possible of the diverse *terroirs* of Senegal, it also shows and enacts the legitimacy of the connection and *métissage* script.[42]

In this respect, the founding moment of Senegal's postcolonial state, the Senghorian moment, is still an important legacy. Senghor is not the major reference when it comes to "national heroes": he ranks sixth in the *open* question of heroes of Senegalese history (see table 7.3). But when asked in interviews what should be remembered of him, it is these two domains of religion and ethnicity that are constantly quoted. Senghor did set an example without which one cannot understand some views of Senegalese on religious or cultural pluralism up to nowadays. For instance, in my Dakar survey, the question about the possibility of having, in the future, a president of Senegal from a minority group, shows that for 71 percent of respondents a Catholic president is still possible. This figure is quite high, if we compare this with a female president (48.8 percent), a *métis* president (46.4 percent), a *casté* president (45.9 percent), a president who does not speak Wolof (38.8 percent), and finally a president who does not speak French (7.4 percent). This 71 percent is definitely a legacy of Senghor's presidency.[43]

This Senghorian legacy is often explained by the fact that he was from a double minority, Catholic and Serer, in a predominantly Muslim and Wolof country, and that he started his political career as the deputy of the former subjects of the hinterland. But Senghor's dealing with religion and *terroirs* cannot only be explained by his (and Dia's) astute political strategy or mere pragmatism, nor only by the preexisting pattern of collaborative practices inherited from the colonial accommodation with the Sufi orders. A close examination of Senghor's writings and his evolving political thought of the 1930s–1950s show that it was part of a broader theoretical project of complementarity, i.e., combining the rational secular state with the spiritual dimensions of religions, in short, reason with faith, as well as combining centralized Jacobin state nationalism with the cultural celebration of local patrias and their moral communities, in short, unity with diversity.[44]

The Senghorian Project

Senghor repeatedly criticized the Western dichotomization of politics and religion. Inspired by socialism, he nonetheless complained about the total absence of God in the writings of Engels and the late Marx. He wrote in 1953 that he managed to reconcile his Christian faith with his socialist ideology thanks to the British Labour party: "Like in our country, their political acts start and end with prayers."[45] As for Islam, it is no surprise that Senghor, focusing on the spiritual dimension of religion, was keen on African Sufism, while not using the word: "An abstract and formal Islamism, a degenerated Islam, is a danger for us. Black Muslims should try to restore its mystical and humanist leaven, tuning it to our soul. That is what West African Islam is beginning to do."[46] Senghor thus saw Christianity and Islam as convergent forces that could lead to a third revolution, a spiritual one, overcoming the materialism of both capitalism and communism.[47] For him, faith and ethics were to complement discursive reason, lost in "the Sahel of rationalism."[48]

Regarding nationalism and ethnicity, the Senghorian initial project was also one of complementarity. Senghor's conception of the nation was indeed one of a modern political construct, a product of the "common will to live together."[49] He therefore distinguished the nation, which stands above, from the local *patries* or *provinces* that were to be organized and disciplined by the nation.[50] He stressed that "to achieve its goal, the nation must animate with its faith all its members, all individuals beyond their *patries*. It must turn individuals into persons, that is, into conscious wills: *souls*." However, Senghor could not be satisfied with the dichotomy between the nation and the cultural patrias, and would thus add: "Far from denying the realities of the patria, the Nation will rely on their virtues, their very nature as realities, that is their emotional force. It will unite the virtues of the patria or, most often, will choose among them those which, by reason of the climate, history or race, have a common denominator, or those who have a universal value."[51] His Jacobinism, at least in his writings, was moderate, as he was well aware of its dangers: "One cannot handle men as firewood. Above all, we will be careful not to fall into one of the temptations of the nation-state, that is, the uniformisation of persons across the patrias. The archetype implies the impoverishment of the persons, their reduction to robot-individuals, a loss in sap and juice. Richness stems from the diversity of the patrias and the persons, from their *complementarity*."[52] Arguably, for all his Jacobinism and modernist stance, Senghor never forgot his "provincial heritage"[53] and the French ideology of *"petites patries."*[54]

Senghor's theoretical views on religion and nation-building cannot be easily separated.[55] For him, nation and *laïcité* were similar encompassing frameworks, neutral spaces that stand above the diverse ethnicities for the former and diverse faiths for the latter. The articulation is clearly hierarchical and beyond discussion, as the state sets the rules of the game. But this never meant for Senghor that the nation and *laïcité* should overlook the cultural patrias and the religious faiths, for these moral communities are incomparable reservoirs of ethical values, *"suppléments d'âmes"* of the modernization project.

Beside Senghor's theoretical project linking both issues and articulated *before* Senegal's independence, I argue here that there is a common pattern of relations between the state, on the one hand, and religious and ethnocultural groups, on the other hand, in postcolonial Senegal.

De Jure "Equal Respect" and De Facto "Proportionate Equidistance"

Senghor's legacy is one of a policy of "equal respect" and "proportionate equidistance" toward religious and cultural groups. Inheriting an intrinsically contradictory model of an imperial colonial state,[56] the leadership had to make the choice of prolonging or halting preexisting compromises. The heyday of the independence era, the imperatives of national unity, the modernist enthusiasm, and the feeling that the postcolonial state's legitimacy was granted—and, unlike the colonial state that was compelled to develop indirect rule, did not have to be earned—all pleaded for a shift in state policy.[57] The postcolonial state was thus more Jacobin and secular than its colonial predecessor: in the name of national unity, the decades-old *statut personnel* for Muslims and Muslim courts was suppressed. Regional political parties, allowed (if not encouraged) under late colonial rule, were now forbidden. Thus, two spheres of autonomy from the central and secular state were altogether suppressed. However, despite this sharp Jacobin turn in two key domains, the Senegalese postcolonial state was not a straightforward replica of the French Jacobin metropolitan model, but rather displayed more continuity with its colonial predecessor state.

First of all, the Senegalese state is rhetorically, and since 2001, constitutionally friendlier to cultural pluralism than its French metropolitan model. The postcolonial state was indeed wary of potential "micronationalism" and dismissed regionalist claims,[58] but the state cultural apparatus and Senghor himself encouraged cultural expressions of ethnicity.[59] The new constitution of 2001, in its preamble, officially recognizes "components" of the nation and their "cultural specificities," which would be a heresy in France. The national population census asks a question on "ethnic" belonging that is not allowed in France. Regarding linguistic policy, French was given all the attention. Although spoken at the time by a mere 15 percent of the population, the constitution of 1963 confirmed its status of sole official language and did not even mention any other Senegalese languages. However, in 1978, six languages (Jola, Mandinka, Pulaar, Serer, Soninke, and Wolof) were listed by the constitution, and given the symbolic status of *langues nationales*. This first step of recognition was merely symbolic, but it was nonetheless a clear departure from the French monolingual model. Under President Diouf, more concessions were made. Alphabetization schemes in *langues nationales* led to the liberalization of the media and gave birth to private radio stations more keen on using *langues nationales*, especially Wolof in urban areas. A scheme of progressive introduction of the *langues nationales* in public primary schools was set up in 1998 and implemented in 2002 under President Wade, who was much more sympathetic to the use of Wolof in the realm of officialdom. The new constitution of 2001 also extended the possibilities for minority languages not yet listed in 2001 to be recognized as *langues nationales*, provided that they were codified.[60] This multilingualism was liberal: state recognition of *langues nationales* implied no formal duties for the state. It was mainly a matter of tolerating these languages in public institutions—not an obligation.[61]

Second, if the model of French *laïcité* is constitutionally entrenched,[62] there are some distinctions to be made. Senghor made it clear that Senegalese secularism could not be like French metropolitan secularism,[63]

Religious and Cultural Pluralism in Senegal

prolonging the line of argument made by French colonial administrators before him.[64] But it was not merely for pragmatic reasons like his predecessors but also out of an unwavering attachment to the educational task of religions and the key role they play to "humanize" society, as we have seen.[65] Moreover, the Senegalese state differs sharply from the French one in that it was born *laïc*, as a colonial superimposition on a religious society, and did not have to emancipate itself violently from the dominance of a religious majority such as in France. Thus, from Senghor's period to the present, it is consensual among Senegalese political elites that "The state must support religions and brotherhoods in order to help Senegalese to better live their faith."[66] So, if we consider Michael Walzer's discussion of Charles Taylor's distinction between "Liberalism 1" (state neutrality) and "Liberalism 2" (in which the state offers guarantees of survival and support to all "forms of life" in society), Senegal, in religious matters, is closer to the Liberalism 2 model.[67] State support for pilgrimages of both religions, going back to colonial times in the case of the *Hajj*, is a perfect illustration. In line with Senghor's insistence on the commonalities of the Muslim and Catholic faiths, interviewees typically value the common religiosity of Senegalese Catholics and Muslims.[68] Finally, political discourse is replete with religious references and metaphors. The postcolonial trajectory of the Senegalese state is thus, classically, one of progressive vernacularization, cautiously initiated by Senghor and then increased by his successors.

But vernacularization in a context of a plurality of cultural traditions is always tricky. Senghor's most significant legacy is in fact less, in the vernacularization of politics, process itself, which was after all quite limited, than in his careful policy of making sure that concessions made to majority groups—religious or linguistic—would not happen at the expense of minorities. He managed to put checks on both majorities—the Muslim majority and Wolof language majority—thus giving the Senegalese state a peculiar legacy of standing above the majority rather than being exclusively in the hands of the dominant Islamo-Wolof core. The Senghorian state was widely described as sticking to neutrality, even artificially, above religious and cultural differences.[69] One sign of this is that some of the fiercest critics against the Senghorian tackling of religious and ethnocultural issues came from nationalist intellectuals accusing him of disregarding Wolof's clear linguistic dominance and refusing to make it the official language (to the benefit of French), or from some Muslim circles criticizing the anti-Muslim nature of the Family Code. Paradoxically, then, political entrepreneurs of the "majority" have under Senghor more often been in the position of asking the state for more recognition of its "forms of life" and institutionalization of its practices (religious holidays like Magal to be officially recognized, Wolof language to be co-officialized with French) than minorities.[70]

Senghor stubbornly stuck to a policy of de jure "equal respect" so that any move toward giving more rights to the majority (whether the Muslim or Wolof-speaking majority) were followed with equivalent ones for the minorities.[71] That is how we can understand his insistence on religion, rather than Islam per se, and cultural patrias, rather than the Wolof ethnicity per se. As a result of this equal respect policy, by sticking to French language and to *laïcité*, however redefined in a more friendly way, Senghor managed to frame the debates in a three player game (the state, the majority, the minorities) rather than a two-player binary zero-sum game (majority holding the state against minorities). The Catholic minority has remained active in the state apparatus,[72] especially in the school system. As a result, despite a dynamic Islamo-Wolof homogenization process in society,[73] religious and cultural "minorities" have usually found in the state apparatus an ally more than an enemy.

At the same time, the state did not alienate the dominant groups in Senegalese society by applying a policy of de facto "proportionate equidistance." Beyond official "equal respect," the Senegalese state does pay attention to numerical weight: the Wolof marker in politics is indeed a dominant one, and the two main Sufi orders symbolized by the cities of Touba and Tivaouane are incomparably more important than Poponguine in politics. From Senghorian times to nowadays, the crafting of the government, while never acknowledged as such, does take into account criteria such as ethnicity and religion, so that at least one Catholic or one Joola, for instance, is part of the government, which shows equal respect but also their relatively marginal role.[74] One also has concrete examples of this "proportionate equidistance" in assessing the size of state delegations to religious festivals or to the *journées culturelles* in the *terroirs*. The size and quality of the delegation typically give rise to comments and serve to assess the level of consideration by the state, together with the level of state funding and media coverage. The event is also the perfect occasion for the groups involved to voice claims (more time for the language on national radio and television channels, more sons of the region appointed ministers, more funding given to the religious or cultural group, more attention paid to the religious ceremonies of the brotherhood). Whether it is for religious or cultural ceremonies, delegations of state officials are expected to publicly display the state's respect for the local culture or religious group. But respect and consideration work both ways. The community organizing its own cultural festival recognizes the legitimacy of the state and the insertion of the community in the wider framework of the nation, making the celebration of one's parochialism fit in the official state-backed nationalist paradigm just as the religious group recognizes the legitimacy of the secular state during its ceremonies.[75]

Breach in Equidistance?

"Proportionate equidistance" is not always easy, but it is the cornerstone of the Senegalese pattern of relation between the state and religious or cultural groups. The word *equidistance* is the one that constantly emerged in interviews as the only legitimate script for state policies in managing pluralism. Significantly, criticism of recent evolution in this domain under President Wade relies on the argument of equidistance, describing what is felt as breaches in equidistance. Typically, his ostentatious affiliation to the Muriddiya and its political manipulation have not been criticized, at grassroots levels, in French republican style for a breach in separation between state and religion—a dangerous departure from *laïcité* mixing the temporal and the spiritual—but for a violation of equidistance and fairness.[76] Wade is not criticized for his apparent religiosity but for his supposed "favoritism" toward the Murids.[77] Likewise, a statement by President Wade in 2001 in which he said that the government would "promote literacy of civil servants in Wolof" sparked off fierce debate. The president had to issue a statement the following day and put the blame on the forgetful journalist: the president had meant "in Wolof *and the other langues nationales*," but the French journalist had only written down "Wolof."[78] Like the highly politicized official marks of support by the state to various brotherhood subgroups, the language debate is a good example of the difficulties for the state to be equidistant from equally recognized and dignified languages as well as proportionate to their relative numerical weight when concrete decisions are to be made.[79]

Conclusion: Informal Accommodation and Its Limits

Despite its theoretical justifications and its ritualized features, the policy of equal respect has not been properly institutionalized. Rather, it amounts to informal consociational *practice* and *spirit* in the backyard of the republican state. By "consociational spirit" we mean something different from Arend Lijphart's definition of consociationalism,[80] which implies some degree of institutionalization and formal procedures, as well as recognized legal autonomy of communities. This is not the case in Senegal, where all these consociational practices are absent from the constitution and the legal framework.[81] Are we able yet to properly theorize situations and models where informality seems to be the way choices are made concerning the parameters of national identity and secularism? This may not be theoretically satisfying: what are the guidelines for implementing "proportional equidistance," which in fact amounts to a series of de facto choices made in the shadows? Fuzziness always proves hospitable to domination, while fairness requires clear rules. However, it could be argued to the contrary that the informality of this set of practices is the key to its resilience and adaptation, as mutual accommodations and political compromises are constantly reworked. In this fluid setting, neither definite conclusions nor definitive count can be made by stakeholders. As a result, some potential conflicts and bitter polarization are certainly avoided. Still, one can ask oneself who is actually participating in these informal compromises, since such matters often do not give rise to public debates.

Moreover, in the absence of formal rules for this loosely defined "proportional equidistance," no tools to measure its violations are provided nor is the voicing of claims from disadvantaged groups always guaranteed.[82] The conflict in Casamance is a case in point. The discourse of autochthony and cultural reinvention of *terroir* that one can find in all regions and among all communities in Senegal turned political in this southern region in the 1980s for many reasons.[83] One major line of the moral argument by supporters of the MFDC was to invoke the lack of respect and consideration from northerners representing the state toward Casamançais people and especially Joola. This discourse included all other grievances (social, economic, administrative, educational) in a convenient claim: "lack of consideration." Confronted with such grievances and the guerrilla of the MFDC, the Senegalese state resorted to an array of responses: military, patronage, and cooptation, but also to a symbolic policy to rebind Casamance to the rest of Senegal. New marks of respect and symbolic gestures of consideration for Casamance and the Joola *terroirs* were necessary for the state to try and regain its legitimacy affected by the war against the MFDC.[84] It has also been argued that the conflict has somehow enabled the Joola to "earn respect" from the state and the rest of the population.[85] The conflict in Casamance (and one could add many other examples) seems to show that, despite official discourses of "equal respect" by the state, respect from the state is never automatically granted but earned, and that—and in this respect Senegal is no exception—considerable conflict can emerge as a result of perceptions of not being respected equally. But it also shows that the state is still the strongest actor in the game, the one that sets the rules and decides the boundary between what is open for discussion and what is not. CIRCOF members promoting a revision of the Family Code and MFDC members fighting for independence have learned it at their expense.

Notes

1. I wish to thank Mamadou Diouf and Alfred Stepan for inviting me to participate in this project, and Vincent Foucher for his valuable comments. This study is based on my fieldwork in Senegal between 2003 and 2007 for my PhD dissertation on intercommunity relations and joking kinships in Senegal.
2. See Hesseling, *Histoire politique du Sénégal*; Diouf, *Sénégal, les ethnies et la nation*; Villalón, *Islamic Society*, pp. 43–60; Cruise O'Brien, "The Shadow Politics of Wolofisation"; Cruise O'Brien, Diop, and Diouf, *La construction de l'Etat au Sénégal*; Gellar, *Democracy in Senegal*, pp. 124–139.
3. Cruise O'Brien, Diop, and Diouf, *La construction*.
4. "Ethnicity" is understood here as emic labels that individuals use to make statements about themselves in terms of belonging and cultural origin or to classify others in daily life, whether it is based on patronymics, language, genealogy, or even physical features. Ordinary essentialisms crystallized in those stereotypes do not preclude flexible processes of identifications and creative plays on these labels.
5. I borrow this oxymoron from Ndiaye, "Une minorité confessionnelle," p. 612.
6. The notions of "proportionate equidistance" and "equal respect" in Senegal are not without analogies with India. However, as Rajeev Bhargava has argued, "principled distance" and "equal respect" in India's distinctive model of secularism allow for further state intervention within the realm of religion, including reform of religious practice or implementation of

antidiscrimination measures. See Bhargava, "What Is Secularism For?" For the notion of "rituals of respect," see Stepan, "Rituals of Respect: Sufis and Secularists in Senegal."

7. Of course, there are important differences too: the degree of institutionalization, the economic and political clout, and the levels of attendance at the gathering of the brotherhoods are incomparably higher than those of cultural associations and (neo)traditional institutions of the *terroirs*.

8. Cruise O'Brien, "Le sens de l'état au Sénégal."

9. Cruise O'Brien, *The Mourides of Senegal*; Copans, *Les marabouts de l'arachide*; Coulon, *Le marabout et le prince*; Diouf, "L'administration Sénégalaise"; Villalón, *Islamic Society*; Searing, "*God Alone Is King*"; Cruise O'Brien, *Symbolic Confrontations*; Robinson, *Paths of Accommodation*; Babou, *Fighting the Greater Jihad*; Diouf and Leichtman, *New Perspectives*.

10. Ndiaye, *L'éthique ceddo*; Diouf, *Histoire du Sénégal: Le modèle Islamo-Wolof*.

11. See Coulon, "The Grand Magal in Touba." On the dynamism of political/religious movements in recent years see Audrain, "Du 'ndigël avorté'"; Samson, *Les marabouts de l'Islam politique*; and Havard, "Le 'phénomène' Cheikh Bethio Thioune." On reformism in postcolonial Senegal, see Loimeier, "Dialectics of Religion and Politics in Senegal."

12. The survey ($n = 338$) was conducted in March 2006 in Dakar and its suburbs. The capital was chosen in order to avoid close connection to a locality or a single community. The sample was built using quotas (age, ethnicity, religion, education, gender, and occupation) in order to fit the stratification of the diverse population of the Dakar region. Despite these guidelines, and because of the relatively small scale of the sample and the descriptive statistics approach chosen, the results should not be generalized by inference to the population of the Dakar region as a whole. More details about the survey can be found in Smith, *Des arts de faire société*.

13. The classification in three spheres was not built into the question but emerged in the analysis of the results. It is somewhat arbitrary as some religious leaders can also be described as heroes of cultural patrias, but I chose to privilege their religious dimension here. Ideally, this survey should be repeated over time in order to avoid conjunctural bias (i.e., a cultural event celebrating a character a few days before the survey). But more than the actual ranking, what is interesting here is the fact that heroes from the three spheres figure in the top list.

14. Heroes that were quoted less than ten times (2.96 percent) are not presented in this table. The following heroes were also quoted, with scores between 3 percent (ten quotations) and 1 percent (three quotations): Blaise Diagne, Samory Touré, Sane Mone Faye, Koli Tengella Ba, Alpha Molo Balde,

Mamadou Lamine Dramé, Abdou Diouf, "tirailleurs," Ndiadiane Ndiaye, Amari Ngone Sobel Fall, Meissa Wali Dione, Serigne Saliou Mbacké, Abdoul Aziz Sy Dabakh, Saidou Nourou Tall, Abdoulaye Wade, Fodé Kaba Doumbouya, Cheikh Ibra Fall, Galandou Diouf, and the "femmes de Nder."

15. In its history school programs, the Senegalese state has popularized some if these heroes (Lat Dior, Amadu Bamba, Alboury Ndiaye, El Hadj Omar, and, since the conflict in Casamance, Aline Sitoe Diatta who remarkably comes third). One also notices the total absence of "colonial figures" such as Faidherbe, for instance, which the Senghorian state had celebrated.

16. For 96.7 percent of respondents, relations between communities in Senegal are very good/good/rather good, and for 3.3 percent rather bad/bad/very bad. This result is significant even if we take into consideration the conformist tendency to give a positive reply and the Senegalese pervasive nationalist discourse that declares good intercommunity relations a matter of national pride.

17. The question was, "If very good/good/rather good, in your opinion, what is the main reason?"

18. Of the respondents, 68.9 percent replied *yes* to the question "Is Senegal different from other African countries?", 11 percent replied *no*, and 20.1 percent replied *I have no idea*.

19. In the survey, questions were also asked on affiliation to Sufi orders, the use of political *ndiggël*, and on membership in religious associations (*dahira*) and secular associations, but the results cannot be developed here.

20. Robinson, *Muslim Societies*.

21. See Diarra and Fougeyrollas, *Relations interraciales*; Fougeyrollas, *Où va le Sénégal?*, pp. 56–68; and my survey on stereotypes among schoolchildren in Guediawaye (July 2003) in Smith, *Des arts de faire société*, pp. 808–815.

22. On the intersection of ethnicity and religion, see, for instance, Villalón, *Islamic Society*; Searing, "'No Kings, No Lords, No Slaves'"; Ngaïde, "Les marabouts face à la 'modernité'"; Marut, "Les particularismes"; Foucher, "Church and Nation"; Dramé, "Migration, Marriage and Ethnicity."

23. When cleavages do seem to be mutually reinforcing at the local level, e.g., over land issues, it is quite remarkable that this polarization does not scale up to the national level. For instance, the struggle around the "ranch Dolly," offered to the Khalife Générale of the Murids by President Wade, has pitted Haalpulaar Tijan herders against Wolof Murid farmers at the local level, but has not led to the emergence of such a cleavage nationally. It could also be argued that the conflict in Casamance has not scaled up also because no nationwide polarization allowed for it. For a discussion of similar dynamics in southwest Nigeria of crosscutting cleavages and the reasons for the

nonpolitization of religion *within* Yoruba communities, see Laitin, *Hegemony and Culture*.

24. Back in 1990, Peter Ekeh famously lamented that the study of kinship had run out of fashion in studies of African postcolonial politics; see Ekeh, "Social Anthropology." For studies in Senegal demonstrating the importance of kinship and political imagination in local political arenas, see Schmitz, "Un politologue chez les marabouts"; Van Hoven, *L'oncle maternel est roi*; Dahou, *Entre parenté et politique*; and Galvan, *The State Must Be Our Master of Fire*.

25. For reports on Poponguine or Fadiouth, for instance, see "Une famille, deux religions," *Le Soleil*, October 23, 2001; "Sénégal," *Syfia International*, September 1, 2001. In Fadhiout and in at least one location in Ziguinchor, Muslims and Christians are buried in a common cemetery.

26. Vengroff, Creevey, and Ndoye, "Islamic Leaders," table 2. I am grateful to Alfred Stepan for this document.

27. Of course, one can always argue that statements on tolerance are biased because of political correctness or the wish to give a good image of oneself and one's country, but it is the comparative ranking between categories that is interesting.

28. For instance, the Serer and Haalpulaar, the Serer and Joola, the Laobe and the Moors, the Fulbe and the Jakhanke, the Fulbe and the Balant, and the Fulbe and Smiths are joking partners. The alliances are known as *kal* and *gàmmu* in Wolof, *dendiraagu* in Pulaar, *maasir* in Serer, *kallengooraxu* in Soninke, *sanaawuyaa* in western Mandinka, and *agelor* in Joola (Fogny). Cf. Smith, *Des arts de faire société*, 69–90. For a review of recent work on joking kinships in West Africa, see Canut and Smith, "Pactes." Joking behavior is by no means automatic. It is up to the individual to choose to practice "joking kinship" with his interlocutor, and to his interlocutor to accept or contest this "frame" for the interaction. See Launay, "Practical Joking"; Fouéré, *Les relations à plaisanteries en Afrique (Tanzanie)*; and Smith, *Des arts de faire société*.

29. For an overview of the old functionalist argument and recent attempts at revamping it, see Smith, *Des arts de faire société*, pp. 93–98, 730–762.

30. Smith, *Des arts de faire société*, pp. 347–396. In my survey, although 57 percent of respondents stated that the *kal* or *gàmmu* do resolve conflicts, only 18.2 percent of respondents recalled a conflict resolved by them or by somebody using the *kal* or *gàmmu* and were able to provide evidence.

31. The 2006 survey shows that in the sample, 17.9 percent practice it "everyday," 28.4 percent "often," 30.3 percent "sometimes," 11.7 percent "seldom," and 11.7 percent "never." For an analysis of these varying degrees and arts of practice, see Smith, *Des arts de faire société*, pp. 232–301.

Religious and Cultural Pluralism in Senegal

32. See Diarra and Fougeyrollas, *Relations*, p. 264; Fougeyrollas, *Où va le Sénégal?* p. 56.
33. Villalón found that Tukulor and Joola administrators enjoyed much better relationships with the predominantly Serer population of the Fatick region—because of the joking kinships between these groups—than their Wolof counterparts. See Villalón, *Islamic Society*, p. 54. See also Galvan, "Joking Kinship"; and De Jong, "A Joking Nation." The same argument has been provided about Serer administrators in Casamance. See Smith, *Des arts de faire société*, pp. 503–548, for a discussion of these arguments.
34. Smith, *Des arts de faire société*, pp. 162–228; and Smith, "La nation 'par le côté.'"
35. The relation between the Murid and Tijan leadership is often described as a subtle joking relationship, for the patronyms Sy and Mbacke are *kal* and the founders Al Haj Malik Sy and Shaykh Amadu Bamba have indeed some kinship ties.
36. Michael Walzer, in a completely different context, has insightfully stressed the fact that "low altitude" or horizontal universalisms can stem from local parochialisms and not only from an a priori "high altitude" philosophical universalism "from above." For him the "low altitude" universalism is more open to pluralism than the "high altitude" one: its "vision of peace" not only "includes others," it also accepts the "alterity of the other." See Walzer, "Universalismes et valeurs juives" and "Les deux universalismes." For an interpretation of joking kinships in this vein, see Smith, "Les cousinages de plaisanterie."
37. Diagne, *Comment philosopher en Islam?*
38. On this expression, originally coined by Homi Bhabba, but used in the Senegalese context as referring to nonelite cosmopolitanism, see Diouf, "The Senegalese Murid Trade Diaspora." For a review of the different meanings associated with this concept, see Werbner, "Vernacular Cosmopolitanism."
39. "Poponguine: Clochers et minarets en parfaite harmonie," *Le Soleil*, October 23, 2001.
40. Senghor, *Ce que je crois*, pp. 10–16.
41. Abdou Diouf once said that, on handing over power to him, Senghor told him he was anxious that this succession might be seen as a succession from a Serer to a Serer (because of President Diouf's patronym, traditionally associated with the Serer), and that it is why he presented himself, from the start, as a mixture of groups. Conference by Abdou Diouf, IEP Paris, January 23, 2004.
42. In a political speech in 1961 in his own Serer *terroir* of Sine, Senghor told his audience "il n'y a pas de patrie sans terroir. La nation se nourrit des sucs

et des sèves du terroir. Enracinement donc, mais nécessaire dépassement. C'est une chance pour moi d'avoir échappé à cette pureté, à cette solitude du sang, puisque je suis né au croisement des sangs serer, peul et malinké. Grâce à Dieu, des centaines de milliers de Sénégalais ont eu le même sort heureux d'être des métis des races Sénégalaises." CD, *Senghor itinéraire d'un chef d'etat*, RFI, 1993, track 6.

43. Of course, replies to this question do not say anything about actual votes, but they do shed light on the legitimacy or illegitimacy of certain "minority" traits. Other traits included Tukulor (80.8 percent), Peul (74.6 percent), Joola (73.7 percent), Casamançais (73.4 percent), Mandinka (71 percent), Soninke (67.8 percent). As we see, ethnicity or religion does not seem to be too critical as long as the candidate can speak Wolof (and French).

44. On Senghor's intellectual formation and political thought, see Hymans, *Léopold Sédar Senghor: An Intellectual Biography*; Vaillant, *Black, French and African*; and Diagne, *Léopold Sédar Senghor*.

45. Senghor, *Liberté 2*, p. 107. Senghor wrote that "I opted for the left-wing about 1930. It was the year that I lost my Catholic faith." Cf. Hymans, *Léopold Sédar Senghor*, p. 263. Criticizing the French Catholic bourgeois in the 1930s for having forgotten the ideal of social justice, and criticizing Marxism in the 1950s for having forgotten God and fallen into materialism, Senghor logically reconciled his positions by proclaiming to be a *"socialiste croyant"* and to be the heir of the ethical trend of French socialism.

46. Senghor, *Liberté 1*, p. 55.

47. Senghor, *Nation et voie Africaine du socialisme*, p. 69.

48. Senghor, *Liberté 2*, p. 107. Mamadou Dia said in a similar vein: "The USSR managed to build a socialist society, but at the expense of religion, of soul." Quoted approvingly by Senghor, *Nation et voie Africaine du socialisme*, p. 67.

49. "If the Nation brings the *patries* together, it is to transcend them. The Nation is not like the *patrie*, a product of natural determinations, hence expression of the environment, but will of construction (. . .) It is the state which realises the will of the Nation and guarantees its permanence . . . it tosses the patrias and remoulds the individuals into the archetype." Senghor, Ibid., pp. 23–24.

50. Senghor preferred the words *patrie, province, pays, terroir*, or *race* to that of *ethnie*. He equated the precolonial kingdoms of West Africa, and later "ethnies," to the *provinces* of France. See, for instance, Senghor, *Liberté 1*, p. 46, and Senghor, *Nation et voie Africaine du socialisme*.

51. Ibid., p. 23.

52. Ibid., p. 25. In the same text, he significantly warns against two diseases of the state: *assimilation* and *imperialism* (Ibid., p. 24). In his famous conference of 1937 in Dakar, "*Le problème culturel en AOF*," he had already laid the justifications for bilingualism and criticized excesses of assimilation. See Senghor, *Liberté 1*, pp. 11–21.
53. See Hymans, *Léopold Sédar Senghor: An Intellectual Biography*, pp. 25–32, for the importance of Barrès and Mistral on Senghor in his early years in France. Hymans argues that this provincial and neo-traditionalist moment was crucial to Senghor's conceptualisation of *Negritude*, but also of messianic provincial patriotism. Later made compatible with socialism and the modernisation project, this intellectual moment seems to have immunized Senghor against full-blown Jacobinism. See also Vaillant, *Black, French and African*, p. 105.
54. For the argument that Senghor and many Senegalese cultural entrepreneurs of the *terroirs* are heirs to the ideology of "*petites patries*" of the French Third Republic, see Smith, *Des arts de faire société*, pp. 679–705.
55. In fact, Senghor himself often dealt with the two issues simultaneously, as if he wanted to show that his views on those issues were coherent. See Senghor, *Nation et voie africaine*, pp. 41–69 where he starts with the nation and finishes with religion, and Senghor, *Liberté 1*, pp. 304–307 where he deals with religion but finishes with nation.
56. See Diouf, "The French Colonial Policy"; Wilder, *The French Imperial Nation-State*.
57. I am focusing here on Senghor's views that were finally implemented, but one should not forget that there were many alternatives possible at the time, such as the political project of Mamadou Dia or the views of Cheikh Anta Diop.
58. As seen, the Senegalese constitution, since 1963, forbids political parties to identify with any religion, race, ethnic group, or language. During the presidential electoral campaign of February 2007, this article was summoned at least twice to censor some TV spots by opposition candidates allegedly calling to their fellow ethnics to vote for them. But the constitution has not prevented religious parties from being officially recognized in recent years, which shows that the state has a much tougher hand on ethnocultural claims than religious ones. However, these religious political parties performed poorly in the 2000, 2001, and 2007 elections.
59. On Senghor's passion for local historiographies, see Smith, "Merging Ethno-Histories in Senegal." On his deliberate use of joking alliances with his Joola, Peul, or Toucouleur audiences, and the legacy of this effective blackmail, see Smith, *Des arts de faire société*, pp. 403–441.

60. From 2001 to 2005, Hassaniya, Balant, Mankañ, None, Manjak, Bedik, Bassari, Baynuk, and Safi have been codified, bringing the number of *langues nationales* temporarily to fifteen, all constitutionally on an equal footing.
61. Although the constitution of 2001 states that *"Toutes les institutions, publiques ou privées, ont le devoir d'alphabétiser leurs membres et de participer à l'effort national d'alphabétisation dans l'une des langues nationales"* (*Constitution de la République du Sénégal* du janvier 7, 2001, article 22), this remains wishful thinking.
62. See articles 1 and article 24 of the 1963 constitution.
63. "It's here the occasion to denounce (. . .) the confusion (. . .) between *laïcité* and *laïcisme*: between the *laïcité* of a Jules Ferry, which was neutrality, thus respect for beliefs, all beliefs, and *laïcisme* (. . .) which is now only a means of electoral propaganda" (Senghor, *Liberté* 2, p. 106); "'Laïcité,' for us, is neither atheism nor anti-religious propaganda. I give as just one piece of evidence the articles of the Constitution that guarantee the autonomy of religious communities. Our Constitution goes further; it turns these religious communities into auxiliaries of the state in its education task, its cultural task. For religion is an essential part of Culture" (Senghor, *Liberté* 1, p. 422).
64. Cruise O'Brien, "Towards an 'Islamic Policy'"; Harrison, *France and Islam in West Africa*; Diouf, "The French Colonial Policy"; Robinson, *Paths of Accommodation*; and Grandhomme, "La politique musulmane de la France au Sénégal (1936–1964)."
65. Senghor, interview, 1980.
66. Farba Senghor, Minister of Agriculture, *Walfadjri*, April 28, 2003.
67. Taylor, *Multiculturalisme: Différence et démocratie*.
68. Interviews in Guediawaye, Summer 2003 and Fall 2004. Abbé Jacques Seck, for instance, officially celebrates how the dynamism of Islam in Senegal encourages the Christian minority to practice more (*Sud Quotidien*, March 27, 2003).
69. For a long time more Catholic than Muslim ceremonies were recognized as official holidays, although Catholics are only a 5 percent minority.
70. Most non-Wolof cultural activists or public figures interviewed staunchly rejected the word *minority*, finding it derogatory, and argued that together, *minorities* constitute a majority. They also preferred the word *respect* or *consideration* to that of *tolerance*, for respect and consideration are not conditioned to numerical weight and imply dignity, while tolerance ascribes a passive status to both the group that is *tolerated* and the group that *tolerates*. Interviews with Babacar Sedikh Diouf, Théodore Ndiaye, Martin Faye, Abba Diatta, Cheikh Hamidou Kane, Yero Doro Diallo, Nouha Cissé (2004), Abbé Diamacoune Senghor, Bertrand Diamacoune (2005), and Abbé Jacques Seck

(2006). For a similar argument about India that *respect* and *equal respect* mean much more than just *tolerance* or basic secularism, see Bhargava, *The Promise of India's Secular Democracy.*

71. Linguistic policy is a clear example of this. Senghor refused to favor Wolof at the expense of other languages, and when forced to make concessions to his critics—and also because he came to realize that the future of the Serer language could be at risk—he made sure to include other languages. For instance, on October 10, 1975, two decrees of codification were issued, one for Wolof *and* one for Serer, the one for Serer being in fact the first (n°75-1025), and Wolof the second (n°75-1026) . . . Cf. Dumont, *Le Français et les langues Africaines au Sénégal,* p. 267. Senghor used to list the *langues nationales* alphabetically, thus putting Wolof at the end, and kept downplaying its numerical dominance, insisting rather on the richness and numerical importance of Pulaar. See Senghor, "Préface," p. 13.

72. Despite being the staunchest supporter of *laïcité*, the mainstream of the Catholic minority does not call for further secularization of society or for religion to be confined to the private sphere. On the contrary, it claims the necessity to be active in society, socially, morally, and politically. Interviews with René Ndoye (2003), Théodore Ndiaye (2004), and Abbé Jacques Seck (2006). On this, see Ndiaye, "Une minorité confessionnelle."

73. On Wolofization see Swigart, "Cultural Creolisation"; Ndiaye, *L'éthique ceddo*; Cruise O'Brien, "The Shadow Politics of Wolofisation"; McLaughlin, "Dakar Wolof"; Dreyfus and Juillard, *Le plurilinguisme au Sénégal*; and Smith, "La nationalisation par le bas."

74. In fact, this informal but careful equilibrium is cast in the more acceptable language of regional cooptation and patronage. This is a sensitive issue, for when one region is absent from the government, the political clientèle of this region can react vehemently.

75. On the magal, see Coulon, "The Grand Magal"; on *journées culturelles*, see De Jong, "Politicians of the Sacred Grove"; Smith, *Des arts de faire société*, pp. 625–632.

76. See Kane, "La république couchée," for a good example of such a reaction by intellectuals. This is not to say that the separation of religion and politics is not formulated by ordinary (nonelite) citizens. In my 2006 survey in Dakar, the practice of political *ndiggël* was deemed negative by 62 percent of respondents and positive by only 10 percent (and 27 percent did not declare themselves). The most often provided justification for the negative answer was this sentence in Wolof: *"diine ak politik du benn"* ("politics and religion are different," literally "politics and religion are not one"). This type of statement testifies to the "mutual space giving" of religion and political institutions that

Alfred Stepan calls "twin tolerations." See Stepan, "The World's Religious Systems and Democracy: Crafting the 'Twin Tolerations.'"

77. In the 2007 presidential election, Wade significantly lost in the cities of Tivaouane and Medina Baye, strongholds of the Tijanniya, whilst he got an overwhelming majority in Touba. For a discussion of the new relationship between the state and Touba under Wade, see Gervasoni and Gueye, "La confrérie mouride."

78. "Wolofisation de l'administration: La présidence met en cause RFI," *Walfadjri*, June 19, 2001.

79. In some ways, the Wade presidency highlighted some of the important differences in the accommodation of religious and cultural pluralism. Controversies about the nature of the relations between the state and the brotherhoods, as well as sporadic tensions between brotherhoods, though nothing new, are on the increase. Conversely, the issue of cultural separatism seems to be receding as the Casamance rebellion has failed. For more developments on this issue, see Smith, "Le pluralisme Sénégalais."

80. Lijphart, *The Politics of Accommodation*.

81. The constitution never lists the religious orders or the "components" of the nation mentioned in the preamble. The well-entrenched collaboration with Sufi orders appears nowhere in the constitution, and neither does the informal accommodation with the traditional institutions of the Lebu community, for instance.

82. Especially given the hegemonic ideology of *maasla* (polite silencing of conflicts), and *jamm* (peace), sometimes at all cost.

83. See Faye, "L'instrumentalisation de l'histoire"; Lambert, "Violence and the War of Words"; Foucher, "Les 'évolués,' la migration, l'école"; Marut, "Le problème casamançais est-il soluble dans l'état-nation?"; Diouf, "Between Ethnic Memories"; and Awenengo-Dalberto, "Les Joola, la Casamance et l'état (1890–2004)."

84. I refer here to such initiatives as the rehabilitation of Joola heroine Aline Sitoe Diatta and other Joola figures and the reinvention of joking pacts between the Joola and Serer. See De Jong, "A Joking Nation"; Awenengo-Dalberto, "Les Joola," pp. 447–452; and Smith, *Des arts de faire société*, pp. 555–619.

85. Pierre Atepa Goudiaby, for instance, argued that "Thanks to our brave fighters, before one used to say '*kii joola rekk la*' [he's 'only' a Joola], now one says '*kii joola de!*' [he's a Joola!! (positive)]" (my translation and spelling). See *Le Soleil*, December 11, 2004, quoted by Awenengo-Dalberto, "Les Joola," p. 503.

Religious and Cultural Pluralism in Senegal

Bibliography

Audrain, Xavier. "Du 'ndigël avorté' au Parti de la Vérité. Evolution du rapport religion/politique à travers leparcours de Cheikh Modou Kara (1999–2004)." *Politique Africaine* 96 (2004): 99–118.

Awenengo-Dalberto, Séverine. "Les Joola, la Casamance et l'état (1890–2004). L'identisation joola au Sénégal." Thèse de doctorat, histoire, Université Paris-VII, 2005.

Babou, Cheikh Anta. *Fighting the Greater Jihad: Amadu Bamba and the Founding of the Muridiyya of Senegal 1853–1913.* Athens: Ohio University Press, 2007.

Bhargava, Rajeev. "What Is Secularism For?" In *Secularism and Its Critics*, ed. Rajeev Bhargava, 486–542. Oxford: Oxford University Press, 2004.

_____. *The Promise of India's Secular Democracy.* Oxford: Oxford University Press, 2010.

Canut, Cécile and Etienne Smith. "Pactes, alliances et plaisanteries: Pratiques locales, discours global." *Cahiers d'Etudes Africaines* 184 (2006): 687–754.

Copans, Jean. *Les marabouts de l'arachide.* Paris: Le Sycomore, 1980.

Coulon, Christian. *Le marabout et le prince: Islam et pouvoir au Sénégal.* Paris: Pédone, 1981.

_____. "The Grand Magal in Touba: A Religious Festival of the Mouride Brotherhood of Senegal." *African Affairs* 98 (1999): 195–210.

Cruise O'Brien, Donal B. "Towards an 'Islamic Policy' in French West Africa." *Journal of African History* 8 (1967): 303–316.

_____. *The Mourides of Senegal: The Political and Economic Organization of an Islamic Brotherhood.* Oxford: Clarendon Press, 1971.

_____. "The Shadow Politics of Wolofisation." *Journal of Modern African Studies* 36 (1) (1998): 25–46.

_____. "Le sens de l'etat au Sénégal." In *Le Sénégal contemporain*, ed. M. C. Diop, 501–506. Paris: Karthala, 2002.

_____. *Symbolic Confrontations: Muslims Imagining the State in Africa.* London: Hurst, 2003.

Cruise O'Brien, Donal B., Momar Coumba Diop, and Mamadou Diouf. *La construction de l'état au Sénégal.* Paris: Karthala, 2003.

Dahou, Tarik. *Entre parenté et politique: Développement et clientélisme dans le Delta du Sénégal.* Paris: Karthala, 2004.

De Jong, Ferdinand. "Politicians of the Sacred Grove: Citizenship and Ethnicity in Southern Senegal." *Africa* 72 (2) (2002): 203–220.

_____. "A Joking Nation: Conflict Resolution in Senegal." *Canadian Journal of African Studies* 39 (2) (2005): 389–413.

Diagne, Souleymane Bachir. *Léopold Sédar Senghor, l'art Africain comme philosophie.* Paris: Riveneuve Editions, 2007.

———. *Comment philosopher en Islam?* Paris: Panama, 2008.

Diarra, Fatoumata and Pierre Fougeyrollas. *Relations interraciales et interethniques au Sénégal.* Dakar, Senegal: IFAN, 1969.

Diouf, Makhtar. *Sénégal, les ethnies et la nation.* Dakar, Senegal: NEAS, 1998.

Diouf, Mamadou. "L'administration Sénégalaise, les confréries religieuses et les paysanneries." *AfricaDevelopment* 27 (2) (1992): 65–87.

———. "The French Colonial Policy of Assimilation and the Civility of the *Originaires* of the Four Communes (Senegal): A Nineteenth Century Globalization Project." *Development and Change* 29 (1998): 671–696.

———. "The Senegalese Murid Trade Diaspora and the Making of a Vernacular Cosmopolitanism." *Public Culture* 12 (3) (2000): 679–702.

———. *Histoire du Sénégal: Le modèle Islamo-Wolof et ses périphéries.* Paris: Maisonneuve and Larose, 2001.

———. "Between Ethnic Memories and Colonial History in Senegal: The MFDC and the Struggle for Independence in Casamance." In *Ethnicity and Democracy in Africa*, eds. B. Berman, D. Eyoh, and W. Kymlicka, 218–239. Oxford: James Currey, 2004.

Diouf, Mamadou and Mara Leichtman, eds. *New Perspectives on Islam in Senegal.* New York: Palgrave Macmillan, 2009.

Dramé, Aly. "Migration, Marriage and Ethnicity: The Early Development of Islam in Precolonial Middle Casamance." In *New Perspectives on Islam in Senegal*, eds. M. Diouf and M. Leichtman, 169–188. New York: Palgrave Macmillan, 2009.

Dreyfus, Martine and Caroline Juillard. *Le plurilinguisme au Sénégal: Langues et identités en devenir.* Paris: Karthala, 2004.

Dumont, Pierre. *Le Français et les langues Africaines au Sénégal.* Paris: Karthala, 1983.

Ekeh, Peter. "Social Anthropology and Two Contrasting Uses of Tribalism in Africa." *Comparative Studies in Society and History* 32 (4) (1990): 660–700.

Faye, Ousseynou. "L'instrumentalisation de l'histoire et de l'ethnicité dans le discours séparatiste en Basse Casamance (Sénégal)." *Africa Spectrum* 29 (1) (1994): 65–77.

Foucher, Vincent. "Les 'évolués,' la migration, l'école: Pour une nouvelle interprétation du nationalisme Casamançais." In *Le Sénégal contemporain*, ed. M.-C Diop, 375–424. Paris:,Karthala, 2002.

———. "Church and Nation: The Catholic Contribution to War and Peace in Casamance (Senegal)." *Le Fait missionnaire: Missions et sciences sociales* 13 (2003): 7–40.

Fouéré, Marie-Aude. *Les relations à plaisanteries en Afrique (Tanzanie): Discours savants et pratiques locales.* Paris: L'Harmattan, 2008.

Fougeyrollas, Pierre. *Où va le Sénégal? Analyse spectrale d'une nation Africaine.* Paris: Anthropos, 1970.

Galvan, Dennis. *"The State Must Be Our Master of Fire": How Peasants Craft Culturally Sustainable Development in Senegal.* Berkeley: University of California Press, 2004.

———. "Joking Kinship as a Syncretic Institution." *Cahiers d'Etudes Africaines* 184 (2006): 809–834.

Gellar, Sheldon. *Democracy in Senegal: Tocquevillian Analytics in Africa.* London: Macmillan, 2005.

Gervasoni, Olivia and Cheikh Gueye. "La confrérie mouride au centre de la vie politique Sénégalaise: Le "Sopi" inaugure-t-il un nouveau paradigme?" In *L'Islam politique au sud du Sahara,* ed. Muriel Gomez-Perez, 621–639. Paris: Karthala, 2005.

Grandhomme, Helene. "La politique musulmane de la France au Sénégal (1936–1964)." *Canadian Journal of African Studies* 38 (2) (2004): 237–278.

Harrison, Christopher. *France and Islam in West Africa, 1860–1960.* Cambridge, Mass.: Cambridge University Press, 1988.

Havard, Jean-François. "Le 'phénomène' Cheikh Bethio Thioune et le djihad migratoire des étudiants Sénégalais 'Thiantakones.'" In *Les voyages du développement,* eds. F. Adelkhah and J. F. Bayart, 309–336. Paris: Karthala, 2007.

Hesseling, Gerti. *Histoire politique du Sénégal.* Paris: Karthala, 1985.

Hymans, Jacques-Louis. *Léopold Sédar Senghor: An Intellectual Biography.* Edinburgh: Edinburgh University Press, 1971.

Kane, Ousseynou. "La république couchée." *Walfadjri,* May 8, 2000.

Laitin, David. *Hegemony and Culture: Politics and Religious Change Among the Yoruba.* Chicago: University of Chicago Press, 1986.

Lambert, Michael. "Violence and the War of Words: Ethnicity vs. Nationalism in the Casamance." *Africa* 68 (4) (1998): 585–602.

Launay, Robert. "Practical Joking." *Cahiers d'Etudes Africaines* 184 (2006): 795–808.

Lijphart, Arend. *The Politics of Accommodation: Pluralism and Democracy in the Netherlands.* Berkeley: University of California, 1968.

Loimeier, Roman. "Dialectics of Religion and Politics in Senegal." In *New Perspectives on Islam in Senegal,* eds. M. Diouf and M. Leichtman, 237–256. New York: Palgrave Macmillan, 2009.

Marut, Jean Claude. "Les particularismes au risque de l'Islam dans le conflit Casamançais." In *L'Afrique politique,* 147–160 Paris: Karthala, 2002.

———. "Le problème Casamançais est-il soluble dans l'état-nation?" In *Le Sénégal contemporain,* ed. M.-C. Diop, 425–458. Paris: Karthala, 2002.

McLaughlin, Fiona. "Dakar Wolof and the Configuration of an Urban Identity." *Journal of African Cultural Studies* 14 (2) (2001): 153–172.

Ndiaye, Augustin Simmel. "Une minorité confessionnelle dans l'etat laïc. Point de vue d'un chrétien." In *Le Sénégal contemporain,* ed. Momar-Coumba Diop, 601–616. Paris: Karthala, 2002.

Ndiaye, Malick. *L'éthique ceddo et la société d'accaparement ou les conduites culturelles des Sénégalais d'aujourd'hui*. Dakar, Senegal: P.U.D, t. 1, *Le Goorgi*, 1996, t. 2, *Les Moodu Moodu*, 1998.

Ngaïde, Abderrahmane. "Les marabouts face à la 'modernité.' Le *dental* de Madina Gounass à l'épreuve." In *Le Sénégal contemporain*, ed. M. C. Diop, 617–652. Paris: Karthala, 2002.

Robinson, David. *Paths of Accommodation: Muslim Societies and French Colonial Authorities in Senegal and Mauritania, 1880–1920*. Athens: Ohio University Press, 2000.

_____. *Muslim Societies in African History*. Cambridge, Mass.: Cambridge University Press, 2004.

Samson, Fabienne. *Les marabouts de l'Islam politique: Le Dahiratoul Moustarchidina Wal Moustarchidaty un mouvement néo-confrérique Sénégalais*. Paris: Karthala, 2005.

Schmitz, Jean. "Un politologue chez les marabouts." *Cahiers d'Etudes Africaines* 23 (1983): 329–351.

Searing, James. *"God Alone Is King": Islam and Emancipation in Senegal. The Wolof Kingdoms of Kajoor and Bawol, 1859–1914*. Oxford: James Currey, 2002.

_____. "'No Kings, No Lords, No Slaves': Ethnicity and Religion Among the Sereer-Safen of Western Baol, 1700–1914." *Journal of African History* 43 (2002): 407–430.

Senghor, Léopold Sédar. *Nation et voie Africaine du socialisme*. Paris: Présence Africaine, 1961.

_____. *Liberté 1: Négritude et humanisme*. Paris: Seuil, 1964.

_____. *Liberté 2: Nation et voie Africaine du socialisme*. Paris: Seuil, 1971.

_____. Interview, in *Ethiopiques* (January 1980): 5–11.

_____. "Préface" in P. Dumont, *Le Français et les langues Africaines au Sénégal*. Paris: Karthala, 1983, 7–20.

_____. *Ce que je crois*. Paris: Grasset, 1988.

Smith, Etienne. "Les cousinages de plaisanterie en Afrique de l'Ouest, entre particularismes et universalismes." *Raisons Politiques* 13 (2004) : 157–169.

_____. "La nation 'par le côté': Politique des cousinages au Sénégal." *Cahiers d'Etudes Africaines* 184 (2006): 907–965.

_____. "Merging Ethno-Histories in Senegal: Whose Moral Community?" In *Recasting the Past: History Writing and Political Work in Twentieth Century Africa*, eds. D. Peterson and G. Macola, 213–232. Athens: Ohio University Press, 2009.

_____. "La nationalisation par le bas, un nationalisme banal? Le cas de la Wolofisation au Sénégal." *Raisons Politiques* 37 (2010): 65–77.

_____. *Des arts de faire société: Parentés à plaisanteries et constructions identitaires en Afrique de l'Ouest (Sénégal)*. Thèse de doctorat de science politique, Institut d'Etudes Politiques de Paris, 2010.

_____. "Le pluralisme Sénégalais à l'épreuve de la Wolofisation: Quel avenir pour le modèle Islamo-Wolof dans le Sénégal post-alternance?" In *Le Sénégal de Wade*, ed. Vincent Foucher. Paris: Karthala, forthcoming 2012.

Stepan, Alfred. "The World's Religious Systems and Democracy: Crafting the 'Twin Tolerations.'" In *Arguing Comparative Politics*, 213–255. Oxford and New York: Oxford University Press, 2001.

_____. "Rituals of Respect: Sufis and Secularists in Senegal." *Comparative Politics* (forthcoming 2012).

Swigart, Leigh. "Cultural Creolisation and Language Use in Post-Colonial Africa: The Case of Senegal." *Africa* 64 (2) (1994): 175–189.

Taylor, Charles. *Multiculturalisme: Différence et démocratie*. Paris: Champs-Flammarion, 1997.

Vaillant, Janet. *Black, French and African: A Life of Léopold Sédar Senghor*. Cambridge, Mass.: Harvard University Press, 1990.

Van Hoven, Eduard. *L'oncle maternel est roi: La formation d'alliances hiérarchiques chez les Mandingues du Wuli (Sénégal)*. Leyde: CNWS, Université de Leyde, 1995.

Vengroff, Richard, Lucy Creevey, and Abdou Ndoye. "Islamic Leaders' Values and the Transition to Democracy: The Case of Senegal." Unpublished manuscript, University of Connecticut, 2005.

Villalón, Leonardo A. *Islamic Society and State Power in Senegal, Disciples and Citizens in Fatick*. Cambridge, Mass.: Cambridge University Press, 1995.

Walzer, Michael. "Les deux universalismes." *Esprit* 187 (1992): 114–133.

_____. "Universalisme et valeurs juives." *Raisons Politiques* 7 (2002): 53–78.

Werbner, Pnina. "Vernacular Cosmopolitanism." *Theory, Culture & Society* 23 (2-3) (2006): 96–98.

Wilder, Gary. *The French Imperial Nation-State: Negritude and Colonial Humanism Between the Two World Wars*. Chicago: Chicago University Press, 2005.

[8]

Islam, the "*Originaires*," and the Making of Public Space in a Colonial City

Saint-Louis of Senegal[1]

MAMADOU DIOUF

This chapter examines the formation of a social group, the nineteenth- and twentieth-century Muslim traders from Saint-Louis of Senegal, by reconstructing the biography of one its prominent members, Hamet Gora Diop. The group was a moral community with a civic culture that drew not only on Islamic religious resources but on the political, economic, and social rights conferred on them by their citizen status as *originaires*.[2] By constantly making claims based on their citizenship rights, they initiated a twofold process, inserting themselves in the colonial narrative and fabricating a world of their own through a daily engagement with colonial policy and knowledge as well as with traditional moral and social prescriptions.

It is certainly not easy to explore the individual history of each member of the *doomu ndaar* community.[3] However, their professional and philanthropic activities, as well as the economy and management of their respective households, provide precise indications of their cultural, economic, and political characters and the social networks they put in place. The symbols, the myths, the rituals, the infrastructures, and the spaces and places with which they were associated have produced an urban civility with various manifestations. This civility borrowed proudly from three sources: the Senegambian traditions, especially Wolof and Halpulaar; the religious, aesthetic, and erotic library and imaginary of the Moors, which

Islam, the "*Originaires*," and the Making of Public Space in a Colonial City

ensured a connection with the North African, Egyptian, and Middle Eastern Arabic and Muslim literary world; and, finally, the administrative, political, and institutional resources of the Senegalese colony. By collaborating with the colonial administration, and adeptly using French legislation and their civil rights,[4] they managed to create an autonomous civic space for themselves. Educated in the arts and sciences as well as the Islamic court system, they also had perfect knowledge of the arcane colonial administrative system and a mastery of the professional rules that governed commercial activities.[5] Their very respectable level of education predisposed them to an active participation in the moral, theological, and political debates that outlined the civic[6] and political culture of both the Senegalese colony and Saint-Louis civil society.[7] Their imagination,[8] supported by a scriptural and literary Islamic modernity, submitted the hegemonic pretensions of the colony's civilizing mission to regular criticism. It introduced a civility made from a multiplicity of heritages, whose core remains, without contest, an Arab and Muslim textuality.[9] In some way, they had the dexterity to outline a native and Wolof version of assimilation through a series of operations creating hybrid and vernacular versions of Islamic, colonial, Moor, and Senegambian libraries.

The Arabic script was simultaneously the instrument of protest and reassessment of French cultural authority and of affirmation of their individual and collective identity. The paradox is that this constant and stubborn quest for an autonomous identity, antagonistic to the status of native—a status given by the colonial ethnographic classificatory system—demanded either total assimilation to or exclusion from the French colonial public space. Compared to the French metropolitan citizens established in the Senegalese colony, the *originaires* of Saint-Louis were natives and citizens whose identity was strongly determined by the administrative, political, and economic grammar of the French colonial empire. Such an identity exists and expresses itself through three written expressions: professional, religious, and intellectual. The first and second can be found in the development of a culture of petition writing to protect the commercial interests of local traders against the colonial administration and the merchants, and the third is present in the philanthropic activities and religious discussions that constituted the community's main avenues for public expression.

To sketch the portrait of Hamet Gora Diop, placing him in the precise context of the second half of the nineteenth and twentieth centuries, several archives were consulted and compared to the works of researchers.[10]

They are H. G. Diop's accounting records from 1882 to 1908, rescued by the family,[11] and the oral traditions of both the family and the Senegalese Sufi brotherhoods. In addition, the biographies, life stories, and studies of the commerce and economic success of traders during the colonial period were examined.[12]

The oral traditions concerning H. G. Diop come from three sites of memory: the religious brotherhoods, the family, and the griots. The first, kept up by the Sufi marabouts, remembers the pious man and his religious charity, his gifts and acts of philanthropy toward the poor and toward Muslim institutions (mosques and Qur'anic schools), in particular. In addition, it celebrates the richness of his personal library and the role that the books he owned played in the intellectual and religious education of marabouts such as Al Hadj Malick Sy, the founder of the Tijanyya zawiya of Tivaouane, and Amadu Bamba Mbacke from the Muridiyya brotherhood. The family memories dwell on his pilgrimages to Mecca, his piety, and especially his charitable works for the poor and marginalized of Saint-Louis and Médine, in Upper Senegal. The griots' memories magnify his social works and the help he constantly brought to the poor, individually and collectively.

The three memories reveal as much about the forms and formulas of mental representations of an era as they do about the material bases that support them. They allow us to sketch the contours of the community of Saint-Louis professional traders and to uncover their way of life and socialization. They furnish the keys to understanding the cultural and historical formations constructed by the elite of Saint-Louis through their daily engagement with colonial ethnography, politics, and Senegambian social and moral traditions.

The Murid and Tijaan oral traditions tie the name of H. G. Diop to the founders of the two brotherhoods as a philanthropist. He participated financially and materially in their agendas, especially in the construction of religious institutions (mosques and Qur'anic schools). He also lent them the books he frequently went to buy in Egypt and in Palestine. H. G. Diop's decisive intellectual and material contribution to the building of the Senegalese Sufi brotherhoods is conceded in their respective memories and historical narratives through a paradoxical operation that domesticates and subordinates the literate Muslim community of Saint-Louis to the dominant narrative of Senegalese Islamization, *Islam Noir* (Black Islam). While the former spirituality permanently compromises the rules and procedures of colonial political and cultural governance and the religious and erotic oriental libraries of Mauritania, North Africa, and Egypt, it stubbornly refuses the transactions instituted by the Sufi brotherhoods' rule of submission to the marabouts. Majestically intellectual and lettered, this spirituality survives still in the religious celebrations and ceremonies organized by the descendants of H. G. Diop in the Minbaar mosque, and in which all the religious brotherhoods of Senegal participate. This spirituality, formulated and put into action, declares a universal, scriptural, and literary religious modernity. Disdainful of native transactions, it fiercely faced the metropolitan and Christian facets of the colonial society. By inscribing it in a secondary position, the brotherhood's oral traditions regarding H. G. Diop cut that spirituality off from both its social identity and the singularity of its spiritual trajectory in order to conceal the urban, lettered, and colonial aspects of Senegalese Islam. On the other hand, the oral traditions directly generated by his social and religious interventions unearth a very Islamic culture and a doctrinal mode of spirituality—defined by readings and commentaries of texts both situated in opposition to the local Sufi religiosity, which was profoundly rooted in the repertoires of saints, of holy places, and of interventions and miraculous intercessions.

Places of Trade and Religious Frontiers

The commercial space in which Hamet Gora Diop operated was circumscribed by two poles: Saint-Louis to the west, where the River Senegal opened onto the Atlantic Ocean, and Médine, in Khasso, at the confluence of the rivers Senegal and Kolombiné. Saint-Louis was at the center of the colonial space, dominating the economy of the Senegal River Valley. Trade was the main activity of the town, from its beginnings in 1650. Trade networks, products, and procedures changed considerably from the foundation of Saint-Louis to the early twentieth century. Traces of those various changes are still visible in the topography of the town.[13] The second pole of the commercial geography is the Upper Senegal region, with Médine at its center, a fluvial port from which Hamet Gora Diop wove his trade network.

The economic history of Saint-Louis is divided into two eras. French companies that held a monopoly on trade dominated the first era, from the founding of the town to approximately the end of the eighteenth century. The Africans and the Métis were often, in this framework, employees of the companies.[14] Economic liberalism characterized the second era, which started after 1780. Saint-Louis trade is divided into three spheres controlled by three socioprofessional groups: the merchants, the "natives," and the administrators. This "tripartite"[15] would be at the origin of the very tense relationships between European merchants and traders (African or Métis), with regard to their respective places in the commercial colonial framework. In 1854, as Faidherbe became governor of Senegal, these quarrels shook the colony.[16]

The dawning of the Faidherbian regime imprinted a new rhythm onto the economic, political, and social trajectories, following the defeat of El Hajj Oumar in the Upper River and the progressive institution of the French military and trade machine along the Senegal River. This new conjuncture announced "the French Islamic policy" (*la politique Musulmane Française*) by a restructuring of *l'école des Otages* (the school of chiefs' sons) copied from the Algerian model (1856), the installation of Islamic courts (1857), and the distribution of grants to Saint-Louis Muslims so they could make the pilgrimage to Mecca (1860–1861). These policies "gave some legitimacy to Muslims who operated within the French sphere."[17] Even better, it diverted them from joining the Senegambian Muslim leaders fighting French colonial expansion by including them in the colonial project. The French Muslim policy provided the Saint-Louis Muslims a solid basis for playing the role of indispensable intermediaries both in the political and commercial relations with the hinterlands as well as in the elaboration of the colony's economic strategies.[18]

Two distinct periods are identified in the Upper Senegal River economy of the nineteenth century. The first was especially marked by the Umarian jihad and its consequences on the entire region. The struggles between the Al Hajj Umar Tall troops and the anti-jihadists, locals allied with the French, had brought about the collapse of the region's economy, the quasi-generalized[19] abandonment of agricultural activities and a generalized famine.[20] The only group "who did not suffer significantly were the members of the St. Louisian commercial community. They often acquired new dependents in the crisis as [the] 1862 deposition about pawning attests."[21] H. G. Diop's father was probably one of those beneficiaries.

The rapid growth of the trade economy that characterizes the second half of the nineteenth century is reflected in the reports of the colonial residents of Bakel and Médine and in the creation of colonial military and fiscal administrations in the region. In 1879, the colonial administration, to ensure better conditions for their expansion toward the Sudan, began a policy of public works to complete the consolidation of their establishments.[22] Their commercial influence, assured of a solid base, projected itself on a hinterland that was still under the control of the *Toucouleur* empire of Amadu Sheikhu.

This quick sketch of the economic geography of the region where Hamet Gora Diop ran his trade operations shows that the commercial space in Upper Senegal is an important crossroad of trade routes, hence its attractiveness for the Saint-Louis trade community and merchants. However, it seems that, despite the favorable context, the traders did not know the same success they enjoyed in the first half of the nineteenth century.[23]

The rapid development of trade observed in the second half of the nineteenth century is reflected in official correspondence.[24] The opening of the Niger route had generally benefited the colony's commerce, and had benefited even more the "naturals established between the Senegal and the Niger."[25] This opinion contrasts strongly with the president of the Saint-Louis Chamber of Commerce's observation, noting the trader's difficult situation with regard to the new economic circumstances—a constantly deteriorating environment recognized by the Saint-Louis traders, notably in their petitions.[26] It is in this difficult context for Saint-Louis traders, however, that Hamet Gora Diop attained his commercial success, at a moment when colonial trade had almost definitely reoriented itself toward the west, with the progressive emergence of the peanut production region in Western Senegambia. This displacement has been wrongly interpreted by almost all authors as the result of the trading crisis in the River Valley, particularly that of Arabic gum, whose terms of trade with the "guinea cloth" brought about the ruin of several traders.[27] The Toucouleur Empire's control of economic routes in the north and south, the linking of the Jula to the colonial trading network, and the western orientation of the Amadou state were not perceived as alternative networks.

By filling this new gap, H. G. Diop was able to at once avoid the fate of his principal colleagues in the old networks and at the same time maximize his profits by diversifying his trading activities. The new economic geography corresponds to a spiritual geography bounded by the Berber and Moor marabouts from Qaddiriyya (in the north), Halpulaar from Tijaniyya (in the east), and further toward the east, the mythical horizon of Egyptian-Islamic letters.

The interweaving of these two geographies illuminates the Saint-Louis trajectory and the Islamic and trade theories and practices that dominated the landscape of the colonial city.[28]

Hamet Gora Diop: Biography of a Trader and Notable Saint-Louis Citizen

H. G. Diop was born in Saint-Louis in 1846 to Gora Diop Fabineta and Tabara Ameth Seck.[29] It is not easy to reconstruct in a precise manner the genealogical family tree, but it is possible to retrace the social and familial context in which he was immersed his entire life. The available genealogical tree tell us Demba Diop was the first generation, father of Gaura Diop Fabineta (1807–1877) in the second generation, who is the father of H. G. Diop (third generation).[30] The grandfather is attributed with the role of founding ancestor of the Diop family. Was he the first in his family to have attained public notoriety by becoming a *doomu ndaar* or the first in his family to reside in Saint-Louis, at the end of the eighteenth century? It is difficult to answer those two questions. The information about Demba Diop is not very precise. The Diop may have come from the province of Kokki, in the kingdom of Kajoor. The Kokki province gained a reputation very early as a stronghold of the Senegambian Muslim community as much for the educational role as for the political and sometimes military role played by certain marabouts.[31] The accounts of family life provide, however, two pieces of very valuable information: Gaura Fabineta's membership in the "Most respected 'Important' Muslim families" and his closeness to the colonial administration.[32]

By favoring a double geography, Senegambian and colonial, and giving to each a strong Islamic spirituality, the *doomu ndaar* community provided itself with a way to erase the singularities attached to the diversity of the places of origin of its members. It could, in this way, compose an identity and culture distinct from these places and from the sources and resources strongly tied to stories, places, and multiple historical circumstances. Islam and the Wolof language were the main means of production of the forms, languages, and alternative versions of religiosity. The space of elaboration was the neighborhood of Sindoné, in the southern part of the island of Saint-Louis largely dominated by Christians, and the Métis in particular.

The father's notoriety and his unquestionable belonging to the *doomu ndaar* community is confirmed by the role he played in the religious and professional education of his son, as well as in the building of his networks of matrimonial alliances, friendship, and business. The community to which the father belonged was structured around two circles: the first was that of the Muslim community whose members constituted the leadership of the commercial and economic networks. The second was that of the Christian Métis living in the same neighborhood in the south of Saint-Louis.

The first circle was that of the *doomu ndaar*. Gaura Fabineta, erudite Muslim, belonged to the generation that had benefited from the Faidherbian Muslim policy, inspired by the Algerian model. Allied with the colonial bureaucracy, he was able to move into trading operations and to accumulate a small amount of capital, thanks to the metropolitan French and Metis colonial firms' trust. Gaura Fabineta participated actively in the networks of the Moor Muslim cleric Sheikh Saad Buh's (1850/51–1917)[33] Qaddiriyya branch, who had established his *zawiya* in Nimzat in the 1880s and of Sheikh Siddiyya al Kébir (1780–1868) and his grandson Sheikh Siddiyya Baba who began to impose himself on the political scene in the beginning of the 1880s until his death in 1924. With him, Boutlimit's *zawiya* became the center of a powerful coalition that regrouped his Moor and Saint-Louis disciples on the one hand and the French colonial administration's agents on the other.[34] Sheikh Saad Buh, recognized authority on the *fiqh* (Islamic law) and the initiation to Sufism, rejected the holy war and violence with an extraordinary steadfastness. That same rejection is also found in his regular correspondence (starting in 1867) with the Saint-Louis Muslim community as well as with the colonial authorities whom he visited often in Saint-Louis starting in 1872. To the first group, he offered his religious expertise and his spiritual powers, and to the second, his authority within the Muslim community. By building himself a powerful network of influence between 1870 and 1880, he constructed for himself an incontrovertible position of economic, political, and religious mediator.[35] Gaura Fabineta was a regular in Saad Buh's circles and one of his correspondents, but he was even closer to Sheikh Siddiya al Kébir and his grandson Siddiyya Baaba.[36] Like Saad Buh, Siddiyya al Kébir was hostile to holy war and ready to work with the colonial administration. He had managed to make Boutlimit the center of a powerful education, intermediation, and trade network, attracting, like the rival network, a large number of students from Saint-Louis. Siddiyya Baba continued his grandfather's work by reinforcing relationships with the colonial administration through frequent visits to Saint-Louis, starting in the 1890s.[37]

The second circle was that of the Métis. This group was strongly represented in the southern neighborhood of the island, where certain *doomu ndaar* families were established and with whom they constituted the "native" community. In this second circle, Gaura Fabineta belonged to the Devès network, originally headed by Gaspard and then by his son Justin, beginning in the year 1875. Gaspard Devès was Gaura Fabineta's partner[38] and Justin Devès was H. G. Diop's.[39] The power of the Gaspard Devès network and the support he garnered from the Muslim community of Saint-Louis is attested to by his election as mayor of Saint-Louis (1875–1880) and the leadership positions he held both at the Chamber of Commerce and in the General Council of Senegal.

The *doomu ndaar* were tightly linked to the Métis with whom they shared the same economic interests, hostility toward French merchants, and a public declaration of their indigenous French identity, that of *originaires*. Some of them, among the most influential, lived in the Sindoné, in the southern sector of the island mainly occupied by the Catholic *originaires* and the agents of the colonial administration.[40]

Constant association and negotiation with the Métis, as well as the support of the colonial administration, had constituted the two most solid pillars of the processes of accumulation and education of the *doomu ndaar* society of Saint-Louis. Leaning against a Christian space whose center was the Catholic Church in Saint-Louis, its members had managed to obtain the construction of a mosque in the northern sector of the island, in which they were the majority, all the while creating a public and private Islamic space in the southern neighborhood. They bought residential buildings for their families and dependents and attempted, in most cases with success, to establish mosques and philanthropic institutions to display, at the heart of the colonial space, their mode of religiosity and civility. This was the case for H. G. Diop with the Minbaar mosque. The neighborhood of Sindoné had become the site of a constant reassembling of several ethnic peculiarities, such as the numerous variations of Wolof, Halpulaar, *Soninke*, Moor, and *Manding* cultures. The Wolof language, the Islamic literary, philosophical, and erotic imagination, the tradition of petition writing and civic and citizen actions, and the imperial theories and practices had ended up reconfiguring these cultures into a unique identity. Thus, in this crossroads, was formed a personal subjectivity, strongly religious, whose history is not yet written. If we trust the testimonial collected by Moussa Diop, "the Sindoné neighborhood (South) became the incontestable bastion of an Arabo-Muslim intelligentsia renowned throughout the country. There they taught mathematics, astronomy, literature, versification and other scientific disciplines. Saint-Louis could validly vaunt itself on being the city of

Islam, the "*Originaires*," and the Making of Public Space in a Colonial City

knowledge, the center of erudition, the high place of Islamic culture that received the badge of honor for having offered its generous hospitality to eminent Muslim clerics who had marked Senegalese religious life with an indelible seal."[41]

The *doomu ndaar* were not content to simply use the institutions put into place by the colonial administration. They constantly maneuvered to inscribe, on the colonial architecture, a modernity carried by a religious infrastructure (mosques, tribunals, philanthropic, and social works) and a universal language: Arabic, and two languages for communication, Wolof and, to a lesser degree, *Hassaniyya*. The search for institutions belonging to the group seems to have played a considerable role in the creation of their social identity by keeping a distance between the French colonial pole, essential to the creation of the difference with the Senegambians, and the Muslim and native Wolof pole, essential for establishing a distinction with other social groups in the colony, the French in particular. Gaura Fabineta was an influential member of this group that began, in the first half of the nineteenth century, to obtain an Islamic representation in colonial institutions, after having imposed the presence of Islam in the colonial space.

The *doomu ndaar* had participated in operations of assembly, hybridization, and alteration of available resources by configuring their own civic space (the mosque and the compounds of their leaders) to elaborate a civility that had very quickly imposed itself as one of the components of the colony's French imperial identity, in particular, after the Umarian episode, against the proponents of holy war. From 1860 to 1880, the issues that preoccupied the *doomu ndaar* were debated within the confines of the mosques, in particular, the Grande Mosquée Nord. During the course of these debates, the unfailing support of Hamet NDiaye Hann and Bou el Moghdad was put into question by certain members of the community. In the beginning of the twentieth century, many of their meetings were held in the complex of the Minbaar mosque, as in 1905, for example, when the Muslim and Métis leadership met on the issue of the restoration of the Islamic court, and in 1913 on the question of the citizen rights of *originaires*.[42] The incorporation of their own government institutions and idioms in the colonial governance infrastructure offered them the possibility of avoiding the authoritarian logic of the colonial administration. They were governed, and therefore represented in the colonial architecture, doubly—once by the recognition of their community institutions that offered them a political space for deliberation, which continuously shaped a Saint-Louis voice, and then by their constant recourse—which they did not hesitate to use—to colonial institutions to defend their interests.

Faidherbe's nomination to the position of governor of Senegal in 1854 and the testing of the theories and practices drawn from the French Islamic policy in Algeria played a decisive role in outlining the contours of the *doomu ndaar* community. All this was done to insist on the fact that both the colonial administrators as well as the colonial institutions played a central role in the development of new discourses and new practices as well as in the introduction of new religious, domestic, and public arts likely to help in the configuration of an indigenous autonomous modernity that participated fully in the colonial modernity.

In addition to Gaura Fabineta, the main leaders of the communities were all traders, colonial administration collaborators, and lettered Muslims.[43] They were all connected to the religious and economic networks of Sheikh Saad Buh and Sheikh Siddiyya and maintained tight relationships with the commercial milieu of the Métis. The name that crops up often is that of Hamet NDiaye Hann.[44] Renowned expert in Islamic sciences, Hamet NDiaye Hann's father, Ndiaye Hann, originally from the Fouta Toro, was the first to assert a moral leadership of the Saint-Louis Muslim community, with the title of *Tamsir* (Tafsir). His son inherited this function before becoming the main interpreter for the colonial administration. Other names follow: Bou El Moghdad Seck,[45] who replaced Hamet Ndiaye Hann in his role as principal interpreter of the colonial administration; Amadu Ndiaye Mabeey, one of the teachers of the future Al Hajj Malick Sy, founder of the Tijaan zawiya from Tivaouane; Massamba Jeery Dieng, from Kajoor, who had a reputation for great piety; and Alaji Kamara, who was the main Saint-Louis host of Amadu Bamba Mbacke, the future founder of the Murid brotherhood of Touba and his second initiator in the way of the Qaddiriyya. With other notables, they not only theorized the compatibility between Islam and French domination, they were the main promoters of the *doomu ndaar* 1843 petition requesting the institution of a Muslim court and recognition of the title of *Tamsir*. Arabic and Wolof languages, professional and political activities, and religious demonstrations and philanthropy became the expressions of an Islamic and colonial cosmopolitanism fed by the creation of a French and oriental library whose main sources are Egypt, the Middle East, and North Africa. General Faidherbe created the Muslim Tribunal in 1857 and the colonial administrative commission to organize pilgrimages to Mecca to fortify a strong Muslim mobilization against the Umarian propaganda. These creations guaranteed a permanent renewal of the philosophical, scientific, and theological resources of a library that kept fueling vigorous secular and religious debates and controversies. If NDiaye Hann was the first *Tamsir*, his son Hamet NDiaye Hann was named the first *qadi* of the newly installed Muslim tribunal. He kept his prerogatives as *Tamsir* but abandoned his role of main interpreter to Bou El Moghdad Seck. The former inaugurated the pilgrimages to Mecca organized by the French colonial administration and became the second *qadi* and *Tamsir* at the death of Hamet NDiaye Hann in 1879.

As actors interested in the definition of the nature of the Saint-Louis public sphere, the notables of Saint Louis attempted to subtract their domestic space from colonial intervention, all the while mobilizing to include it in the same Islamic civic cultural institutions, so as to exclude inheritance, the control of orphans, and civil status from the scope of republican law. The identification and organization of the theories and practices of this civic, Muslim-inspired, culture were governed by the desperate will of the *doomu ndaar* to defend their moral community by any means, including legal means, political mobilization, participation in elections, and petitions to the metropolitan and colonial administrations, at the crossroads of a French civility taken from the French Civil Code and the indigenous Islamic civility. This double move toward exclusion and inclusion places the civic community of the *doomu ndaar* in a fragile stability.

H. G. Diop grew up in this environment of disputation, negotiation, and (re)construction of the *doomu ndaar* community. Born in the Sindoné neighborhood, he was first initiated into the Qur'an by an erudite and notable Muslim father engaged in the discussions that shook his community in the first half of the nineteenth century. It is said in *La Biographie* that Gaura Fabineta's knowledge of books and the richness of his library had facilitated relationships of esteem and friendship with the Moor marabouts who had taken sides with the Senegalese colony, Sheikh Saad Buh, Sheikh Siddiyya al Kebir, and his grandson, Sheikh Siddiyya Baaba.[46] To complete his education, he joined the school of a disciple of Mor Massamba Jeery Dieng to perfect his mastery of the Qur'an and Arabic literature. He continued his courses by starting "theological studies taught by leading religious experts from Saint-Louis and Mauritania with a particular focus on religious sciences . . . mathematics and astronomy"[47]—among them, the *qadi* Hamet NDiaye Hann, Ndiaye Sarr, and Amadu Ndiaye Mabeey.

Islam, the "*Originaires*," and the Making of Public Space in a Colonial City

At the end of his studies, H. G. Diop began a trade career in the service of his father and at the same time joined the economic networks of the Devès as well as the religious networks of the Moor Sheikhs. His father's death was a turning point in his life. Shaped by the *doomu ndaar*'s civic community, he began to participate and contribute, in return, to the production and public display of their civic culture. Effectively, if the father had been part of the first generation of the Saint-Louis community that negotiated the civic, administrative, and political contours of the Senegalese colony with Faidherbe, it is H. G. Diop's generation that put to the test the signs of an identity that was being forged in the unstable compromise between religious belonging, indigenous cultural traditions, and the political economy of a colony in full expansion.

The Contours of a Culture and Civic Community

To measure H. G. Diop's fortune, the only elements we have are his real estate investments, his travels, and his philanthropic actions, all pieces that communicate his affluence. The affluence of a notable *doomu ndaar* was reflected as much in his real estate acquisitions as in his philanthropic interventions.[48]

H. G. Diop's charity work came from the same Islamic model as his commercial activities, a model for the notable person who has succeeded. He had gone several times on a pilgrimage to Mecca, visited Alexandria and Jerusalem, scrupulously respected his religious duties, and bought books to build up his library. He frequently received books and prayer beads from the three cities cited previously. This important library gained him the friendship of the marabouts, most significantly those from the large religious brotherhoods: Qaddiriyya, Sheikh Saad Buh, and Sheikh Siddiyya Baaba; Tijaan, El Hajj Malick Sy, and Murid; and Amadu Bamba Mbacke. Notable, rich, and pious, he consecrated a part of his fortune to building mosques, notably in Médine (The Little Mosque), in Saint-Louis (*Minebaar*), and contributed financially to the construction of the large mosques in Tivaouane and Touba, without forgetting to come to the aid of his religious leader friends.[49] In Rosso, his philanthropic actions were jointly the expression of a religious culture of sharing, charity, and obligation to the poor on the one hand, and of the munificence and generosity of the *doomu ndaar* in the "bush." He became renowned for his donations to the sick and handicapped, and during the drought that occurred in Mauritania in 1890 and the famine of 1903, he gave large donations of millet and money. He also decided to give an annual donation in cash to the Moor clerics on the eve of the month of Ramadan. In Saint-Louis, his philanthropy competed with the Christian and colonial interventions for the creation of a civic Saint-Louis culture and, within that culture, for locating Islamic institutions within the colonial public space. All the interventions, in Rosso, Médine, and Saint-Louis, became common knowledge in the western Sudanese region, circulating both in the commercial as well as religious networks and reinforcing H. G. Diop's reputation and respectability.

H. G. Diop's social interventions in Khasso, however, combined philanthropy with the construction of infrastructures to support his religious action. At the center of the large territory he occupied was *La Petite Mosquée*, whose prayer room floor and courtyard were covered with white sand that he had sent from Saint-Louis after the rainy season. He created Qur'anic schools tightly attached to the mosque and paid the fees for the instructors, who were sometimes imams.[50] In the heart of the religious compound, he had a well dug in order to supply water to the neighboring houses.

La Petite Mosquée and H. G. Diop's home held several functions: a place for religious education; for philosophical, theological, and political debates; and for settling any type of quarrel and for reinforcing cooperation between the members of the Muslim community. These places attracted famous western Sudanese experts in the various Islamic sciences and religious subject matter. The mosque was also the preferred place for business meetings, religious ceremonies, weddings, and funerals. Numerous Qur'an recitation sessions and introductions to the law or theology were organized there, particularly during the month of Ramadan. These attracted people from the entire region, all ethnicities combined.[51] Just as in Rosso, H. G. Diop's social activities were centered on helping the handicapped and the poor by providing gifts in cash and in kind, and interceding in domestic, ethnic, commercial, and religious disputes.[52]

H. G. Diop's economic, social, religious, and political activities at the mobile frontier of the French imperial expansion testify to a logic of domination of a space, a community, and a civic culture by Islam. He participated actively in the production of a transethnic and profoundly universalist and assimilationist Islam that was strongly inspired and commanded by a Saint-Louis civility characterized by munificence, grace, compassion, and an exceptional capacity for engagement with the diverse versions of Halpulaar, *Fulani, Manding,* Arab, and Moorish Islam—an Islam, in other words, that seemed to be engaged in a race to fill the void created by the colonial conquest.

In Saint-Louis, his hometown, he adroitly managed to build religious infrastructures to carry out his charity work and social actions, thereby taking the envied position of "one of the most prestigious benefactors of Islam . . . recognized protector of the oppressed, educator, mediator when needed and provider of asylum to the poor and the old."[53] The creation of the Minbaar religious compound seems to fall within the context of a competition with the Catholic and administrative formulas and the colonial policies of the civilizing mission.[54] The compound was "a fort that once belonged to *signares*.[55] Persuaded that in the evolution of Islam there could not be any historical monument more impressive than the mosque, he had one built in the vast courtyard of the fort. The structure of the edifice located in the residential neighborhood of the South, in Leybar Street (Bancal), far from the Christian zone, was composed of a prayer room, topped by a library that was the envy of all Saint-Louis, because of the variety and richness of its volumes"[56] and "a room decorated with Persian rugs and perfumed with incense imported from the Asian countries. It was in this room that the scholars passing through, as well as those from Saint-Louis, would debate theological questions until late at night."[57] Minbaar had become the meeting place for the notables of Saint-Louis and for the Muslim community, as much for the celebration of ceremonies specific to different sects and brotherhoods as for the common religious gatherings, as well as deliberations on political, economic, and social questions so as to form a common front against the colonial authorities. Even more so than the deliberations, the library encouraged meetings and debates.[58] Next to the mosque, still inside the fort, residential buildings were built to welcome the marabouts and religious dignitaries visiting Saint-Louis for the first time. To ensure the religious complex of Minbaar would be financially sustainable, H. G. Diop rented ten rooms in the building on Neuville Street to pay for the maintenance work, reparations, and property tax. He was at the service of the *doomu ndaar* civil community and wanted to ensure that the Muslims passing through were given a space as well as reasons for civility at the service of the expansion of a lettered and tolerant Islam, where the education of agents was conducted in an intellectual environment and in a tradition of debate and deliberations.

Islam, the "*Originaires*," and the Making of Public Space in a Colonial City

His support of the marabouts took the form of donations, loans of books, access to the Minbaar compound and the use of its facilities for ceremonies, commemorations, and religious debates. He also offered them financial and administrative assistance toward the acquisition of real estate, in the cases, for example, of Sheikh Thioro Mbacke, brother of Amadu Bamba; of Mamadou Ciss, a marabout related to Al Hajj Umar; and of Cheikh Buh Kunta, of the Qaddiriyya of Ndiassan branch; as well as toward the preparation for a pilgrimage to Mecca.[59] While he did not join the two brotherhoods, Tijaan and Murid—who saw, at the end of the nineteenth century, an increase in enrollment among the Wolof—he supported their expansion through cash and in-kind donations. His financial assistance for the construction of the big mosques at Tivaouane and Touba was constant and significant.

The relationship with the various brotherhoods, in particular the founders of the Tijaan and Murid, encouraged the birth, in Saint-Louis, of a civic Islamic space and the construction of a "ritual community"[60] that spread beyond the limits of the *doomu ndaar* community to encompass all the Muslims in the Senegambian region. The education and the gatherings owed much to the Minbaar religious compound. Sheikh Saad Buh and Sheikh Siddiyya stopped there to pray and to meet their peers and their disciples. Al Hajj Malick Sy was a regular there, and Amadu Bamba Mbacke came during his second stay in Saint-Louis in 1892, on his way to exile in 1895, and at his return from Mauritania in 1907. Both he and H. G. Diop, his brother's friend, were members of the powerful religious network of Sheikh Siddiyya Baaba. The story says that in order to foil the prohibition set on Al Hajj Malick Sy and his disciples from performing the *wazifa* (litanies and chants to glorify the Prophet) every night, he opened the doors of the mosque to them. Supposedly, the first celebration of the Prophet Muhammed's birthday (*Gàmmu*) was celebrated in the Minbaar complex.[61]

Hamet Gora Diop died in 1910, after accomplishing four pilgrimages to Mecca and ensuring the financial autonomy and sustainability of the most important legacy in his eyes, Minbaar. The religious complex was one of the most significant expressions of the *doomu ndaar* community and their civic culture that blossomed in the heart of the colonial space, in cooperation and competition with its political, economic, cultural, and sometimes religious ambitions. His biography follows rather perfectly the contours of the formation of the civic community to which he belonged.

Islam, the "*Originaires*," and the Making of Public Space in a Colonial City

The *doomu ndaar's* religious practices, style of life, and consumption evidenced the will to introduce a rhythm and an indigenous civility into the colonial modernity. Choosing as much the modes of their inclusion as those of their exclusion from colonial society and its activities, they buttressed themselves with their prerogatives and the defense of an Islamic identity. Their commercial success as well as their education—strongly rooted in a perfect mastery of Arabic, of one of its dialectical variants, the Moor *Hassaniyya*, of their soft and sensual intonations, and of their poetry—offered them universal and literary formulas linked to the Arab and Muslim world. They created for themselves a civic culture of deliberation. The encouragement of the colonial authorities and the search for a collective representation encouraged the development of a culture of petition writing and a systematic recourse to the rule of law, lawyers, and justice. The systematic search for representation and representativeness configured a public space whose contours were produced jointly by the colonial administration and the *doomu ndaar* notables.

Adding up their civic culture and moving away at the same time from the humanism and universalism of the enlightenment philosophy, they invested the public space with their liturgical chants; their Turkish, Moroccan, and Eastern-inspired clothes; their burnooses and incense; their matrimonial practices, particularly polygamy; and the regularity of their prayers—all of which resulted in the quasi-permanent occupancy of religious complexes. Thus emerged a Saint-Louis–style humanism that was essential in the colonial context to maintaining the civic community and its singular practices: its ceremonies and commemorations, its commemorative plaques written in golden Arabic letters, and its deliberations—both with respect to the colonial administration and to the Senegambian religious circles. The emblems were produced by matrimonial alliances; Islamic expertise; professional activities; a mastery of the Arabic script and language and religious literature; a strong participation in civic and civil activities demanded by the colonial and community authorities; and a civility that was reflected in the style of life, décor, and decoration of the body (particularly for women) and the type of life, dress, food, and ways of walking, feeling, and talking. Distinctively Saint-Louisian, the contours and grammar of the civic community were constantly reconfigured in the colonial town. The civic power of the *doomu ndaar*, essential to the construction and manifestation of their citizenship rights within their communities and in front of the colonial administration, rested on the clear

Islam, the "*Originaires*," and the Making of Public Space in a Colonial City

idea they had of their roles and their functions. The community was created, therefore, in the social actions and charity work i.e., the acts of generosity that established the notables as a reference and recourse in the face of the colonial administration. In competition with Christian philanthropy, the *doomu ndaar* notables imposed their civility as a pivotal organizing principle of the colonial society of Saint-Louis. The Abbé Boilat's violent recriminations and indictments of the small population of Catholics for appropriating not only their baptismal and marriage ceremonies but also Islamic amulets attest to this fact.[62]

Notes

1. A shorter and more condensed version of this chapter focusing on the biography of Hamet Gora Diop has been published in Dennis D. Cordell, ed., *The Human Tradition in Modern Africa*, New York: Rowman and Littlefield, 2011.
2. The *originaires* are also called the inhabitants. Although they received citizenship rights very early, including the right to vote, they consistently refused to submit themselves to the French Civil Code for religious reasons. They thereby were able to conserve their "particular status" by permanently reinforcing this religious identity. On this question, see Diouf, "The French Colonial Policy of Assimilation."
3. Literally the "children of Saint-Louis." This qualification is the autoportrait of the notables of Saint-Louis (the *doomu ndaar*).
4. On this distinct culture, see Le Châtelier, *L'Islam dans l'Afrique Occidentale*, chapter 4, in particular; and Abbé Boilat, *Esquisses Sénégalaises*.
5. Concerning the history of trade and the diasporas of trade, see the following works: Cohen, "Cultural Strategies"; Curtin, *Economic Change in Precolonial Africa*; and *Cross-Cultural Trade in World History*; Lovejoy, *Caravans of Kola*; and *Salt of the Desert Sun*.
6. This notion goes back to the historical approach to the definition of "civic culture—a set of orientations towards a specific set of social objects and processes," Almond and Verba, *The Civic Culture*, p. 12, and the particular characteristics of a "civic community"—"active participation in public affairs; equal rights and obligations for all; respect and trust between members; and, finally, the embodiment of these qualities in voluntary associations" (Putnam, *Making Democracy Work*, pp. 86–91) tested by Ruth Watson, *Civil Disorder Is the Disease of Ibadan*, questioning the origin and the development in time of norms and values covered by the two notions, pp. 3–4.

7. See Robinson, *Paths of Accommodation*, in particular chapters 5 and 6.
8. Hastings, *The Construction of Nationhood*, notably chapter 1.
9. The transcription of the Wolof language with Arabic characters and the genealogical reconstructions that tie the notable northern Senegambian Islamic families to those of the first Arab communities that joined the Prophet Muhammad are the best illustrations.
10. In addition to the studies already cited and the more general ones on the history of Senegal and Senegambia, I would like to mention Bathily's dissertation *Guerriers* (Vol. 2 in particular) and Robinson's *The Holy War of Umar Tal*, both of which focus on the region where H. G. Diop carried out his commercial activities.
11. I owe the remarkable work of indexing the names of people, places, and products mentioned in the H. G. Diop registers to my friendship with Makane Fall, whom I thank here.
12. Diop, E., *La Biographie de El Hadj Ameth Gora DIOP* is dated "Saint-Louis 1950" but seems to have been rewritten several times in the following twenty years.
13. For a description of the city, see Faidherbe, "Notice sur la colonie du Sénégal"; Durand, *Voyage au Sénégal*; Archives Nationales du Sénégal (ANS), "Correspondance de Huzzard à Portal"; and Rousseau, "Le site et les origines de Saint-Louis."
14. Lamiral, *L'Afrique et le peuple Africain*; Delcourt, *La France et les etablissements Français au Sénégal*; and Ly, *La compagnie du Sénégal*.
15. Marcson, "European-African Interactions."
16. On this subject, see Barrows, "General Faidherbe."
17. Robinson, *The Holy War of Umar Tal*, p. 215.
18. El Hadj Souleymane Diop, "Le difficile problème du commerce au Sénégal," Saint-Louis, n.d., p. 6. Only the outline and the first ten pages of the first chapter of the manuscript were recovered.
19. On this theme, Robinson, *The Holy War of Umar Tal*, pp. 239–240; Cissoko, "La guerre sainte umarienne dans le Khasso" (note 1), pp. 717–721; Cissoko, *Contribution à l'histoire politique du Khasso*, pp. 718–721; and Bathily, *Guerriers, tributaires et marchands*, Vol. 2, pp. 517–557.
20. Robinson, *The Holy War of Umar Tal*, pp. 239–241. See also Saint-Martin, *L'empire toucouleur*.
21. Ibid., p. 240.
22. Bathily, *Guerriers*.
23. Ibid., Vol. 2, p. 635; and Archives Nationales du Sénégal (ANS), 15G 6bis.
24. ANS, 15G 6 bis.
25. Ibid.
26. ANS, "Pétition à M. Léon D'Erneville"; "Pétition des traitants du Haut Fleuve"; and "Réclamation des traitants de Médine."

27. See particularly the articles by Pasquier and Robinson cited in this study.
28. Diop, I., *Les lumières d'une cité*, p. 104. The reference to the respect of Muslim rules in commercial practice elevated to the dignity of holy war would not pass unnoticed in the charged context of the last two decades of the nineteenth century, characterized by the transition from the military holy wars to the brotherhood's religious and political orientations. H. G. Diop distanced himself from these two approaches all the while participating in the Islamic reconstructions aimed at rebuilding the Wolof communities in the face of crises provoked by the ruin of the Western Senegambian kingdoms and the start of the French territorial conquests.
29. Diop, E., *Biographie* (p. 1), is precise on the year of birth. However, I. Diop, *Les lumières d'une cité*, is content to propose "around 1840," p. 89.
30. See Diop, I., *Les lumières d'une cité*, pp. 91 and 259, for the genealogical framework. It is interesting to note that in the text, the genealogical reference to the name refers to the first name of the mother for identification, Gaura Fabineta, illustrating the dominant matrilineal framework of Wolof kinship, whereas the genealogical framework uses the father's name, Gaura Demba, taking heed of the Muslim patrilineal rule for naming. This oscillation, perceptible throughout the text, reflects the diversity of oral sources and the periods considered. It seems that the first name composed of that chosen by the mother gives way to a composition that joins the father's name, probably at the end of the nineteenth century in Saint-Louis. This slip is an indication of the changing social rules in Saint-Louis.
31. On the education system, see Kâ, *L'enseignement Arabe au Sénégal*. It is interesting to note that the exhumation of this double Muslim and aristocratic origin has a precise function in the construction of respectability and reputation in an urban society that is, in the middle of the nineteenth century, a post-slavery society and whose Wolof and Halpulaar constituents are ethnicities structured around social inequality and political domination. This double origin from the Wolof provinces of Kajoor, Jolof, and from Waalo or Halpulaar in Fouta Toro seems to have been very sought after by notable Muslim families in Saint-Louis.
32. Diop I., *Les lumières d'une cité*, p. 90.
33. On Saad Buh, see Marty, "L'Emirat des Trarzas"; Hamès, "Shaykh Sa'ad Buh 1850–1917"; and on his biographical, political, economic, and religious work, see Robinson, *Paths of Accomodation*, pp. 178–193.
34. On Siddiya Babba, see also Robinson, *Paths of Accommodation*.
35. He would have played a primary role in the selection of the first *Tamsir* (leader of the Muslim community of Saint-Louis) and the first *qadi* (judge of the Muslim courts established in 1857), Hamet NDiaye Hann (1813–1879), and in the introduction of the family of Doudou Seck, known under the

name of Bou el Mogdad (1826–1880). He had become the main agent and interpreter for the colonial administration in the management of relationships with Senegambian kingdoms and the Moor tribes and the most active Muslim adversary of Al Hajj Umar Tall. Like Hamet NDiaye Hann whom he replaced in the position of interpreter in the colonial administration, when the former was named *qadi*, he had a perfect mastery of Arabic and of the Moor dialect, *Hassaniyya*.

36. Diop, I., *Les lumières d'une cité*, pp. 95–96.
37. Robinson, *Paths of Accommodation*, p. 182.
38. *Les lumières de Ndar* considers that the success of Gaspard Devès rested on the tightness of his relationships with the "best Muslim families on the island," the institution of a commercial network that depended on the "indigenous traders," the breadth of his activities, and his marriage to a *négresse*, the mother of his children, Hyacinthe and Justin, p. 96.
39. Still according to *Les lumières d'une cité*, Justin Devès, "merchant, lawyer and businessman, was of the generation of Ahmed Gaura," and the collaboration between the two men "ended up giving the two families a certain complicity," p. 97.
40. According to *Les lumières de Ndar*, "the first catholic missionaries chose, upon their arrival in Senegal, the southern neighborhood of the island to implant their first parish. Some Métis such as Devès, Carpot, Crespin, D'Erneville and some *signares* although Christianized and living in a community between the Place de l'Eglise and Repentigny Street (zone said to be *keur-thiane*, a distortion of the French word "chrétien") had stayed very attached to the dignitaries and Muslims of the south. However, in no case would they adventure themselves to go live in the sector included between Leybar Street (Bancal) and the southern point. This place was almost a sacred and protected territory. All of this corroborates the validity of a popular belief that says that a divine benediction was hidden somewhere in the famous neighborhood of Sindoné," pp. 90–91.
41. Ibid.
42. Robinson, *Paths of Accommodation*, pp. 130–136.
43. *Les lumières d'une cité* offers biographical sketches of (1) Mor Massemba Diery Dieng (1826–1900), who was educated at Kokki and in Mauritania and was the father-in-law of El Hajj Malick Sy and Amadu Bamba Mbacke; (2) Alaji Camara (1829–1889), who was born in Guinea, trained in the Islamic schools of Fouta Jallon, Kankan, and Timbuktu, initiated in the way of Qaddiriyya, and impregnated with esoterism and mysticism, settling definitively in Saint-Louis after living in many trading posts along the Senegal River; and (3) Qadi NDiaye Sarr (1822–1903), pp. 171–189.

44. See note 47 for a few biographical indications.
45. See note 48 for a few biographical indications. The family of Bou el Moghdad was originally from Waalo. He played a central role in the production of a library that fit in the colonial architecture and for which it became a support structure. This orientation, in a certain measure, explains the tonality of this Islam resolutely opposed to the "Black Islam" (Islam Noir).
46. Diop, E., *La biographie*, pp. 1–2.
47. Diop, I., *Les lumières d'une cité*, p. 94.
48. Diop, E., *La biographie*, p. 3.
49. This orientation is probably the explanation for the *doomu ndaar*'s interest in leaders of holy wars and the resistants to colonial rule in the western Sudan region of Amadou Sheikhou, Samory Touré, and Mamadou Lamin Drame to whom he may have provided direct or indirect assistance. Did he share their conviction that holy war was the appropriate way to expand Islam, only to change his mind after their failure and his return to Saint-Louis? This is, in any case, the position put forth by *Les lumières d'une cité*, p. 133.
50. Ibid. These imams had been recruited from all ethnic groups represented in the region: Halpulaar, *Fulani*, Moor, and *Manding*. H. G. Diop worked in this way to minimize the conflicts provoked by the ethnic diversity of the region by strongly advocating a shared Muslim identity.
51. Ibid., p. 129.
52. Ibid., p. 125.
53. Ibid., p. 140.
54. At least this is the position of the author of *Les lumières d'une cité*, p. 137.
55. *Signares* were African or Métis women who lived as concubines and had business relationships with the Europeans trading on the west Atlantic coast since the time of the Portuguese. Their business and sexual relationships are the origins of the Métis community. They had adopted at the same time the lifestyle and style of their partners, including their religious practices. See Boulègue, *Les Luso-Africains de Sénégambie*; Brooks, "The *Signares* of Saint-Louis and Gorée," pp. 14–44; and Brooks, *Eurafricans in Western Africa*.
56. Diop, I., *Les lumières d'une cité*, p. 137. The transformation of a *signare* compound into a Muslim compound represents an enlightening symbol of the competition to define the civic rule in Saint-Louis.
57. Ibid., p. 140.
58. Ibid., p. 138.
59. Ibid., p. 140.
60. Cohen, *Customs and Politics in Urban Africa*, the conclusion in particular.
61. Diop, I., *Les lumières d'une cité*, pp. 147–148.
62. Diouf, "The French Colonial Policy of Assimilation."

Bibliography

Almond, Gabriel and Sidney Verba. *The Civic Culture: Political Attitudes and Democracy in Five Nations*. London: Sage Publications, 1989.

Archives Nationales du Sénégal, "Correspondance de Huzzard à Portal: 1B6, 13 avril 1822."

———, "Pétition à M. Léon D'Erneville des traitants de Médine et Bakel, 27 septembre, 1885."

———, "Pétition des traitants du Haut Fleuve adressée au Gouverneur du Sénégal et dépendances, Saint-Louis, 26 décembre, 1892."

———, "Président de la Chambre de Commerce au Directeur de l'Intérieur Saint-Louis: 15G 6 bis, 11 décembre 11, 1885 (32)."

———, "Réclamation des traitants de Médine, 10 août, 1886."

Barrows, Leland. *General Faidherbe, the Maurel and Prom Company, and the French Expansion in Senegal*. PhD dissertation. Los Angeles: University of California Los Angeles, 1974.

Bathily, Abdoulaye. *Guerriers, tributaires et marchands*. Dakar, Senegal: Université de Dakar, 1985.

Boilat, Abbé David. *Esquisses Sénégalaises*. Paris: Karthala, 1853/1984.

Boulègue, J. *Les Luso-Africains de Sénégambie XV–XIXème siècle*. Dakar, Senegal: Département d'Histoire, Université de Dakar, 1972.

Brooks, George. "The *Signares* of Saint-Louis and Gorée: Women Entrepreneurs in Eighteenth-Century Senegal." In *Women in Africa: Studies in Social and Economic Change*, eds. N. J. Hafkin and E. G. Bay. Stanford, Calif.: Stanford University Press, 1976.

———. *Eurafricans in Western Africa: Commerce, Social Status, Gender, and Religious Observance from the Eighteenth Century*. Athens: Ohio University Press, 2003.

Cissoko, Sekene Mody. "La guerre sainte umarienne dans le Khasso." In *Mélanges offerts à Raymond Mauny. Le sol, la parole et L'ecrit*. Paris: Société Française d'Histoire d'Outre-mer, 1981.

———. *Contribution à l'histoire politique du Khasso dans le Haut Sénégal des origines à 1854*. Paris: L'Harmattan, 1986.

Cohen, Abner. "Cultural Strategies in the Organization of Trading Diasporas." In *The Development of Indigenous Trade and Markets in West Africa*, ed. C. Meillassoux. Oxford: Oxford University Press, 1972.

———. *Custom and Politics in Urban Africa: A Study of Hausa Migrants in Yoruba Towns*. Berkeley: University of California Press, 1969.

Curtin, Phillip. *Economic Change in Precolonial Africa, Senegambia in the Era of the Slave Trade*, Vol. 2. Madison: University of Wisconsin Press, 1975.

———. *Cross-Cultural Trade in World History*. Cambridge, Mass.: Cambridge University Press, 1984.
Delcourt, A. *La France et les etablissements Français au Sénégal entre 1713 et 1763*. Mémoire de l'IFAN n.17, Dakar, Senegal: IFAN, 1952.
Diop, El Hadj Souleymane. *La biographie de el Hadj Ameth Gora DIOP dit Ameth GUEYE Cheikh 1846–1910*. Dakar, Senegal, 1950.
———. "Le difficile problème du commerce." Saint Louis, n.d. Only the outline and the first ten pages of the manuscript were recovered.
Diop, Iba Amett. *Les lumières d'une cité: Ndar*. Dakar, Senegal: Presses Universitaires de Dakar, 2003.
Diouf, Mamadou. "The French Colonial Policy of Assimilation and the Civility of the *Originaires* of the Four Communes (Senegal): A Nineteenth Century Globalization Project." *Development and Change*, special issue 29 (4) (1998): 671–696; and in *Globalization and Identity: Dialectics of Flows and Closures*, eds. B. Meyer and P. Geschiere, 671–696. New York: Palgrave Macmillan, 2006.
Durand, L. Jean-Baptiste. *Voyage au Sénégal, 1785 et 1786*. 2 vols. Paris: H. Agasse, 1803.
Faidherbe, Louis L. "Notice sur la colonie du Sénégal," *Annuaire du Sénégal et Dépendances*. Saint-Louis: 1885.
Hamès, Constant. "Shaykh Sa'ad Buh 1850–1917," *Islam et sociétés au Sud du Sahara* 4 (1990): 133–136.
Hastings, Adrian. *The Construction of Nationhood: Ethnicity, Religion and Nationalism*. Cambridge, Mass.: Cambridge University Press, 1997.
Kâ, Thierno. *L'enseignement Arabe au Sénégal*. PhD dissertation. Paris: Université de Paris Sorbonne, 1982.
Lamiral, M. *L'Afrique et le peuple Africain considérés sous les rapports avec notre commerce et nos colonies*. Paris: Desseme, 1786.
Le Châtelier, Alfred. *L'Islam dans l'Afrique Occidentale*. Paris: G. Steinheil, 1899.
Lovejoy, Paul E. *Caravans of Kola: The Hausa Kola Trade 1700–1900*. Oxford: Oxford University Press, 1980.
———. *Salt of the Desert Sun: A History of Salt Production and Trade in the Central Sudan*. Cambridge, Mass.: Cambridge University Press, 1986.
Ly, A. *La compagnie du Sénégal de 1673 à 1696*. Paris: Présence Africaine, 1958.
Marcson, Michael D. *European-African Interactions in the Precolonial Period: Saint-Louis du Senegal*. PhD dissertation. Princeton, N.J.: University of Princeton, 1976.
Marty, Paul. *L'Emirat des Trarzas*. Paris: Leroux, 1919.
Putnam, Robert, D. *Making Democracy Work: Civic Traditions in Modern Italy*. Princeton, N.J.: University of Princeton Press, 1993.

Robinson, David. *Paths of Accommodation: Muslim Societies and French Colonial Authorities in Senegal and Mauritania, 1880–1920*. Athens: Ohio University Press, 2000.

———. *The Holy War of Umar Tal: The Western Sudan in the mid-Nineteenth Century*. Oxford: Oxford University Press, 1985.

Rousseau, R. "Le site et les origines de Saint-Louis." *La Géographie*, n.2, T. XLIX; 1925: 116–128; 3T. XLIX, 1925: 282–301; T. XLIX, 4, 1925: 424–438.

Saint-Martin, Yves-Jean. *L'empire toucouleur*. Paris: Karthala, 1975.

Watson, Ruth. *"Civil Disorder Is the Disease of Ibadan": Chieftaincy and Civic Culture in a Yoruba City*. Athens: Ohio University Press, 2003.

[9]

Stateness, Democracy, and Respect

Senegal in Comparative Perspective[1]

ALFRED STEPAN[2]

Introduction

In this chapter, I will attempt to make four interrelated contributions to the comparative literatures on secularism, human rights, citizenship, and democratization using Senegal as my primary case.

First, Senegal has been ranked by some authorities as the leading democracy in the Islamic world since 2000. The country has been brilliantly written about by anthropologists and historians, but many of Senegal's experiences and creations have not been sufficiently incorporated into modern democratization theory. Overcoming this lacuna is a major goal of this chapter. Second, much of the standard literature on religion and politics, building on France and the United States, implies that secularism, with a complete separation of church and state, is the most conducive institutional arrangement for democracy building and the protection of human rights. But, I will show how, and why, three of the countries with large Muslim populations that are performing best in the democratic world (India, Senegal, and Indonesia) violate, and I will argue appropriately violate, these French and American "lessons." Empirical democratic theorists must abandon the idea of a singular secularism and advance research concerning "the multiple secularisms of modern democracies."[3] I hope my observations about Senegal's social construction of a version of secularism they call *"laïcité well understood and properly practiced"* will encourage new thinking about alternative formulas for rights protection and democratization in polities where religions are practiced robustly.

Third, virtually every long standing democracy in the world (e.g., Japan, India, the United Kingdom, France, the United States) respects certain basic norms, but has distinctive historical origins and institutional features that facilitated the growth, and the support, of democracy in that country. Analogously, it is my conviction that human rights in the countries of the world are on firmer ground if they can be defended as being consistent with the highest and most cherished values of that society.

I have argued elsewhere that all religions are "multivocal." By that I mean that all religions in the world at some time have had aspects in their doctrines and practices that are in tension with democracy, and some aspects that are "usable" for democracy.[4] Within this multivocal situation, it has proved very important for the emergence of a greater consensus on democracy if authoritative actors *from within* the religious tradition, and *from within* the country, make effective public arguments against the most salient and influential nondemocratic doctrines and practices in their community. External democracy and human rights advocates, if they are present at all, are almost always more effective if they have been invited by major domestic democratic actors and movements in a clearly supplementary role. In such an invited, supplementary capacity, the chances that democracy as an institution, and human rights as a value, will be rejected because they are "alien" to the culture, and a "foreign imposition," can be diminished.[5]

Building on the aforementioned theoretical and empirical perspectives, I will advance the argument in this chapter that where specific human rights violating practices are defended as being *an intrinsic part of that country's religion*, the most efficacious actions are *independent but coordinated state and religious campaigns* against such practices. More explicitly, I will attempt to show why such coordinated policies are *unlikely* to be possible in a society with a pattern of high religious practice and high respect for religious leaders if the state has adopted a "religiously hostile" form of secularism, *but quite possible* if state and religions have developed patterns of mutual respect. To support this argument, I will show how, and why, such campaigns came about in 95 percent Muslim Senegal in areas such as anti-AIDS policy and anti-female genital mutilation policy. I will also show how and why, given the tacit Sufi-religious and secular-state cooperation, there is no space or demand in Senegal, unlike in Pakistan, for foreign-funded, Wahhabi-like fundamentalist *madrasas*, with their rights-eroding practices.

Fourth, "institutions do matter," and I have devoted much of my scholarly life to studying them, but "respect" matters, too, and is more difficult for institutionalists to study. I will try to gain some leverage on this elusive subject in this essay, because what I have come to call "rituals of respect" were crucial in Senegal to the emergence of a more democratic and rights-respecting polity.

In a world where many polities are marred by intolerant and violent state and societal behavior, especially in areas concerning religion, passive tolerance or noninterference is a positive value. But, mutual public respect for the rights of the "other," between religiously or ethnically different groups, and between the state and all religions in the society, if it could be attained, would be of even greater social and political value.

Much of the classic literature on "rituals" focuses on an individual's rite of passage, such as birth, puberty, or death.[6] However, the types of rituals I will focus on in this chapter are quite different. My concern is not with once-in-a-life time "individual transitions" from one stage to the other, but with recurrent, reciprocated, public performances. These rituals of respect must be "public, repeated, and reciprocated" because one of their major functions is to produce assurance of a common knowledge among all relevant actors. Michael Suk-Young Chwe, in an innovative and broad-ranging book, argues that ritual messages must not only be sent, but sent in such a way that it becomes very clear that "people are aware that other people also receive it. In other words, it is not just about people's knowledge of the message; it is also about people knowing that other people know about it, the 'metaknowledge' of the message."[7] Almost all the Senagalese rituals of respect that I will discuss are structured so as to produce, reproduce, and extend such "common knowledge" about mutual respect.

Indeed, such performances in Senegal are often designed precisely to demonstrate group recognitions of mutual dignity. Such "rituals of respect" are thus "performative" in that they have significant political implication because they involve repeated active participation in reciprocal gestures of respect between state and society, and between different religious, ethnic, or linguistic groups.

Conceptually and historically, the origins of such rituals in any society are less important than their persistence. Their origins theoretically could be, and empirically are, highly diverse in motivation and/or conjuncture, ranging from military opponents wishing to send a sign of coexistence or even eventual possible cooperation, to religious groups desiring to acknowledge the oneness of humanity. Whatever their origins, when these rituals of respect are mutually valued, and persistently repeated, they can be transformative and contribute to a virtuous cycle of social relations in the polity.

As is well known, in John Rawls's classic work on liberalism, an "overlapping consensus" in society is virtually only generated by liberal public argument; he also initially argued that such consensus is best achieved by "taking religion off the agenda."[8] But where religion is central to potential conflicts, and in polities where many of the participants in a possible conflict are deeply religious and illiterate, and/or have poor access to public systems of communication and media, such liberal public argument is highly unlikely to occur. But such a context, if it can be socially constructed, can be conducive to the emergence of the "twin tolerations" that I have defined as entailing a sufficient degree of autonomy from religion for democracy not to be constrained by theocrats, and a sufficient degree of autonomy of religion from the state for religious citizens and organizations to exercise their religious rights and their rights of expression, not only in their places of worship, but in civil and political society as well.[9] Could "rituals of respect" play a role in generating such a normative and behavioral consensus for peace and tolerance? Could rituals of respect contribute to fostering an overall political context in which basic rights of religions, and eventually a democratic state, are respected, and independent but coordinated state and religious human rights policy reforms are possible?

The structure of the presentation is straightforward. Part I briefly makes the case that Senegal ranks near the top among the world's poor countries in indicators relating to "stateness," social peace, civilian control of the military, religious toleration, civil liberties, democracy, and human rights.

Part II draws on excellent historical work to document the social construction of first "accommodation," and then growing mutual Sufi/French respect, in two different "political geographies" within Senegal, the interior and the coastal towns.

Part III analyzes how "rituals of respect," especially in the area of religion, contribute to Senegal's overlapping consensus concerning the "twin tolerations."

Part IV examines the role of such rituals in contributing to cooperation between the state and religions in key contemporary policy areas of direct concern for human rights.

The conclusion attempts to explore why, emerging from the ground up, Senegal's rights-enhancing system increasingly worked for Sufis and secularists alike, and to suggest theoretical and policy implications that might be applicable elsewhere.

Part I: Senegal: Political and Human Rights in Comparative Perspective

My stress on a "package" of political processes such as "stateness," credible constraints on bureaucratic impunity, and civilian control of the military, comes from my historical and comparatively based understanding that it is a theoretical and political mistake to focus only on "human rights" by themselves. This is a mistake because, while human rights *as values* may be "universal" and "inalienable," they cannot *as practices* be effectively protected unless there is a "usable state" and some form of rule of law that, among other things, credibly establishes horizontal and vertical checks on the state apparatus itself. In the modern world, a democracy, of course, is nether a sufficient, nor in all cases a necessary, condition for a rights-respecting political system. However, in terms of constitutionally embedded citizen's rights, and constitutionally crafted and constrained institutions of governance to protect such citizens' rights, democracy would seem to be a better starting point than any other type of political system.[10] Senegal ranks well on a number of the key dimensions indicating a reasonably workable social and political consensus and nonviolation of basic human rights. Let us see.

Senegal is not now, and has never been, a "failed state." As Linz and Stepan have argued elsewhere, where there is no state, there can be no protected human rights, no law boundedness, and of course, no democracy.[11] In 2006, the magazine *Foreign Policy*, in collaboration with The Fund for Peace and Carnegie Endowment for International Peace, created their second annual Failed States Index. Twenty states, including four of Senegal's West African neighbors (Guinea, Sierra Leone, Liberia, and Ivory Coast) were listed in the worst category, "critical." Twenty additional states, including four more of Senegal's West African neighbors (Togo, Burkina Faso, Cameroon, and Nigeria) were in the next worst category, "in danger."[12]

Senegal was in neither category. While it has not threatened to produce "statelessness," I would be remiss not to mention the on-off armed conflict with some separatist implications for the last twenty-five years in Casamance.[13]

Senegal is also highly unusual in that, like India, it has never been ruled by a military regime, and has therefore been free of all the problematic "prerogatives" such regimes often leave both in civil society and the state concerning patterns of acceptable civil-military relations.[14] In Latin America since World War II, eighteen of the twenty countries have experienced direct military rule.[15] Latin America is not exceptional. In sub-Saharan Africa, more than thirty newly independent countries have had major military involvement in their governments.[16] In Asia, some countries that are now democratic, such as Indonesia, Korea, the Philippines, and Taiwan, have had recent periods of military rule; some once-democratic countries, such as Pakistan and Thailand, have been under military rule, and Bangladesh underwent military tutelage.

Within the set of the world's nondemocratic regimes, some have almost no constraints on state violence against its citizens, whereas some nondemocratic regimes, in interaction with their societies, have established a degree of rule of law in which citizens have some civil liberties, if not political rights, and state employees do not have unchecked discretionary authority, but act within some mutually recognized norms. One standard indicator of such variation is Freedom House's civil liberties scale that goes from 1 (the best score) to 7 (the worst score). From 1972–2006, fifty-seven countries have at one time or another received a score of 6 or 7 on civil liberties. In contrast, Senegal never received a score worse than 4 in any one of these years.[17]

With no religious freedom in a polity, both human rights and the "twin tolerations" suffer. The Religion and State Codebook ranks 152 countries in the world on measures of "discrimination and/restrictions against religions." On this index, Senegal had a better ranking than all but two of the European Union's twenty-seven members. Saudi Arabia ranked 152.[18]

In attempting to rank countries on a democracy scale, the political scientist Ted Gurr created Polity, which has a twenty-one-point scale running from minus ten to plus ten.[19] For the last two editions of this scale, in 2000 and 2004, Senegal received a score of plus eight, the third highest score possible. Senegal's average score for 2000 and 2004 was the highest of the forty-three Muslim-majority countries included in the Polity scale.[20]

Senegal's comparatively superior wealth cannot explain this top ranking among the Muslim-majority countries. Indeed, thirty-two of the forty-three other Muslim-majority countries have a higher per capita income than Senegal's $1,300.[21] Moreover, since countries below $1,500 per capita income that have competitive elections are highly unusual, Senegal merits classification as one of the world's few "great electoral overachievers."[22]

How did this come about? What was the role of resistance, mutual accommodations, or even respect?

Part II: French Colonists and Sufis: The Social Construction of Mutual Respect

From Colonial Military Conflict and Jihad to Mutual Accommodation: Rural Senegal

One of the founders of modern democratization theory, Dankwart Rustow, argued that conflicting groups, if they come to the conclusion that they cannot completely defeat their opponents, occasionally implicitly accommodate each other.[23] Historians of the French conquest of the interior of Senegal note that the French military almost completely destroyed the system of traditional African kingship in the interior of the country. Islamic, largely Sufi military, leaders stepped into the vacuum this created, some of them declaring jihad against the French. However, eventually, both the French and the Sufis realized that they could not dislodge the other and arrived at a Rustovian accommodation. The distinguished British political anthropologist Donal B. Cruise O'Brien comments: "France was short of legitimacy in Senegal, short also of staff and money, and it made good sense to support the local Muslim leaderships.... [Sufi orders] may have in the nineteenth century been identified by the French policy makers as instruments of holy war, but in the twentieth century colonial setting it was quite possible to come to an understanding on the solid ground of shared material interests."[24] The French could not develop agriculture in a hostile interior, but they could, and did, grant substantial landholdings with great peanut-growing potential to major Sufi orders, especially to the Murids, to do so.

The French did this, according to an excellent study by David Robinson, because "the Murids were already a necessary part of the infrastructure of central Senegal. They helped solve major problems of agricultural production, labor supply, and social control."[25] In return, the Sufis not only generated Senegal's major source of revenue but the charismatic founder of the most influential Sufi order, Amadu Bamba of the Murids, sealed the reciprocal relationship (which he saw as allowing Islam in general, and his Sufi order in particular, to grow) by getting his followers to accept a long, mutually beneficial process of accommodation with the French.[26] In a critical letter that helped reinforce the incipient Murid/French rituals of respect, Bamba wrote: "I have decided to give . . . some advice to my Muslim brothers in order that they not be drawn into wars . . . The French government, thanks to God, has not opposed the profession of faith but on the contrary has been friendly toward Muslims and encouraged them to practice [their religion]."[27] Part of the reason that this rural accommodation evolved was due to a prior, quite different, but eventually reinforcing, urban process involving voting.

Voting: The Urban Dialectic of Citizen Conquest and Colonial Concession

Historical studies of the gradual, but powerful, emergence of citizens' rights in countries such as the United Kingdom, the United States, and India give great importance to the relatively early creation by local peoples of patterns of representation, whether by elections or parties. Such instruments of self-representation increased local people's sense of their rights, just authority, and their power to negotiate with colonial authorities. Comparativists should add Senegal to this list.

For comparativists there are some important, but little noted, political processes. Political authority in the major urban coastal settlements in what came later to be called the "Four Communes" of Senegal in the late eighteenth and early nineteenth centuries had periods of sharp discontinuity. The permanent local residents, some black and some mixed-race Creoles, appeared to have used such periods to increase their role in the management of the cities and to express their grievances. For example, the British occupied the commune of Gorée in Senegal from 1758–1763. But "when the French reoccupied Gorée in 1763 they found . . . a Catholic African acting as mayor."[28] When the French Revolution destroyed the Old Regime, the local residents of the then most important commune, Saint-Louis, sent a register of grievances to the Assembly in Paris, and a Colonial Council "composed of local residents elected by their fellow citizens" emerged.[29]

Residents of Senegal seized the opportunity of the revolution of 1848 to send a representative to Paris to petition for the right to elect a deputy to the new National Assembly. The petition was granted, and from 1848 until independence in 1960, any time France held elections for the Assembly, the Four Communes of Senegal elected a deputy to a seat in the French Assembly.[30] From 1848 to 1914, the deputy was either white or creole. But as the franchise widened, Black Senegalese constituted a clear electoral majority. From 1914 until independence, *all* the Senegalese deputies to the French Assembly were black Africans. In 1879, a General Council was created, and in the judgment of Johnson, this "gave the Four Communes effective institutions of local government controlled by the urban inhabitants."[31]

In 1946, two years after Gaullists took power following the fall of Vichy France, Senegal won the right to elect an additional deputy from the previously unrepresented interior to the Assembly in Paris. The elected deputy from the interior until independence in 1960 was Léopold Sédar Senghor, the distinguished poet who went on to become Senegal's first president, and also an elected member of the Academy of France.[32]

Comparatively and interpretively, I draw four conclusions from this emergence of voting in Senegal. First, contested campaigns, with rules of the game, for nationally important elections, have been an intrinsic part of political life in the Four Communes since the mid-nineteenth century, more so than in any former colony of the Middle East, Africa, or Asia, with the possible exception of India. But even India never elected members to the British Parliament in London. While these elections were initially urban, some of the electoral traditions eventually spilled over to rural Senegal.

Second, the literature often refers to French "assimilation" policies that "gave" elections to the Senegalese as an overall part of their colonialization policy. The term *gave* does not adequately capture the process that I prefer to call a "dialectic between citizen conquest and colonial concession." As Crowder stresses, "Senegal is the exception . . . the other territories of French Black Africa did not elect deputies until 1946."[33] One reason such rights were "acquired" so early by Senegal is that, again and again, such rights were demanded. Significantly, there were a number of French efforts to take away these acquired rights, all of which failed.[34] The Senegalese social scientist Mamadou Diouf is particularly useful in showing the numerous strategies devised by the Senegalese to retain their political rights. In a convincing and revisionist argument, Diouf helps us advance the general argument about "respect."[35] Beyond military accommodation, there can be "won" and "earned" respect. For Diouf, "assimilation" implies "the loss of a historical initiative and of cultural creativity, because of total subordination to the metropolitan culture." Diouf rejects the appropriateness of the use of the term *assimilation* for what occurred in the Four Communes because the local population, black, mixed, and white, was able to fight back and create a new and original culture. He calls this process "acculturation," which he defines as "the *re-creation* of a culture and society in the context of a colonial experience, an *original* production built on the continual reorganization of precolonial and colonial experiences."[36]

Part of this original production of a culture in the Four Communes was the successful political and legal struggle to retain the full French legal code giving Senegalese inhabitants of the Four Communes rights as citizens, including voting rights, while also retaining some aspects of Muslim personal law. This combination was refused by the French to Algerians, so Algeria never attained the Senegalese-type of voting status within colonial rule. One of many successful moves in the struggle to retain the right to vote involved the decision by the Four Communes to voluntarily pay extra taxes to support France in the Franco-Prussian war of 1871; but the Communes then petitioned Paris that, as taxpayers, their right of representation could not be cancelled. The chief French administrator in Senegal supported the petition, adding that the Senegalese also paid a "blood tax, which none of the other colonies pay, by fighting in our colonial armies."[37] Before agreeing to fight in World War I, the first black-elected deputy from Senegal to the French Assembly, Blaise Diagne, stipulated that the Senegalese would adhere to all the obligations of citizenship, such as military service; but he also proposed a law stipulating that, in return for such military service, France would ever after recognize the full citizenship rights of Senegalese. This demand was met in the French Citizenship Law of 1916, and in a series of other laws called the Blaise Diagne Laws.[38]

Third, voting in Senegal, given how it emerged, helped create incentives for inclusion in a religious sense as well. The majority-elected deputy for the constituency of the rural interior of Senegal, Léopold Sédar Senghor, was a "double minority." He was a Catholic, when more than 90 percent of his constituents were Sufi Muslims, and a linguistic and ethnic Serer, when the majority of his constituents spoke Wolof and did not consider themselves ethnically Serer. This electoral reality, in a context where elections had firmly established themselves as the "major game in town," deepened Senghor's interest in preserving Senegal as the religiously and ethnically tolerant polity it was becoming.[39]

Fourth, Senegal's early and persistent voting created incentives for a more inclusive polity, geographically speaking. In many of the developing countries in the world, rural populations are politically abandoned by the capital cities. But, in a context such as existed in Senegal, where votes play a major part in producing political authority, political leaders have more incentives not to completely neglect the countryside than "sultanistic" or military leaders might have. For example, by 1951 a new electoral law tripled the number of people who could vote and "the balance of the electorate was shifting from the old communes to the countryside."[40] Senghor became the first major politician to campaign throughout the interior, attending some 450 meetings, traveling ten thousand kilometers, and meeting with traditional village and religious leaders in the lead-up to the 1951 elections. The hinterland was by then so electorally important that in 1951, even though Senghor's party lost in the two largest towns of Dakar and Saint-Louis, it still "won 41 of the 50 seats for Senegal's territorial council."[41] In addition, in Senegal, since the countryside is deeply influenced by Sufi religious leaders (the marabouts), secular state leaders and national politicians, since the universal male and female enfranchisement in 1956, have had incentives to develop forms of cooperative relations with such rural religious leaders.

Part III: Rituals of Respect

Let us now turn to our main interest. How did "rituals of respect" help shape and reinforce Senegal's exceptional degree of overlapping consensus on religious, ethnic, and even electoral matters?

The Secular State and Sufis

France and the United States are often taken as the two major examples of long-standing democracies where there is the greatest legal separation of religion and state. Such separation is often seen as a necessary part of, or at least conducive to, modern democracies. However, these two countries' forms of separation of religion and state are polar opposites in their origins and consequences. The concept of *laïcité* was created in France in 1905 as a clerically hostile form of "freedom of the state from religion." The driving spirit of separation of church and state in France has its origins in the French Revolution's struggles to reduce the power of the Catholic Church.[42] In contrast, the First Amendment of the U.S. Constitution, with its antiestablishment and religious freedom clauses, was passed as a clerically friendly form of "freedom of religion from the state."[43]

However, the clerically hostile form of French *laïcité* does not actually apply to state-religion relations in Senegal, despite the fact that the opening articles in the constitutions in both countries refer to *laïcité* and are virtually identical. It is hard to conceive that France's religiously hostile brand of secularism would have contributed, in a society with intense involvements with the discussion and practice of religion, to the emergence of Senegal's socially constructed overlapping consensus with its emphasis on respect. Note how the second president of Senegal, Abdou Diouf, in essence gives a new interpretation to *laïcité*:

> Laïcité in itself is a manifestation of respect of others. It acts in this way if it is laïcité well understood and properly practiced. Such laïcité cannot be anti-religious, but neither if it is a true laïcité can it become a state religion. I would say further that such a laic state cannot ignore religious institutions. From the fact that Citizens embrace religion flows the obligation for the state to facilitate the practice of that religion, as it does for all other vital activities of citizens . . . Respect of religion does not only mean tolerance, it does not mean only to allow or to ignore, but to respect the beliefs and practices of the other. Laïcité is the consequence of this respect for the other, and the condition of our harmony.[44]

Given the profoundly different normative and empirical implications of *laïcité* in France and Senegal, it should be clear why I argue that democratic theorists should speak not of "secularism" as a singular democratic universal, but instead of the "multiple secularisms of modern democracies."[45]

India, with its Muslim minority of 140 million citizens, and heavily Muslim majority Indonesia and Senegal, are some of the highest-ranked democracies in the developing world.[46] None of them has either a U.S.- or French-style notion of secularism as separation of religion and the state.

Stateness, Democracy, and Respect

All three have variants of the Indian invention of "equal respect, principled distance, and equal (and substantial) support for all religions."[47] Such financial support on the part of the state in Senegal (and also in India and Indonesia) certainly violates French or U.S. ideas of a strict separation of religion and state, but does not violate citizens' human rights or violate the necessary spheres of autonomy that I have identified as the "twin tolerations" that modern democracies need. Indeed, the strong majority of religious leaders and followers alike in these three countries have arrived at a mutual accommodation with, and even support of, the democratic and secular state.[48] This is so, despite the fact that all three countries have versions of the secular state that can impose some normative and constitutional constraints on religious majoritarianism, and on possible religious violations of human rights.[49]

In Senegal, rituals of respect contribute to the twin tolerations in numerous reinforcing ways. One of the rituals relates to state representation at religious ceremonies, and vice versa. At the major religious ceremonies of any of the three major Sufi orders (Murid, the most politically influential; Tijan, the most numerous; and Qadir, the oldest), or of the influential Catholic minority, a significant number of cabinet-rank officials of the secular state will attend, along with the leading authorities of all the other religions.[50] The tradition of state officials attending such religious ceremonies informally began in the nineteenth century, but by the twentieth century, Marcel de Coppet, Governor General of French West Africa (1936–1938), mandated such attendance. According to Christian Coulon, a leading French scholar of such ceremonies, De Coppet did so because attendance "symbolized the existence of a relationship of mutual recognition between the religious power of the marabouts and the power of the colonial government, following a period of extreme suspicion between the two blocs."[51]

At their recent annual pilgrimage (called the Grand *Mággal*) more than one million Murids (around 10 percent of Senegal's entire population) converged on their holy city, Touba. The government was represented by eleven ministers, almost half the cabinet.[52] Building on the work of the influential British anthropologist Victor Turner, Coulon goes on to argue that the Grand *Mággal* creates what Turner would call a "communitas," through which all the people who participate in such an event "come to think of themselves as a homogeneous unit, a communion of individuals who may be of varying status but who nonetheless, in particular circumstances, perceive of themselves as forming a distinct community."[53]

Such participation by leading secular leaders in constant rituals of respect is seldom found in the secular state of France, where in their version of *laïcité*, officials of the secular state at the most might attend a religious event such as a funeral. But, *laïcité* became transformed in colonial, and even more, in independent, Senegal. Mamadou Diouf's concept of "acculturation" works both ways, in this case not only on the Sufi orders but also on the secular French colonial, and now on contemporary secular, African Senegalese officials.

An important point to stress is that the government not only participates in and provides important logistical, health, technical, and financial support for this Murid ritual, but for all similar pilgrimages, such as the *Gámmu* of the Tijaan Sufi order to Tivaoune, and of the Catholic annual pilgrimage to Popenguine.[54] The secular state in Senegal, as does the secular state in India, helps some of their Muslim citizens fulfill their obligation of making, if possible, a pilgrimage to Mecca in their lifetimes by subsidizing their airfares. In Senegal, the secular state also supports pilgrimages by Catholics to the Vatican.

In keeping with Chwe's point that a key part of rituals is the production of "common knowledge that everybody knows that everybody knows," the religious leaders often begin such ceremonies with a detailed public acknowledgment of the state agencies that have contributed to making the ceremony possible.[55] This shows everyone, including possible religious and political competitors, how powerful and respected the religious leader is. The acknowledgment also helps it be known to everyone, including possible political and religious competitors, how powerful and beneficent the secular state leaders are.[56] As their part of this process of mutual recognition and coparticipation in rituals of respect, leading figures from the Sufi orders and the Catholic Church will be present at all major events of the secular state.

Rituals of Respect Between Religions (and Between All Human Beings)

We turn now to "rituals of respect" between the different religions themselves. If there are intense problems at this level, there can be great conflict and intolerance, even if state policy opposes such intolerance.

Though Islam is a universal religion, there are many streams of interpretation, and concrete political practices within it, as there are in all such religions.⁵⁷ Sufis are not necessarily tolerant or peaceful at all times and in all places. However, some leading scholars of Islamic life in Senegal, such as the philosopher and historian of Islam Souleymane Bachir Diagne, stress that within Senegal, a central part of the taught and lived Sufism is that "God is in every human being," regardless of religious affiliation.⁵⁸ Diagne argues that "Sufism is, by the very nature of its metaphysics (founded on the notion that every being is longing after the One Necessary Being which sustains its very existence) particularly tolerant to different ways of worship. One of the main Sufi beliefs is that all spiritual paths are a quest for the same divine reality under the different representations they make of it . . . These metaphysics have attracted a great opposition from what may be considered as a literalist understanding of Islam."⁵⁹ Thus for Diagne, and many Sufi religious marabouts I have interviewed, violence against another human being, because of religious disputes or differences, is morally repugnant.⁶⁰

Diagne approvingly endorses a paper of Abdul Aziz Kébé, the Official Coordinator of Communications of the Tijaan Order of Tivaouane, that stresses the "absolute ontological gender equality" of males and females.⁶¹ In a private correspondence with me, Kébé also stressed that Fatwas were seldom given in contemporary Senegal on major social or political issues and that, in any case, they are only learned legal opinions, not absolutely binding moral obligations, because even major Islamic scholars can, and do, contradict each other.⁶²

Islam, like all world religions is of course "multivocal."⁶³ However, again and again in my interviews with Senegalese religious and political leaders, they chose to emphasize those parts of the Qur'an's multivocality that urges tolerance as a response to diversity. For example, a professor of Arabic read to me a number of Qur'anic verses (Suras) that emphasize that God created diversity in the universe. For example, Sura 49:13: "We have made of you nations and tribes so that you can know each other"; or Sura 5:48: "If Allah had willed he would have made of you one nation."⁶⁴ Many of them quoted Sura 256, in which God states that "There shall be no compulsion in religion." Some even quoted Sura 18:29: "Whoever wills, let him believe; and whoever wills let him disbelieve." The right of religious "exit" was often stressed as being consistent with these texts.

It is in this context that almost no one I interviewed felt comfortable with the concept of an "apostate" and all felt comfortable with the fact that the famous Catholic Cardinal Thiandoum of Dakar came from a Muslim family. In general, in Senegal, there are strong normative codes against forms of physical attacks on the body as a form of punishment, even religious punishment.[65]

This "Senegalese Sufism" contributes to the numerous "rituals of respect" between religions in Senegal, and within, and between, the Islamic Sufi orders in Senegal. Examples of such rituals between the once very influential Catholics and the Sufis abound. In the city of Popenguine, both Sufis and Christians helped build each others' mosque and church.[66] In Fadiouth, after the Catholic church was destroyed in a hurricane, it was rebuilt with the physical and financial help of the Muslims.[67] In the two cities of Ziguinchor and Fadiouth, there is a common cemetery for Muslims and Catholics.

There is also a "Senegalese Catholicism" in that, whereas in France Catholics disliked the imposition of *laïcité* in 1905, in Senegal, the Catholics are the greatest defenders of Senegal's *"laïcité bien comprise."*[68]

Within the Sufis, Donal B. Cruise O'Brien asserts that the three major Sufi orders have "well established procedures of co-existence," that "state leadership in Senegal encourages devotional togetherness on a national scale," and that the two great Sufi "tomb-shrines of Touba and Tivaouane, have become centers for the reconciliation of intractable national disputes."[69]

Surveys are not very abundant in Senegal, but those that we have are consistent with the account we have advanced so far of widespread tolerance of "other" religious and ethnic groups. Three political scientists from the University of Connecticut interviewed 200 Islamic religious leaders and a national sample of 1,500 respondents. They constructed a tolerance measure based on responses to twelve questions. The religious leaders were by no means tolerant across the board; for example, only 12 percent of them were tolerant of "drug addicts." But 98 percent of religious leaders were tolerant of "people from other ethnic groups," and 92 percent were tolerant of "people from another religious group." Among the general population, 87 percent were tolerant of other ethnic groups, and 78 percent were tolerant of other religious groups.[70] Pew surveyed seventeen Muslim majority countries concerning whether democracy "could work" in their country or was only "a Western way." The country where the highest percentage of respondents felt democracy "can work here" was Senegal, 87 percent.[71]

Stateness, Democracy, and Respect

Part IV: State/Religion Policy Cooperation and Conflict Concerning Contemporary Human Rights Reforms

President Léopold Sédar Senghor, when he spoke at the inauguration of the Murids' Great Mosque at Touba in 1963, captured the sense of how even the leader of the Senegalese secular state could participate in the spirit of a Victor Turner–like "communitas." Indeed, in his speech he indicated that such communitas and *laïcité* even entailed state/religion codesign and co-implementation of major social policies:

> Last Monday, the Head of State attended the great national pilgrimage of Popenguine. Today, he is attending the inauguration of the Great Mosque of Touba. This double attendance will astonish only those who keep ignoring the realities of Africa. For us, Senegalese, it constitutes the basis of our national policy. . . . I have always found support, advice and comfort among you. . . . Laïcité, for us, is neither atheism nor antireligious propaganda. I give as just one piece of evidence the articles of the Constitution that guarantee the autonomy of religious communities. Our Constitution goes further; it turns these religious communities into auxiliaries of the state in its education task, its cultural task. For religion is an essential part of culture.[72]

The constant mutual public displays of respect between religions and the state has facilitated policy cooperation even in some sensitive areas of human rights abuses. It has also facilitated an atmosphere where religious leaders have felt free to make arguments *from within Islam* against practices and policies that violate human rights. When I argued in the "Twin Tolerations" that all religions are "multivocal," I also drew the conclusion that this necessarily implied, *contra* John Rawls, that it would be mistake to "take religion off the agenda."[73] I did so because proponents of some human rights–violating policies often use religious arguments to support their positions. There thus must be a counterresponse in defense of rights put on the agenda.

Ideally, this response is not only from abroad, in the name of "universal human rights." The most effective counterresponse is by a local authoritative figure, who, from within the core values of the religion and culture of the country, makes a powerful, religiously based argument against the specific practice that violates human rights. Let us look at some examples of Senegalese state/religion policy cooperation in the area of human rights.

The Campaign Against Female Genital Mutilation

A variety of national and international feminist and human rights movements wanted to ban the practice of female genital mutilation (FGM) but had been countered by powerful religious-based attacks. In the end, secular movements in the government, and some national and international non-governmental organizations (NGOs), were greatly helped by religious leaders. N'Diaye, the Secretary General of the National Association of Imams of Senegal (ANIOS), publicly argued that there is nothing in the Qur'an commanding the practice, and that there was no evidence that the Prophet had his own daughters circumcised.[74] A law banning female circumcision was passed in 1999. To avoid the law being a dead letter, ANIOS enlisted the help of government health authorities to train imams how to speak authoritatively about the health problems circumcision presents and to help with anti-FGM talks by imams on radio and television. Since patterns of female circumcision are closely related to perceptions of marriage eligibility, the government, ANIOS, and national and international women's rights organizations worked together with entire adjacent villages to develop policies of "coordinated abandonment" of female circumcision in order to preclude jeopardizing marriage prospects within participating villages.[75]

Despite this law banning FMG, it helps make the law an increasing social reality if the most authoritative religious bodies in the country continue to campaign against the practice so that it is increasingly delegitimated in the religious norms and social practices of the country. To help advance this crucial goal, Professor Abdoul Aziz Kébé, coordinator for the Tivaouane-based largest Sufi order in Senegal, the Tijaans, wrote a powerful forty-five-page attack on FGM. The report systematically argues that FGM is a violation of women's rights, bodies, and health, with absolutely no justification in the Qur'an or in approved Haddiths. Kébé argues that not only is there no Islamic justification for FGM but that given current medical knowledge, and current Islamic scholarship, there is a moral obligation for communities and individuals to bring a halt to FGM. The report was distributed by Tijaan networks, secular ministries, and the World Health Organization.[76]

Female circumcision is still a problem in Senegal, with an estimated 28 percent of women from the ages of 15 to 49 having undergone FGM, according to the United Nations Children's Fund (UNICEF). However, the same source lists Egypt at 96 percent. Senegal's three contiguous Muslim majority countries have much higher rates than its own: Mali, 92 percent;

Guinea, 95 percent; and Mauritania 71 percent. It should be acknowledged that ethnic traditions, as well as social policy are important. The Wolof traditionally have not practiced FGM. However, it is worth noting that among ethnic groups that have a high rate of FGM, the rates inside Senegal are lower. For example, the Pulaar in neighboring Mali have more than a 90 percent rate and the Pulaar in Senegal have a 62 percent rate.[77]

Anti-AIDS Policies

Another area of policy cooperation between religious and secular authorities concerns AIDS. A United Nations Development Program report on anti-AIDS policies in Muslim majority countries notes the following:

> In Senegal, when political leaders realized that a change in sexual behavior was necessary to contain HIV/AIDS they undertook multiple strategies, an important one of which was to enlist the support of religious leaders. Religious leaders were given training to equip them with knowledge for advocacy work. HIV/AIDS then became a regular issue of Friday prayer sermons in mosques throughout the country and religious leaders talked about HIV/AIDS on television and radio. Brochures and information were distributed through religious teaching programmes. Since the early 1980s, Senegal has managed to keep their HIV prevalence rates low, less than 1%.[78]

Some observers may think that the Muslim pattern of male circumcision alone accounts for this low AIDS rate. However, they should bear in mind that AIDS rates in some other Muslim majority African states, where male circumcision is also the norm, such as Chad, Guinea, Eritrea, Mali, and Djibouti, are two to five times higher. This is, of course, not to speak of the extremely high AIDS rates in some non-Muslim states such as South Africa, 21 percent, and Botswana, 37 percent.[79]

Tacit Cooperation Between Sufis and Secularists: Education

In social policies, cooperation does not always have to be explicit. Tacit cooperation can be quite useful. In the 1980s, as the Iranian Revolution, Saudi

Arabian money, and Wahhabi influences gained greater weight in the Islamic world, there were numerous articles about some trends in Senegal that seemed to be going in a more Islamist direction, using the term to mean in a more fundamentalist direction.[80] It appeared that there could be some tensions and even conflicts between Sufi Islam and Islamists. This seems less of a prospect today. By and large, neither the secular state nor the Sufis wanted to block political Islam by repression, because this would go against their prevailing spirit of religious tolerance, and also against their belief that fundamentalists grow best under repressive politics. However, neither the secular state nor the Sufis went out of their way to facilitate Islamist expansion.[81] A brief examination of Islamist, or what some call fundamentalist, schools or *madrasas* illustrates this point.

In Senegal, the state provides free public schooling for close to 85 percent of all primary school age children.[82] Furthermore, since 2003 state schools have offered religious instruction (using authorized textbooks that are never Wahhabi in spirit), with the informal approval of secular and Sufi teachers alike. More and more parents are increasingly sending their sons, and now their daughters, to these tolerant, accredited, and democracy-compatible, schools.

Some parents still elect to send their children to private, often Franco-Arabic, schools. However, the Senegalese pattern of state-religious relations allows the state to partially fund such private religious schools. In return, the state regularly inspects such schools. The only schools the state does not supervise are the Qur'an-based schools, which some parents use as a complement, seldom a full substitute, for state education. But most of the traditional religious teachers in such schools practice Senegalese rituals of respect, and in any case, view Saudi Arabian-style schools as culturally alien competitors.[83] In this overall Senegalese context, fundamentalist schools, as well as Iranian and Saudi Arabian aid in the education sector, find little space or demand.[84]

Not Even Tacit Cooperation but Implicit Acceptance

Sometimes the fact that the state has a form of secularism, but, as in India and Indonesia, is in no way antireligious, allows the government to take a policy initiative in the area of human rights that the religious leaders might not originate, or even oppose, but to which such leaders eventually accede simply because the law has been duly passed by the organs of a democratic state of which they are full participating members. In 1973, for example, after years of debate and opposition by many religious leaders, the Senegalese parliament passed a revised Family Code enhancing women's rights in the areas of divorce and inheritance. The code still remains controversial, many of the Muslim leaders calling it a "Women's Code." Worse, when it was issued, the Khalife Générale of the Murids pronounced that the family code would not be enforced in the Holy City of Touba. At the time, Touba was a very small new settlement, and the government turned a blind eye. However, now that Touba is the second most populous city in Senegal, this is increasingly problematic. In 2003, a group of imams created a pressure group, CIRCOF, to reverse the code. However, in an interview, a leader of CIRCOF acknowledged that, given the resistance of the state, CIRCOF had few prospects of success. He seemed unhappy, but reconciled, to this result.[85]

Limits of State/Religion Cooperation: Polygamy

Polygamy is proving one of the most intractable issues for human rights advocates and feminist groups. Female education reduces the rate, but it is still substantial in Senegal; 49 percent among women with no instruction, 34 percent for women with a primary education, and 27 percent for women with at least a secondary education.[86] The Family Code introduced a partial reform, in that it allowed women to ask for divorce, and made men entering into marriage sign a statement as to whether they agreed to enter a monogamous marriage or not. If men signed the affirmation that their marriage would be monogamous, they could be legally charged with breaking the law if they became polygamous. Feminists correctly argue, however, that for social reasons, there is not sufficient enforcement of this law.[87] Here we must observe what Max Weber would call "an inconvenient truth." Some African political systems under periods of nondemocratic leadership, such as Tunisia, or Turkey under Atatürk, simply abolished polygamy. But under a democracy such as Senegal's, until public opinion changes more strongly against polygamy, the practice might be eroded but not completely legally abolished.

Conclusion

The historical pattern in Senegal of French and Sufi mutual accommodation in the rural areas, and the urban dialectic between French colonial "concessions" and Senegalese "citizen's voting conquests," helped socially construct a workable consensus concerning once quite conflictual divisions within Senegalese society. This consensus contributed to Senegal's never having a failed state, never having a military coup, never having a period where the state (French or Senegalese) ruled with no constraints on its ability to violate citizens' human and political rights, and never producing political leaders who were able to successfully use religious or ethnic differences to create regime-destroying conflicts to advance their interests.

That Senegal actually has a socially constructed, overlapping consensus, is itself the consensus view many leading scholars of Senegal. The historian Andrew F. Clark speaks of a balance in Senegal "between religion and politics that has served both sides exceedingly well."[88] Donal B. Cruise O'Brien comments that "the strength of the Senegalese state, its connections with social networks and institutions, has been assured above all by Sufi Muslim intermediation."[89] Mamadou Diouf talks about the "social creativity" of nineteenth-century Muslim and Catholic indigenous cultures in the four major communes, a creativity that resulted in a "two sided religiosity. . . . whose civility is the product of a compromise and of revisions of cultural outlooks."[90] Leonardo A. Villalón begins his important monograph on Sufis with the statement that "socio-political cleavages based on religion, whether between Muslim and non-Muslim or between Sufi orders, are virtually nonexistent."[91] Why was this rights-enhancing regime accepted by both secularists and Sufis?

Three conclusions, with comparative implications for what I call "the multiple secularisms of modern democracies," would seem to have emerged strongly from this chapter. First, in a polity such as Senegal (which in its religious intensity of belief and practice is closer to India and Indonesia than it is to France), this overlapping consensus could not have emerged if the French had tried to impose a religiously hostile separation of religion and state. Any attempt to impose French-style secularism in Senegal would have met resistance and blocked cooperation. With their powerful, but limited military resources, French colonialists could probably have put down major jihads, but they would have been subjected to some internal criticism from the electorally based republican institutions, and most importantly, without accommodation, they could not have peacefully and productively developed the peanut economy in the interior of Senegal or received the black Senegalese military support they so valued in World War I. The French thus dropped "hard secularism" and aspired to be an "Islamic power" in Senegal. To further this goal, they gradually adopted, and were "seen" to have adopted, the numerous policies we have documented; they supported pilgrimages of influential Sufis to Mecca, they created a Muslim tribunal in 1857 (even after giving Senegal a deputy and the right to vote), they gave some financial support for Mosque construction, they supported Arabic language training for Islamic schools, and increasingly they attended major Sufi ceremonies and were seen to give public respect to marabouts.[92] All of these policies violated 1905 French-style *laïcité*, but none of them violated human rights, democratic values, or what I call the "twin tolerations."

Second, Senegal's overlapping consensus would not have emerged if Sufi leaders had violated *all* of the many possible versions of democratic secularism, by trying to impose a complete fusion of religion and state of the sort that much of political Islam often attempts. Senegal is possibly the only country in the world where Sufis are not only the overwhelming majority of the population but have never been systematically repressed, marginalized, or controlled by state authorities. The outlines of this possible future were already clear in the early twentieth century. However, this future would have been put in jeopardy if a major Sufi leader such as Amadu Bamba had struggled for a fusion of religion and state. The French would not have accepted such fusion, and the effort to create this fusion would have required a jihad, which probably would have been unsuccessful. In fact, *Bamba made a virtue of the non-fusion of religion and state.* As Robinson argues, "Bamba put a premium on autonomous Muslim communities that would live, work and reproduce themselves in conditions of stability."[93] Bamba, who in the interior of Senegal had great prestige for not submitting to France, struggled not to be involved in the direct administration of state policies, and thus was not seen by fellow Muslims as the collaborative ally of the French colonial state.

Third, *laïcité*, "well understood and properly practiced," not only worked for the secularists but for the Sufis as well. Indeed, Senegal must be included with India when human rights activists and democratic theorists alike reconsider "the multiple secularisms of modern democracies."

Notes

1. I would like to acknowledge the great intellectual support, during all stages of this article, of Etienne Smith, who was finishing his doctorate at Sciences Po in Paris on "joking kinships" in Senegal. Etienne Smith was an immense help with the bibliography and history of Senegal, and helped me arrange and conduct more than twenty interviews with religious, political, and civil society leaders, some in Wolof, in Senegal.
2. This chapter was originally published in Thomas Banchoff and Robert Wurthnow, eds., *Religion and the Global Politics of Human Rights*.
3. I will develop this argument in greater general detail in an article, "The Multiple Secularisms of Modern Democracies," being prepared for the Social Science Research Council Working Committee on Secularism. An early version, with the above title, was presented at SSRC on February 12, 2007, in New York, and at the Globalism Seminar at Columbia University, November 3, 2007. Here I will concentrate on Senegal. I am building upon the work of Eisenstadt, "Multiple Modernities"; Kaviraj, "An Outline of a Revisionist Theory of Modernity"; and the articles by Rajeev Bhargava listed in the bibliography.
4. I develop this argument in more detail in "The World's Religious Systems and Democracy: Crafting the 'Twin Tolerations.'" See Stepan, *Arguing Comparative Politics*, pp. 213–254, esp. pp. 227–229. Henceforth, this article will be cited for brevity simply as Stepan, "Twin Tolerations."
5. For example, Abdullahi An-Na'im, one of the major contemporary Islamic political theorists and an advocate of human rights everywhere in the world, argues that each specific society must argue against human rights violations in their own society, drawing upon usable and authoritative arguments in their own tradition, or such arguments will be rejected. "The Muslim world and the *ulama* in particular have been unable and unwilling to embrace the [human rights] debate for the simple reason that so much of it has been dominated by external actors and agents." But he insists that "We can assert our religious or cultural justification of these rights, instead of the 'take it or leave it' attitude of Western secular advocates of human rights." See the interview in Noor, "Muslims Must Realize," p. 6.
6. See, for example, van Gennep, *The Rites of Passage*, and Turner, *The Ritual Process*.
7. See Chwe, *Rational Ritual*, p. 9. Almost all the Senegalese rituals of respect that I will discuss are structured to produce, reproduce, and extend, such "common knowledge" about mutual respect. I thank my colleague Macartan Humphreys for bringing Chwe's book to my attention.

8. John Rawls, *Political Liberalism*.
9. See Stepan, "Twin Tolerations."
10. In the previously cited interview (see endnote 5), the Islamic political theorist and human rights advocate, Abdullahi An-Na'im, is emphatic on this point: "Human rights, as the term is defined today, can only be protected when there are certain legal and political institutions at work ... You need the basic fundamentals of democracy and democratic institutions to be in place at least—an open and democratic government that is genuinely representative, a working judiciary that is credible and independent, a security and law and order apparatus that is not politicized, etc. Without such institutions and political norms in place, it is hard to imagine human rights being promoted and protected by anyone." See An-Na'im in Noor, ed., *New Voices of Islam*, p. 10. Some countries, like most mid-nineteenth-century Scandinavian polities, did not necessarily have all these democratic institutions in place but managed to be rights-protecting. However, the general point about a usable state with some constraints on its own actions is certainly one worth stressing.
11. See Stepan and Linz, *Problems of Democratic Transition and Consolidation*, chapter 1.
12. See "The Failed States Index," *Foreign Policy*, May/June, 2006, pp. 50–58. International relations theorists often allude to the difficulty of maintaining stability, due to negative spillover effects, if a state lives in a "hard neighborhood." From this perspective, Senegal's stability is of special note. Senegal is in an especially hard neighborhood. For example, eight of its thirteen other fellow members in the Economic Community of West African States are classified in the Failed States Index in the two most endangered categories. Also see, "Special Report: Responding to War and State Collapse in West Africa," United States Institute for Peace, January 21, 2002.
13. See Humphreys and Mohamed, "Senegal and Mali."
14. On the negative effects on many democracies of such "prerogatives," which can occasionally last for decades after direct military rule see the chapter "The Military in Newly Democratic Regimes: The Dimension of Military Prerogatives" in Stepan, *Rethinking Military Politics*.
15. See Valenzuela, "Presidencies Interrupted."
16. See, for example, the data complied and monitored by Arthur S. Banks for Africa under the categories of "military government" or "military civilian government" in his *Cross-National Time-Series Data Archive* (CNTS), Databanks International, Binghamton, N.Y., June 2005.
17. Computed from data contained in the annual reports produced by Raymond D. Gastil, ed., *Freedom in the World: Political Rights and Civil Liberties*.

18. For a discussion of the database, see Jonathan Fox, "World Separation."
19. The polity twenty-one-point scale goes from minus ten, to zero, to plus ten.
20. For 2000, see Monty G. Marshall and Keith Jaggers, *Polity IV Project*, Integrated Network for Societal Conflict (INSCR) Program, Center for International Development and Conflict Management (CIDCM), University of Maryland, College Park (www.bsos.umd.edu/cidcm/polity). Unfortunately, we observed key parts of the February 2007 presidential election and believe that some presidential abuses of power should merit a lower ranking in the next Polity ranking. See Stepan's February 2007, Project Syndicate op-ed type column that appeared in numerous countries before the election, "Senegal's Imperiled Rituals of Respect."
21. See Stepan and Graeme B. Robertson, "An 'Arab' More than a 'Muslim' Electoral Gap."
22. For the concept of electoral "overachievement" and "underachievement" in comparison to a country's GNP, see Ibid.
23. See Dankwart Rustow, "Transition to Democracy."
24. See Cruise O'Brien's classic article "Renegotiating the Senegalese Social Contract," in *Symbolic Confrontations*, p. 194.
25. See Robinson, *Paths of Accommodation*.
26. Amadu Bamba sealed this process of accommodation with a letter to his followers in 1910. Malik Sy, the leader of the Tijaniyya, the largest Sufi order in Senegal, arrived at a similar accommodation. For a detailed account of these mutual French–Sufi accommodations in the interior of Senegal see Ibid., pp.194–227.
27. Ibid., pp. 221–222.
28. See the very valuable book by Johnson, *The Emergence of Black Politics in Senegal*.
29. Ibid., pp. 40–41.
30. The two major breaks in this continuous electoral history were the two authoritarian periods in France, the Second Empire of 1852–1870 and the Vichy government during Nazi-occupied France.
31. Johnson, *The Emergence of Block Politics in Senegal*, p. vii.
32. The standard biography of this major leader in English is Vaillant, *Black, French and African*.
33. Michael Crowder, *Senegal*, p. 6.
34. An entire chapter is devoted to such French attempts in Crowder, Chapter 3, "French Reaction Against Assimilation", in Ibid., pp. 21–34.
35. Diouf, "The French Colonial Policy of Assimilation."
36. Ibid., p. 8. Emphasis added.
37. Johnson, *The Emergence of Black Politics in Senegal*, p. 44.

38. See Diouf, "The French Colonial," p. 693.
39. For this important and creative period in Senghor's life, see the chapter "Master Politician" in Valliant, *Black, French and African*, pp. 214–242.
40. Ibid., p. 238.
41. Ibid., p. 239.
42. The anticlerical struggle during the revolution in France was such that about 3,000 priests were guillotined and much church property was confiscated. During the thirty-five-year struggle (1870–1905) leading up to the 1905 law on secularism, about 15,000 Catholic schools were closed. For the contrast between French and U.S. secularism, see Kuru, "Secularism, State Policies, and Muslims in Europe." France is the only country in Europe to pass a law banning headscarves in public schools. All but two members of the Stasi Commission recommended this ban. See "Le Rapport de la Commission Stasi sur La Laïcité," *Le Monde*, Décembre 12, 2003, pp. 17–24, for the report and an analysis.
43. Indeed the U.S. pattern of separation of church and state is labeled "philo-cléricale" by a leading contemporary French scholar; see Lacorne, "La séparation de L'Église et de l'état aux États-Unis."
44. Reprinted in a large paperback printing with the constitution of Senegal and commentaries edited by Me Doudou Ndoye, a former Minister of Justice. Dakar: EDJA, 2001, pp. 48–49.
45. See my manuscript referred to in endnote 3 for greater elaboration of this point.
46. For example, in the most recent ranking of all the countries in the world on a democracy scale in Ted Gurr's *Polity*, of the forty-three Muslim-majority countries ranked, Senegal and Indonesia received the highest scores, and India has been ranked at that level for over thirty years.
47. For this model in India, see Bhargava, "The Distinctiveness of Indian Secularism." For the moral and political theory behind India's secularism, see Bhargava's "Political Secularism." Also see the volume Bhargava edited, *Secularism and Its Critics*, especially the articles by Bhargava, Akeel Bilgrami, and Amartya Sen.
48. For numerous tables supporting this assertion for India, see chapter 2 in Stepan, Linz, and Yadav, *Democracies in Multinational Societies*. One of our most counterintuitive findings in India, for both Hindus and Muslims, is that the greater the intensity of religious practice, the greater the intensity of support for democracy. In India, the responses of Hindus and Muslims were statistically the same. These three authors also wrote the questions on religion and democracy for the *State of Democracy in South Asia*. Delhi: Center for the Study of Developing Societies, 2006. The study included surveys and reports covering India, Pakistan, Bangladesh, Sri Lanka, and Nepal.

49. In Senegal, they call their model "laïcité bien comprise," in Indonesia, "pancasila" (state of five principles), and in India, simply "secularism." In my current research into these three countries, I am examining the distinctive versions of secularism that have emerged and the contributions they make to the countries' ability to manage democratic politics. For Indonesia, two basic books for the history and evolution of pancasila are Azyumardi Azra, *Indonesia, Islam, and Democracy*; and Ramage, *Politics in Indonesia*.
50. Catholics now constitute only 5 percent of the population but they have been very important in the political and social history of Senegal because they probably, at the beginning of the nineteenth century, constituted a majority of the population of Saint-Louis, the most important commune in Senegal at the time. The first president of independent Senegal from 1960–1980, Léopold Senghor, was a Catholic.
51. Coulon, "The Grand Magal in Touba," quote from p. 202.
52. See Momar Dieng, "Onze ministres chez Serigne Saliou: Quand la république prend d'assaut la capitale du Mouridisme," *Walfadjiri*, April 23, 2003.
53. Coulon, "The Grand Magal in Touba," p. 205. The book of Victor Turner that Coulon is referring to is *Dramas, Fields and Metaphors*, especially the famous chapter on "Pilgrimages as Social Processes," pp. 166–230. See also Turner, *The Ritual Process*.
54. For extensive discussion and documentation of this point, see Samb, *Comprendre la laïcité*, pp. 140–144.
55. See Chwe, *Rational Ritual*, pp. 13–16.
56. For an excellent illustration of how this works at local and national Tijan rituals, see Villalón, "Sufi Rituals as Rallies."
57. An example of great variation in state regulatory practices in Muslim majority countries is found in the Religion and State Codebook that ranks 152 states on various measures of discrimination and/or restrictions against religions. Among the 152 states, Saudi Arabia ranked worst, 152nd, on the discrimination/ restrictive measures; Senegal ranked 12th. For a discussion of the database, see the previously cited Fox, "World Separation of Religion and State."
58. Interview with Stepan, November 29, 2006, Paris. Diagne comes from a long line of Sufi preachers and is an occasional preacher himself. Diagne was formerly at the University of Dakar and an advisor to the president of Senegal, Abdou Diouf. In January 2008, he joined Columbia University as a professor of Philosophy, French, and African Studies.
59. Souleymane Bachir Diagne, "Islam in Senegal," p. 5.
60. When I told S. Bachir Diagne of these interviews, he commented to me that they were in no way exceptional but reflected modal opinions in Senegal.

Stateness, Democracy, and Respect

On the same day, in his April 5, 2007, public lecture at Columbia University, Bachir developed the theological and ethical underpinning in Sufism, especially as understood and practiced in Senegal, of the imperative of nonviolence in religious disputes.

61. As quoted in Diagne, "Sufism and the Deconstruction of the Macho Ego." The paper he is referring to is a ninety-three-page argument on the fundamental equality of men and women. See Abdoul Aziz Kébé, "Argumentaire religieux musulman sur l'equité de genre," Fonds des Nations Unies Pour la Population and Government of Senegal, Ministère de la Famille, du Développement Social et de la Solidarité Nationale (Dakar, Senegal: 2003). Some of the characteristic statements in this document are that the soundest Islamic jurisconsulates in fact argue that "women have the right to participate in public life," "to issue judicial decisions," and to arrive at "personal interpretations" concerning proper Islamic life (p. 53). He also argues that "it is inappropriate to quote haddiths and specific verses referring to domestic life and to extend their effects to the domain of public life; all misunderstandings and injustices in matters of gender equality and social construction come from this" (p. 23).
62. E-mail in answer to my questions about Fatwas on June 27, 2007. Also an interview in Dakar, Senegal, December 4, 2006.
63. On "multivocality" in all the world's religions, see Stepan's article on the "Twin Tolerations," pp. 223–226, on the "intolerant" and the "tolerant" aspects of multivocality in Islam, see, pp. 233–237.
64. Interview with Abdoul Aziz Kébé, University Cheikh Anta Diop, December 5, 2006.
65. The political scientist and comparativist H. E. Chehabi, who was born in Iran, visited Senegal in 2005. Upon returning, he told Stepan and Linz he was amazed at the fact that the concept, apostate, almost did not exist in ordinary Islamic speech in Senegal. Stoning to death or cutting off of hands for supposed crimes against Islam are not only illegal in Senegal but also theologically unsupported by Senegalese Sufis and culturally offensive to Senegalese traditional customs.
66. See the article in a Dakar newspaper significantly entitled "Une Famille, deux religions," *Le Soleil*, October 23, 2001.
67. *Syfia International*, September 1, 2001.
68. This was repeatedly emphasized to me throughout a four-hour conversation in Dakar with Abbé Jacques Seck, who from 1977–2000 was assigned by the Cardinal of Dakar to be a member of the Commission for Muslim-Christian Dialogue in Senegal. Abbé Seck said that the Catholic radio shows of the sort allowed in Senegal would be inconceivable in the Arab countries he had visited

such as Tunisia or Morocco. Seck also stressed that Catholics did not only want to be "tolerated" in Senegal, but "respected," and that on the whole they were.

69. See Cruise O'Brien, *Symbolic Confrontations*, pp. 12–13.
70. See Vengroff, Richard, Lucy Creevy and Abdou Ndoye, "Islamic Leaders' Values and the Transition to Democracy: The Case of Senegal," unpublished manuscript, University of Connecticut, 2005.
71. See The Pew Global Project Attitudes, February, 3, 2005. The same report says that Pew polled twelve Muslim majority countries as to whether it was "very important to live in a country with honest multiparty elections," and Senegal polled the highest.
72. Senghor, *Liberté 1: Négritude et humanisme*, pp. 422–424. Elsewhere in the same volume he asserts, "Union and cooperation between religions is a national, and vital, necessity. . . . Religious leaders understand this by collaborating for nation-building and by making religious cooperation one of the primary principles of their actions" (p. 307).
73. See Stepan, "Twin Tolerations," pp. 227–229.
74. See the long feature article in one of Senegal's leading newspapers, Habibou Bangré, "Croisade musulmane contre l'excision: Les imams rétablissent la vérité sur cette tradition," *Walfadiri*, June 8, 2004.
75. Ibid. A similar social policy of public pledges renouncing foot-binding in nearby Chinese villages with high patterns of intermarriages proved useful.
76. See Abdoul Aziz Kébé, "Argumentaire religieux musulman pour l'abandon des MGF's." Dakar: Organisation Mondiale de la Sante, décembre 2003.
77. All FMG rates from UNICEF statistics (Multiple Indicator Cluster Servers, MICS 1995/2005) available at www.childinfo.org/areas/fgmc/tables.php.
78. "The Role of Religious Leaders in the Fight Against HIV/AIDS," United Nations, UNDP, November 30, 2006, p. 19.
79. See table 4 in UNICEF, www.unicef.orf/french/sowco5/Table4 F.xls.
80. For a review of this literature, see Loimier, "L'Islam ne se vend plus."
81. For example, Gellar in his *Senegal*, p. 98, writes that "During the mid 1980s, relations with Iran worsened because of Iran's attempt to foster radical fundamentalist movements in Senegal. In January 1984, Senegal expelled Iranian diplomats from the country and broke diplomatic ties, which were not resumed again until February 1989 . . . By this time, Iran under President Rasanjani had reduced its efforts to export its revolution to Black Africa in general and to Senegal in particular."
82. Republique du Sénégal, Ministère de l'Education, *Situation des indicateurs de l'education, 2000–2005*, octobre 2005.
83. Hefner and Zaman have recently edited an invaluable book that reviews *madrasas* in eight different countries; see their *Schooling Islam*. In terms of

state involvement in the consensual development of a moderate curriculum, these eight countries vary from the low involvement of Pakistan to the high involvement of Indonesia and India. In his introduction, Hefner asserts that "No comparison better illustrates the contextual relativity of modern Islamic education than that of Pakistan and India . . . the situation in the madrassas in the two countries could hardly be more different," p. 23. Unfortunately, Senegal was not included in the study, but at the primary and secondary level, Senegal would seem to be close to India and Indonesia, and completely different from Pakistan, especially from the situation in Pakistan's Northwest Frontier Providence where there are only about 1,400 registered, but 15,000 unregistered, madrassas. See ibid., pp. 85–86.

84. The preceding two paragraphs are based on talks with an official from the Ministry of Education and to the headmaster and some school teachers in a major private Franco-Arabic school in Dakar, December 12, 2007, that I visited with my Columbia colleague Ousmane Kane. They told us that visits by authorities occur regularly, often once a month. I also interviewed a marabout in Touba who was a son of the former Khalife Générale of the Murids. The marabout happened to teach the history of Islam in a state school and felt the new materials being developed were acceptable. The marabout also taught in a Qur'anic-only school.

85. Interview with Imam Mbaye Niang, at his "Unfinished Mosque of the Airport," on December 9, 2006. The imam is also the president of a small political party, MRDS, which includes Catholics, and stressed that "when one creates a party, one must respect the constitution."

86. See Fatou Sow, "Les femmes, l'état et le sacré," in M. Gomez-Perez, ed., *L'Islam politique au sud du Sahara*. Paris: Kartala, 2005, pp. 283–307, esp. p. 302.

87. For the views of a prominent feminist, human rights advocate, medievalist, and former minister of culture on these and other issues, see Penda Mbow, "L'Islam et la femme Senegalaise," *Ethiopiques: Revue Négro-Africaine de literature et de philosophie*, numéros 66–67, 2001. See also Sow, "Les femmes, l'état et le sacré."

88. See Clark, "Imperialism, Independence, and Islam in Senegal and Mali."

89. See Cruise O'Brien, "Sufi Symbolism and the State in Senegal, 1975–81," in *Symbolic Confrontations*.

90. Cruise O'Brien, *Symbolic Confrontations*," p. 694.

91. See Villalón, *Islamic Society and State Power in Senegal*, p. 2.

92. For a documented and convincing discussion, see chapter 4, "France as a 'Muslim Power'," in Robinson, *Paths of Accommodation*, pp. 75–96. See also Cruise O'Brien, "Towards an 'Islamic Policy' in French West Africa."

93. Robinson, "The Murids: Surveillance and Collaboration," p. 200.

Bibliography

Azra, Azyumardi. *Indonesia, Islam, and Democracy: Dynamics in a Global Context.* Jakarta, Indonesia: Solstice Pub., 2006.

Bhargava, Rajeev. "The Distinctiveness of Indian Secularism." In *The Future of Secularism,* ed. T. N. Srinivasan, 20–53. Oxford and Delhi: Oxford University Press, 2006.

———. "Political Secularism." In *The Oxford Handbook of Political Theory,* eds. John S. Dryzek, Bonnie Honig, and Anne Phillips, 636–655. Oxford and New York: Oxford University Press, 2006.

———. *Secularism and Its Critics.* Oxford and Delhi: Oxford University Press, 1998.

Chwe, Michael Suk-Young. *Rational Ritual: Culture, Coordination, and Common Knowledge.* Princeton, N.J.: Princeton University Press, 2001.

Clark, Andrew F. "Imperialism, Independence, and Islam in Senegal and Mali." *Africa Today* (46) (3–4) (1999): 149–167.

Coulon, Christian. "The Grand Magal in Touba: A Religious Festival of the Mouride Brotherhood of Senegal." *African Affairs* (98) (1999): 195–210.

Crowder, Michael. *Senegal: A Study of French Assimilation Policy.* London: Methuen, 1960.

Cruise O'Brien, Donal B., ed. *Symbolic Confrontations: Muslims Imaging the State in Africa,* 193–213. New York: Palgrave, 2003.

———. "Towards an 'Islamic Policy' in French West Africa." *Journal of African History* 8 (1967): 303–316.

Diagne, Souleymane Bachir. "Islam in Senegal: The Religion of the Rosary." Unpublished manuscript, Chicago, 2007.

———. "Sufism and the Deconstruction of the Macho Ego." Unpublished manuscript read and distributed at Columbia University, April 5, 2007.

Diouf, Mamadou. "The French Colonial Policy of Assimilation and the Civility of the *Originaires* of the Four Communes (Senegal)." *Development and Change* 29 (4) (1998): 671–696.

Eisenstadt, S. N. "Multiple Modernities." *Daedalus* (Winter 2000): 1–29.

Fox, Jonathan. "World Separation of Religion and State into the 21st Century." *Comparative Political Studies* 39 (June 2006): 537–569.

Gellar, Sheldon. *Senegal: An African Country Between Islam and the West.* Boulder, Colo.: Westview Press, 1950.

Hefner, Robert W. and Muhammad Qasim Zaman. *Schooling Islam: The Culture and Politics of Modern Muslim Education.* Princeton, N.J.: Princeton University Press, 2007.

Humphreys, Macartan and Habaye ag Mohamed. "Senegal and Mali: A Comparative Study of Rebellions in West Africa." In *Understanding Civil War: Evidence and Analysis*, Vol. 1, *Africa*, eds. Paul Collier and Nicholas Sambanis, 247–302. Washington, D.C.: World Bank, 2005.

Johnson, G. Wesley, Jr. *The Emergence of Black Politics in Senegal: The Struggle for Power in the Four Communes, 1900–1920*. Stanford, Calif.: Stanford University Press, 1971.

Kaviraj, Sudipta. "An Outline of a Revisionist Theory of Modernity." *European Journal of Sociology* 46 (December 2005): 496–526.

Kuru, Ahmet T. "Secularism, State Policies, and Muslims in Europe: Analyzing French Exceptionalism." *Comparative Politics* 40 (2008): 1–19.

Lacorne, Dennis. "La séparation de l'Église et de L'état aux États-Unis: Les paradoxes d'une laïcité philo cléricale." *Le Débat* (Novembre-Décembre 2003): 63–79.

Loimier, Roman. "L'Islam ne se vend plus: The Islamic Reform Movement and the State in Senegal." *Journal of Religion in Africa* 30 (May 2000): 168–190.

Noor, Farish A. "Interview with An-Na'im, Abdullahi: 'Muslims Must Realize That There Is Nothing Magical About the Concept of Human Rights.' " In *New Voices of Islam*, ed. Farish A. Noor, 5–14. Leiden: ISIM, 2002.

Ramage, Douglas E. *Politics in Indonesia: Democracy, Islam and the Ideology of Tolerance*. London and New York: Routledge, 1995.

Rawls, John. *Political Liberalism*. New York: Columbia University Press, 1996.

Robinson, David. "The Murids: Surveillance and Collaboration." *Journal of African History* 40 (1999): 193–213.

———. *Paths of Accommodation: Muslim Societies and French Colonial Authorities in Senegal and Mauritania, 1880–1920*. Athens: Ohio University Press, 2000.

Rustow, Dankwart. "Transition to Democracy: Toward a Dynamic Model." *Comparative Politics* (April 1970): 337–363.

Samb, Djibril. *Comprendre la laïcité*. Dakar, Senegal: Les Nouvelles éditions Africaines du Sénégal, 2005.

Senghor, Lépold Sédar. *Liberté 1: Négritude et humanisme*. Paris: Seuil, 1964.

Stepan, Alfred. *Arguing Comparative Politics*. Oxford: Oxford University Press, 2001.

———. *Rethinking Military Politics: Brazil and the Southern Cone*. Princeton, N.J.: Princeton University Press, 1988.

Stepan, Alfred and Juan J. Linz. *Problems of Democratic Transition and Consolidation: Southern Europe, South America, and Post-Communist Europe*. Baltimore and London: Johns Hopkins University Press, 1996.

Stepan, Alfred, Juan J. Linz, and Yogendra Yadav. *Crafting State-Nations: India and Other Multinational Democracies*. Baltimore and London, John Hopkins University Press, 2011.

Stepan, Alfred and Graeme B. Robertson. "An 'Arab' More Than a 'Muslim' Electoral Gap." *Journal of Democracy* 14 (July 2003): 30–44.

Turner, Victor. *Dramas, Fields and Metaphors: Symbolic Action in Human Society.* Ithaca, N.Y.: Cornell University Press, 1974.

———. *The Ritual Process: Structure and Anti-Structure.* Chicago: Aldine Publishing Company, 1969.

Vaillant, Janet G. *Black, French and African: A Life of Léopold Sédar Senghor.* Cambridge, Mass.: Harvard University Press, 1990.

Valenzuela, Arturo. "Presidencies Interrupted." *Journal of Democracy* (October 2004): 5–19.

Van Gennep, Arnold. *The Rites of Passage.* Chicago: University of Chicago Press, 1960.

Villalón, Leonardo A. "Sufi Rituals as Rallies: Religious Ceremonies in the Politics of Senegalese State Society Relations." *Comparative Politics* 26 (July 1994): 415–437.

[10]

Negotiating Islam in the Era of Democracy

Senegal in Comparative Regional Perspective

LEONARDO A. VILLALÓN

The "Compatibility" of Sufism and Democracy, and the Senegalese Case

There may be no more vexed contemporary political question than the future of democracy in the Muslim world. Among many scholars and other analysts considering the empirical record, pessimism runs deep. Thus the reputable Freedom House survey of the world in 2001 could confidently diagnose a democracy "deficit" or "gap" among Muslim countries. And the implicit explanation for that diagnosis was an apparent "incompatibility" between the belief system of Islam and the core elements of a culture of democracy.[1] The incompatibility argument has deep roots, and in American political science is found in such explicit statements as Huntington's[2] assessment of Islam as "not hospitable to democracy."

More nuanced observers of the Muslim world, however, have noted that the negative correlation between a Muslim majority population and a democratic political system does not always hold, and have consequently suggested the need to disaggregate the Muslim world in various ways. Thus Stepan and Robertson,[3] for example, point out that the democratic gap is more an "Arab" than a "Muslim" one. Others have suggested that perhaps certain specific variants of Islamic theology might be compatible with democracy, even while some others are not. In the sub-Saharan African context, the version of Islam known in the old colonial category as *"l'Islam noir,"*[4] and now more often labeled "African Islam,"[5] is often evoked to explain the greater "tolerance" and "peacefulness" of those Muslim societies. In African settings where political contexts are less peaceful—say northern Nigeria or Sudan—this is often explained as a result of the fact that other—imported—forms of Islam have made significant inroads.

In this view, "African Islam," understood as a syncretic form of classical Sufism, appears to be a particularly (or even uniquely) fruitful Islamic foundation on which to build a democratic political order. The overwhelming dominance of this religious form in Senegal is thus invoked to explain the country's notable political exceptionalism, and in turn the Senegalese case lends strong support to this hypothesized correlation. Thus, to take a recent example, Gellar's effort to apply Tocqueville to Senegalese democracy notes without critiquing the Frenchman's negative views of Islam as "rigid" and "unbending," but argues that they do not apply in Senegal, whose Islam is instead "tolerant" and flexible."[6]

There is no doubt much validity to this perspective, and indeed the role of Sufi Islam in explaining Senegalese political exceptionalism is an argument that I have myself developed at some length.[7] It merits noting, however, that this analysis focused more on the specific social structures and organizational forms developed by Senegalese Sufism rather than on any ideological or religious aspect of Sufism as a belief system—though the latter has certainly not been absent.[8]

Rather than focusing on the exceptionalism of Senegal in this chapter, however, I would like to examine Senegal from a comparative regional perspective, in light of democratic developments in some of its Muslim Sahelian neighbors.[9] I find that this comparison highlights some of the less exceptional qualities of Senegal, at least as compared to its neighbors. Or, perhaps better stated, the comparison highlights some common patterns across the region in terms of the evolving relationship between Islam and democracy, and I believe that seeing how these patterns apply to Senegal may help us to nuance and better understand the current dynamics of the Senegalese case.[10]

Two initial observations—each central to the main thematic concerns of this volume—should be made as a point of departure for this comparative exercise. First, it merits noting that the hypothesis that the relative tolerance of Sufism produces a greater affinity for a democratic political system than other forms of Islam is simply a variant of a "compatibility" argument. For various reasons, I find this general approach unsatisfying, or at least in need of careful nuancing.[11] Sufism has many faces, and many possible postures may be justified in the name of a Sufi ideology. That is, like any religious tradition, Sufism is, in Stepan's terms,[12] also "multivocal." Given that both Sufism and democracy are essentially contested terms, any broad statement about their relationship risks disintegrating into a debate on the definition of either, or both.

The multivocality of Sufism is clear even from a cursory view of the history of religion in the Senegambian region. As a well-known Senegalese Islamic intellectual and owner of a major media company noted in response to a question about the relationship between Sufism and the state in Senegal, the answer depends on which face of Sufism you consider.[13] There is a tradition and a history in Sufism of dialogue and engagement with political authority, and in Senegal it is this face that is represented by the historical figure of El Hajj Malik Sy and his Tijani *zawiya* in Tivaouane. There is a parallel Sufi tradition of retreat from worldly concerns and withdrawing from the political realm; Shaykh Amadu Bamba's Murid order was built on this tradition. But there is yet another tradition, he insisted, represented by the mid-nineteenth-century jihad of El Hajj Umar Tall, which finds in Sufi Islam the inspiration for militancy and armed struggle in defense of the faith. Indeed, the jihads that swept West Africa in the late eighteenth and the nineteenth century were in almost all cases led by leaders rooted squarely in the Sufi tradition, a tradition on which they based the inspiration for their movements of militant reformism.

This variation in the political stances of Sufism is even apparent within a given Sufi order—witness the varying political postures that led the French to alternately regard the Tijaniyya in West Africa as dangerous or accommodating in different times and places.[14] My point here is to stress the need for caution in any generalizing about the impact of Sufism on a given political outcome, such as democracy.[15]

A second initial observation relates to the timing of the arrival of democracy in Senegal. Despite its frequent designation as a "rare democracy" on the African continent in the first three decades of independence, from the added perspective of another two decades it is clear that in fact Senegal was less exceptional than it often seemed. To be sure, the regime of Léopold Sédar Senghor (1960–1980) and the first decade of that of his designated successor, Abdou Diouf, were marked by significant stability, relative nonrepression, and a greater tolerance of opposition than most other regimes on the continent.

But these regimes were not democratic, at least not in any sense we would today be willing to use the term. Like elsewhere on the continent, Senegal moved quickly after independence to the consolidation of a de facto single-party regime under the *Parti Socialiste* (PS), and when it did take the exceptional move of reauthorizing opposition parties (indeed, to mandate them constitutionally) in the mid-1970s, it did so within carefully circumscribed rules that ensured that they could not in fact accede to power.[16] Strikingly, then, as economic conditions deteriorated and political frustration increased throughout the decade, Senegal ended the 1980s in a political situation not much different than that of many other regimes on the African continent. Following the declaration of another PS victory in the 1988 elections, massive social mobilization and violent protests led to the announcement of a "state of emergency," the imprisonment of opposition leaders, and police repression of street protests.[17]

As old regimes on the continent began to crumble under demands for democratization in the late 1980s and the early 1990s, the Senegalese regime also found itself pressured to "democratize." And indeed, faced with calls for a "national conference" or a "transitional government" on the model of some neighboring countries, the ruling PS was obliged to make significant concessions to the opposition, notably by embarking on a series of fundamental and profound revisions of the electoral process. The 1993 elections were thus the first really "democratic" ones in independent Senegal in many senses, and the first held in a context in which all parties were in agreement on the rules of the game.[18] Because they nevertheless did not produce an alternation in power, however, the decade of the 1990s remained politically uncertain and marked by periodic troubles. But by the 1998 legislative elections, the strong showing of the opposition made it clear that they had learned important lessons, and indeed in 2000, forty years after independence, Senegal finally experienced its first electoral transition of power with the victory of Abdoulaye Wade in presidential elections.

Considering this historical evolution, then, the point to emphasize here is that a consideration of the relationship between religion and "democracy" in the Senegalese case (as opposed to its relationship with stability or with a relatively benevolent single-party-dominant regime) can really only be explored beginning in the 1990s—because that is the point when Senegal in fact launched itself on a process of substantive procedural democratization.

Negotiating Islam in the Era of Democracy

Senegal in Regional Perspective

In the broad outlines of its history and from the perspective of recent democratization, a comparison of Senegal with its Sahelian neighbors, Mali and Niger—two Muslim countries that also experienced democratic transitions in the early 1990s—reveals similarities that suggest some fundamental characteristics in the relationship of Islam and democracy in the region. In demographic terms, the three countries are quite similar: all have populations of some twelve to fourteen million, of which the best estimates would suggest some 90–95 percent are Muslim. All three came to independence in 1960 as a result of the dissolution of France's West African colonial empire. Mali and Niger both quickly followed the common African model of postindependence authoritarianism, with single-party regimes giving way to military ones (in 1968 in Mali and in 1974 in Niger), which were to last until finally toppled in a context of popular mobilization in the early 1990s.[19] In all three countries, the political liberalization in the name of democracy that was embraced in the early 1990s resulted in a rapid expansion of religious influence in public life, and very similar fundamental debates about the appropriate role and place of religion in a democratic political order.

From the perspective of almost two decades, it is now clear that the democratic openings in the Muslim Sahel, like those across Africa, marked the *beginning* of a process of reform, and not its culmination. Thus, in both Mali and Niger, the first elected governments were themselves tasked with elaborating much of the core institutional and legal infrastructure of the new democratic state. And while the situation was somewhat different in Senegal given the significant negotiation and reforms that had occurred in the 1990s, it is still striking that the aftermath of the 2000 presidential elections was immediately consumed by debates concerning the fundamental restructuring of the entire political system.[20] Indeed, immediately upon coming to office, Abdoulaye Wade declared his intent to break with the existing regime by drafting a completely new constitution, which was in fact done within the year.[21]

Such "democratic transitions" thus open the door to longer-term and perhaps more fundamental political transformations, with unintended and unanticipated consequences.[22] Specifically in the Sahel, the newly liberalized contexts opened the door to the organization and mobilization of new social groups, and empowered them in their efforts to exert control over the agenda and shape the outcomes of reform. This bore the potential for standoffs when the societal agenda included elements that are difficult to reconcile with the Western-derived, but now globally dominant, conception of democracy that was espoused by the prodemocracy activists.

Specifically in the Sahelian countries, whose dual heritage is reflected in their variously being qualified by the adjectives "Muslim" or "francophone," the notion of democracy that was embraced by the reformers and reflected in the first elected governments quickly brought a confrontation between two different worldviews and visions of the political order: the secular and the religious. The opposition activists and "intellectuals" who took the lead in demanding reform in these countries in the name of democratic change were almost universally rooted in the secular worldview imbued by the francophone education that defined them. Unsurprisingly, therefore, the immediate reaction of many religious elites was to view the intentions of the activists with suspicion, and often to explicitly oppose what was presented as the democratic agenda. And yet, quite strikingly, this initial opposition was rather quickly abandoned as religious groups became cognizant of their demographic advantages in the new democratic game. That is, significant evidence from the region shows that in a newly liberalized context, with the fundamental pillars of the old regimes called into question, and with the weight of influence among the masses of the population on their side, religious groups saw an opening, and took it.

In an insightful critique of a Rawlsian perspective that posits democracy as an arrangement to be built on a "liberal argument," rather than emerging from a "democratic bargaining" process among value systems, Stepan has suggested that *"liberal arguing* has a place in democracy, but it would empty meaning and history out of political philosophy if we did not leave a place for *democratic bargaining,* and for some forms of non-liberal public argument within religious communities, in such democratic bargaining."[23] In fact, I believe, it is precisely such a historical process that is—tentatively and imperfectly, but perceptibly—taking place in the Muslim Sahelian countries. In the Muslim countries of the Sahel, issues that began as debates or arguments about democracy in the early 1990s have moved gradually into a process of democratic "bargaining" or "negotiation" on how to adapt the core of democracy to their varying Islamic and African visions for a good social and political order.

Democratization in all three countries has entailed significant changes in both the religious and the political spheres, and the intersection of these dynamics is shaping the outcomes of processes of democratic "negotiation" or "bargaining." While these dynamics are of course constrained by individual histories and specific social contexts—and notably in Senegal by the extraordinary weight of the clericalized maraboutic Sufi system—a comparative consideration reveals some strikingly similar patterns in the region. First, the democratic liberalization of the public sphere has brought, in turn, significant transformations in the religious domain—indeed in some real sense one might speak of a "democratization" of religion.[24] The rise of many new religious movements, with wide variations in ideology and theology, in the newly liberalized contexts, has fed a public questioning of established authorities and a challenging of religious orthodoxies. There is thus now an extensive public debate and negotiation *among* religious groups. Secondly, the liberalization of political life has opened the door to religious actors, and to an increased and more assertive role for religion in public life. Thus in both Mali and Niger we quickly saw the politicization of several key issues that were put on the agenda by the concerns of religious groups, issues for which striking parallels were to emerge in Senegal.

The Muslim Public Sphere: Democracy and Religious Change

In both Niger and Mali, the arrival of democracy immediately gave rise to a veritable explosion of religious associations. The corporatist old regimes had, in each case, allowed only a single authorized religious association—the *Association Islamique du Niger* (AIN) and the *Association Malienne pour l'Unité et le Progrès de l'Islam* (AMUPI)—each closely affiliated with the respective single party. The liberalization of associational life that allowed for official recognition of voluntary social organizations, however, quickly brought out in each case a wide multiplicity of religious voices in the public sphere, with wide variations in ideology.[25] In addition, in the democratic context even the francophone and "secular" elite increasingly tend to insist publicly on their own faith, and endeavor to find "Islamic" arguments in support of social or political positions they have long supported in the name of "republican" values. Among some francophones, in addition, we have seen the rise of groups with a reformist religious ideology, at times close to the Egyptian Muslim Brotherhood, which insists on individual responsibility in the practice of religion and which tends to draw individuals with a scientific or technical background—doctors, pharmacists, engineers, and the like.

Among "arabisants," that is those whose education has been religiously oriented and most often Arabic-based, new religious associations of a Salafist or Wahhabi inspiration have emerged, emphasizing faithfulness to the original textual sources of Islam and the imitation of the *sunna* of the Prophet and the early Muslim community. Interestingly, in each country a few "arabisant" intellectuals, sometimes Arabic teachers or university professors, have presented themselves as "moderates," capable of interpreting Islam in ways supportive of public policies intended to address social and developmental problems. Frequently embraced by governments and nongovernmental organizations (NGOs), these religious voices have become increasingly influential in their pronouncements or activities on social policy initiatives in such fields as health (e.g., HIV/AIDS prevention) and legal reform in defense of women's rights.

In the context of this religious effervescence, however, the historical Sufi orders remain an important part of the religious landscape. While institutionalized Sufi organizations have never had the same dominant role in Mali or Niger as they have had in Senegal, Sufi forms of religiosity have nevertheless been widespread at the popular level, and various organized Sufi movements—notably of the Tijaniyya order—have a public presence. Importantly, however, faced with critiques by various other movements, Sufi groups find themselves under fire, and in the resulting debate they are undergoing various changes. There is now emerging a conscious discourse on Sufism in the region, and critical reflection on its meaning.

Considering the Senegalese case from the perspective of its neighbors' dynamics in the religious domain, important parallels are discernible. To be sure, the history of the extraordinary dominance of the institutionalized Sufi system in Senegal constrains and determines the parameters of religious developments. Nevertheless, it is also clear that the past two decades have also witnessed a new religious dynamism and an evolving pluralism of religious voices in Senegal. This is reflected in the increased public religiosity of the francophone elite who dominate the state apparatus and public life. Thus, looking back at the changes of the past several decades, one long-time observer of Senegal notes that "One of the most interesting phenomena has been the growing tolerance of religion on the part of Senegal's Western-educated intelligentsia who had embraced antireligious Marxist ideologies in their youth . . . By the end of the [twentieth] century, it was increasingly difficult to find Senegalese intellectuals and politicians willing to express antireligious views in public."[26]

Negotiating Islam in the Era of Democracy

This phenomenon underpins the increased public role for arabophone intellectuals, who are increasingly called on to pronounce themselves in public domains from which religious figures had been previously excluded. Thus one might point in the Senegalese case to such individuals as the Arabic professor Abdoul Aziz Kébé, who has emerged as a Muslim public intellectual, in demand both because of his wide knowledge of Islam and Arabic and because he is also fully fluent in French. Kébé was one of the founders of the *Réseau Africain des Organisations Islamiques pour la Population et le Développement* (African Network of Islamic Organizations for Population and Development), which is sponsored by the United Nations Population Fund (UNFPA) to add a religious perspective to policies in the fields of health and gender.[27]

Importantly, in the era of democratic debate, Senegal has also witnessed both the expansion of anti-Sufi, Islamist, movements explicitly critical of the prevailing patterns, and the rise of new movements *within* the Sufi orders but that nevertheless borrowed from Islamist critiques to push for changes in leadership and in organization.[28]

As elsewhere in the Muslim world, the main locus of the Islamist movement was within the universities. Since the 1980s, we have seen the expansion of the *Jama'atou Ibadou Rahmane*, leading by 2002 to the founding of a formal student organization, the *Mouvement des Elèves et Étudiants Jama'atou Ibadou Rahmane* (MEEJIR). The unprecedented adoption of a form of veiling by young university women calling themselves "Sunnite" was the most visible manifestation of the dynamism of these movements in the 1990s.[29]

These movements were important, to be sure, but they also had a limited popular appeal outside the class of young intellectuals. More significant were movements growing out of the maraboutic system itself. Perhaps the most visible of these was the *Dahiratoul Moustarchidina wal Moustarchidaty*, an offshoot of the Tijaniyya order that adopted an unprecedented contestary political stance in the 1993 elections.[30] A parallel movement within the Murid order was the *Hizbut Tarqiyyah*, which started as a Murid students' association at the University of Dakar.[31]

In response to these developments, there has been an interesting emergence of a new public debate about "Sufism" and what it entails. This is particularly striking given that despite the historical omnipresence of discourse about the various Sufi orders (*tariqas*) and their religious hierarchy, the abstract notion of "Sufism" has been notably absent from public debate, and the term itself has been rarely used in Senegal. A new and younger generation of marabouts, however, is now self-consciously discussing the "modernization" of Senegalese religious structures and practices by evoking Sufism as a guiding principle. Thus a young grandson of the founder of the Murid order, Seriñ Fallou Dieng, has recently attracted significant media attention speaking in the name of a group calling itself the *Cercle des Intellectuels Soufis du Sénégal* (Circle of Senegalese Sufi intellectuals). Dieng is openly critical of both individuals and specific practices within the Murid order, while claiming a close attachment to it. He insists that his critiques draw on "true Sufism" as opposed to the corrupted prevailing practices in Senegal.[32]

An argument paralleling these concerns, and developing them at some length, is found in a book recently published in Senegal whose title reflects a similar ambivalence: *Le Soufisme: Avantages et Inconvénients* (Sufism: Advantages and Inconveniences).[33] Mansour Sall, the author, is the caliph of a well-known Tijani maraboutic family from the town of Louga, and currently heads a group of schools that bear his father's name: *Complexe Scolaire Serigne Abass Sall*. He is thus from the classic Senegalese religious establishment. In his book, however, as well as in his discourse, he undertakes a conscious examination of Sufism as both doctrine and practice that is uncommon, and rather surprising, in the Senegalese context.[34]

Sall distinguishes between two types of Sufism, which he (rather idiosyncratically) terms "philosophical Sufism" and "Sunnite Sufism." His purpose in writing the book, he says, is to "distinguish Sunnite Sufism which means the adoration of God and the application of the Qur'an and the Sunnah, from philosophical Sufism which simply means associationism and the cult of personalities, things that are forbidden in Islam." And he continues: "I have nothing against Sufism, as such, but what I cannot tolerate is to see Muslims led into error and exploited in the name of a Sufism which is nothing more than paganism and idolatry."[35] Sall thus represents a kind of "Sufi reformism," critical of the established maraboutic system in Senegal, but also interested in promoting a "good" Sufism rooted in Sunni Islam.

For Sall, the dangers of African Sufism extend into the political domain given the "corruption" of the religious leadership by the state. This, he pointedly argues, has given rise to the reformist and anti-Sufi movements that criticize not only the religious errors of the Sufi leadership but the fact that by their collaboration with political power they undercut the development of democracy: "This situation [of misguided Sufi leadership] has recently created a reaction on the part of certain Muslims who publicly preach the idea that the [Sufi] sects are harmful not only because they lead to associationism, but also because they distort emerging African democracy."[36] Sufism as practiced in Senegal, he is thus suggesting, is actually *antidemocratic* because the close alliance and dependence of the religious elite on the state does not leave room for free religious debate able to challenge the state.

Sall suggests a link between the evolving religious debate about "true" Islam and the authority to speak for it on one hand, and the politics of democracy and liberalization on the other. Within the parameters marked by its historical legacy of strongly institutionalized Sufi orders, Senegal thus—like its neighbors—gives every indication of experiencing a "democratization" of religious discourse in the sense of a new possibility for public challenges to established religious authority, and this phenomenon would itself appear to be directly linked to the democratization of the political sphere over the past two decades or so.[37]

The Political Sphere: Religious Agendas in the Democratic Context

A democratic opening in a widely religious social context opens the door to increased religious influence in politics. To the surprise of the political class of reform-minded francophone intellectuals who led the movements in favor of democratization, the transitions in Mali and Niger very quickly empowered religious groups to pursue their agenda in the political sphere. As these groups realized the potential benefits of their demographic advantage in electoral contests, the power of popular opinion forced political actors to align themselves more with popular (religious) sentiment and away from the secular values of the francophone promoters of democracy. The functioning of democracy in these countries has thus raised a number of issues for debate/negotiation that were unanticipated at the time of the transition. These include fundamental questions about the nature of the state (the meaning of "secularism"); a set of related policy issues concerning the management of society (notably family law and related gender issues); and—more quietly but with long-term implications—an emerging negotiated compromise about the shaping of new citizens (the role of religiously based education).

The dynamic of religious empowerment in a democratic opening is also clearly discernible in Senegal. Thus at the level of direct religious challenges to the established political order, for example, we see the political emergence of the Moustarchidine movement during the 1993 electoral campaign and the creation of a political party linked to the movement, the *Parti de l'Unité Républicain* (PUR) in 1998, explicitly credited to the opportunity presented by the changed political context.[38] Likewise, the one deputy in the National Assembly after 2001 who might be said to support an "Islamist" position, the Imam Mbaye Niang, also explicitly claimed that the initiative for the founding his party, the *Mouvement pour la Réforme et le Developpement Sociale* (MRDS) shortly after the 2000 transition, was a direct reaction to the democratic opening, which seemed to present a new opportunity for religious voices to be heard in political affairs.[39]

There has, of course, always been a great influence of the religious on politics in Senegal, but in fact this has actually been manifested primarily by the great influence of individual religious leaders on the politics of distribution and access to resources. From the colonial era and on into the independence period, the extent of the religious elite's impact on having religious values shape public issues was significantly circumscribed, in the name of secularism, *laïcité*. The 2000 elections, however, were for the first time contested by two candidates who campaigned on openly religious appeals, Cheikh Abdoulaye Dièye and Ousseynou Fall. While the latter was a political unknown with a limited impact, Dièye had a long and known political itinerary, first as an organizer of Murid students in France in the 1970s, and then in the 1990s as the founder of his own political party, the *Front pour le Socialisme et la Démocratie* (FSD).[40] In the 2000 campaign, under the Arabic slogan "Allahu wahidun!" (God is one), Dièye made religious issues campaign themes, taking the unprecedented step of questioning the use of the word *laïque* (secular) in the constitution, and calling for the reform of Senegalese family law along Islamic lines.

While neither of these two religious candidates got any significant support in terms of votes in the election—a fact that some interpreted as a sign of the victory of secular "citizenship" at the time[41]—what is quite striking in retrospect is that a number of issues that in Senegal had appeared to be "settled" on the "secular" side were reopened and called into question in the electoral process. Thus despite the broad de facto "accommodation" of the Senegalese elite on the relationship between religion and politics that Stepan[42] points to, there is also today significant anxiety and constant

Negotiating Islam in the Era of Democracy

critiques by Senegalese francophone intellectuals about what they see as increased religious power and the erosion of the secular nature of the state, fears that have been mounting regularly since the election of Abdoulaye Wade. And there are consequently striking parallels in Senegal to the issues that have become points of contention between secular and religious worldviews in Mali and Niger, including *laïcité*, family law, and education.[43]

Questioning the Secular State

A major fundamental debate raised in the process of democratization, and particularly of writing constitutions, concerns the nature of the state itself. Influenced by their colonial heritage, the democratizers in the former French colonies have widely shared a French republican vision of the state as "*laïque, démocratique, et sociale,*" and these terms have regularly been borrowed directly into African constitutions. In the religious context of the Sahelian countries, however, the notion of secularism or *laïcité* has, inevitably, been controversial. Indeed the word itself tends to provoke strong negative reactions among religious actors, and there is an ongoing public debate in the region on its meaning. In both Mali and Niger, the concept of *laïcité* was challenged and debated at their respective "national conferences," and while the overwhelming dominance of francophone secular groups in those events ensured the continuity of secularism, the issue remains a hotly contested one.[44]

In Senegal, and despite the great weight of the religious elite in politics, the ideal of secularism has historically been a major pillar of the state. Nevertheless, in the context of the strongly entrenched religious powers on which they built much of the political foundations for their regimes, it is noteworthy that both Presidents Senghor and Diouf periodically found themselves obliged to explain what they presented as the distinctive Senegalese vision of *laïcité*.[45] While these explanations were clearly intended to allay the suspicions of the religious elite, they also reflected the extremely strong attachment to the principle of secularism among the Senegalese intellectual and political elite.

It was hence completely unexpected and indeed shocking to many when, in early 2001, the term itself did not appear in the first draft of the new constitution. As one distinguished Senegalese legal scholar noted about the draft, "Despite Article 24 and its efforts at specifying [freedom of religion and the separation of religion and the state], Senegalese of all confessions were frightened when at the phase of elaborating the new constitution the word *laïcité* was not included in the project."[46] Faced with an immediate explosion of public controversy, notably in the francophone press and among intellectuals and the political class, the term was ultimately reinstated in the final draft of the constitution that was presented for approval in a referendum. The reasons for this curious episode remain unclear, but it is striking that this highly symbolic issue should be publicly raised in the wake of the first democratic transition in the country, and it is difficult not to imagine that in the new context of electoralism there was some calculation about the possible political advantage that might be gained from removing the term.

Beyond the symbolism of terminology, there is also now across the region a major substantive debate about the meaning of secularism, and about the implications of various interpretations for public affairs and political life. The point of departure of these discussions is inevitably French legal tradition, and the difficulties of discussing the issue in the Sahelian countries is a product of the francophone intellectual tradition—in which the vast majority of the political class has been educated—and the centrality to that tradition of a particularly strong ideology of secularism, what Kuru[47] has labeled "combative secularism."

In the public debate that has emerged, there is a broad range of positions in all three countries. The strong French version of "combative" anticlerical *laïcité*, however, almost never works itself into public discourse in the era of democracy. The dominant discourse about *laïcité* in the region today, rather, distances itself from the French version, while insisting instead on the importance of religious freedom and the circumscription of state interference in religious thought or practice. It is this vision that Senghor and Diouf proposed in their various speeches in defense of secularism and which is celebrated in Samb's[48] book, whose cover proclaims "the non-aggressive, and indeed non-militant—character of Senegalese secularism [*"laïcité à la Sénégalaise"*] and especially that it does not smell of any anti-religious tendency, especially in political discourse."

Today the majority of the political class—seeing themselves as defenders of the separation of religion and state but recognizing that only a posture that does not threaten religious power is politically viable—thus espouses this "moderate" secularism. Among some religious groups, however, a stronger argument suggests that if *laïcité* is to allow the full exercise of religion, then the state must not only refrain from interference, but must work proactively to ensure the conditions that allow for religious practice: the construction of mosques in public workplaces and schools; hours in official services scheduled around prayer times; the weekend moved to Thursday and Friday; or state funding of religious education.

Much of the francophone elite is distinctly uncomfortable with this argument,[49] and Western observers at times see it as a latent threat to the democratic system. But in fact, I would suggest, this discussion must be seen as a very product of democracy. Public opinion matters in a democracy, and political elites must be careful to align themselves with it. In the religious context of the Sahel, then, the rise of religious influence in politics is the normal outgrowth of the liberalization of political systems, in Senegal no less than in its neighbors.

Regulating the Family

While sexuality and the family are at the center of debates about the role of religious values and culture in shaping legislation across many religious traditions, family law is particularly sensitive in Muslim contexts. In the democratic context, then, it is not surprising that debates in this domain should quickly emerge as central. While I cannot here develop at length the complex and ongoing history of this debate in each case, the essential point is that in both Mali and Niger the development of a "family code" was put on the agenda at the instigation of secular groups—notably women's, human rights, and legal associations—as a core ingredient in the development of a democracy, and that the specific legislation proposed by these groups borrowed heavily from French family law. In each of these countries, as a result, religious groups objected, and there has subsequently been a long and still-inconclusive debate about what form of family law the country should adopt.[50]

In contrast to Mali and Niger, Senegal in fact has a family code in effect, which was passed in 1972 by President Senghor's government, and with his close involvement. Even at the time it was highly controversial, and the major religious figures in the country, convoked under the umbrella of a *Conseil Supérieur Islamique du Sénégal*, strongly opposed it. Given both the international and the domestic context, however—and specifically the fact that Senghor and the National Assembly (composed then exclusively of deputies from his party) could safely defy public opposition—the code was passed. Clearly, however, in the current context of competitive democratic elections, no such legislation would be viable today. While criticisms of the code surfaced periodically in Senegal over the years, this seemed largely a settled debate, and discussion tended to center on critiques by the secularists that the legislation was in fact only rarely enforced.[51]

The simmering discontent of religious groups on the issue, however, bubbled to the surface shortly after the election of Aboulaye Wade. In the post-alternance context of electoral empowerment, and with the new government clearly opening the door to discussions of previously unchallengeable issues, religious groups saw an opening and attempted to seize it. Thus, in 2002, a group calling itself the Comité Islamique pour la Réforme du Code de la Famille au Sénégal (CIRCOF) launched a public campaign to reinvigorate the debate and push for reforms to the 1972 Family Code in order to bring it into line with Islamic law.[52] Under the leadership of the lawyer Babacar Niang, a well-known political figure (and one-time presidential candidate) who had been active in the radical parties of the Left before rallying to the Islamic movement, a complete alternative to the code, entitled Code du Statut Personnel Islamique, was proposed.

Unsurprisingly, this proposal sparked an extraordinary reaction against it by the secular elite in Senegal and provoked anxiety from outside observers; one RFI article for example portrayed the proposal as an "Islamist attack on *laïcité*." Indeed, as Brossier[53] points out in the title of her thesis, the issue of the family code in fact raised the "redefinition of *laïcité* as a stake in the process of democratization." And Niang himself wrote a long article in defense of the reform proposal, provocatively entitled "La *laïcité*? Parlons-en" ("Secularism? Let's talk about it").[54]

No doubt recognizing the Pandora's box that would be opened by allowing the debate to continue, President Wade cut off public discussion of the issue when he forcefully declared that the family code would never be reformed while he was president. The issue was thus moved to the back burner, but it is certainly not dead. Today both proponents and opponents of reform point out that the current code is mainly characterized by the fact that it is almost universally ignored in Senegal. And indeed this fact is clearly central to the little popular mobilization around the issue; for the vast majority of Senegalese, the code is simply irrelevant. But it is this very fact that is sure to keep the issue alive; efforts to extend its application will inevitably be met by resistance given the gap between its prescriptions and the prevailing values and preferences of Senegal's Muslim majority.

While the varying historical contingencies of how the issue has evolved mean that the state of the debate is different in each country, the fundamental political issue is strikingly similar in each. If the secular states of the Sahel are to attempt to create a legal infrastructure to regulate the family affairs of their overwhelmingly Muslim societies in the context of a democratic system, this must be done in negotiation with the representatives of prevailing cultural and religious values. It is clear that if the outcome of such a negotiation is to be "democratic," in the sense that it is seen as legitimate and reflecting of their values by the majority of the population, it will require compromises with ideal notions of "democracy" such as those derived from Rawlsian liberal argument.

Redefining Education

Less prominent as a debate in the public sphere, but potentially with very significant long-term impact and consequences, is a strikingly parallel and unprecedented set of changes in the relationship of the state to religious education on which all three Sahelian countries have embarked in recent years. These changes have also been given their impetus from the liberalization of political systems and the consequent social and religious transformations underway. In all three countries, recent innovations are reforming and reinforcing the parallel nonstate systems of education built on Arabic language and religious instruction, and these reforms are being undertaken in the name of "giving parents the educational system they want," and defended as the actions of a democratic state sensitive to the needs of its citizens.[55]

The stage for these reforms was set by a confluence of factors. The core underlying factor concerns the maladaptation of the francophone system of education inherited from the colonial period and maintained into the postcolonial context as part of the ideology of the secular republic. This system was built on the need to create a francophone elite primarily to staff the state apparatus, and it has maintained this ideological underpinning; schools were intended to create a citizenry imbued in a French "republican" culture, and only an infinitesimally small percentage of the population ever complete secondary education. The results of this are unsurprising—the vast majority of parents across the Sahel have seen the official state schools as at best unattractive options, and indeed have often actively resisted efforts to enroll their children.

The resulting low school enrollment rates across the region were only made worse by the economic crises and the implementation of structural adjustment programs in the 1980s, which further diminished state capacity to support schools, only further adding to their unattractiveness to local populations. Throughout this same period, however, and strengthening from the end of the Cold War, the United Nations Educational, Scientific, and Cultural Organization's (UNESCO) "Education For All" and similar campaigns placed significant international pressures to expand school enrollment rates across Africa.[56] Particular pressure was put on states to increase girls' school enrollments, something singularly unattractive to many parents given the social risks involved.

This situation of strong pressures and low state capacity offered an opportunity for some advocates to push for the strengthening of religious educational institutions, and for bringing them into the system overseen by the state. These were typically a coalition of state agents in the historically small "directorates of Arabic education" in the ministries of education and the "directorates of religious affairs" most often housed in ministries of the interior. In the context of strong pressures to increase school enrollment rates, these advocates found allies, sometimes reluctant allies, among other sections of the state. This was clearly facilitated by political systems that, as a result of electoral processes, had been gradually growing more receptive to religious concerns.

In Mali, the period since the democratic transition of the early 1990s has seen an expansion of the system of religious schools known locally as *médersas* (*madrasas*) and an increased concern by the state in capturing them.[57] Over the course of fifteen years, in a series of incremental steps, a formalized *médersa* system, incorporation of the official state curriculum and French language as well as religious education and Arabic through the secondary school level, has thus been put in place. Comparable dynamics have led to a parallel evolution in Niger. In contrast with Mali, Niger had a formally recognized state system of "Franco-Arabic" schools starting from the late colonial period, but they were historically very poorly served and marginalized in comparison with the francophone state schools. As in Mali, however, the confluence of the pressures noted before and the era of democracy opened up opportunities for change. Capitalizing on the pressures to increase school enrollment, a major project to expand and strengthen Franco-Arabic education was launched, leading to a rapid expansion in the number of state-funded *madrasas* in Niger: from 180 in 2001 to some 700 by 2007.[58]

Negotiating Islam in the Era of Democracy

Among the many innovations that caught the prodemocracy civil society by surprise in post-*alternance* Senegal was the decision in 2002 by President Wade to introduce religious education within the public school system around the country. The idea had actually been suggested much earlier, in a major national consultation on education (*États-généraux de l'éducation*) in 1981, but had never been implemented due to the hostility of state functionaries to the idea. As a result, argues the official in the division of Arabic of the ministry of Education now implementing the reforms, the educational system remained based on a philosophy of *laïcité* that had been "imposed or adopted from the colonial period, but never *adapted* to Senegalese reality," and consequently a significant portion of the population strongly resisted state efforts to entice school enrollment.[59]

The problem faced by the new government after the democratic *alternance*, then, was how to "get the population to participate in the educational project of the state." Following a tour of schools around the country by the minister of education and representatives of the division of Arabic in the ministry, the proposed solution was to "offer something closer to what the population demanded" in terms of education. Religious education in public schools was thus mandated, and moreover—quietly and much less noticed in the public debate—the October 2002 reforms also included the creation of a system of *public* Franco-Arabic schools around the country. By 2007–2008 some seventy-two of these schools were functioning in every region except Dakar. These reforms, the ministry reports, were a significant factor in the declared success in raising the primary school enrollment rate from the 69 percent where it was stagnated at the time of the *alternance* in 2000 to some 85 percent by 2007.[60]

Within the specificities of the historical and social contexts of each country, these recent innovations share fundamental similarities. All of these changes grow out of shifts in power relations between the partisans of the francophone secular state and those with a more religious vision, shifts that have been driven by the process of public debate in the context of liberalized political systems. These innovations also clearly represent negotiated compromises—although at times still hotly debated ones—in the sense that the educational reform projects have all on the one hand strengthened French language and state curricular supervision, but on the other hand have also entailed state support for religious instruction.

Reconsidering Islam and Democracy in Senegal: Lessons from the Sahel

In contrast to the widespread depiction of the Senegalese case as exceptional, in some very fundamental respects the interaction of religion with the political in the era of democratization in Senegal largely parallels the situation in its neighbors. If for much of the postcolonial period the social structures of Senegalese Sufism were important elements of the country's long stability and relative nonrepressiveness, with the democratic opening of the 1990s, and in the current international context, a new and open public debate has been launched about religion in public life.

All three Muslim Sahelian countries that embarked on processes of democratization since the early 1990s have witnessed a very similar evolution in the debate on the role of religion in a democratic system. First, in all three, the role of religion in the public sphere has significantly expanded. This public presence has, in turn, produced a "democratization" of the religious sphere in the sense of a possibility for new voices to challenge established authorities and there has been a proliferation of debates on the interpretation of religious truths. As we have seen, the increased power of religion in public life has produced strikingly parallel patterns of politicization of a number of issues: the meaning of secularism in a democratic system; the relative role of local cultural and religious values versus "international" conceptions of human rights in shaping the legal framework governing family life; and the role of religious values in defining the educational system shaping the worldview of an emerging citizenry.

In all of these countries, this process has at times produced difficult and acrimonious debates and occasionally long stalemates on these issues between, on one side, the proponents of an ideology rooted in the French educational system and political culture inherited from colonialism and, on the other, those whose political orientation is rooted in the religious culture of the overwhelmingly non-francophone and Muslim societies. While the early processes of transition were largely led by the former, it is the latter who have gradually gained in influence in the open public debate that a liberalized political context has brought. Neither side, however, has displaced the other. Instead, we see that the stark oppositions are being subtly eroded, and these contentious and difficult political issues are being incrementally negotiated. Gradually and unevenly these countries appear to be experimenting with compromise solutions to the sharp debates that pit "secularists" against "Islamists."

What is there to make of this process and of the "normality" of Senegal in this respect, rather than its exceptionalism? For some observers of Senegal, both domestic and international, the fact that democracy has brought changes that are marked by an erosion of some of the "secular" and francophone ideology of the state raises alarms and questions about the future viability of its model of "success." A closer comparison with the processes in its neighbors, however, suggests that rather strikingly it is accommodation and bargaining that are taking place. The give and take of democracy over time, all indications suggest, is gradually moving the state and the political regime closer to the population and to local cultures and realities. The result, of course, will be that it will be more rooted in religious values than many of the secularists would like. Religious values will certainly continue to figure prominently in debates and outcomes of legislation on gender and sexuality. There are increased incentives for politicians to make religious appeals to get elected, and they will thus promise more religiously oriented state outcomes in schools and other institutions of public life. In short, given the deeply religious societies on which Sahelian democracy is being constructed, these countries are far more likely to evolve in the direction of American rather than French democracy. Along with its neighbors, Senegal seems to be defining one end of the spectrum of possibilities for negotiating and instituting democracy in Muslim contexts.

Notes

1. Karatnycky, "The 2001 Freedom House Survey."
2. Huntington, "Will More Countries Become Democratic?"
3. Stepan and Robertson, "An 'Arab' More than a 'Muslim' Electoral Gap."
4. Monteil, *L'Islam noir*.
5. Westerlund and Evers Rosander (eds.), *African Islam and Islam in Africa*.
6. Gellar, *Democracy in Senegal*, p. 108.
7. Notably in Villalón, *Islamic Society and State Power in Senegal*.
8. See Villalón, "Sufi Modernities in Contemporary Senegal" and the other contributions to the edited volume by van Bruinessen and Howell, which collectively develop the theme of the compatibility of Sufism and "modernity."

9. For a more extended comparative consideration of three Sahelian cases, see Villalón, "From Argument to Negotiation." The arguments in this chapter draw in part on this article.
10. Much of the comparative aspect of this paper is based on research for a project, entitled "Negotiating Democracy in Muslim Contexts: Political Liberalization and Religious Mobilization in the West African Sahel," funded by the Carnegie Scholars program of the Carnegie Corporation of New York. I gratefully acknowledge this support, which allowed significant fieldwork in Senegal, Mali, and Niger in 2007 and 2008.
11. A basic premise of this chapter is that approaching the issue of the relationship of religion to politics in terms of "compatibility" misframes the question and is ultimately misleading. For an eloquent discussion of a similar argument, see Bayat, *Making Islam Democratic*, especially his first chapter: "Islam and Democracy: the Perverse Charm of an Irrelevant Question."
12. Stepan, "The World's Religious Systems and Democracy."
13. Sidi Lamine Niasse, owner and editor of the *Walfadjri* newspaper and media group, speaking to an academic audience at the West African Research Center in Dakar, Senegal, June 2003.
14. For a collection of essays that collectively demonstrate the wide multiplicity of meanings in the politics of the Tijaniyya—the most widespread and important Sufi order in West Africa—see Triaud and Robinson, *La Tijaniyya*.
15. For a rich and insightful discussion of the varied political positions of Sufi movements in several African contexts, see Loimeier, "Sufis and Politics."
16. The electoral process was fully controlled by the state apparatus, for example, and the secret ballot was "optional," making it easy to impose sanctions on those rare voters who chose to exert that option rather than publicly demonstrate their support for the incumbent party.
17. Young and Kanté, "Governance, Democracy, and the 1988 Senegalese Elections."
18. Villalón, "Democratizing a (Quasi) Democracy."
19. Space considerations preclude an account of the political histories of these two countries or of their processes of democratization. For my own discussion of each of these, see Villalón and Idrissa, "Repetitive Breakdowns" and "The Tribulations of a Successful Transition." Neither Mali nor Niger have received anywhere near the degree of scholarly attention that Senegal has attracted.
20. Changes concerning the type of regime ("presidential" vs. "parliamentary" variants of the French Fifth Republic hybrid model), the electoral system, the role of decentralized institutions, the organization of the legislature and the very existence of its second chamber, as well as more fundamental questions about relations with and among key social and economic actors, were all put on the agenda by the new government of Abdoulaye Wade.

Negotiating Islam in the Era of Democracy

21. It is true that this new constitution of 2001 in fact resembled the old one in many respects—and gradually came to resemble it even more with successive amendments—but the important point is that drafting a new constitution put all aspects of the political system on the agenda for discussion and eventual change and reform. On the 2001 constitution, see Ndoye, *La Constitution Sénégalaise.*
22. VonDoepp and Villalón, "Elites, Institutions."
23. Stepan, "The World's Religious Systems and Democracy."
24. For discussions of the changing public roles of Islam in new political contexts, see Salvatore and Eickelman, *Public Islam.* A nice collection of case studies of these dynamics in African contexts is available in a special thematic issue on "Islam and African Muslim Publics" of the *Journal for Islamic Studies,* ed. Abdulkader Tayob (Vol. 27, 2007).
25. Excellent descriptions by local scholars of this diversity of religious associations in each country are available in Hassane, Diarra, and Makama, "Etude"; Magassa and Guindo, "Etat des lieux"; Magassa, "Islam et démocratie"; and Diakité, "La dynamique sociale." I am grateful to Professors Hassane, Magassa, and Diakité for making copies of these works available, and indeed for many extended discussions and shared insights.
26. Gellar, *Democracy in Senegal,* pp. 112–113.
27. Interview with Abdoul Aziz Kébé, July 2007, Dakar. Professor Kébé maintains a Web site on interreligious dialogue at www.aazizkebe.unblog.fr. On the network see the UNFPA's Senegal Web site at www.unfpa.sn/news/news3.htm.
28. See Villalón, "Senegal: Shades of Islamism on a Sufi Landscape?" for a longer discussion of these trends.
29. Augis, "Dakar's Sunnite Women."
30. Villalón and Kane, "Senegal."
31. Sène, "Islam as a Site of Agency, Mediation and Resistance."
32. Interview with *Seriñ* Fallou Dieng, Dakar, January 10, 2008.
33. Sall, "*Le Soufisme: Avantages et inconvénients.*"
34. The thrust of the argument of his book as sketched in this chapter was also developed by Sall in an interview with the author, January 7, 2008, Dakar, Senegal.
35. Author's translations from French. The reference to "associationism" refers to the Islamic theological error of *shirk,* attributing God's divine qualities to any other being or thing. Citation from p. 12.
36. Ibid., p. 138.
37. It may merit noting that one other interreligious dynamic clearly linked to democratization in Senegal and which currently provokes much concern is the growing rivalry between the two major Sufi orders, the Murids and the Tijanes, which grows out of an apparent preference for the Murids on the

part of President Abdoulaye Wade, and is in fact a major aspect of the politics of religion in Senegal under Wade. It is, however, very much a political rivalry rather than an ideological or theological one.

38. In an interview with the author, two current leaders of the movement insisted that the party was founded explicitly to take advantage of the opening provided by democratization in the 1990s, and argued that although the party has not actually contested any elections, it has stood ready to so do should it feel that none of the other alternatives are acceptable. Dakar, January 9, 2008.
39. Author's interview with Imam Mbaye Niang, Dakar, Senegal, January 8, 2008.
40. Gellar, *Democracy in Senegal*, p. 119–123.
41. Diop, Diouf, and Diaw, "Le Baobab a été déraciné."
42. Stepan, "Rituals of Respect: Sufis and Secularists in Senegal."
43. Space considerations preclude any significant discussion of these issues in the Malian and Nigerien cases.
44. Interestingly, however, in the context of a more difficult democratization in Niger, the word *laïque* was replaced with a statement of the "non-confessional" nature of the state and the affirmation of the "separation of the state and religion."
45. Samb, *Comprendre la laïcité*.
46. Ndoye, Doudou, *La Constitution Sénégalaise*, p. 49.
47. Kuru, "Secularism."
48. Samb, *Comprendre la laïcité*.
49. See Dièye, "La laïcité"; and Kane, "Politique et religion au Sénégal" for two academic discussions of the issue.
50. Schulz, "Political Factions, Ideological Fictions"; Villalón, "The Moral and the Political."
51. Sow Sidibé, "Senegal's Evolving Family Law."
52. A particularly thorough and useful discussion of this issue, linking the issue of reform of family law directly to the question of *laïcité* and the process of democratization, is available in Brossier, "Les débats sur la reforme du Code de la Famille au Sénégal."
53. Ibid.
54. Published in *Le Jour*, no. 65, Dakar, Senegal, July 2003. This paper is identified as a *"mensuel d'informations generales d'analyses, et de réflexions Islamiques."* I am grateful to Erin Augis for kindly providing me with a copy of this article.
55. The discourse surrounding these reforms is virtually identical in each of the three countries. My discussion of these educational reforms is based on interviews with the state officials in charge of such programs, as well

as interviews with and visits to religious schools involved in the process, in Dakar, Bamako, and Niamey in January and February 2008.
56. UNESCO, *Education for All: Is the World on Track?*
57. Sanankou and Brenner, *L'enseignement Islamique au Mali*; Brenner, "The Transformation of Muslim Schooling in Mali."
58. Author's interview with an official in the Ministry of Religious Affairs, Niamey, Niger, February 5, 2008.
59. Author's interview with the head of the Division of Arabic Education, Ministry of Education, Dakar, Senegal, January 8, 2008.
60. Ibid.

Bibliography

Augis, Erin. "Dakar's Sunnite Women: The Politics of Person." In *L'Islam politique au sud du Sahara: Identités, discours et enjeux*, ed. Muriel Gomez-Perez, 309–326. Paris: Karthala, 2005.

Bayat, Asef. *Making Islam Democratic: Social Movements and the Post-Islamist Turn.* Stanford: Stanford University Press, 2007.

Brenner, Louis. "The Transformation of Muslim Schooling in Mali: The Madrasa as an Institution of Social and Religious Mediation." In *Schooling Islam: The Culture and Politics of Modern Muslim Education*, eds. Robert W. Hefner and Muhammad Quasim Zaman, 199–223. Princeton, N.J.: Princeton University Press, 2007.

Brossier, Marie. "Les débats sur la reforme du Code de la Famille au Sénégal: La redéfinition de la laïcité comme enjeu du processus de démocratisation." Mémoire (thesis) for DEA in Etudes Africaines, option Science Politique. Université Paris I, 2004.

Diakité, Drissa. "La dynamique sociale des mouvements confessionnels: Tendances et enjeux majeurs pour le développement du Mali." Unpublished manuscript, prepared as part of multiauthor report entitled *Etude nationale prospective: "Mali 2025."* PNUD/Futurs Africains, 1998.

Dièye, Abdoulaye. "La laïcité à l'epreuve des faits au Sénégal: Approche juridique." Paper presented at a conference on "Islam and the Public Sphere in Africa." Sponsored by the Institute for the Study of Islamic Thought in Africa (ISITA), Program in African Studies, Northwestern University. May 17–19, 2007.

Diop, Momar Coumba, Mamadou Diouf, and Aminata Diaw. "Le Baobab a été déraciné: L'alternance au Sénégal." *Politique Africaine* 78 (2000): 157–179.

Gellar, Sheldon. *Democracy in Senegal: Tocquevillian Analytics in Africa.* New York: Palgrave Macmillian, 2005.

Hassane, Moulaye, Marthe Diarra, and Oumarou Makama. "Etude sur les pratiques de l'Islam au Niger." Niamey: République du Niger, Ministère de l'Interieur et de la Décentralization, Direction Générale des Affairs Politiques et Juridiques, Direction des Affairs Coûtumières et Religieuses, and DANIDA: Bureau de Cooperation Danoise-Niger. Unpublished document, 2006.

Huntington, Samuel. "Will More Countries Become Democratic?" *Political Science Quarterly* 99 (2) (Summer 1984): 193–218.

Kane, Ousseynou. "Politique et religion au Sénégal: Les nouveaux paradigmes." Paper presented at a conference on "Islam and the Public Sphere in Africa." Sponsored by the Institute for the Study of Islamic Thought in Africa (ISITA), Program in African Studies, Northwestern University. May 17–19, 2007.

Karatnycky, Adrian. "The 2001 Freedom House Survey: Muslim Countries and the Democracy Gap." *Journal of Democracy* 13 (1) (January 2002): 99–112.

Kuru, Ahmet T. "Secularism, State Policies, and Muslims in Europe: Analyzing French Exceptionalism." *Comparative Politics* 4 (1) (2008): 1–19.

Loimeier, Roman. "The Secular State and Islam in Senegal." In *Questioning the Secular State: The Worldwide Resurgence of Religion in Politics*, ed. David Westerlund, 183–197. New York: St. Martin's Press, 1996.

———. "Sufis and Politics in Sub-Saharan Africa." In *Sufism and Politics*, ed. Paul L. Heck, 59–101. Princeton: Markus Wiener Publishers, 2007.

Magassa, Hamidou. "Islam et démocratie en Afrique de l'Ouest: Le cas du Mali." Bamako: Friedrich Ebert Stiftung, 2005. Unpublished document.

Magassa, Hamidou and Moussa Guindo. "Etat des lieux de l'Islam au Mali." Bamako: Fondation Friedrich Ebert, 2003. Unpublished document.

Monteil, Vincent M. *L'Islam noir*. Paris: Seuil, 1964.

Ndoye, Doudou. *La Constitution Sénégalaise du 7 Janvier 2001 commentée, et ses pactes internationaux annexés*. Dakar: Les Editions Juridiques Africaines, 2001.

Sall, Mansour, *"Le Soufisme: Avantages et inconvénients."* Dakar: NIS, 2007.

Salvatore, Armando and Dale E. Eickelman, eds. *Public Islam and the Common Good*. Leiden, Netherlands: Brill, 2004.

Samb, Djibril. *Comprendre la laïcité*. Dakar: Les Nouvelles Editions Africaines du Sénégal, 2005.

Sanankou, Bintou and Louis Brenner, eds. *L'enseignement Islamique au Mali*. Bamako: Editions Jamana, 1991.

Schulz, Dorothea E. "Political Factions, Ideological Fictions: The Controversy Over Family Law Reform in Democratic Mali." *Islamic Law and Society* 10 (1) (2003): 132–164.

Sène, Ibra. "Islam as a Site of Agency, Mediation, and Resistance: Hizbut Tarqiyya (Senegal), 1975–2002." Paper presented at the annual meeting of the African Studies Association. Washington, D.C.: October 30–November 1, 2003.

Soares, Benjamin F. "Saint and Sufi in Contemporary Mali." In *Sufism and the Modern in Islam*, eds. Martin van Bruinessen and Julia Day Howell, 76–91. London: I. B. Tauris, 2007.

———. "Islam in Mali in the Neoliberal Era." *African Affairs* 105 (418) (2005): 77–95.

Sounaye, Abdoulaye. "Instrumentalizing the Qur'an in Niger's Public Life." *Journal for Islamic Studies* 27 (2007), Thematic Issue: "Islam and African Muslim Publics": 211–239.

Sow Sidibé, Amsatou. "Senegal's Evolving Family Law." *University of Louisville Journal of Family Law* 32 (2) (1994): 421–430.

Stepan, Alfred. "Rituals of Respect: Sufis and Secularists in Senegal in Comparative Perspective." *Comparative Politics* 44 (4) (July 2012): 379–401.

———. "The World's Religious Systems and Democracy: Crafting the 'Twin Tolerations,'" Chapter 11 of *Arguing Comparative Politics*, 213–253. Oxford: Oxford University Press, 2001.

Stepan, Alfred and Graeme B. Robertson. "An 'Arab' More Than a 'Muslim' Electoral Gap." *Journal of Democracy* 14 (3) (July 2003): 30–44.

Triaud, Jean-Louis and David Robinson, eds. *La Tijaniyya: Une confrérie musulmane à la conquête de l'Afrique*. Paris: Karthala, 2000.

UNESCO. *Education for All: Is the World on Track?* EFA Global Monitoring Report. Paris: UNESCO, 2002.

Villalón, Leonardo A. "Democratizing a (Quasi) Democracy: The Senegalese Elections of 1993." *African Affairs* 93 (371) (April 1994): 163–193.

———. *Islamic Society and State Power in Senegal: Disciples and Citizens in Fatick*. Cambridge: Cambridge University Press, 1995.

———. "The Moral and the Political in African Democratization: The *Code de la Famille* in Niger's Troubled Transition." *Democratization* 3 (2) 1996: 41–68.

———. "Senegal: Shades of Islamism on a Sufi Landscape?" In *Political Islam in West Africa: State-Society Relations Transformed*, ed. William F. S. Miles, 161–182. Lynne Rienner Publishers, 2007.

———. "Sufi Modernities in Contemporary Senegal: Religious Dynamics Between the Local and the Global." In *Sufism and the Modern in Islam*, eds. Martin van Bruinessen and Julia Day Howell, 172–191. London: I. B. Tauris, 2007.

———. "From Argument to Negotiation: Constructing Democracies in Muslim West Africa." *Comparative Politics* 42 (4) (July 2010): 375–393.

Villalón, Leonardo A. and Abdourahmane Idrissa. "Repetitive Breakdowns and a Decade of Experimentation: Institutional Choices and Unstable Democracy in Niger." In *The Fate of Africa's Democratic Experiments: Elites and Institutions in Comparative Perspective*, eds. Leonardo A. Villalón and Peter VonDoepp, 27–48. Bloomington: Indiana University Press, 2005.

_____. "The Tribulations of a Successful Transition: Institutional Dynamics and Elite Rivalry in Mali." In *The Fate of Africa's Democratic Experiments: Elites and Institutions in Comparative Perspective*, eds. Leonardo A. Villalón and Peter VonDoepp, 49–74. Bloomington: Indiana University Press, 2005.

Villalón, Leonardo A. and Ousmane Kane. "Senegal: The Crisis of Democracy and the Emergence of an Islamic Opposition." In *The African State at a Critical Juncture: Between Disintegration and Reconfiguration*, eds. Leonardo A. Villalón and Phillip Huxtable, 143–163. Boulder: Lynne Rienner Publishers, 1998.

VonDoepp, Peter and Leonardo A. Villalón. "Elites, Institutions, and the Varied Trajectories of Africa's Third Wave Democracies." In *The Fate of Africa's Democratic Experiments: Elites and Institutions in Comparative Perspective*, eds. Leonardo A. Villalón and Peter VonDoepp, 1–26. Bloomington: Indiana University Press, 2005.

Westerlund, David and Eva Evers Rosander, eds. *African Islam and Islam in Africa: Encounters Between Sufis and Islamists*. Athens: Ohio University Press, 1997.

Young, Crawford and Babacar Kanté. "Governance, Democracy, and the 1988 Senegalese Elections." In *Governance and Politics in Africa*, eds. Goran Hyden and Michael Bratton, 57–74. Boulder, Colo.: Lynne Rienner, 1992.

Glossary

Adat: Tradition, customs
Addiya: Religious offerings
Adhan: Call to prayer
Alal: Wealth
Amal (plural *a'amal*): Work, religious tasks
Baraka/Barke (Wolof): Blessings, gift of grace
Batin: Sufi Islam esoteric knowledge
Bid'a: Innovation in religion
Cosaan: Tradition
Daara: Rural Qur'an school (combining teaching and agricultural production)
Dahira/Daayiras: Religious associations, urban Sufi order prayer group
Dar Al Islam: Land ruled by Islam/inhabited by Muslims
Dar al-kufr/Dar al-harb: Land of the Infidels
Dhikr: Litany of prayers
Din: Religion
Fiqh: Islamic jurisprudence
Fitna: Division within Islam
Gàmmu: Wolof for *Mawlid* (or *Mawlud*)
Griot: Praise singer, musician, and oral historian
Gris-Gris: Amulets
Hadith: Collections of oral traditions of the words and deeds of the Prophet Muhammad

Glossary

Hajj: Pilgrimage to Mecca. One of the five prescriptions of Islam. Also the title acquired by a man who made the pilgrimage. For a woman it is *Ajja*

Hijab: Veil, headscarf

Hijra: Migration of the Prophet Muhammad from Mecca to Medina in 622 C.E.

Imam: Head of a mosque. He leads the prayers

Imam Ratib: Principal imam, leads the Friday and key religious ceremonies prayers

Jihad: To strive or struggle in the context of religious war or personal struggle within oneself against all sorts of temptations or against poverty

Jum'a: Friday prayer or Friday mosque

Khalife Générale: Head of one of the Sufi orders of Senegal

Mággal: Pilgrimage to and celebration of the Prophet Muhammad (*Mawlud* by the Tijaniyya of Tivaouane) or of Amadu Bamba Mbacke (by the *Murridiyya* of Touba)

Marabout: Muslim religious erudite (Qur'an school teacher or Sufi order leader)

Masjib: Mosque, place of prostration

Mawlid: Celebration/commemoration of the birthday of the Prophet Muhammad

Muqqadam: Representative of important Sufi leaders

Ndiggël: Sufi leader political instruction/religious ordinance

Njebbel: Initiation rite into a Sufi order

Sharî'a: Islamic law

Shaykh (Arabic) or *Seriñ* (Wolof) or *Ceerno* (Halpulaar): religious and spiritual guide

Sokhna: Daughters or wives of Sufi leaders

Sunnah: The body of Islamic law based on the words and deeds of the Prophet Muhammad and his successors

Taalibe: Disciple

Teranga: Hospitality

Ummah: The Muslim community

Wahhabi: Reformist Islamic movement named after the founder of Saudi Arabia, Mohammad Ibn Abd al-Wahhab (1703–1792)

Wali: Holy man, saint

Wazifa: Sufi repetition of sacred phrases

Wird: Prayer formula specific to each Sufi order in Senegal

Zawiya: Headquarters/sacred site of a Sufi order

Ziyara: Visit and renewal of allegiance to a spiritual leader and a holy site

Contributors

ERIN AUGIS is an associate professor of sociology at Ramapo College, where she teaches in the sociology, women and gender studies, and Africana studies programs. She lectures and publishes articles on American race relations, African immigrants in the United States, migratory flows within Africa, and her principal area of research—Sunni reformist women in West Africa. Augis is currently completing her book manuscript, "Dakar's Sunnite Women: Activism and Subjectivity in Senegal's Islamic Reform Movement," which is a longitudinal ethnography of young women's engagement in Dakar's Sunnite movement in the new millennium.

CHEIKH ANTA BABOU is an associate professor of history at the University of Pennsylvania in Philadelphia. Babou teaches African history and the history of Islam in Africa. His research focuses on mystical Islam in West Africa and Senegal and on the new African diaspora. Babou has published extensively on the Muridiyya Muslim order of Senegal and the Senegalese diaspora. His book *Fighting the Greater Jihad: Amadu Bamba and the Founding of the Muridiyya of Senegal, 1853–1913* was published by Ohio University Press in 2007. Babou's articles have appeared in *African Affairs, Journal of African History, International Journal of African Historical Studies, Journal of Religion in Africa, Africa Today,* and other scholarly journals in the United States and in Europe. He has presented papers at international scholarly meetings on

Islam and the transnational migration of West African Muslims. His current research examines the experience of West African Muslim immigrants in Europe and North America.

BETH A. BUGGENHAGEN is an assistant professor of sociocultural anthropology at Indiana University, Bloomington. Her research interests include circulation and value, diaspora and transnationalism, neoliberal global capital, gender, and Islam and visuality. She is the editor (with Anne-Maria B. Makhulu and Stephen Jackson) of *Hard Work, Hard Times: Global Volatilities and African Subjectivities*. (Berkeley: University of California Press, 2010). Buggenhagen is currently working on a book manuscript, "Prophets and Profits: Gender and Islam in Global Senegal," on the global circuits of Senegalese Muslims and the politics of social production.

SOULEYMANE BACHIR DIAGNE is a professor at Columbia University in the departments of French and philosophy. His field of research includes history of logic, history of philosophy, Islamic philosophy, African philosophy, and literature. Two of his many publications have been recently translated into English: *Islam and Open Society: Fidelity and Movement in the Philosophy of Muhammad Iqbal* (Dakar: Codesria, 2011) and *African Art as Philosophy: Senghor, Bergson, and the Idea of Negritude* (London: Seagull Books, 2011).

MAMADOU DIOUF is the Leitner Family Professor of African Studies and History in the Middle East, South Asia, and African Studies and History departments, and director of the Institute of African Studies at Columbia University in New York. His primary research has focused on the colonial and postcolonial, urban, and cultural history of Senegal and francophone West Africa as well as the intellectual history of the African enclaves of the Black Atlantic. He is the author of many articles, book chapters, and books, including *Le Kajoor au 19ème siècle: Pouvoir ceddo et conquête coloniale* (Paris: Karthala, 1990); *Histoire du Sénégal: Le modèle Islamo Wolof et ses périphéries* (Paris: Maisonnueve and Larose, 2001); and *La construction de l'état au Sénégal* (with D. Cruise O'Brien and M. C. Diop; Paris: Karthala, 2002); coeditor of *New Perspectives on Islam in Senegal: Conversion, Migration, Wealth, Power, and Feminity* (with Mara Leichtman; New York: Palgrave Macmillan, 2010); and *Rhythms of the Afro-Atlantic World: Rituals and Remembrances* (with Ifeoma C.K. Nwankwo; Ann Arbor: University of Michigan Press, 2011).

Contributors

JOSEPH HILL has been a visiting assistant professor and postdoctoral fellow in anthropology at the Department of Sociology, Anthropology, Psychology, and Egyptology at the American University in Cairo since 2008. His primary research project, begun in 2001, focuses on a global Sufi Islamic network, the disciples of Shaykh Ibrahim Ñas, who call themselves "Taalibe Baay" in the Wolof language of Senegal. Although Ñas's disciples are scattered around the world, this fieldwork has primarily concentrated on Senegal and Mauritania, but more recently has included the Taalibe Baay communities in Cairo, Egypt, and New York. Hill's current academic writings are about the Taalibe Baay, the followers of Shaykh Ibrahim Ñas, the relationships between religious and secular governance, Islamic women leaders, and the use of languages (Wolof, Arabic, French) in Islamic oratory. His publications include "'All Women Are Guides': Sufi Leadership and Womanhood Among Taalibe Baay in Senegal." Hill is currently working on a manuscript called "Hidden Authorities: Taalibe Baay Women as Sufi Leaders in Senegal."

ETIENNE SMITH is currently a postdoctoral research scholar at the Committee on Global Thought at Columbia University, where he teaches African politics and history. His research interests focus on ethnicity, joking kinships, cultural nationalisms, and intellectual history in Senegambia and Mali. Smith's recent publications include *L'Afrique: Histoire et défis* (Paris: Ellipses, 2009) and numerous articles on history and politics.

ALFRED STEPAN is the Wallace Sayre Professor of Government, director of the Center for the Study of Democracy, Toleration, and Religion, and codirector of the Institute for Religion, Culture, and Public Life at Columbia University. He is a fellow of the American Academy of Arts and Sciences and of the British Academy. He is the coauthor of *Crafting State Nations: India and Other Multinational Democracies* with Juan J. Linz and Yogendra Yadav (Baltimore: Johns Hopkins University Press, 2011), author of *Arguing Comparative Politics* (Oxford: Oxford University Press, 2001), and the coauthor of *Problems of Democratic Transition and Consolidation: Eastern Europe, Southern Europe, and Latin America* (Baltimore: Johns Hopkins University Press, 1996), with Juan J. Linz.

Contributors

LEONARDO A. VILLALÓN is director of the Center for African Studies and associate professor of political science at the University of Florida. His research has focused on Islam and politics and on democratization in West Africa, with special attention to the Sahelian countries of Senegal, Mali, and Niger. His publications include *Islamic Society and State Power in Senegal: Disciples and Citizens in Fatick* and numerous others works on politics and religion in West Africa. The chapter in this volume builds on research carried out from 2007 to 2009 with the support of a grant from the Carnegie Scholars program of the Carnegie Corporation of New York.

Index

Abbasid caliphs, 38
Abderraziq, Ali, 38–40
Abduh, Muhammad, 3
acco, 27
African Islam, 4, 30, 240
ahir ("apparent") truths, 27, 102, 105–108, 111–113, 115
AIDS, 29, 46, 206, 223
AIN (Association Islamique du Niger), 245
Al Afghani, Jamal Ad-Din, 3, 38
al Kébir, Siddiyya, 187
al-Amîn, Muḥammad, 109
alcohol, 129–130, 134
al-Falah Collège, 75, 80
Algeria, 3, 8, 31n6, 74–75, 86, 127–128, 184, 214
Al-Hallaj, 3
Alidou, Ousseina, 81
Al-Jabri, Mohammed, 3
Allawi, Ali A., 40–41
almaamiyya, 43

AMUPI (Association Malienne pour l'Unité et le Progrès de l'Islam), 245
An Na'im, Abdullah Ahmed, 41–42
ANIOS (Association Nationale des Imams et Oulemas du Sénégal), 222
An-Na'im, Abdullahi, 228n5, 229n10
anti-AIDS policies, 29, 46, 206, 223
anti-female genital mutilation (FGM) policies, 29, 46, 86, 206, 222–223
apostates, 2, 219, 233n65
"apparent" (ahir; zâhir) truths, 27, 102, 105–108, 111–113, 115
"Arab Spring", 100
Arabic, 75, 138, 181, 189–190, 196, 198n9
assimilation, 28, 128, 181, 193, 213–214
assimilés, 44
Association de Quinze, 86
Association des élèves et étudiants Musulmans du Sénégal, 84
Association des étudiants Musulmans de l'Université de Dakar, 84

Association Islamique du Niger (AIN), 245
Association Malienne pour l'Unité et le Progrès de l'Islam (AMUPI), 245
Association Nationale des Imams et Oulemas du Senegal (ANIOS), 222
Ataturk, Mustafa Kemal, 31n6
Augis, Erin, 23, 26
Averroes (Ibn Rusch), 3, 38
Avicenna (Ibn Sina), 3, 38

ba ("hidden") truths, 27, 66, 102, 105–108, 111–113, 115
Ba, Màbba Jaxu, 111
Baay Faal, 118n32
Baba, Siddiyya, 187
Babou, Cheikh, 6, 27
Badawi, Abdullah, 3
Badis, Al-Azhar Ben, 33n48
Bahrain, 81
Bamba, Amadu (Amadu Bamba Mbacke), 4, 10, 44, 61, 63, 128–129, 132, 190, 195, 212
baraka (*barke*): marabout's identity and, 12; religion-based media and, 51, 53–54, 60, 62, 64; seeking during *Mawlid*, 105; shifting emphasis from, 21
bâtîn ("hidden") truths, 27, 66, 102, 105–108, 111–113, 115
Baubérot, Jean, 47–48
BDS (Bloc des Masses Sénégalaises), 17
Ben Badis, 3
Benin, 81–82
bida, 76
Black Islam, 9, 184, 240
Bloc des Masses Sénégalaises (BDS), 17
boroom dëkk, 109
Boumédienne, Houari, 3, 31n6
Bourguiba, Habib, 3, 42
Bouteflika, Abdel Aziz, 3
Brigade de la Fraternité Musulmane, 74
broadcast media, 51–53
Buckley, Liam, 65
Buggenhagen, Beth, 20, 22, 24–26, 80
Buh, Saad, 187
Buso clan, 132

caliphate: abolition of, 25, 39; recasting function of, 21; restitution of, 40–41
Casset, Mama, 64–65
ceerno (shaykhs), 43
Cekkeen, 110–113
Cercle des Intellectuels Soufis du Sénégal, 248
Chehabi, H. E., 233n65
China, 79
Christianity, 29, 45, 77, 140, 153, 156–158, 161–162, 217–218, 220
Chwe, Michael Suk-Young, 207, 218
CIRCOF (Comité Islamique pour la Réforme du Code de la Famille), 20, 86, 165, 225, 254
circuits, 51, 55
Cissé, Aliou, 106–107
Cissé, Hassan, 107, 119n41
cloth and clothing, 52, 55, 59, 64–66, 79
Code du Statut Personnel Islamique, 86
Collectif des Associations Islamiques au Sénégal, 86
colonial administration, 8–11, 14; challenge to French secularism, 42–44; Islamization, 43; mutual accommodation, 211–212; voting, 212–215
Comité Islamique pour la Réforme du Code de la Famille (CIRCOF), 20, 86, 165, 225, 254

Index

Complexe Scolaire Serigne Abass Sall, 248
Conseil Supérieur Islamique, 16–17
constitution, 16, 160, 174n81, 261n21
Coppolani, Xavier, 127–128
cosmology, call for new, 37–38
Coulon, Christian, 4–6, 217
Creppell, Ingrid, 12
currency devaluation, 58, 78

daar al Murid, 28, 129
daara, 74
Dahiratoul Moustarchidina wal Moustarchidaty, 247
da'iras (*daayiras*), 5, 57–58, 62, 104, 109, 115, 138
dawa, 76
De Coppet, Marcel, 217
De Gaulle, Charles, 15–16
decline of religions, 1
democracy, 205–259; "compatibility" of Sufism and, 239–242; Family Code, 253–257; human rights reforms, 221–225; mutual respect, 211–215; questioning the state, 251–253; regional perspective, 243–245; religious agendas in, 249–253; religious change and, 245–249
Devès, Gaspard, 188, 200n38
Dia, Mamadou, 16–18, 31n6, 31n7, 44–47, 131
Diagne, Abd al-Qadir, 74
Diagne, Aichatou Fall, 87–88
Diagne, Blaise, 13, 214
Diagne, Souleymane Bachir, 17, 24–25, 219, 232n60
Dieng, Massamba Jeery, 190
Dieng, Seriñ Fallou, 248
Dièye, Abdoulaye, 250
Digital Solidarity Fund, 80

Diop, Daam, 103–105, 113–115
Diop, Hamet Gora, 181–193, 195
Diouf, Abdou, 4–5, 15, 19, 23, 36, 46, 85, 134–135, 157, 216, 241–242
Diouf, Mamadou, 28, 213–214
discursive expression, 22–23, 100
discursive space, autonomy of, 10, 12
Djamil, Mansour Sy, 20
Djamil, Moustapha Sy, 18
doomu ndaar, 28, 180, 186–192, 194–197, 201n49
Drame, Mamadou Lamin, 8
drought cycle and environmental crisis of 1970s, 19–20, 56

education, 223–224, 255–257
Egypt: influence on Sunnite groups, 75, 79; reformist women, 82–83; secularism, 99; Sufi associations, 3
Egypt (Ndour), 53
Ekeh, Peter, 168n24
electoral code, 135–136
ethnicity, 29
Exposition de l'Art Nègre (1966), 57–58

Fabineta, Gaura Diop, 186–188, 190
Faidherbe, Louis, 184
Failed States Index, 209, 229n12
Fall, Abd al-Qadir, 74
Fall, Ousseynou, 250
falsafa, 100
Family Code, 16–17, 20, 23, 46, 85–88, 161, 225, 253
Fatma, Cheikh Mbacke Gainde, 17, 130, 133
Fatton, Robert, 4
female genital mutilation (FGM), 29, 46, 86, 206, 222–223
Filali-Ansary, Abdou, 40
fiqh, 75, 100, 187

Index

Foire Afro-Arabe, 80
Fortier, François-Edmond, 64
Foundation Cheikhul Khadim, 138
France, 8–10, 15–16, 27; bans on religious signs and symbols, 54; economic history of Saint-Louis, 183–184; handshaking, 90–91; lying at work, 91; migration of Murids to, 57–58; mutual accommodation, 211–212; private capital, 57; roots of social contract, 127–129; secularism, 43–44, 86–87, 160–161; veiling, 89, 231n42; voting, 212–215
Frearon, J. D., 11
Freedom House's civil liberties scale, 210
freedom of conscience, 41–42
French Union, 15–16
Front pour le Socialisme et la Démocratie (FSD), 250
Fuuta Tooro, 43

Gambia, 65
Gellar, Sheldon, 4
Ghana, 81–82
globalization, Sunnite women and, 77–84
Great Britain, 126, 212
groundnut production, 14, 16, 18–20, 55–56, 130
Gueye, Lamine, 16–17, 31n7
Gueye, Meissa, 64
Gurr, Ted, 210

hajj (pilgrimage to Mecca), 17, 44, 161, 184, 190–191, 195
handshaking, 26, 90–91
Hann, Hamet NDiaye, 189–191, 199n35
Hansen, Thomas B., 126–127
Harakat al-Falah, 75, 84

Hassaniyya, 189, 196
haya (modesty in dress and relations with opposite sex), 26, 76, 90–91
"hidden" (*ba*; *bâtîn*) truths, 27, 66, 102, 105–108, 111–113, 115
hijab (veil), 26, 75, 81–83, 89, 231n42
Hill, Joseph, 20, 26–27
Hirschkind, Charles, 54
Hirschmann, Nancy, 82
HIV/AIDS, 29, 46, 206, 223
Hizbut Tarqiyyah, 138, 247
hospitality (*teranga*), 149–151
human rights, 206–208, 229n10; cooperation and conflict concerning reforms to, 221–225; political rights and, 209–211

Ibn Al-Arabi, 3
Ibn Rusch (Averroes), 3, 38
Ibn Sina (Avicenna), 3, 38
identity: creating a Senegalese modernity, 15; marabouts' dual, 12; private accumulation and, 80; public display of, 10; religious, of brotherhood units, 12–13; Sunnite women, 83–84
ijtihad, 42
independent media, 53, 59–60
India, 38–39, 126, 165n6, 216–217, 231n48, 232n49
institutionalized in-group policing, 11
inter-brotherhood cooperation, 13, 19
International Monetary Fund, 58, 78, 133
Internet, 53, 59, 76, 79
Iran, 29, 77, 79, 234n81
Islamization, 42–44
Islamo-Wolof model, 7, 9, 24, 28, 147, 149, 152, 161–162; defined, 32n27; modernization, 15–22; theorizing, 10–15

Index

Ivory Coast, 81–82
Izala movement, 81

Jama'at Ibad ar-Rahman, 75, 85
Jama'at Ibadu Rahman, 84
Jama'atou Ibadou Rahmane, 247
Jamiyat al-Islah (Bahrain), 81
Jaxate clan, 132–133
jihad, 8
jikko, 61, 65
jinn, 105, 113, 120n55

kalante (joking kinship), 148–151, 154–157, 168n28, 169n33, 169n35
Kamara, Alaji, 190
Kébé, Abdul Aziz, 219, 222, 247
Keïta, Seydou, 65
Khalîfa, 107–109
khalifatullah, 39
Khalife Générale, 12, 22, 54–55, 61, 106–107, 225
kinship, 29, 148–150, 153–157
Kunta, Bachir, 143n29
Kuru, A., 46
Kuwait, 75, 79–80

La Petite Mosquée (Médine), 192–193
Laay, Seydinâ Limâmu, 44
Laayeen, 44
laïcité, See secularism (*laïcité*)
laicité bien comprise (well-understood secularism), 25, 36, 42–48, 227
Laitin, D. D., 11
Lamine Gueye law, 13
Lamp Fall FM Dakar and Touba, 60
language, 149–150, 157, 160–161, 163, 173n71, 189–190
Le Blanc, Marie Nathalie, 81
Le Chatelier, Alfred, 49n19

Le Soufisme: Avantages et Inconvénients (Sufism: Advantages and Inconveniences) (Sall), 248
Lebanon, 57
Les Allées du Centenaire, 79
Les laïcités dans le monde (Secularities in the World) (Baubérot), 47
Libya, 79
L'Islam et les fondements du pouvoir (Islam and the Foundations of Power) (Abderraziq), 38–39
L'Islamisme et la science (Renan), 37–38
lying, 91

Maam Jaara Buso, 138
Mabeey, Amadu Ndiaye, 190
madrasas, 207, 224, 256
Mággal, 54, 60–63, 131–132, 138, 140, 217
mahdism, 44
Mahmood, Saba, 82–83
Mali, 19, 30, 43, 59, 131, 243, 249, 253, 256
marabouts: during colonial period, 43; creation of theocratic states, 8; *ndiggël*, 32n40; postcolonial state, 15–16; relationship to *taalibe*, 13–14, 18, 75; social contract, 6, 9–12; women as, 81; worldly, 22
Marché H.L.M. (Habitations Loyers Modéré), 59
Marché Sandaga, 59
Marty, Paul, 127, 141n8
Masquelier, Adeline, 81
Matlabul Fawzayni, 138–139
matrilineage, 8
Mauritania, 107
Mawlid (*Gàmmu*), 102–105, 195
Mbacke, Abdou Lahat, 19, 56, 131–134

Index

Mbakke, Amadu Bamba (Amadu Bamba), 4, 10, 44, 61, 63, 128–129, 132, 190, 195, 212
Mbacke, Falilou, 19, 23, 130–132
Mbacke, Mortalla, 61, 135
Mbacke, Moustapha, 17
Mbacke, Moustapha Falilou, 133
Mbacke, Saliou, 61
Mecca, 17, 44
MEEJIR (Mouvement des Elèves et étudiants Jama'atou Ibadou Rahmane), 247
Meriboute, Zidane, 2–3, 31n7
Méridien President Hotel, 80
Metcalf, Barbara, 126
Métis, 187–189, 200n40
metropolitains, 44
MFDC (Mouvement des Forces Démocratiques de Casamance), 164–165
Miran, Marie, 81–82
mission civilisatrice, 28, 49n19
"moderate" Muslims, 100–101, 118n21
modesty in dress and relations with opposite sex (*haya*), 26, 76, 90–91
Moghdad, Bou el, 189
Moorish Islam, 9
Morocco, 3, 8, 79, 86
Mouvement des Elèves et étudiants Jama'atou Ibadou Rahmane (MEEJIR), 247
Mouvement des Forces Démocratiques de Casamance (MFDC), 164–165
Mouvement pour la Réforme et le Developpement Sociale (MRDS), 250
Mudimbe, V. Y., 17
Muhammad (Prophet), 40, 102
multiparty democratic system, 15, 22
multivocal nature of religions, 2, 19, 206, 219, 221, 241

muqaddams, 109–113
Murid order (Muridiyya), 4, 6, 13, 17, 19–20; current president's connection to, 47; economic power of, 55–60; financial autonomy of, 138–139; founding of, 44; H. G. Diop and, 182, 190, 192, 195; migration of, 21–22, 26, 56–58; mutual accommodation, 211–212; percentage of population, 144n37; policy of cultural compromise, 27; religion-based media, 51–52, 55, 60–63; rituals of respect, 217–218; state politics and social contract, 125–141
music, 52–53, 60, 79
Muslim Brotherhood, 23
Muslim intellectual response, 42

Nandy, Ashis, 1
Ñas (Niasse), Ibrahim, 17, 27, 101, 106
Nasser, Gamal Abdel, 3
National Domain, 23
"national heroes", 149–150, 157, 166n14, 167n15
ndiggël, 13–14, 20, 22, 32n40, 56, 138
Ndour, Youssou, 53
Negritude, 130, 142n16, 171n53
neoliberalism, 23, 77–84, 88, 91–92, 102
NGOs (nongovernmental organizations), 78, 222, 246
Niang, Maitre Babacar, 86–87
Niang, Mbaye, 250
Niass, Al-Hadj Abdoulaye, 106–107
Niass, Tidiane, 109
Niasse (Ñas), Ibrahim, 17, 27, 101, 106
Niasse, Sidi Lamine, 260n13
Niger, 19, 30, 77, 81, 243, 249, 253, 256

Index

Nigeria, 107
Njolofeen, 110–114
nongovernmental organizations (NGOs), 78, 222, 246

O'Brien, Donal B. Cruise, 4–6, 141n1, 211, 220
Organisation de la Conférence Islamique (OCI), 41, 80
originaires, 16, 18, 28, 44, 180–197, 197n2

Pakistan, 31n6, 207, 234n83
Palestinian nationalist struggle, 80
Parti de l'Unité Républicain (PUR), 250
Parti Démocratique Sénégalais (PDS), 19, 24, 135
Parti Socialiste (PS), 15, 19, 134–135, 242
patrias, 30, 41, 148–153
PDS (Parti Démocratique Sénégalais), 19, 24, 135
peintures sous verre (reverse glass painting), 65
petition writing, 181, 185, 188, 190, 196
philanthropic activities, 181, 188–190, 192–194
photography, 52, 54–55, 60, 63–66
Pinney, Christopher, 65
pluralism, 147–165; breach in equidistance, 163; de jure "equal respect" and de facto "proportionate equidistance, 159–163; leadership practices, 156–158; overview, 147–148; religion, state and patrias, 149–153; Senghorian project, 158–159; social uses of kinship, 153–156
political Islam, 1–5, 9, 14, 30, 224, 227

political philosophy, call for new, 38–41
Polity scale, 210
polygamy, 85–86, 225
Ponty, William, 49n20, 128
Poole, Deborah, 66
"proportional equidistance", 147–165
PS (Parti Socialiste), 15, 19, 134–135, 242
PUR (Parti de l'Unité Républicain), 250

Qadir order (Qadiriyya), 43, 137, 143n29, 190, 192, 217
qadis, 44, 85, 191, 199n35
Qarawiyyin university, 33n48

radio, 51, 53–55, 59–60
Radio Al Hamdoulilah, 60
Radio Dunyaa, 51, 60
Radio Touba Hizbut Tarqiyyah, 60
Radiodiffusion Television Senegalaise (RTS), 59–61, 104
Refah party (Turkey), 81
Religion and State Codebook, 210, 232n57
religion-based media, 25–26, 51–67; global circuits, 55–59; Islam in public sphere, 51–55; *Mággal* videos, 60–63; portrait photography, 63–66
religious governance, 99–124; engagement and disengagement with state authority, 102–105; mystical language and competing truth claims, 105–108; overview, 99–102; resolving local conflicts, 108–116
Renan, Ernest, 25, 37–38
republican model, 28, 147
Réseau Africain des Organisations Islamiques pour la Population et le Développement, 247

respect, 206–209; rituals of, 215–220; social construction of mutual, 211–215
"restricted literacy", 14, 18
reverse glass painting (*peintures sous verre*), 65
riba, 57
Rida, Rashid, 74–75
rituals of respect, 29, 215–220; overview, 215; between religions, 218–220; between secular state and Sufis, 215–218
Robinson, David, 211–212
Rosander, E. E., 4
Roume, Ernest, 128
Roy, Olivier, 83
RTS (Radiodiffusion Television Senegalaise), 59–61, 104
Rumi, 3
Rustow, Dankwart, 211

Saalum-Saalum, 113
Sahel, 243–244, 258–259
Saint-Louis, 28, 180–197; biography of H. G. Diop, 186–192; economic, social, religious, and political activities, 192–197; economic history of, 183–186; overview, 180–183; photography, 64; schools, 49n18
sal Khawarizwi, 3
Salafism, 30, 74–75, 99, 101
Sall, Mansour, 248–249
Sarr, Ndèye Faty, 87–88
Sarr, Rabi, 90
Saudi Arabia, 74–75, 77, 79–80
Sayyid, Hâdî wuld, 109
Seck, Abbé Jacques, 233n68
Seck, Bou El Moghdad, 190, 199n35
Seck, Tabara Ameth, 186

A Secular Age (Taylor), 37
secularism (*laïcité*), 1, 4, 215–218; Diouf's interpretation of, 216; global circuits, 55–59; hiddenness as resistance and disengagement, 105–108; intellectual responses to, 37–42; Islam's new publicity, 51–55; local governance, 108–116; overview, 36–37, 99–102; performing sovereignties, 102–105; practical response to, 42–46; questioning the state, 251–253; religious media, 59–66; Senegalese exceptionalism, 46–48; Senghor's views on, 158–159; well-understood, 25, 36, 42–48, 227; world of Islam and, 36–48, 51–67, 99–117
Senegal: democracy, 239–259; exceptionalism, 6, 18–20, 25, 30, 47, 149–150; mutual accommodation in rural, 211–212; political and human rights, 209–211; regional perspective, 243–245; religious and cultural pluralism, 147–165; respect, 205–227; Saint-Louis, 180–197; secular age and world of Islam, 36–48, 51–67, 99–117; social contract, 125–141; Sunnite women, 73–92; well-understood secularism, 42–46
Senghor, Léopold Sédar, 15, 17–19, 23, 31n7, 42, 44–47, 130–131, 157–159, 213–215, 221, 241–242
separation of church/mosque and state, 16, 29, 44, 47, 84, 215–216
seriñ (shaykhs), 43
sharî'a: adoption of in kingdom of Tekrûr, 43; caliph as protector of, 39; multiple interpretations of, 100; need for freedom of conscience,

Index

41; reform of Family Code, 17, 86; Sunnite movement, 77
shaykhs (*seriñ*; *ceerno*), 43
signares, 194, 201n55
Sindoné neighborhood, 188, 191
siyâsa, 100
Smith, Etienne, 18–20, 28–29, 228n1
social contract, 9–14, 19, 125–141; in crisis, 131–137; golden age of, 130–131; Islam and national culture, 5–7; overview, 125–127; redefining, 131–140; roots of, 127–129; Sufi orders' role of social moderator, 47; women and future of, 22–24; youth and, 22–24
social networking, 59
Sow Fall, Aminata, 64–65
Stepan, Alfred, 2, 9–10, 23, 29–30, 36, 46
Stepputat, Finn, 126–127
"success story" concept, 6
succession disagreements, 106–107
Sudan, 79
"Sufi-secular mutual respect", 37, 46
Sufism: as antidote to political Islam, 1–5; overview of in West Africa, 7–10; secular state and, 215–218; social construction of mutual respect, 211–215
Sunnite movement, 23–24
Sunnite women, 73–92; Family Code reforms, 84–88; globalization, 77–84; Islamist women's agency, 77–84; moral issues at work, 89–92; nature of faith, 84–88; neoliberal ethics, 77–84; origins of Sunnite movement, 74–77; overview, 73–74; sexuality, 84–88
Sy, Abdou Aziz Jr., 47
Sy, Al Hajj Malick, 10
Sy, Babacar, 17–18, 23
Sy, Malick, 182, 241
Sy, Tidiane, 17

taalibe: *ndiggël*, 32n40; relationship to marabout, 13–14; relationship to marabouts, 18, 75; social contract, 6, 11; wasteful spending of tithes, 74
Taalibe Baay community, 99–124; engagement and disengagement with state authority, 102–105; mystical language and competing truth claims, 105–108; overview, 99–102; resolving local conflicts, 108–116
Tall, Al Hajj Umar, 7–8, 13
Tall, Seydou Nourou, 13, 16
Tamsir, 190–191, 199n35
tawhid, 76
Taylor, Charles, 36–37
tchador, 79, 89
technocracy, 19
Tekrûr, kingdom of, 43
television, 51, 53–55, 59–60, 79
teranga (hospitality), 149–151
Thiandoum (Catholic cardinal), 2
Tijan order (Tijaniyya), 17, 20, 23, 43, 47, 137; H. G. Diop and, 182, 190, 195; religious change, 246–247; rituals of respect, 217–218
Tijanyya Ñasen (Niassen), 20
Tivaouane, 17
tobacco, 129–130, 134
Torodo, 43
Touba, 129, 133–135, 137
Toucouleur Empire, 185
trade liberalization of 1997, 20, 58
Triaud, Jean Louis, 126–127
Trimingham, J. S., 4

Tunisia, 3, 33n48, 42
Turkey, 31n6, 39, 54, 79, 81

UCAD (Université Cheikh Anta Diop), 75, 90–91
Umar al Fûtî, 43
UNACOIS (Union Nationale des Commerçants et Industriels du Sénégal), 139
UNESCO (United Nations Educational, Scientific, and Cultural Organization's), 256
UNICEF (United Nations Children's Fund), 222
Union Culturelle Musulmane, 75
Union Nationale des Commerçants et Industriels du Sénégal (UNACOIS), 139
Union Progressiste Sénégalaise (UPS), 15–17
United Nations Children's Fund (UNICEF), 222
United Nations Educational, Scientific, and Cultural Organization's (UNESCO), 256
United States, migration of Murids to, 58
Université Cheikh Anta Diop (UCAD), 75, 90–91
UPS (Union Progressiste Sénégalaise), 15–17

Vaillant, Janet, 18
veil (*hijab*), 26, 75, 81–83, 89, 231n42
vernacularization, 2, 6, 18
videos, 51–52, 54–55, 59–60
Villalón, Leonardo A., 5, 19, 30
voting, 260n16

Wade, Abdoulaye, 19–20, 23, 47–48, 53, 86, 136–137, 157, 163
Wahhabi Islam, 29–30, 207, 224
Walf TV, 59
Walzer, Michael, 161, 169n36
Wârjâbî (king of Tekrûr), 43
Weiner, Annette, 64, 66
well-understood secularism (*laicite bien comprise*), 25, 36, 42–48, 227
women: as actors in power struggle, 22; future of social contract and, 22–24; Murid migrant, 26; portrait photography, 63–64, 66; power of, 8; Sunnite, 26, 73–92
World Bank, 58, 78, 133

youth, future of social contract and, 22–24

zâhir ("apparent") truths, 27, 102, 105–108, 111–113, 115
zawiyas, 3, 182, 187, 190, 241

GPSR Authorized Representative: Easy Access System Europe, Mustamäe tee 50, 10621 Tallinn, Estonia, gpsr.requests@easproject.com

www.ingramcontent.com/pod-product-compliance
Lightning Source LLC
Chambersburg PA
CBHW021357290426
44108CB00010B/273